LUKE THE PHYSICIAN

AND OTHER STUDIES IN THE HISTORY OF RELIGION

PLATE XXII.

Old Turkish Art: the Door of the Sirtchali Mosque in Konia.

LUKE THE PHYSICIAN

AND OTHER STUDIES IN THE HISTORY OF RELIGION

by

William M. Ramsay

WIPF & STOCK · Eugene, Oregon

Wipf and Stock Publishers
199 W 8th Ave, Suite 3
Eugene, OR 97401

Luke the Physician and Other Studies in the History of Religion
By Ramsay, William M.
Softcover ISBN-13: 978-1-6667-2598-8
Hardcover ISBN-13: 978-1-6667-2053-2
eBook ISBN-13: 978-1-6667-2054-9
Publication date 5/6/2021
Previously published by Baker Book House, 1908

This edition is a scanned facsimile of the original edition published in 1979.

PREFACE

THE papers republished in this volume have appeared in various Magazines, *Contemporary Review*, *Expositor*, *Journal of the Royal Asiatic Society*, *Geographical Journal*, to the editors of which my thanks are tendered. Most of them have been profoundly modified and much enlarged; but only in the last, which is made up of six older articles, is there any essential change in the original opinions. Elsewhere, the alterations which have been introduced are intended to render more precise and emphatic the views formerly stated. Even the first article, which has been little changed in expression, has been greatly enlarged. Only in the sixth article (first published in 1882) have the additions been indicated.

The last article stands in much need of help and criticism from more experienced scholars. In writing it I felt the depths of my ignorance; but the first steps had to be taken in the subject. The most striking result was reached at the last stage, and is stated only in a footnote and the Table of Contents and Index. The pagan temple-grave became the Christian church-grave or *memorion;* and the pagan θύρα appears as the church doorway on gravestones in Isauria. The great Anatolian writers of the fourth century are full of information, which yet remains to be collected and valued. Professor Holl's *Amphilochius von Iconium* is the one great modern study in its department. The humble essays which conclude this volume and my former series of *Pauline and other Studies* tread in his footsteps; but I am mindful of the poet's advice, *longe sequere et vestigia semper adora*.

I am indebted for the very interesting series of photographs, not merely to my wife, but also to Miss Gertrude Lowthian Bell, Mr. J. G. C. Anderson, Senior Censor of Christ Church, Oxford, and Professor T. Callander, Queen's University, Canada; and I am grateful to them for permitting me to adorn my preface with the names of such experienced and successful explorers, and my book with views so skilfully taken in spite of the ink-black shadows cast by that pitiless sun.

The Index is largely the work of my wife.

W. M. RAMSAY.

ABERDEEN, 31*st October*, 1908.

CONTENTS

I
LUKE THE PHYSICIAN 1

II
THE OLDEST WRITTEN GOSPEL 69

III
ASIA MINOR: THE COUNTRY AND ITS RELIGION . . 103

IV
THE ORTHODOX CHURCH IN THE BYZANTINE EMPIRE . 141

V
THE PEASANT GOD: THE CREATION, DESTRUCTION AND RESTORATION OF AGRICULTURE IN ASIA MINOR . 169

VI
THE RELIGION OF THE HITTITE SCULPTURES AT BOGHAZ-KEUI 199

VII
THE MORNING STAR AND THE CHRONOLOGY OF THE LIFE OF CHRIST 217

VIII

A CRITICISM OF RECENT RESEARCH REGARDING THE NEW TESTAMENT 247

IX

THE HISTORICAL GEOGRAPHY OF THE HOLY LAND . . 267

X

ST. PAUL'S USE OF METAPHORS DRAWN FROM GREEK AND ROMAN LIFE 283

XI

THE DATE AND AUTHORSHIP OF THE EPISTLE TO THE HEBREWS 299

XII

THE CHURCH OF LYCAONIA IN THE FOURTH CENTURY 329-410

    Introduction: The District and its Ecclesiastical Organisation 331

    I. Chronological Arrangement of the Documents . 334

    II. A Bishop of the Church Reorganisation after Diocletian 339

    III. The Presbyters: their Relation to Bishops and Deacons 351

    IV. Crosses and Christian Monograms as the Origin of Ornament (also No. 42) . . . 368

    V. The Church Manager or Oikonomos . . 369

		PAGE
VI.	The Church in the Decoration of Tombs: the Christian Grave in Isauria was a Miniature Church	370
VII.	Distinction of Clergy and Laity: its Early Stage	387
VIII.	Deaconesses	393
IX.	Martyrs	395
X.	Curses on Christian Graves	395
XI.	Virgins or Parthenoi in the Lycaonian Church	397
XII.	Heretic Sects	400
XIII.	High-Priest of God	403
XIV.	Christian Physicians	403
XV.	Quotations from the New Testament	366 and 406
XVI.	Slaves of God	407
INDEX		411

ILLUSTRATIONS

PLATES

	TO FACE PAGE
I. On the Byzantine Military Road: the Pass leading to Dorylaion	106
II. On the Central Trade Route: the Source of the Maeander	106
III. On the Central Trade Route: the Falls at Hierapolis	108
IV. The City, Rock and Castle of Kara-Hissar . .	112
V. The City, Rock and Castle of Sivri-Hissar . .	116
VI. Roman Milestone on the Syrian Route . . .	116
VII. Archaic Sepulchral Monument in Phrygia: November weather	120
VIII. The Tomb of King Midas: a Phrygian Holy Place	124
IX. The Grave of an Ancient Phrygian Chief . .	128
X. The Broken Grave of an Ancient Phrygian Chief .	132
XI. Phrygian Rock-tomb of the Roman Time . .	136
XII. The Site of Pisidian Antioch and the Sultan-Dagh	140

	TO FACE PAGE
XIII. The Monasteries and Churches at Deghile, on the Mountain above Barata	140
XIV. Church and Memorial Chapel on the Summit of the Kara-Dagh: from the west	158
XV. Church on the Summit of the Kara-Dagh: from the south-east	158
XVI. The Throne of the Anatolian God, near Barata .	160
XVII. Ruins of Double-arched West Door of Church at at Bin-Bir-Kilisse (Barata)	160
XVIII. Monastery at Deghile on the Mountain above Barata, showing brickwork used as ornament in a stone building	124
XIX. Church at Deghile on the Mountain above Barata: North Arcades of the Nave	164
XX. Church at Barata: South Arcades of the Nave and Apse	164
XXI. The God and the King at Ibriz	174
XXII. Early Turkish Art: Door of the Sirtchali Mosque in Konia	*Frontispiece*
XXIII. Early Turkish Art: Zazadin-Khan near Konia .	192
XXIV. The Gate of the Virgin-Goddess: looking over the Limnai	192

FIGURES IN THE TEXT

		PAGE
1.	Plan of the Entrance to the Hittite Palace at Euyuk	207
2.	Relief at Euyuk. Procession of Worshippers, headed by the Chief Priest and Priestess, approaching the Goddess	208
3.	The Warrior Goddess of the Hittites with her Favourite and Priest	210
4.	The Chief Priest of the Goddess of Ephesus	213
5.	Apollo the Pastoral God of Lystra on a Third-century Votive Relief	216
6.	The Christian Star as a Decorative Dove and Leaf on the Grave of a Third-century Christian Virgin at Nova Isaura	328
7.	The Symbol of the Cross as a Decorative Element on a Lycaonian Grave	330
8.	Christian Architectural Decoration on the Grave of a Physician at Nova Isaura	330
9.	The Monogram of Christ as a Decorative Element on a Lycaonian Grave	368
10.	Architectural Decoration (the entrance of the church) on the Grave of a Third-century Bishop at Nova Isaura	371
11.	Christian Architectural Decoration and Church Screen on the Grave of a Bishop at Nova Isaura, A.D. 300	379

	PAGE

12. Christian Architectural Decoration on the Grave of a Fourth-century Deacon at Nova Isaura . . . 383

13. Christian Architectural Decoration on the Grave of a Fourth-century Bishop at Nova Isaura . . . 384

14. Anthropomorphic Lycaonian Christian Grave-stone, showing Cross and Rosette (Monogram) as corresponding Decorative Elements 410

ERRATA AND ADDENDA.

P. 109, l. 6, *for* " the Frontispiece " *read* " Plate III ".
P. 203, *note, for* " Hermann " *read* " Humann ".
P. 273, *note* 1, *read* " Quarterly Statement for 1895 ".
P. 281, *note* 2, *for* 200 *read* 250-5.
P. 328, fig. 6, *for* " symbol of the Cross " *read* " Christian Star ".
Pp. 340, l. 17, 341, l. 1. This reading and interpretation will be defended in *Expositor*, December, 1908.

I.
LUKE THE PHYSICIAN

I.

LUKE THE PHYSICIAN

It has for some time been evident to all New Testament scholars who were not hidebound in old prejudice that there must be a new departure in Lukan criticism. The method of dissection had failed. When a real piece of living literature has to be examined, it is false method to treat it as a corpse, and cut it in pieces: only a mess can result. The work is alive, and must be handled accordingly. Criticism for a time examined the work attributed to Luke like a corpse, and the laborious autopsy was fruitless. Nothing in the whole history of literary criticism has been so waste and dreary as great part of the modern critical study of Luke. As Professor Harnack says on p. 87 of his new book,[1] "All faults that have been made in New Testament criticism are gathered as it were to a focus in the criticism of the Acts of the Apostles".

The question "Shall we hear evidence or not?" presents itself at the threshold of every investigation into the New Testament.[2] Modern criticism for a time entered on its task with a decided negative. Its mind was made up, and it

---

[1] *Lukas der Arzt der Verfasser des dritten Evangeliums und der Apostelgeschichte*, Leipzig, Hinrichs, 1906. In order to avoid frequent reiteration of the personal name, we shall speak, as a general rule, of "the Author" simply.

[2] The bearing of this question is discussed in the opening paper of the writer's *Pauline Studies*, 1906.

would not listen to evidence on a matter that was already decided. But the results of recent exploration made this attitude untenable. So long as the vivid accuracy of Acts xxvii., which no critic except the most incompetent failed to perceive and admit, was supposed to be confined to that one chapter, it was possible to explain this passage as an isolated and solitary fragment in the patchwork book. But when it was demonstrated that the same lifelike accuracy characterised the whole of the travels, the theory became impossible. Evidence must be admitted. All minds that are sensitive to new impressions, all minds that are able to learn, have become aware of this. The result is visible in the book which we have now before us. Professor Harnack is willing to hear evidence. The class of evidence that chiefly appeals to him is not geographical, not external, not even historical in the widest sense, but literary and linguistic; and this he finds clear enough to make him alter his former views, and come to the decided conclusion that the Third Gospel and the Acts are a historical work in two books,[1] written, as the tradition says, by Luke, a physician, Paul's companion in travel and associate in evangelistic work. This conclusion he regards as a demonstrated fact (*sicher nachgewiesene Tatsache*, p. 87). It does not, however, lead him to consider that Luke's history is true. He argues very ingeniously against attaching any high degree of trustworthiness to the work, and hardly even concedes that the early date which he assigns to it entails the admission that it is much more trustworthy than the champions of its later date would or could allow. That is the only impression which I can gather (see below, p. 32) from the Author's

[1] He hints at the possibility that a third book may have been intended by Luke, but never written. See below, p. 27.

language in this book. On the other hand, in a notice of his own book (*Selbstanzeige*),[1] he speaks far more favourably about the trustworthiness and credibility of Luke, as being generally in a position to acquire and transmit reliable information, and as having proved himself able to take advantage of his position. I cannot but feel that there is a certain want of harmony here, due to the fact that the Author was gradually working his way to a new plane of thought. His later opinion is more favourable.

Some years ago I reviewed Professor McGiffert's arguments on the Acts.[2] The American professor also had felt compelled by the geographical and historical evidence to abandon in part the older criticism. He also admitted that the Acts is more trustworthy than previous critics allowed; he also was of opinion that it was not thoroughly trustworthy, but was a mixture of truth and error; he also saw that it is a living piece of literature written by one author. But from the fact that Acts was not thoroughly trustworthy, he inferred that it could not be the work of a companion and friend of the Apostle Paul; and he has no pity for the erroneous idea that the Acts could fail to be trustworthy if it had been written by the friend of Paul. I concluded with the words: "Dr. McGiffert has destroyed that error, if an error can be destroyed". But what is to Professor McGiffert inadmissible is the view that Professor Harnack champions.

The careful and methodical studies of the language of Luke by Mr. Hobart[3] and Mr. Hawkins[4] have been thoroughly used by the Author. He mentions that Mr. Haw-

---

[1] In the *Theologische Literaturzeitung* (edited by himself and Professor Schürer), 7th July, 1906, p. 404.
[2] The review is republished in *Pauline Studies*, 1906, p. 321.
[3] *Medical Language of St. Luke*, Dublin, 1882.
[4] *Horae Synopticae*, 1899.

kins seems to be almost unknown in Germany (p. 19), and expresses the opinion (p. 10) that Mr. Hobart's book would have produced more effect, if he had confined himself to the essential and had not overloaded his book with collections and comparisons that often prove nothing. I doubt if that is the reason that Mr. Hobart's admirable and conclusive demonstration has produced so little effect in Germany. The real reason is that the German scholars, with a few exceptions, have not read it. That many of his examinations of words prove nothing, Mr. Hobart was quite aware; but he intentionally, and, as I venture to think, rightly, gave a full statement of his comparison of Luke's language with that of the medical Greek writers. It is the completeness with which he has performed his task that produces such effect on those who read his book. He has pursued to the end almost every line of investigation, and shown what words do not afford any evidence as well as what words may be relied upon for evidence. The Author says that those who merely glance through the pages of Mr. Hobart's book are almost driven over to the opposite opinion (as they find so many investigations that prove nothing). This description of the common German "critical" way of glancing at or entirely neglecting works which are the most progressive and conclusive investigations of modern times suggests much. These so-called "critics" do not read a book whose results they disapprove. The method of studying facts is not to their taste, when they see that it leads to a conclusion which they have definitely rejected beforehand.

The importance of this book lies in its convincing demonstration of the perfect unity of authorship throughout the whole of the Third Gospel and the Acts. These are a history in two books. All difference between parts like Luke i. 5-ii. 52 on the one hand, and the "We"-sections of Acts on the other hand—to take the most divergent parts—is a mere trifle in comparison with the complete identity in language, vocabulary, intentions, interests and method of narration. The writer is the same throughout. He was, of course, dependent on information gained from others: the Author is disposed to allow considerable scope to oral information in addition to the various certain or probable written sources; but Luke treated his written authorities with considerable freedom as regards style and even choice of details, and impressed his own personality distinctly even on those parts in which he most closely follows a written source.

This alone carries Lukan criticism a long step forwards, and sets it on a new and higher plane. Never has the unity and character of the book been demonstrated so convincingly and conclusively. The step is made and the plane is reached by the method which is practised in other departments of literary criticism, *viz.*, by dispassionate investigation of the work, and by discarding fashionable *a priori* theories.

Especially weighty, in the Author's judgment, is the evidence afforded by the medical interest and knowledge, which mark almost every part of the work alike. The writer of this history was a physician, and that fact is apparent throughout. The investigations of Mr. Hobart supply all the evidence—I think the word "all," without "almost," may be used in this case—on which the Author relies. Never was a case in which one book so completely exhausts the subject and presents itself as final, to be used and not to be supplemented even by Professor Harnack. It is doubtless only by a slip, but certainly a regrettable slip, that the Author, in his notice of his own book published in the *Theologische Litera-*

turzeitung, makes no reference to Mr. Hobart, though he mentions other scholars from whose work he has profited.

The Author has up to a certain point employed the plain, simple method of straightforward unprejudiced investigation into the historical work which forms the subject of his study, a method which has not been favoured much by the so-called critical scholars of recent time. So far as he follows this simple method, which we who study principally other departments of literature are in the habit of employing, his study is most instructive and complete. But he does not follow it all through; *multa tamen suberunt priscae vestigia fraudis*. If we read his book, we shall find several examples of the fashionable critical method of *a priori* rules and prepossessions as to what must be or must not be permitted. These examples are almost all of the one kind. Wherever anything occurs that savours of the marvellous in the estimation of the polished and courteous scholar, sitting in his well-ordered library and contemplating the world through its windows, it must be forthwith set aside as unworthy of attention and as mere delusion. That method of studying the first century was the method of the later nineteenth century. I venture to think that it will not be the method of the twentieth century. If you have ever lived in Asia you know that a great religion does not establish itself without some unusual accompaniments. The marvellous result is not achieved without some marvellous preliminaries.

Professor Harnack stands on the border between the nineteenth and the twentieth century. His book shows that he is to a certain degree sensitive of and obedient to the new spirit; but he is only partially so. The nineteenth century critical method was false, and is already antiquated. A fine old crusty, musty, dusty specimen of it is appended to the

Author's *Selbstanzeige* by Professor Schürer, who fills more than three columns of the *Theologische Literaturzeitung*, 7th July, 1906, with a protest against the results of new methods and a declaration of his firm resolution to see nothing, and allow no other to see anything, that he has not been accustomed to see: " These be thy gods, O Israel".

The first century could find nothing real and true that was not accompanied by the marvellous and the "supernatural". The nineteenth century could find nothing real and true that was. Which view was right, and which wrong? Was either complete? Of these two questions, the second alone is profitable at the present. Both views were right—in a certain way of contemplating; both views were wrong—in a certain way. Neither was complete. At present, as we are struggling to throw off the fetters which impeded thought in the nineteenth century, it is most important to free ourselves from its prejudices and narrowness. The age and the people, of whatever nationality they be, whose most perfect expression and greatest hero was Bismarck, are a dangerous guide for the twentieth century. In no age has brute force and mere power to kill been so exclusively regarded as the one great aim of a nation, and the one justification to a place in the Parliament of Man, as in Europe during the latter part of the nineteenth century; and in no age and country has the outlook upon the world been so narrow and so rigid among the students of history and ancient letters. Those who study religion owe it to the progress of science that they can begin now to understand how hard and lifeless their old outlook was. But we who were brought up in the nineteenth century can hardly shake off our prejudices or go out into the light. We can only get a distant view of the new hope. The Author is one of the first to force his way out into the light of day;

but his eyes are still dazzled, and his vision not quite perfect. He sees that Luke always found the marvellous quite as much in his own immediate surroundings, where he was a witness and an actor, as in the earliest period of his history; but he only infers, to put it in coarse language, "how blind Luke was".

What was the truth? How far was Luke right? I cannot say. Consult the men of the twentieth century. I was trained in the nineteenth, and cannot see clearly. But of one thing I am certain: in so far as Professor Harnack condemns Luke's point of view and rules it out in this unheeding way, he is wrong. In so far as he is willing to hear evidence, he comes near being right.

Practically all the argument, in the sense of facts affording evidence, stated by the Author has long been familiar to us in England and Scotland. What is new and interesting and valuable is the ratiocination, the theorising, and the personal point of view in the book under review. We study it to understand Professor Harnack quite as much as to understand Luke: and the study is well worth the time and work. Personally, I feel specially interested in the question of Luke's nationality. On this the Author has some admirable and suggestive pages.

That Luke was a Hellene is quite clear to the Author. He repeats this often; and if once or twice his expression is a little uncertain, as if he were leaving another possibility open, that is only from the scientific desire to keep well within the limits of what the evidence permits. He has no real doubt. The reasons on which he lays stress are utterly different from those which have been mentioned by myself in support of the same conclusion, but certainly quite as strong if not stronger; it is a mere difference of idiosyncrasy which makes him lay stress on those that spring from the thought and the inner temperament of Luke, while I have spoken most of those which indicate Luke's outlook on the world and his attitude towards external nature. But just as I was quite conscious of the other class and merely emphasised those which seemed to have been omitted from previous discussions of the subject,[1] so the Author's silence about the class which I have mentioned need not be taken as proof that he is insensible to such reasons. But those reasons appeal most to the mind of one who has lived long in the country and has felt the sense impressions from whose sphere they are taken. Perhaps they are apt to seem fanciful to the scholar who has spent his life in the library and the study.

The sentimental tone and the frequent allusion to weeping, which is characteristic of Luke, is characteristic also of the Hellene: *dort und hier sind die Tränen hellenische* (p. 25). Mark and Matthew have hardly any weeping: there is more in John; but Luke far surpasses John. Such ideas and words as "injury" (an inadequate translation of the Greek ὕβρις, Acts xxvii. 10, 21), "the barbarians,"[2] are characteristically Greek. "Justice did not suffer him to live" (Acts xxviii. 4) is exactly the word of a Hellenic poet: the words are put in the mouth of the Maltese barbarians, but they are only the expression in Greek by Luke of their remarks in barbaric speech and their attitude to Paul; and they are the Hellenised thought of a Hellene. To Pindar or Aeschylus Justice and Zeus are almost equivalent ideas.

In an extremely interesting passage, p. 100 f., the Author sketches the character of Luke's religion. He recognises

---

[1] *St. Paul the Traveller*, pp. 21, 205 ff.
[2] Both are confined to Paul and Luke in the New Testament.

with correct insight the fundamental Hellenism of Luke's Christianity. To put the matter from a different point of view, Luke had been a Hellenic pagan, and could not fully comprehend either Judaism or Christianity. As in Ignatius, so in Luke, we see the clear traces of his original pagan thought,[1] and we detect the early stage of the process which was destined to work itself out in the paganisation of the Church. The world was not able to comprehend Paulinism, and the result of this inability to understand the spiritual power was the degrading of spiritual ideas into pagan personal deities conceived as saints. It was not possible for even Luke to spring at once to the level of Paulinism; that would need at the best more than a single life, even supposing that there had been unbroken progress. As it happened, there supervened a degeneration in the level of thought and comprehension, after the first impulse communicated by Jesus had apparently exhausted itself, until the Christian idea had time slowly to mould the world's mind and impart to it the power of comprehending Paulinism better. After the first generation of Pauline contemporaries and pupils had died, we see little proof that Paulinism was a living power until we come down to Augustine, and then it appeared only for a moment.

I confess, however, that the Author, while he catches this undeniable characteristic of Luke's religious comprehension, seems to miss the elements in his thought that were capable of higher development. These were only germs, and the

[1] I do not mean to imply that the Author expresses exactly this opinion in this form about Luke; he pictures Luke's idea as a definite hard fact; to me it always comes natural to regard a man's ideas as a process of growth, and to look before and after the moment. The Author isolates the moment. On Ignatius see *Letters to the Seven Churches*, p. 159 ff.

weakness of the Author's view seems to be that he recognises only the fully articulated opinion and is sometimes blind to ideas which were merely inchoate. Hence I cannot but regard the estimate (on p. 101) of Luke's Paulinism, *i.e.*, of his failure to grasp Paulinism, as too hard and too thin.

I may give an example to illustrate what I think was the case. Like the Author, I think that the story in Luke i., ii., is dependent on an oral not a written report; but unlike him, I think that this report comes from Mary herself.[1] Like Professor Sanday, I should conjecture that it came through one of the women named by Luke elsewhere. Here we have a narrative which comes from a Hebrew source, from a woman thinking in Hebraic fashion, one whose language was saturated with Hebraic imagery. This narrative Luke has transmitted to us in a form which clearly shows its Hebrew origin, and equally clearly shows that it had been re-expressed in Lukan language (as the Author has proved) and transformed by Luke. But also, I venture to believe, it has been re-thought out of the Hebraic into the Greek fashion. The messenger of God, who revealed to Mary the Divine will and purpose, becomes to Luke the winged personal being who, like Iris or Hermes, communicates the will and purpose of God. Exactly what is the difference between the original narrative and the Greek translation, I am not able to say or to speculate; but that there was a more anthropomorphic picture of the messenger in Luke's mind than there was in Mary's I feel no doubt. Yet I believe that Luke was translating as exactly as he could into Greek the account which he had heard. He expresses and thinks as a Greek that which was thought and expressed by a Hebrew.

[1] *Christ Born in Bethlehem*, p. 74 ff.

But, with this qualification, the passage on p. 100 f. appears to me to be most illuminative and remunerative. As regards the Hellenism of Luke the difference between us is one merely of degree. We are really trying to say the same thing, but expressing it through the colouring and transforming medium of our different personalities, and I too imperfectly. The really important matter is this. In the first place, the Author sees clearly and perfectly and finally the first century character of Luke's thought: "He has come into personal relations with the first Christians, with Paul" (p. 103). In the second place, the Author's view that Luke was so incapable of comprehending the spirit of Christianity —for that is inevitably implied in his exposition, pp. 100–102—only brings out into clearer light Luke's inability to evolve from his inner consciousness the picture of Jesus which looks out in such exquisite outline from his historical work. The picture was given·to, and not made by, Luke; and the Author himself shows plainly how it was given him. He had intimate relations with some of those who had known Jesus, and from that, more than from the early written accounts to which he also had access, he derived his conception. Where he altered this conception, it could only be to introduce his own poorer, less lofty ideas, and to betray his want of real comprehension. I do not at all deny that there are in his Gospel (as there are in the other Gospels) traces of the age and the thoughts amid which they were respectively composed; but these are recognised because they are inharmonious with the picture as a whole. They are stains, and not parts of the original picture.

Accordingly, in spite of certain differences, so close does this part of the task bring us, starting from our widely opposed points of contemplation, that the conclusion of this brilliant passage is an expression of Paul's general position in the Jewish and Hellenic world, as Harnack conceives it, which I am able to adopt and to use as my own: "Paul and Luke are counterparts.[1] As the former is only intelligible as a Jew, but a Jew who has come into the closest contact with Hellenism, so the latter is only intelligible as a Hellene, but a Hellene who has personally had touch with the original Jewish Christianity." Usually, in his characterisation of Paul, the Author sees the Jew so clearly, that he sees nothing else; and, as a rule, I find myself in strenuous opposition to his conception of the great Apostle. Here he recognises the very close contact of Paul with Hellenism. We must, then, ask whether that contact had been so utterly devoid of effect on Paul's sensitive and sympathetic mind, as the Author often represents it to have been? To me it seems that, while Luke was the Hellene, who could never fully understand or sympathise with the Jew[2] (though his whole life and thought had been changed by contact with the religion taught by Jews), Paul was the Jew who had sympathised with much that lay in Hellenism and had been powerfully modified and developed thereby, remaining, however, a Jew, but a developed Jew, "who had come into the closest contact with Hellenism".

In the familiar argument about the "We"-passages of Acts, the Author puts one point in a striking and impressive way. In these "We"-passages, as he points out and as is universally recognised, Luke distinguishes carefully between "We" and Paul. Wherever it is reasonably possible, in view of historic and literary truth, he emphasises Paul and keeps the "We" modestly in the background.

[1] *Gegenbilder*, companion and contrasted pictures.
[2] *St. Paul the Traveller*, p. 207.

Now, take into account the narrative in Acts xxviii. 8-10: "And it was so that the father of Publius lay sick of fever and dysentery: unto whom Paul entered in and prayed, and laying his hands on him healed him. And when this was done, the rest also which had diseases in the island came and were cured [more correctly, 'received medical treatment']: who also honoured us with many honours."

In this passage attention is concentrated on Paul, so long as historic truth allowed; but Paul's healing power by prayer and faith could not be always exercised. Such power is efficacious only occasionally in suitable circumstances and on suitable persons. As soon as it begins to be exercised on all and sundry, it begins to fail, and a career of pretence deepening into imposture begins. Accordingly, when the invalids came in numbers, medical advice was employed to supplement the faith-cure, and the physician Luke became prominent. Hence the people honoured not "Paul," but "us".

Here the Author recognises a probable objection, but considers it has not any serious weight, *viz.*, that Luke, like Paul, may have cured by prayer and not by medical treatment. Against this he points to the precise definition of Publius's illness, which is paralleled often in Greek medical works, but never in Greek literature proper; and argues that faith-healers do not trouble themselves, as a rule, about the precise nature of the disease which is submitted to them. He acknowledges that this is not a complete and conclusive answer. He has strangely missed the real answer, which is complete and conclusive. Paul healed Publius (ἰάσατο), but Luke is not said to have healed the invalids who came afterwards. They received medical treatment (ἐθεραπεύοντο). The latter verb is translated "cured" in the English Version; and Professor Harnack agrees. Now in the strict sense ἐθεραπεύοντο, as a medical term, means "received medical treatment"; and in the present case the context and the whole situation demand this translation (though Luke uses the word elsewhere sometimes in the sense of "cure"): the contrast to ἰάσατο, the careful use of medical terms in the passage, and above all the implied contrast of Paul's healing power and Luke's modest description of his medical attention to his numerous patients from all parts of the island, all demand the latter sense. Professor Knowling is here right.

The Author states a careful argument that, since Luke and Aristarchus are twice mentioned together in the Epistles of Paul, and Aristarchus is thrice mentioned in the Acts, the silence of Acts about Luke is to be explained by his having written the book; and that there is no other explanation possible. Aristarchus, an unimportant person, is mentioned in Acts solely because he was in relation with Luke. Luke did not name himself, though he frequently indicates his presence by using the first person. Luke and Aristarchus were Paul's two sole Christian companions on his voyage to Rome. These facts, the triple reference in Acts to a person so unimportant in history as Aristarchus, and the silence about Luke except in the editorial "we," point to Luke as the author.

This argument occurs or appeals to every one who approaches the book with a desire to understand it; it carries weight; but the weight is lessened by the enigmatic silence of Acts about Titus, a person of such importance and so closely alike in influence to Luke. He who solves that enigma will throw a flood of light on the early history of Christianity in the Aegean lands. A conjecture that Titus was a relative of Luke (brother or cousin)[1] is advanced in *St. Paul the Traveller*, p. 390; and as yet I see no other way out of the difficulty, since the only other supposition that suggests itself—*viz.*, that Titus Lucanus was the full name of the author, and that he was sometimes spoken of as Titus simply, sometimes as Lukas (an abbreviated form) —introduces apparently far greater difficulties than it solves.

The attempt on pp. 15-17 to demonstrate that the writer of Acts was closely connected with Syrian Antioch, seems to me a distinct failure. That Luke had some family connection with Syrian Antioch[2] is in perfect harmony with the evidence of his writings, and must be accepted on the evidence of Eusebius and others; but the Author's argument that this influenced his selection and statement of details is anything but convincing. A false inference seems to be drawn in some cases. For example, it is pointed out on p. 16, note 1, that Syrian Antioch is only once alluded to in the Pauline letters (Gal. ii. 11), whereas it is often mentioned in a peculiar and emphatic way in Acts; and the inference is drawn that the emphasis laid on Antioch in Acts cannot be explained purely from the facts and must be due to some special interest which Luke felt in it. This reasoning implies that the importance of different places in the early history of Christianity can be estimated according to the frequency with which they are mentioned in Paul's letters. Without that premise the Author's reasoning in the note just quoted has no validity; but the premise needs only to be formally stated, and its falsity is at once evident.

[1] In the *Expository Times*, 1907, p. 285, Professor A. Souter argues that in 2 Cor. viii. 18 Luke is called " the brother " of Titus. This always seemed to me highly probable; but ἀδελφός might signify "cousin," and it might indicate close friendship and intimacy (*St. Paul the Traveller*, p. 390).

[2] On the character of this connection, see Note at the end of this article.

In the view which I have tried to support, the reason why Syrian Antioch is often mentioned in Acts is not that Luke loved to speak of his own city, but simply and solely its critical and immense importance in the development of the early Church. In Antioch were taken the first important steps in the adaptation of the Church to the pagan world; for the episode of Cornelius does not imply such a serious step, and would have been quite compatible with the maintenance of a really Judaic Church.

The reason why Antioch is rarely mentioned by Paul is that his letters are not intended to give a history of the development of the Church, but to warn or to encourage his correspondents. Only in Galatians i., ii., does Paul diverge into history, and there Antioch plays an extremely important part. It is the scene of action from Galatians i. 21 (where Syria means Antioch) down to ii. 1, and again ii. 11-14; and in these two references how much historical weight is implied!

The Author's further suggestion that Mnason the Cypriote, whom Paul and his companions found living at a town between Caesareia and Jerusalem,[1] may have been the missionary from Cyprus that helped to found the Church in Antioch (p. 16, n. 2), has absolutely nothing in its favour, and is an example of the sort of vague "might have been" which annoys and irritates the plain matter-of-fact English scholar, but which is extremely popular among the so-called "Higher Critics" abroad and at home. Those suggestions of utterly unproved and improbable possibilities lead to nothing, and should never be made, as here, buttresses for an

---

[1] At Jerusalem, as the Author thinks, assigning no value to Western readings. My own view is that even the Accepted Text bears the same sense as the Western (*Expositor*, March, 1895, p. 213 f.).

argument, founded on the Author's observation that among the Antiochian leaders mentioned in xiii. 1, no Cypriote occurs.[1] But we must remember that the first of the list, the outstanding leader of the Antiochian Church, Barnabas, was a Cypriote; and, though he was not one of the missionaries who helped in the original foundation, he came to Antioch immediately after the foundation; and there is no reason to assume that the five leaders mentioned in xiii. 1 must include all the original founders.

The imagined contrast between the importance attached in Acts to Syrian Antioch and Paul's comparative silence about it, is strengthened by the quotation of Acts xiv. 19 as a reference—a confusion of Syrian with Pisidian Antioch, evidently a mere slip, but a slip into which the Author has been betrayed by eagerness to find arguments in favour of a theory.

Not much better seems to me the inference drawn from the first speech of Jesus (Luke iv. 21-27), which begins with "this parable, Physician, heal thyself," and ends with a reference to Naaman, the Syrian. In this the Author finds conclusive proof that Luke was a physician, and that he was keenly interested in Antioch. What connection has Damascus with Antioch? True, we now speak of them both as in Syria. But Syria was not a country. There was no political connection between Damascus and Antioch when that speech was delivered, and as little when Luke composed his history. The two cities were in different countries, under different rule, far distant from one another, and having so far as we know nothing in common. One was the capital of a Roman Province, the other was subject

---

[1] *Ein Cyprier wird nicht genannt.*

to the barbarian King of Arabia. It is only on the map that they look close to one another.

The cases in which I find myself obliged to disagree with the Author are generally of one class, and are due to the fact that he frequently regards as indicative of Luke's individual character details which are forced on the historian by his subject. We have found some examples in the Author's attempted proof that Antioch had a special interest for Luke as his birthplace. On p. 106 he attempts similarly to show that Ephesus had a special interest for him, and is specially marked out among the Churches by him; this supposed interest he explains by the further supposition that Luke settled and wrote either at Ephesus or in a district for which Ephesus had a central significance, and he adds that this country may have been Achaia. Why Ephesus should have a central significance for one who resided in Achaia is not easy to see, except in the sense that it had a central significance for the Gentile Church in general: in other words, that Ephesus was a leading and specially important Church. But, if it was so, does not its importance sufficiently explain the attention and space which the historian Luke devotes to it, without supposing that he had some private and personal love for speaking about the city? Moreover, this assumed residence of Luke in Achaia is not in harmony with the Author's footnote on the same page, in which he says that, while Acts clearly shows the foundation of the Church at Corinth to have been the principal achievement of Paul's second journey, yet Luke himself had no relation to the Corinthian Church.[1] How it could have been possible

---

[1] For my own part I think that Luke had relations with the Corinthian Church (*St. Paul the Traveller*, pp. 284, 390). But this is, as yet, merely matter of opinion.

for Luke to settle in Achaia, and yet not come into any relation to Corinth, but regard Ephesus as the point of central significance for his district, I cannot in the circumstances of the Roman period understand, nor does the Author try to explain. The rest of Achaia communicated with Ephesus only through Corinth; and it is simply incredible that residents in Achaia should disregard Corinth and look to Ephesus.

The Author seeks to prove that Luke felt a special interest in Ephesus mainly from the character of the Ephesian address (Acts xx. 18 ff.); and he mentions (1) the heartfelt tone of affection in which Paul addresses the elders of Ephesus; (2) the way in which Paul's address on that occasion is turned into a general farewell to the congregations of the Aegean district; (3) that he knows and takes notice of the later history of the Ephesian Church.

(1) The facts seem to me only to illuminate Paul's feeling towards Ephesus and to mark out Luke's report as being a trustworthy account of an address which was really delivered; Luke sinks and Paul alone emerges in the report. The words spoken by Paul prove nothing as to Luke's feelings unless the speech is either a fabrication of Luke's, or an unnecessary part of a history of the time, unimportant in itself and not characteristic enough to deserve insertion. Now, if true, the speech throws much light on the character of Paul: it is uttered on a great and unique occasion: it is the one episode in Acts which brings out into clear, strong relief the intense interest which Paul felt in his Churches. In short, it is eminently required in order to complete the picture of Paul's work in the Aegean world, and it was spoken at the moment when Paul was taking farewell of that world in order to enter on the new world of

the West (after consecrating the results of his work in the Aegean world by an offering at Jerusalem intended to cement the unity of all the Churches of the East). The speech is introduced with eminent dramatic propriety. It is historic in its scope and weighty in its matter. He who argues that the words reveal Luke's feelings, not Paul's, is therefore driven back on the other alternative, that the speech was a fabrication of Luke's; but we remember that, on the Author's view, Luke was present and heard the speech. How can we reconcile the contradiction? Luke, a companion and admirer of Paul, listened to the address delivered on such a remarkable occasion; but, in place of reporting the speech which he heard, he presents his readers with a fabricated one.

This contradiction can be reconciled only by declaring Luke to have been a singularly bad historian; and such is the Author's view: Luke was incapable of being accurate, and was untrustworthy as a historian. But is this view natural? Is it reconcilable with the literary skill and the sympathetic insight of the work? Could the man who tells the story of the voyage and shipwreck make such a false account of another great occasion?

(2) The farewell to Ephesus was at some points expressed by Paul as a general farewell, because his audience included representatives of all the Churches, in Achaia, Macedonia, Asia and Galatia; and though these representatives were accompanying him to Jerusalem, yet, when he was explaining that he intended to come no more into those regions (having, as we know, Rome and the West now in view), he naturally began to speak more generally: "Ye all, among whom I went about preaching, shall see my face no more". This is said to all the congregations, Corinth, etc., which,

though absent, were represented by delegates, who would report his farewell.

(3) Considering Paul's past experience elsewhere, it is not strange that he should be able to foresee what dangers from without and from within awaited Ephesus. Further, the Author has just pointed out that the address had already become general; why, then, does he assume that this sentence 29-30 applies only to Ephesus, and shows such a knowledge of later Ephesian history as proves the subsequent acquaintance with, perhaps actual residence in, Ephesus of the historian who composed the address and put it into the mouth of Paul? It might equally plausibly be argued, on the contrary, that this sentence shows ignorance of subsequent Ephesian history, for both John and Ignatius agree that Ephesus was long the champion of truth and the rejecter of error.[1]

In general, one feels that, where the Author is at his best, he is studying Luke in a straightforward way and drawing inferences from observed facts; where he is less satisfactory, he has got a theory in his head, and is straining the facts to support the theory.

He lays much stress on the fact that inconsistencies and inexactnesses occur all through Acts. Some of these are undeniable; and I have argued that they are to be regarded in the same light as similar phenomena in the poem of Lucretius and in other ancient classical writers, *viz.*, as proofs that the work never received the final form which Luke intended to give it, but was still incomplete when he died. The evident need for a third book to complete the work, together with those blemishes in expression, form the proof: see below, p. 27.

[1] *Letters to the Seven Churches*, p. 240 f.

But the Author finds inconsistencies and faults in Luke where I see none. He complains, *e.g.*, that Luke is not disturbed by the fact that Paul was driven on by the Spirit to Jerusalem, and yet the disciples in Tyre through this same Spirit seek to detain him from going to Jerusalem. I cannot feel disturbed any more than Luke; such were the facts; and I can only marvel that the great German scholar thinks we ought to be disturbed. Nor can I blame Luke (as the Author does, p. 81) because Agabus's prophecy, xxi. 11, is not fulfilled exactly as it is uttered. Luke is merely the reporter of what he heard Agabus say; and we can only feel profoundly grateful that he recorded the simple facts, and did not suppress the prophecy or adapt it to the event.

The tendency to regard historical details which Luke narrates as indicative of his personal character often takes the form of blaming the historian for being inconsistent, where the inconsistency (if it be such) was the fault of the facts, not of the narrator. I quote just one example. In xvi. 37 Paul appeals to his Roman rights as a citizen: "one asks in astonishment why he does so only now". One may certainly be quite justified in asking the question, but one is not justified in blaming Luke because Paul did not claim his rights sooner. This is an interesting question. Paul had already several times submitted to punishment from Roman or municipal magistrates without claiming his immunity from such treatment as a Roman. At this point he began to take advantage of his privileged position. Is not this a step in his realisation of the relation of the Church to the Empire?

We take it that Luke is right, and that Paul did not at first reveal his Roman citizenship to the Philippian magistrates. If that is so, it is absurd to blame the historian for telling the truth. The Author, presumably, must hold that Luke is wrong, that Paul did claim his rights earlier, and that Luke either suppressed or was ignorant of the Apostle's earlier appeal. Now the Author's view is that Luke was in Philippi as Paul's companion; the facts therefore must have been known to the historian, but he did not record the first claim. Such conduct would justify the very severe strictures which the Author makes on Luke's inability to tell a story clearly and correctly. But how difficult it is to work out that theory in a reasonable way! If Paul claimed his rights on the preceding day, how did it come that he was beaten in defiance of the privilege of a Roman citizen? And, if the magistrates were convinced by his claim on the morrow, how came they to disregard it on the first day? Or are we to suppose that the beating was an invention of Luke's?

In short, here and generally, we come back to Professor McGiffert's view (as stated above) that, if Luke was a friend and companion of Paul, his history must be accepted as thoroughly trustworthy. The qualities of intellect and heart which are revealed in his work show that he was an exceptionally well-qualified witness and narrator. The Author's theory that Luke was Paul's contemporary and personal friend, and often an eye-witness of the events which he records, but yet was untrustworthy as a recorder even of what he had seen, leads into many hopeless inconsistencies, of which the above is only one slight specimen.

There are clear signs of the unfinished state in which this chapter was left by Luke; but some of the German scholar's criticisms show that he has not a right idea of the simplicity of life and equipment that evidently characterised the jailer's house and the prison.¹ The details which he blames as inexact and inconsistent are sometimes most instructive about the circumstances of this provincial town and Roman colonia.

But it is never safe to lay much stress on small points of inexactness or inconsistency in any author. One finds such faults even in the works of modern scholarship, if one examines them in the microscopic fashion in which Luke is studied here. I think I can find them in the Author himself. His point of view sometimes varies in a puzzling way. On p. 92 the paragraph Acts xxviii. 17-31 is said to be clearly modelled to make it the conclusion of the whole work. On p. 96 the Author confesses his inability to solve the serious problem presented by the last two verses, and suggests the possibility that Luke intended to write a third book. Again, on p. 20 he numerates xx. 5, 6 as part of the "We"-sections, but on p. 105 f. he declares that Luke first met Paul at Troas, accompanied him to Philippi, and there parted from him, to rejoin him after some years, and in fact the meeting took place once more at Troas. But if the reunion only took place at Troas, then xx. 5, 6 cannot be a genuine part of the "We"-sections.

I suspect that inexactness on the Author's part forms the foundation for a charge which he brings against me. He speaks of my theory that Luke was employed by Paul as a physician during his severe illness in Galatia. If I have so spoken it would be a clear example of inexactitude and inconsistency on my own part. I entirely agree with Professor Harnack that Paul first met Luke in Troas, and that Luke never travelled with Paul in Galatia; and I think this is put quite clearly and strongly in my book, *St. Paul the*

---
¹ *St. Paul the Traveller*, p. 220 ff.

Traveller. I may elsewhere have been guilty of this inexactitude and inconsistency; but I cannot remember to have made such a statement. I have doubtless spoken of Luke as being useful as a medical adviser to Paul in travelling, as, *e.g.*, I have said that Luke would have discouraged any proposal to walk sixty miles in two days (Acts xxi. 16),[1] more especially since Paul was liable to attacks of fever; but his fever was not confined to Galatia or to any one journey. Moreover, a traveller may be guided by his physician's advice, even though the physician does not accompany him.

The Author has an object in thus dwelling on the inconsistencies and inexactitudes of which Luke is guilty. He is here preparing to cope with the supreme difficulty in Acts, *viz.*, the disagreement between the narrative of Acts xv. and that of Galatians ii. 1-11, if these are taken (as the Author takes them) to be accounts of the same event, or series of events. These are so plainly inconsistent with one another —for the attempts to represent them as consistent are among the strange things in the history of learning—that, if they depict the same incident, one must be fatally inaccurate. Now, as Paul was present and took part in the incident, his evidence must rank higher, unless he be condemned as intentionally misrepresenting facts, a theory which few adopt and which need not be considered. Luke then must be wrong, where he is in disagreement with Paul. The disagreement can be readily explained by those who regard Acts as the work of a later period: history, as they may reasonably say, had become dimmed by lapse of time, by the growth of prejudice, and by various other causes. But how can those explain it, who maintain (as the Author does) that Acts was written by the friend, coadjutor and personal

[1] In a paper now reprinted in *Pauline and other Studies* (1906), p. 267.

attendant of Paul, the friend of many other persons closely concerned and certain to possess good information? The inconsistency is not in unimportant details, easily caught up differently by different persons: the inconsistency is fundamental and thorough.

To that question the Author has to prepare his answer; and his answer is that Luke was habitually inaccurate and inconsistent with himself. This answer is always a difficulty, against which the Author is struggling with extraordinary dialectic skill throughout his book, but the struggle is vain and success impossible. Luke is not, in the Author's exposition, a single character. He is a double personality, good and bad.

The truth is, as has frequently been pointed out, that the whole problem which governs so completely and so disastrously this and most modern books about Acts is a mere phantom, the creation of geographical ignorance, the result of the irrational North Galatian view. Acts xv. describes a different scene from Galatians ii. 2-11.

On p. 106 f. the Author discusses the relation between Luke and the Gospel of John, and points out that of all the Apostles Luke shows interest in none but Peter and John. The idea that this greater frequency of reference to these two Apostles might be due to their greater importance in the development of Christianity as the religion of the Empire (which I hold to be the truth) is set aside without even a passing glance by the Author. The reason must lie in some accidental meeting of Luke with, or personal relation to, John. It is quietly assumed from first to last that the determining motive of Luke in his choice of events for record or omission lies in personal idiosyncrasy or caprice, never in the importance or insignificance of the events. The

Author says that, considering his predilection for John, it is remarkable that Luke does not mention him in Acts xv., when Paul shows in Galatians ii. that John was one of the three prominent figures in the incident; and the only inference which he draws is that Luke had not read the letter to the Galatians. But, even if that inference were true, it would not be a sufficient explanation, for Luke had abundant opportunity of learning the facts and the comparative authority of the various Apostles from other informants; and the Author fully grants that he made considerable use of oral information. The only justifiable inference which the mere commonplace historian would permit himself to draw is that, according to the information at Luke's disposal, John did not play a prominent part in the incident described in Acts xv., whereas he was prominent in the scene described by Paul (Gal. ii. 2-10).

The view which at present commends itself to me (but which might, of course, be altered by more systematic consideration) is that the writer of the Fourth Gospel knew the Third, but that the writer of the Third did not know the Fourth and had little direct personal acquaintance with its author. The analogies which Dr. Harnack points out are analogies of subject, forced on both by external facts, and not caused by the character of the two writers.

It sounds, at first hearing, strange to us that the Author feels himself as the first to observe that the female element is so much emphasised in Luke, whereas Mark and Matthew give women very small place in the history.[1] This seems such a commonplace in English study, that I felt obliged to

---

[1] *Worauf, soviel ich mich erinnere, bisher noch nie aufmerksam gemacht worden ist. . . . Erst Lukas hat sie* [i.e., *Frauen*] *so stark in die evangelische Geschichte eingeführt.*

be almost apologetic and very brief in referring to the subject in *Was Christ Born at Bethlehem?* (pp. 83-90). Yet when one's attention is called to the fact, it is not easy to refer to any formal and serious discussion of this extremely important side of the evidence about Luke's personality; and it may be that the Author is the first, at least in modern German scholarship, to treat the topic in a scholarly way. The truth seems to be that German scholars have been so entirely taken up with the preliminary questions, such as " Was there a Luke at all ? " that they have never tried to discover what sort of man he was. Even those who championed his reality were so occupied in proving it by what are considered more weighty arguments, that they forgot the mode of proof which seems in my humble judgment to be far the strongest, *viz.*, to hold up to the admiration of all thinking men this man Luke in his humanity and reality. Do his works reveal to us a real man? If so, they must be the genuine composition of a true person; no pseudonymous work ever succeeded or could succeed in exhibiting the supposititious writer as a real personality. Professor Harnack has only half essayed the task. He has entered on it, but never heartily, for he is too much cumbered by prepossessions, by old theories only half discarded, and above all by the hopeless fetters of the North-Galatian prejudice, which inevitably distorts the whole history.

I have pointed out, in the passage just quoted (p. 90), that this attitude of Luke's mind is characteristic of Macedonia (implying thereby that it is not characteristic of Greece proper) : I might and should have added that it is characteristic also of Asia Minor. But there is much to say on this subject, and here I can only refer to the discussion of the effect on subsequent Christian development produced by the

Anatolian craving for some recognition of the female element in the Divine nature (*Pauline and other Studies*, 1906, p. 135 ff.).

"The traditions of Jesus, which lie before us in the works of Mark and Luke, are older than is commonly supposed. That does not make them more trustworthy, but yet is not a matter of indifference for their criticism."[1] So says the Author on p. 113. These are not the words of a dispassionate historian; they are the words of one whose mind is made up *a priori*, and who strains the facts to suit his preconceived opinion. In no department of historical criticism except Biblical would any scholar dream of saying, or dare to say, that accounts are not more trustworthy if they can be traced back to authors who were children at the time the events which form this subject occurred, and who were in year-long, confidential and intimate relations with actors in those events, than they would be if they were composed by writers one or two generations younger, who had personal acquaintance with few or none of the actors and contemporaries.[2] But compare above, p. 4.

There is room, and great need, for a dispassionate and serious examination of the question how far there exist in the Gospels traces of the age in which they were composed, and of the thought characteristic of that time. Such an examination cannot now be conducted to a useful end by one who begins with his mind made up as to what must be later and what cannot be real, for this prejudice must inevitably be of nineteenth century character and hostile to any true

---

[1] *Die Ueberlieferungen von Jesus, die bei Markus und Lukas vorliegen, sind älter als man gewöhnlich annimmt. Das macht sie nicht glaubwürdiger, ist aber doch für ihre Kritik nicht gleichgültig.*

[2] The Author dates Luke's History A.D. 80. For a different reason I argued that Luke iii. 11 was written under Titus. 79-81 (*St. Paul the Traveller*, p. 387).

comprehension of first century realities. I cannot but think and maintain that there are later elements in the Gospels, showing the influence of popular legend, and reminding us that after all the picture of Jesus which stands before us in the New Testament has always to be contemplated through glass that is not perfect and flawless, through a human and imperfect medium.[1] The flaws can be distinguished, but the marvel is that they are so few and so unimportant. The picture is so strong, so simple in outline, and so unique, that it shines with hardly diminished clearness through the medium.

After stating in a general way the position which Professor Harnack takes up in this remarkable book, it is only fair to give some specimens in detail of the arguments on which he relies. As we are in almost entire agreement with the main position of his book, it will conduce to clearness to say that most of the quotations which will be made at the outset are of points which seem to show his method at its best. In the concluding pages some remarks will be made on the method of proof which is employed in the book.

The Author's argument and inferences about the passages in which the first personal pronoun "We" is used are stated most definitely on p. 37 f. After minutely examining Acts xvi. 10-17, and observing the identity in words, construction, tone and thought, with the style of the rest of the Acts and the Third Gospel, he argues that, if the writer of the Acts took this passage from a "Source," he has left nothing in it unchanged except the first personal pronoun: everything else he has recast into his own characteristic vocabulary,

[1] Legend gathers quickly in the East. It is, for example, an interesting study to observe how the historic figure of Ibrahim Pasha has been hidden beneath a crust of legend in the districts of Asia Minor which he held from 1832-40. The name is famous, but the legends gather round it.

syntax and style. Such a procedure is simply inconceivable, and therefore there remains only the position that the writer of the whole book is himself the original composer of these "We"-passages: he is the man whose personal presence in Troas and Philippi with Paul obliges him to speak as a witness of and sharer in the action.

It is possible, the Author argues on p. 38, to go one step farther. The writer did not take this passage, xvi. 10-17, from his own old notebook or diary, and insert it in his history. When he wrote the history twenty to thirty years after the events, he could not possibly have retained in all respects exactly the same style as he used in his old notebook. This passage was written when the Book of the Acts was written; it was composed as part of the whole work, though this does not preclude the view that he had notes written down at the time, with which he could refresh his memory. This argument is absolutely conclusive to every person that has the power of comprehending and appreciating style and literary art; unfortunately many of the so-called "Higher Critics" seem to have become devoid of any such comprehension through fixing persistently their attention on words and details.

Luke was not merely a witness, he took part in the action: "Straightway we sought to go forth into Macedonia, concluding that God had called us for to preach the Gospel unto them," and "we sat down and spake unto the women" (xvi. 10, 13): here the narrator makes himself one of the missionaries to Macedonia. He was not a mere companion, he was an enthusiastic missionary to that country; and on my view (though not on the Author's view) he continued to be specially devoted to that country, except in so far as the still closer personal devotion to Paul called him away.

The Author, on the contrary, is disposed to connect Luke with Ephesus, with Asia and with Achaia (as has been stated above, p. 21). He finds a sufficient proof that Luke was not a Macedonian[1] in Acts xxvii. 2—"we put to sea, Aristarchus, a Macedonian of Thessalonica, being with us" (p. 31). I cannot see any force in this reasoning. On the same principle it might be argued that Luke was not an Asian (which the Author is inclined to believe that he was), because in xx. 4, 5, he speaks of "Asians, Tychicus and Trophimus," who "were waiting for us at Troas".

The remarkable passage, Acts xvi. 9, must detain our attention for a moment, while we apply to it a principle which the Author lays down on p. 11, though he does not apply it to xvi. 9, and would deny the inferences which we shall draw. He points out that, throughout the "We"-passages, Luke distinguishes carefully between "We" and Paul: wherever it is reasonably possible in view of historic and literary truth, he emphasises Paul and keeps the "We" modestly in the background.[2] Now observe in xvi. 10 how the "We" is put forward. The vision was seen by Paul alone, the message was given to Paul alone, "Come over into Macedonia and help us". Yet the narrative continues, "And when he had seen the vision, straightway we sought to go forth into Macedonia, concluding that God had called us for to preach the Gospel unto them". Without any apparent necessity, even without any apparent justification, the writer assumes that, because Paul has been called into Macedonia, Luke shares in the call. There is no other passage in which the "We" is forced in without obvious

[1] In this paragraph I am using the words Macedonian and Asian of Luke in the sense of residing in Macedonia or in Asia, which is not strictly accurate, but is convenient.

[2] See above, p. 15 f.

justification; and on the view stated in *St. Paul the Traveller*, pp. 200-3, there is a justification hidden beneath the surface in this case also, for Luke had played a part in the vision, and was therefore forced to conclude that he as well as Paul was called to Macedonia. Several reasons (which need not be repeated here) are there stated, which point to the idea that the man of Macedonia, whom Paul saw in the vision and recognised at sight as a Macedonian, was Luke; and these are confirmed by the observation now stated.

Every time I read this remarkable passage, xvi. 6-10, I am more and more struck with the intense personal feeling that lies under the words, the hurry and rush of the narrative, and the quiet satisfaction of the conclusion, "God had called us". Luke is here introducing himself, in the moment when he played so important a part in determining the course of Paul's work. The large space which is given to the Macedonian work in the Acts is out of proportion to its importance, and can only be explained by Luke's strong personal interest in it.

The Author gives as an example of the style of the "We"-passages a similar analysis of xxviii. 1-16, a specimen of continuous sea-narrative; his treatment cannot be shortened, but must be studied in full. Only one criticism has to be made on this excellent piece of investigation. It is strange that on p. 44 the Author quotes, as if there were any probability in it, Professor Blass's unjustifiable objection to, and conjectural alteration of, the reading παρασήμῳ Διοσκούροις, "whose sign was the Twin Brothers," given by MSS. and all other editions in Acts xxviii. 11. Neither of them has observed that this dative absolute is the correct technical form, guaranteed by many examples in inscriptions. This has been pointed out, and some examples quoted in an article published long ago in the *Expositor*.¹ There is no detail in which the exact technical accuracy of Luke's expression is more clearly made out than this, and yet Professor Blass would change it into a commonplace relative clause, ᾧ ἦν παράσημον Διοσκούρων, which is Greek so unidiomatic as to be hardly Greek at all.

The author devotes considerable space to statistics about the occurrence of the same words in the "We"-passages and in Luke generally, as contrasted with the rarity or total absence of many of those words in Matthew, Mark and John. It is impossible to abbreviate this argument: the reasoning must be taken as a whole, and seems conclusive, though opinion will always differ a good deal as to the value of such verbal arguments in proving identity of authorship. Personally, I have not as a rule much belief in such arguments, but it must be confessed that the statistics in this case are impressive.

The single sign of difference between the language of the "We"-passages and the rest of Luke lies in the unusually large number of words in the former, which are used nowhere else by Luke. Words which an author uses only once and no more occur throughout the writings of Luke as well as in all the other books of the New Testament; they are distributed in a fairly even way, and in proportion to the amount of the "We"-passages there should be in them about thirty-eight words which occur nowhere else in the Acts and the Third Gospel; whereas

---

¹ Room for it fails in the present volume. In *St. Paul the Traveller*, p. 346, it did not occur to me even to defend this common technical usage (dates by a consul's name, *e.g.*, being always tacked on loosely by this absolute dative in Greek, ablative in Latin): I had not realised how little known the technical and the colloquial Greek of the later Hellenistic and the Roman period was known even to such masters of Greek as the late Professor Blass.

there actually occur 111 of that class. But this is due to the subject-matter. Navigation and voyages play a large part in the "We"-passages, because it was to a large extent on voyages that Luke accompanied Paul in the earlier years of their friendship; and he was by nature interested as a Greek in seamanship. Three-fifths of the words which are peculiar to the "We"-passages are technical terms relating to ships, parts of a ship, naval officers, sea-winds, management of a ship, and matters of navigation generally, and almost all of them are nouns, while the few verbs without exception denote actions required in seamanship. Such words are forced on the writer by his subject; and, as the Author rightly remarks, it is a striking fact that in spite of the novelty of subject in chapter xxvii., describing the shipwreck, the ordinary style and vocabulary of Luke are traceable with perfect clearness even in that long passage (p. 60).

It is, of course, acknowledged by practically all scholars that Luke employed written Sources. These written Sources he has modified and recast so that they assume much of his own style. Now, if any one still continues, in spite of the above-stated proofs from style and vocabulary, to urge that Luke found the "We"-passages in a written Source, and took them over into his book, transforming them into his own style and language, the Author replies by a careful study of the way in which Luke elsewhere uses his written Sources, from which he demonstrates that in spite of the freedom with which Luke handled and touched up his written Source, the original style, syntax and vocabulary still are clearly traceable in the transformed narrative. This is one of the most important and striking parts in the Author's work, and will reward the closest attention.

While every one admits freely as a starting-point that Luke had access to written narratives about many events of which he had not been an eye-witness—for he himself mentions in the opening of his Gospel that there were many such written Sources, founded on information given by eye-witnesses, to which he could have recourse—there is not much agreement as to the extent to which, and the parts of his two books in which, he was indebted to these Sources. But there is at any rate one Source, the character of which is indubitable: for we possess the Source in practically its original form (or a form so near the original as to be equally useful for the immediate purpose of this investigation), and can thus tell exactly how far and in what way Luke used it. Some Sources are more or less a matter of conjecture and inference, as they are lost in the original form and are merely supposed as the foundation of Luke's narrative. But it is practically universally admitted now that Luke employed the Second Gospel: he took a copy of Mark in much the same text and extent as we now possess, and he wrote out three-fourths of it in his own Gospel in much the same order as Mark wrote it. He improved the Greek, he touched it up with explanatory additions and "improvements" or "corrections," and he added greatly to it from other sources of information, oral or written; but the style, syntax and vocabulary of Mark are clearly discernible in the borrowed passages.

The Author exemplifies this in two passages, Mark i. 21-28 (*i.e.*, Luke iv. 30-37) and Mark ii. 1-11 (*i.e.*, Luke v. 17-24). A few verses may be quoted from the first as a specimen of this most luminous and instructive investigation, which ought to be studied by every one in the Author's own words.

| Mark i. 21. And they go into Capernaum, and straightway on the Sabbath day He entered into the synagogue and taught. | Luke iv. 31. And He came down to Capernaum, a city of Galilee, and He was teaching them on the Sabbath day. |

Mark has used the plural "they went after him" in the previous verse, and continues his narrative accordingly. But Luke had the singular in iv. 30 (which belongs to a passage derived from a non-Markan source), " He passing through the midst of them went His way "; and was therefore obliged to change Mark's plural to the singular. Further, in the preceding verses Mark's scene was the shore of the Sea of Galilee, and therefore the simple verb "go" was suitable. But Luke's scene in the preceding passage was at Nazareth, and he marks the change of scene from the hill-country of Nazareth to the lower coast of the lake, "He came down". And, as the readers for whom he wrote did not know the topography of Palestine, he adds to the name Capernaum the explanation "a city of Galilee".[1] Again, Mark was fond of the word "straightway," and often employed it (as in verse 23); but Luke disliked the usage, and often omits the word. Mark allowed the verb "teach" without an object; but this also was not a usage that Luke approved, and he inserted "them" (not very lucidly). The process "was teaching" seemed to Luke to express the facts better than the simple "taught". He found the expression "was teaching" in the following sentence of Mark, and brought it over to this place.

| 22. And they were astonished at His teaching; for He was teaching them as having authority and not as the scribes.[2] | 32. And they were astonished at His teaching, for His word was with authority. |

[1] Luke has already mentioned Capernaum in iv. 23; but there it occurs incidentally in a speech of Jesus, and explanation is unnecessary and would be out of place. Here the topographical explanation is useful and suitable.

[2] The quotations here follow the Authorised Version almost exactly, but

In the second half of the verse the thought is entirely remodelled and transformed into Lukan Greek and Lukan language; the verb had been transferred to the preceding sentence, and change was therefore imperatively required.[1]

| 23. And straightway there was in their synagogue a man in an unclean spirit; and he cried out, saying— | 33. And in the synagogue there was a man which had a spirit of an unclean demon, and he cried out with a loud voice— |

Luke here cuts out the possessive "their," and replaces the preposition "in" (perhaps a literal rendering by Mark from the original Semitic, not very satisfactory in Greek) by "which had"; he defines "unclean" more precisely; he substitutes the more vivid "with a loud voice" for the simple "saying"; and omits "straightway" (compare verse 21).

Verses 24 and 25 are taken over unchanged, except that in 25 Luke changes "out of" into "from".

A comparison like this might be carried out over the whole of the matter common to Mark and Luke. In some places there is distinctly more change than here. But even where there is most change, enough remains to show the character of the Source. Slight alterations to improve the Greek are frequent. Complete refashioning of the thought and expression is rare. Words and phraseology which Luke rarely employs where he is writing freely are retained from the Source. Luke recognised that a certain type of narrative style had been established for the Gospel, and he allowed this to remain. Especially in the beginning of a borrowed paragraph he altered more freely to suit the pre-

occasional slight changes are made to follow the Greek more literally, as here "was teaching," where both Authorised and Revised Versions give "taught" (which is better English in this case).

[1] Similarly, when the Bezan Reviser transferred the idea, "he neglected a region," from Acts xvi. 8 to xvii. 14, he remodelled the former passage.

ceding narrative. From some places it is clear that he did not translate verse by verse, but considered a paragraph or incident as a whole, and transferred touches from one point to another, where they seemed more effective. He studied effect more, or rather, perhaps, he pictured the scene to himself more vividly than Mark did, and lit it up with more vivid forms of language, *e.g.*—

| Mark ii. 3. And they came carrying unto Him. | Luke v. 18. And behold! men carrying. |

It will be best to give one continuous example from the Author, showing the net result over a short paragraph, of Luke's way of treating the Markan original; the capitals indicate non-Markan matter, and the italics matter which is gathered from Mark but occupies a different place in his narrative. The reader observes how Luke in his opening words places the picture before the reader's eye.

MARK II. 1-10.	LUKE V. 17-24.
1. And when He entered again into Capernaum after some days, it was noised that He was in the house.	17. And it came to pass on one of those days that He was teaching; and *there were* PHARISEES AND DOCTORS OF THE LAW *sitting by*, WHICH WERE COME OUT OF EVERY VILLAGE OF GALILEE AND JUDÆA AND JERUSALEM: *and the power of the Lord was with Him to heal.*
2. And many were gathered together, etc.	Nil.
3. And they come, bringing, etc.	18. And behold, men bring, etc.
4. And when they could not come nigh . . . they uncovered the roof, and when they had broken it up, they let down the bed.	19. And not finding by what way they might bring him in, they . . . let him down THROUGH THE TILES.
5. And Jesus seeing their faith, etc.	20. And seeing their faith, He, etc.
6. But there were certain of the scribes sitting there, and reasoning in their hearts.	21. And the scribes and the Pharisees began to reason, saying, Who

7. Why does this man thus speak? He blasphemeth; who can forgive sins but one, God?	is this that speaketh blasphemies? Who can forgive sins, but God alone?
8. And straightway Jesus, perceiving in His spirit that they so reasoned within themselves, etc.	22. But Jesus perceiving their reasonings, etc.
9. Whether is easier, etc.	23. Whether is easier, etc.
10. But that ye may know that the Son of man hath power on earth, etc.	24. But that ye may know, etc.

Mark ii. 1—Luke v. 17. Luke prefixes an introductory sentence in which he describes the general situation and lays stress on the fact that it was for Jesus a day of power (perhaps implying an idea, natural to a physician, that His power was not always equally strong in Him). This sentence is non-Markan, yet most of it actually lies in Mark's account of the incident, and merely needs to be gathered out of what he relates. The last statement regarding the power of Jesus might perhaps be inferred by a physician from Mark ii. 10 f.; but it goes beyond what Mark says.

Moreover, in the first sentence Luke describes the company, Pharisees and doctors of the law, and their origin from numerous distant villages of almost all Palestine. Mark only incidentally mentions in verse 6 that there were scribes present. Luke gives the picture of a large assemblage of learned and distinguished persons. Mark in verse 2 (not reproduced by Luke) tells us of the crowd, but leads us to understand that the crowd was of the ordinary kind, and we should naturally infer (though Mark does not exactly say so) that it mainly consisted of the people of the district and was rather uneducated as a whole, though there was a sprinkling of scribes among them (verse 6).

The two pictures are markedly different. If Mark was the sole authority upon whom Luke here could draw, this passage would certainly suggest that Luke made additions from his own imagination without actual testimony, and that he went at least to the verge, if not beyond the verge, of what is allowable in thus reconstructing a picture from the words of an earlier authority.

The question, then, arises: Had Luke no other authority? The Author seems tacitly to assume that he was dependent solely on Mark; and, if so, one can only say that Luke goes beyond his authority and his picture is less trustworthy. Hence—on the Author's assumption—the general impression that results would be unfavourable to Luke's historical trustworthiness in comparison with Mark.

But is the assumption correct? I cannot think so. Luke claims to have had several authorities (i. 2). The certainty and the detail in which he describes the character of the crowd and its origin from all Palestine seem to me to imply the use of other testimony besides Mark.

One Markan detail is omitted. Luke nowhere states the exact locality; but leaves us to gather from v. 1, 12, 16, that it was near the lake of Gennesaret.

In the sequence of the narrative the frequent use of the simple "and" to connect the sentences is not Luke's own style, but is taken by him from his authority. Various changes are made in the words of Mark to improve the style. Some of these changes are in the direction of a "Biblical style," which Luke seems to have regarded as suitable, and which he did not employ except where he thought the occasion and subject to be suitable; *e.g.*, he does not use it in i. 1-4, but begins at once to employ it in i. 5 ff.; examples here are the introduction of "they began to reason" instead of "they were reasoning" (ii. 6—v. 21), and the form "it came to pass" (17). Other changes are made to avoid words or usages which he disliked: he avoided the phrase "and straightway," he changed the adjective "a man sick of the palsy" (παραλυτικός) into the participle "a man that was palsied" (παραλελυμένος), and so on. He substituted the better Greek word κλινίδιον for the vulgar κράβαττον. He altered Mark's words, "perceiving that they so reasoned within themselves" into "perceiving their reasonings".

The Author rightly remarks that the change from "thy sins are forgiven" to "thy sins are forgiven thee" (twice, ii. 5, 9; v. 20, 23) is difficult to explain. There may be more in this slight addition than meets the eye.

It is also noteworthy that in Mark the scribes "were reasoning in their hearts," and that Jesus perceived "in His spirit that they so reasoned within themselves," whereas in Luke they simply reasoned and Jesus perceived their reasonings. Yet Luke's report of Jesus' words, "What reason ye in your hearts?" shows that the words were not spoken, but only thought. Here the picture given by Mark with such repeated emphasis is exactly the picture that we gather from Luke, when we read his narrative to the end; and it becomes clear that his omission of "in the hearts" was due to stylistic reasons alone, as was his omission of "in His spirit" in v. 22 (which he evidently considered otiose).

The changes from ii. 4 which are introduced in Luke v. 19 are of a more serious kind, and give a radically different picture of the event. It might fairly be said that they have almost the effect of misrepresenting the facts. The same effect is produced in a few other cases; but this is either for the sake of making the situation more intelligible to his readers, who were Western, not Oriental, or possibly because he doubted the accuracy of some detail in the Source. The present case may be taken as a good example. It is briefly noted by the Author, who, however, does not discuss it, but refers in a word to Wellhausen's explanation. The words are fully discussed in my Essay on the Credibility of Luke (*Was Christ Born at Bethlehem?* pp. 58-64); but I may epitomise here what is stated at length there. Mark ii. 4 describes how the bearers of the paralytic stripped off the covering of clay and soil from the (flat) roof of the house, broke a hole in the ceiling, and let down the bed through it. This description was true of the simple Palestinian hut, but was unintelligible to a person who knew only the houses of a Greek or a Roman city. Luke adapts his account of the incident (not to a Greek house, but) to a Roman house, and tells how the bearers of the man who was paralysed went up on the tiled roof,[1] and let the sick man down through the hole (*impluvium*) which was in the roof of the public room (*atrium*) of every Roman house. There was not a hole of this kind in the roof of Greek houses, and Luke therefore wrote for an audience or a single reader (*viz.*, Theophilus, a Roman official [2]) familiar with Roman houses, *i.e.*, living either in Italy or in some Roman colony like Philippi. Perhaps we may assume that the Roman style of house was common in this Roman colony. We could hardly make such an assumption about the Colony Corinth, where probably Greek fashion was dominant; but at Philippi the Roman soldiers were numerous.

There is no question here that Mark states the actual facts, and Luke misrepresents what occurred. The question is whether Luke, familiar only with Greek or Roman houses, misunderstood the description of the incident on the roof of a rustic hut in Palestine, or intentionally stated the

[1] He imitates even the Latin usage, which used the term "the tiles" (*tegulæ*) to indicate the roof.
[2] *St. Paul the Traveller*, p. 388.

facts in this changed way in order to make the scene more easily intelligible to his readers (or his reader, Theophilus), preserving indeed the general character of the scene, but altering the details and the surroundings from Palestinian to Italian. But, after all, how small even in this case is the change!—for though a good many sentences are needed to explain it to the modern reader, it is completed in two or three words in the Greek.

What is most striking as the result of the Author's investigation is (1) the slightness of the changes as a whole that Luke makes in his authority, and the faithfulness with which on the whole he reports his authority, even preserving largely Mark's very simple method of connecting sentences by "and" (καὶ)—a kind of connection which is much rarer in the parts where Luke composes freely.

(2) His almost invariable practice of touching up descriptions of medical matters: on this there will be more to say in the latter part of the present paper.

(3) The way in which, even where he most freely alters, he preserves a certain style of expression, which he evidently considered to be an established and suitable form for the Gospel. We recognise in Luke a marked sense of style and great dramatic propriety in varying the style to suit difference of scene and action. This has been the quality of Luke as a stylist that most impressed me during years of study. There is a certain modulation and freedom in his expression, which varies in obedience to the feeling of the moment and to the changes of scene; and the Author is sensitive to this beyond any other of the German scholars whom I have read. Even Professor Blass, greatest of Lukan editors, has been so taken up with explanation, and attention to readings, and questions of verbal har-

mony, that he has not been sufficiently (if I may venture to say so) alive to this highest quality of style. In the Author's hands this observation leads to very important results regarding the first two chapters of Luke's Gospel. But, before passing to this much controverted topic, I should like briefly to call attention once more to the paragraph Acts xvi. 6-11 as a specimen of this quality in Luke. It has long appeared to me that this is the most remarkable paragraph, from a certain point of view, in the whole of Luke's writings: it is most full of himself and his whole view of history and life and his Pauline comprehension, most instinct with vibrating emotion (*St. Paul the Traveller*, p. 200): "the sweep and rush of the narrative is unique in Acts: point after point, province after province, are hurried over": Paul is driven on from country to country, Galatic Phrygia, Asian Phrygia, the Bithynian frontier, Mysia, the Troad, and he must have been in despair as to what was to be the outcome of this dark and perplexing journey, until at last the vision and the invitation explained the overruling purpose of all those wanderings. We cannot wonder that the commentators have been so perplexed and nonplussed by this paragraph, and that they have had recourse to such shifts to make their way through it; perplexity is the fact or emotion which underlies the whole passage, and that is what the style brings out. The writer felt that breathless, panting eagerness, so to say; and his style is modelled to suit the emotion. The style here and always is almost out of the writer's control: the subject and the emotion compel the style, or, rather, clothe themselves naturally in the suitable words. That is the perfection of style. But it puzzles the commentator. We must here and everywhere in Acts follow truth and life; we must regard the surroundings and the geography.

And, if Paul is here driven on from country to country, if the historian has to hurry over the lands to keep pace with his subject, is not that the whole life of Paul the Christian? Paul thinks imperially: "he talks of Provinces, and, as he marches on in his victorious course, he plants his footsteps in their capitals".[1] It is hardly too much to say that all the rest of right Lukan study is an exposition of the meaning and spirit of that one paragraph where the mind of Luke and the influence of Paul are most perfectly expressed.

Regarding Luke i. and ii., the Author is of the opinion that the historian is dependent entirely on oral tradition, and used no written Source; he regards those chapters as purely legendary. He allows the possibility that the narrative part may depend on an Aramaic written Source translated by Luke himself; but he is not favourably disposed to this view, and he is absolutely convinced that the hymns of Mary, i. 46-55, and Zacharias, i. 68-79, are the free composition of Luke himself, that they were originated in the Greek form, and never had an Aramaic form. The proof lies in the fact that the language and style are so thoroughly Lukan, adapted with extraordinary skill from fragments of the Old Testament (the Septuagint).

Considerable part of this view seems to me highly probable. I have always felt and maintained that Luke regarded this part of his history as being a pure addition made by him to the Gospel as recorded by his predecessors: he had obtained it from oral, not literary sources.[2] He believed,

---
[1] *Pauline and other Studies*, p. 198.
[2] *Christ Born at Bethlehem*, Chap. IV.

however, that those sources were good, and he would not have been satisfied with popular tradition. The man who wrote i. 1-4 could never have gone on to repeat in i. 5 ff. a mere popular tale, or have invented without authority such hymns as those of Mary and Zacharias. Exaggeration and overdoing of a view fundamentally correct is here the character of the Author's opinions.

The Author does not draw the following inferences, but they seem to follow from what he does say. The style of Luke's history is governed according to the gradual evolution of the Christian Church out of its Jewish cradle. It is most strongly Biblical (*i.e.*, taken from the Septuagint Greek) and Hebraistic in describing the birth and early years of Jesus. In describing the life and death and words of Christ it is less Biblical, but still is deeply tinged with Hebraism, while in many parts it shows strong traces of non-Lukan style due to the use of written Sources. In describing the earliest stage of the Palestinian Church after the death of the Lord, it continued to be distinctly Hebraistic, and parts of the Acts even go beyond the later parts of the Gospel in the intensity of the Hebraistic tinge, as if marking the narrowed spirit of the early Church, which had hardly yet begun to understand the universality of Christ's message. In the second half of Acts (except in chap. xv. and in some of the scenes at Jerusalem, where the earlier Hebraistic tone is perceptible) it is most thoroughly Greek and Lukan. The preface to the whole history, Luke i. 1-4, is on the same level as the second half of Acts, in excellent and markedly individual Greek—here we have the true and natural Luke. As the Author says, the problem of the language and style of the Third Gospel taken by itself would be insoluble, but by the aid of comparison with the

Acts, everything is clear. It may be doubted, however, whether the Sources in the Third Gospel could be disentangled, were it not that we can recover the originals independently of Luke, through their survival in the Gospels of Mark and Matthew.

I do not mean that Luke was unconscious of the variation in style: such an assertion would be ridiculous. But he did not originate the variation—his subject originated it; and he did not employ it for mere literary and artistic effect, as the Author definitely maintains, but for historical reasons, as a means of conveying more clearly and effectively his meaning.

Study of the two forms, Hierosolyma and Jerusalem, which appear side by side in Luke's Gospel and Acts, shows both that Luke was conscious of the difference between them, and that he learned from Paul how to employ it for effective presentation of his subject. There is no trace of attention to this difference in the other Gospels;[1] but it is clearly present in the writings of Paul, who probably originated it. The form Jerusalem occurs twice in Galatians, Hierosolyma three times: the latter is in that Epistle clearly a geographical term, the former is hieratic and Judaistic, as it is in Revelation and Hebrews. A similar distinction can on the whole be traced in Luke though it is partly obscured by various causes (notably by uncertainty, and sometimes perhaps by corruption, in the text).

I. Hierosolyma occurs only four times in the Third Gospel,[2] always very definitely in a geographical sense, while

---

[1] They all use only the form Hierosolyma, except that Matthew once has Jerusalem. The latter form is almost confined to Paul and Luke in the New Testament; exceptions are noted above.

[2] Always in passages that have no parallel in the Gospels of Mark or Matthew.

Jerusalem occurs twenty-six times: some of the latter cases are mainly geographical in sense, but the atmosphere of the passage, the spirit of the context, may be regarded as determining the form to be employed. Some of these cases are in passages common either to Mark or to Matthew; and Luke has deliberately altered the form used. But most are in passages or in clauses peculiar to Luke. The following list, taken from the Concordance by Moulton and Geden, tells its own tale.

II. Passages peculiar to Luke: name Jerusalem occurs in Luke ii. five times; Luke x. 30; in xiii. three times; xvii. 11; xix. 11; xxiii. 28; xxiv., five times.

III. Passages common to Luke with Matthew or Mark, or both:—

Luke iv. 9.	Jerusalem.	Mt.		The holy city.
,, v. 17.	,,	Mt., Mk.		omit.
,, vi. 17.	,,	,,	,,	Hierosolyma.
,, ix. 31.	,,	,,	,,	omit.
,, ix. 51.	,,	,,	,,	,,
,, ix. 53.	,,	,,	,,	,,
,, xviii. 31.	,,	,,	,,	Hierosolyma.
,, xxi. 20, 24.	,,	,,	,,	omit.

Thus, while Luke has frequently the form Jerusalem, he uses it only twice in places where Matthew or Mark actually employ the other form. It is a principle of verbal suitability which is peculiar to himself among the Evangelists, one which he almost certainly learned from Paul.[1]

IV. In Acts i.-xii., xv., Jerusalem occurs twenty-five times, Hierosolyma six times.

[1] The idea that Paul adopted it from Luke may be dismissed without hesitation. Their usage cannot be independent of one another, if they were friends and companions. Paul is not likely to have taken it from a predecessor.

V. In Acts xiii., xiv., xvi. ff., Jerusalem occurs fourteen times, Hierosolyma nineteen times (but according to the text of WH., the numbers are twelve and twenty-one). Many of the places where the form Jerusalem is used are markedly hieratic and Hebraising.

While details in some cases are uncertain, the general result of these statistics is clear. Luke did, beyond doubt or question, attach some meaning to the distinction of form. He deliberately and intentionally chose sometimes one, sometimes the other. He was not guided by his Source, for in some few cases he changes the name used in his Source, and in other cases inserts the name where the Source did not use it. The distinction is clearest where he depends on eye-witness, and had no written Source. The distinction has no literary value, but only a historical and real value. It was used as a device to express meaning, not to give external and formal beauty. Professor Harnack, who maintains that Luke aimed at the latter kind of effect alone, without any thought of the former, cannot explain such a fact as this. Finally, Luke took the distinction from Paul, in whose case it would be ridiculous to think of a conscious striving after formal and artistic or rhetorical effect.

A similar case is found in the distinction between the names Saul and Paul. Luke consciously and deliberately uses the former to indicate the Apostle in his character as a Hebrew, the latter in his character as a citizen of the Græco-Roman world. I have little to add to, and nothing to retract from, the exposition of this subject in *St. Paul the Traveller*, pp. 81-8. Here again we have a distinction used by Luke, in regard to which no one can dream of any striving on his part for artistic or literary effect: it originates entirely in the delicate perception of real fact and historic truth. It is, probably, not necessary nowadays to waste time on the old-fashioned idea that Luke depended on two written authorities, in one of which the Apostle was called Saul, while in the other he bore the name Paul.

In respect of Luke's style, I regret to find myself in one important respect holding a view diametrically opposed to that of the Author. The style appears to me natural, unforced, determined by the subject in hand. The Author, on the contrary, takes the view that Luke's style is extremely artificial and elaborated (pp. 80 f., 152), that he paid the most minute and careful attention to form and the external qualities of style, but was careless to the last degree of fact and truth and consistency. It has been pointed out in an earlier part of this article what is the fixed idea and motive that induces the Author unconsciously to exaggerate (as I venture to think) the inconsistencies and the artificiality, the contempt for facts and the devotion to verbal art, that he discovers in Luke. He seems to me to have often been misled by that fixed idea so as to misunderstand Luke's method of narration. For example, he thinks that Luke in Acts xvi. 27 describes the jailer as not having observed the earthquake, but only its consequence, the opened doors. It is quite evident that Professor Harnack has never had the misfortune (or, shall I say, the good fortune? for it is a good preparation for appreciating this passage) to live in a country subject to earthquakes. If he had, he would never think it necessary for the historian to record that a person, who was wakened from sleep by an earthquake (as the jailer was wakened), was cognisant of the fact that an earthquake had occurred, for no person is roused by an earthquake without perceiving it. Luke and his readers knew better about earthquakes; and when he described the earthquake and its consequences, and added that the jailer was wakened, he could reckon on every one of his readers understanding without formal mention that the jailer perceived the earthquake. He who reads Luke without applying practical sense and mother-wit and experience will always misunderstand him; and one of the chief purposes of my *St. Paul the Traveller* was to illustrate the fact that these qualities must be constantly applied in studying Luke. When you think you find an "inconsistency" in Luke, you should look carefully whether you have been sufficiently applying these qualities, before you condemn the supposed fault.

The Author is not disposed to admit that any written Source was used by Luke in the first half of Acts. He rejects with contempt all the numerous speculations about Sources used in the Acts i.-xii. as empty, unmethodical and valueless, excepting only the attempt of Bernhard Weiss to prove that one such written Source can be traced here and there in Acts i.-xv.: Weiss detects numerous inconsistencies, and explains these by the hypothesis that Luke was here only a Redactor, who failed to harmonise his material thoroughly. But, so far as language and style go, the Author finds no part of Acts i.-xv. that can be separated from the rest as showing signs of a different hand and expression, whereas in the Third Gospel the parts common to Luke and Mark, and those common to Luke and Matthew, show such signs distinctly. On the ground of difficulties regarding facts and the treatment of facts, the Author is disposed to consider that Luke used a written Source for the episodes in which Peter plays the chief part; but the Source was Aramaic and Luke translated it himself, so that his own style appears alone in the Greek form.[1] Even in this case, however, the hypothesis that oral information alone was used by Luke cannot (in his opinion) be convincingly disproved.

The Author rightly attaches great importance to the proof that the writer of the Third Gospel and the Acts was a physician. The same personality is felt throughout. The proofs are found in all parts of the work, both those written by Luke as an eye-witness and those which he has borrowed from Sources that are known to us. The Author enumerates six classes of proofs :—

1. The presentation of the subject as a whole to the reader is determined to a certain degree by point of view, aims and ideals of a medical character.

2. Acts of healing are recorded in abundance and with especial interest.

3. The language of the history is coloured by the speech of physicians (in the way of technical medical terms, etc.).

These three proofs, however, are not sufficient. Jesus did much as the great physician and healer ; and it must be the case that the four Gospels should vary in the attention which they pay to this side of His work and character, and that one must go beyond the others in this respect. It would not follow that the one which goes beyond the others was written by a physician. But these proofs are raised to a demonstration by the following reasons :—

4. The description of the several cases of sickness mentioned shows the observation and knowledge that mark a physician.

---

[1] In the Third Gospel the parts common to Luke and Matthew rest ultimately on an Aramaic Source, but the Author considers that Luke used a Greek translation from the original Aramaic, and did not himself translate. See below, p. 74.

5. The language of Luke, even when he is not treating of medical matters and acts of healing, has a medical colour.

6. Where Luke is speaking as an eye-witness, the medical element is specially clearly visible.

The proof of these six propositions lies in the cumulative effect of a great number of small details scattered over the whole of Acts and the Gospel. It is, of course, impossible to give any analysis of such a demonstration. There are few striking cases to quote even as specimens; and one or two samples would give no conception of the strength of the cumulative proof. One of the most effective instances has been quoted above, p. 16.

This topic leads up to a question which I do not remember to have seen adequately discussed. Even in the passages that have been taken over by Luke from the Source which we still possess almost in its original form in the Gospel of Mark, wherever there occurs any reference to illness or medical treatment of sick persons, Luke almost invariably alters the expression more or less, as in v. 18 he changes the term "a paralytic"[1] of Mark ii. 3 to "a man who was paralysed". He could hardly ever rest satisfied with the popular untrained language used about medical matters by Mark.[2]

In some cases the change does not imply really more than is contained in the original Source, and amounts only to a more scientific and medically accurate description of the fact related in the Source. But in other cases a real addition to knowledge is involved, as appears, *e.g.*, from the following examples:—

---

[1] " A man sick of the palsy " in the Authorised Version.

[2] This is the second class of alterations, systematically introduced by Luke into the parts which he takes from Mark, as mentioned on p. 47.

I. *Luke*

1. Mark iii. 1 speaks of a man with a withered hand; Luke vi. 6 adds that it was the right hand: the medical mind demands such specification.

2. Luke viii. 27 adds to Mark v. 2 that the possessed man had for a long time worn no clothes: this was a symptom of the insanity that a physician would not willingly omit.

3. In Luke viii. 55 the physician mentions that Jairus' daughter called for food (*cf.* Mark v. 42). Various other examples occur.

In such cases are we to suppose that Luke simply made these additions without any authority, inventing them as natural and probable? That is the Author's decided opinion (p. 130, n. 4); according to him, these are examples of Luke's carelessness about fact and truth. But why must we suppose that Luke, who in the Author's opinion had access to so many oral sources of information, and who so often used sources of this kind in both books of his history, never had access to any oral authority for any event narrated by Mark?[1] Is it not more natural to suppose that the authorities with whom he had conversed told him sometimes about incidents which Mark records; and that, while he preferred to use Mark's account as his basis, he made additions in some cases from other authorities? Those who reject wholly the possibility that Luke could have had access to any good oral authority possessed of first-hand knowledge of the facts, are justified in regarding those additions as pure invention; but it seems inconsistent in the Author to maintain that Luke's witnesses (whom he admits to be first-rate) confined their statements strictly to matters that Mark omitted. Moreover, Luke is known to have used at least one written Source, apart from Mark; we can trace it where it was employed by both

[1] See above, p. 44.

Luke and Matthew. There were perhaps cases in which Luke gathered information from it, though Matthew did not use it (see below, p. 77).

The question inevitably arises, What effect will this book have on general opinion? The interest and value of the book, as has been already said,[1] seems to lie even more in the evolution of the thought of a striking modern personality, *viz.*, the distinguished Author, than in the study of Luke. It shows the Author on the threshold of the twentieth century thought, yet not able completely to shake off the fetters and emerge out of the narrow methods of the nineteenth century.

It may be doubted whether Professor Harnack's book, highly as we must estimate the ability and the clever ratiocination displayed in it, will change any one's opinion or convince any one who was not already convinced of the truth that Luke the companion of Paul wrote the Third Gospel and the Acts. Its method is too deeply infected with the vice of most modern investigations into questions of the kind: it is too purely verbal; it has too little hold on realities and facts. The history of literary criticism of ancient documents during the last fifty years has demonstrated that by such purely verbal criticism one can prove anything and nothing. Almost all the real progress that has been made comes from the discovery of new evidence, and not from verbal criticism of the old books. It is only by bringing the old books into comparison with facts and life that they can be profitably studied.

It is difficult to think that the Author himself can attach much value to the verbal proofs which he gathers together in his third Appendix, with the intention of showing that the

[1] See above p. 10.

letter of the Council in Jerusalem (Acts xv. 23-29) is the free composition of Luke without any written authority. I cannot imagine that the Author arrived at his opinion on the strength of the verbal evidence, which is singularly weak and conflicting; and, in fact, he confesses on p. 154 that the verbal arguments are perhaps less important than the reasons of fact and history. One feels that his opinion was reached first on the latter ground, and the verbal reasons are mere buttresses added afterwards in the attempt to support the tottering pile. One notes with real regret the special pleading in the comments on xv. 23, where κατά in οἱ κατὰ τὴν Ἀντιόχειαν καὶ Συρίαν is proved to be a Lukan usage (as if any one could doubt this) by comparison with the totally different sense of κατά in Acts ii. 10, Λιβύης τῆς κατὰ Κυρήνην. It needs no demonstration that Luke could use the preposition with an accusative; so could any other Greek speaker from the Danube to the Nile, and from the Atlantic Ocean to the Persian Gulf. And the attempt to make out, in defiance of the plain sense and linguistic usage, that οἱ πρεσβύτεροι ἀδελφοί is the easy reading and οἱ πρεσβύτεροι καὶ οἱ ἀδελφοί the more difficult reading, and therefore more liable to alteration, mixes up argument and meaning in the style of a lawyer pleading a bad case.

The same character attaches to much of the commentary on the following verses. What bearing has it on the question whether the Council or Luke composed the letter that ἀπαγγέλλειν (which is found in verse 27) is used by Luke twenty-five times, by Mark only twice, and John twice?[1] What reason does this give for thinking that the Apostles could not use the word? Paul uses it twice, the Epistle

---

[1] There are some textual differences on this point. Moulton and Geden give it five times in Mark, three times in John.

to the Hebrews has it, the Septuagint has it, Matthew uses it eight times.

Why point out that Matthew and Mark do not use the perfect of ἀποστέλλω; as if that had any, even the remotest, bearing on the question? Both use the verb very frequently, and as a matter of fact Matthew has the perfect passive in xxiii. 37. John uses the verb and its perfect freely. Paul, Peter and Hebrews have it (the first using even the perfect active). Similar remarks rise to one's lips in a good many other parts of this short commentary : many of the notes are absolutely irrelevant, and prove nothing, do not even point towards anything. Why heap them up? They merely weaken the Author's argument, for they show that he has tried every way and found nothing to buttress his case.

But, while the Author spends several pages in this discussion, he does not explain his position on the really important questions that arise about this letter. His position is far more difficult in this instance than that of the more thorough-going "critics," who maintain that Acts was composed by a late writer: they find it quite natural that this late writer should have to make up this document from his own resources. But the Author considers that the historical Luke, the companion of Paul, wrote the Acts, and that Luke was in the closest relations with Paul during the latter part of the very journey in which (he tells us) Paul delivered this letter to all his non-Jewish converts in the Galatian cities as an authoritative guide for their conduct in life. Luke certainly makes it clear and inevitable that this Decree of the Council at Jerusalem was the solution of the difficulty for himself and for all in his position. Now what every one asks from the Author, and what he is bound to furnish, is some explanation of the matter. How does it come that Luke was so entirely ignorant of the words of a Decree which he describes as of such immense importance, and which Paul had in his hands when he met Luke at Troas? Or if Luke knew the words of the Decree, does the Author seriously believe, and wish to make us believe, that the historian threw aside the real Decree and composed a sham one in its place? Finally, the Author must explain what he considers to be the relation between the sham Decree and the real one. Do they state the same thing, or different things? If the same, why does Luke in this case rewrite a document entirely, whereas in other cases (as the Author proves so carefully and so conclusively) he retains so much of his original Source? Or does the Author consider that the Council was a pure fiction, the Decree a mere invention, and the story that Paul carried it to Antioch and delivered it to his Galatian converts an elaborate lie? If that be so, how does he reconcile this with Lukan authorship? He declares that Luke is to the last degree careless of truth and consistency; but such elaborate falsification goes far beyond mere carelessness; it implies wilful intention to mislead.

These are not questions that can be evaded. They must be answered, in order to make Professor Harnack's view intelligible and rational to us, who desire to understand him. It is not sufficient to waive them aside (as the Author does) on the plea that they have been discussed by others; for these others think differently about essential points.

On this question the Author's argument is mainly of words; yet one does not feel that it was through these studies of words that he attained his present opinions. Where the verbal argument of this book possesses demonstrative value, it has more than words to rest on. Thus, in the study of the parts common to Mark and Luke, the reasoning rests on the firm foundation of the original written Source, and investigates the process by which Luke transformed this original into the words of the Third Gospel. In the study of the " We "-passages it has a large extent of varied narrative to deal with, and it cannot wholly neglect the facts. But, when the Author takes small pieces like the song of Mary or the Decree of the Council of Jerusalem, and analyses the language and rests purely on verbal statistics, we fail to find strength in the reasoning.

Take as a specimen with which to finish off this paper, the passage Acts xxviii. 9 f., which is very fully discussed by the Author twice (pp. 11 f. and 123 f.). He argues that the true meaning of the passage was not understood until medical language was compared, when it was shown that the word καθῆψεν, by which the act of the viper to Paul's hand is described, implies " bit," and not merely " fastened upon ". But it is a well-assured fact that the viper, a poisonous snake, only strikes, fixes the poison-fangs in the flesh for a moment, and withdraws its head instantly. Its action could never be what is attributed by Luke the eye-witness to this Maltese viper; that it hung from Paul's hand, and was shaken off into the fire by him. On the other hand, constrictors, which have no poison-fangs, cling in the way described, but as a rule do not bite. Are we then to understand, in spite of the medical style and the authority of Professor Blass (who translates " momordit " in his edition), that the viper " fastened upon " the Apostle's hand (καθῆψεν)? Then, the very name " viper " is a difficulty. Was Luke mistaken about the kind of snake which he saw? A trained medical man in ancient times was usually a good authority about serpents, to which great respect was paid in ancient medicine and custom.

Mere verbal study is here utterly at fault. We can make no progress without turning to the realities and facts of Maltese natural history. A correspondent [1] obligingly informed me years ago that Mr. Bryan Hook, of Farnham, Surrey (who, my correspondent assures me, is a thoroughly good naturalist), had found in Malta a small snake, *Coronella Austriaca*, which is rare in England, but common in many parts of Europe. It is a constrictor, without poison-fangs, which would cling to the hand or arm as Luke describes. It is similar in size to the viper, and so like in markings and general appearance that Mr. Hook, when he caught his specimen, thought he was killing a viper.

My friend, Professor J. W. H. Trail, of Aberdeen, whom I consulted, replied that *Coronella lævis*, or *Austriaca*, is known in Sicily and the adjoining islands; but he can find no evidence of its existence in Malta. It is known to be rather irritable, and to fix its small teeth so firmly into the human skin as to hang on and need a little force to pull it off, though the teeth are too short to do any real injury to the skin. *Coronella* is at a glance very much like a viper; and in the flames it would not be closely examined. While it is not reported as found in Malta except by Mr. Hook, two species are known there belonging to the same family and having similar habits, *leopardinus* and *zamenis* (or *coluber*) *gemonensis*. The colouring of *C. leopardinus* would be the most likely to suggest a viper.

These observations justify Luke entirely. We have here a snake so closely resembling a viper as to be taken for one by a good naturalist until he had caught and examined a

[1] Mr. A. Sloman, Kingslee, Farndon, Chester.

specimen. It clings, and yet it also bites without doing harm. That the Maltese rustics should mistake this harmless snake for a venomous one is not strange. Many uneducated people have the idea that all snakes are poisonous in varying degrees, just as the vulgar often firmly believe that toads are poisonous. Every detail as related by Luke is natural, and in accordance with the facts of the country.

The Author quite fairly quotes this passage as an example of Luke's love for the marvellous. One cannot doubt that the reason for its appearance in Luke's history is that it seemed to the writer a proof of Paul's marvellous powers. We see now that, while it was bound to appear marvellous to Luke, the event was quite simple and natural. No one can doubt, probably hardly any scholar has ever doubted, that the incident is narrated by an eye-witness: it is so vivid and so direct, so evidently a transcript from life, that its character is self-evident. But of what value would mere verbal examination be in this case without investigation of the real facts and surroundings in which the incident occurred? It is the same throughout Luke's history from beginning to end. One may refer to the incidents of the stoning and reviving of Paul at Lystra, and the recovery of Eutychus at Troas, which are not necessarily marvellous, but which both Luke and the public assuredly considered to be so; yet (as is shown in *St. Paul the Traveller*) Luke, while revealing what was the general belief and his own, describes the events simply and accurately, without intruding anything that forces on the reader his own marvellous interpretation.

NOTE.—A word must be added about the meaning of Eusebius's statements as to Luke's origin, τὸ μὲν γένος ὢν τῶν ἀπ' 'Αντιοχείας. In *St. Paul the Traveller*, p. 389, I expressed the opinion that this peculiar phrase, used in preference to one of the simple ways of saying that he was an Antiochian or resided at Antioch, amounted to an assertion that he did not live in Antioch, but belonged to an Antiochian family. Professor Harnack does not say anything that conflicts with my statement (so far as I have observed), though he does not formally agree with it, and, on the whole, rather neglects it; quite probably he may never have observed it. But several others have disputed it, and asserted that Eusebius describes Luke as an Antiochian. Some parallel passages will show that I was right; had Luke been known to Eusebius as an Antiochian himself, the historian would not have said that " by family he was of those from Antioch ". Arrian, *Ind.* 18, mentions Nearchos, son of Androtimos, τὸ γένος μέν Κρὴς ὁ Νέαρχος, ᾤκεε δὲ ἐν Ἀμφιπόλει τῇ ἐπὶ Στρύμονι (compare *Bull. Corr. Hell.*, 1896, p. 471). Nearchos was by family a Cretan, but he resided in Amphipolis, where probably his father settled, and where the son could only be a resident stranger, not a citizen:[1] hence he continued to be "Cretan by family, settled in Amphipolis". Similarly we find in an epitaph of Olympos in Lycia Telesphoros, son of Trophimos, γένει Πρυμνησεοῦς,[2] a resident in Olympos and married to an Olympian woman (*Bull. Corr. Hell.*, 1892, p. 224). As resident strangers acquired no citizenship, it was

[1] Unless an act of the Macedonian king forced the conferring of citizenship.

[2] Though I have no right to decide on such a point, I should be disposed to regard Πρυμνησεούς as the better accentuation: the form is due to rough and coarse local pronunciation of Greek, often exemplified in inscriptions of Asia Minor: many examples of this are quoted in writings on Asia Minor of recent date, *e.g.*, κατεσκεούασαν for κατεσκεύασαν, where ου must be regarded as a representation of the sound of W. In Πρυμνησεούς it represents either W or the modern pronunciation F. See, *e.g.*, *Histor. Geogr. of As. Min.*, p. 281; *Studies in Eastern Provinces* (1906), p. 360.

necessary to have some method of designating them in the second or third generation: had Telesphorus himself migrated from Phrygian Prymnessios, he would have been called Πρυμνησσεὺς οἰκῶν ἐν Ὀλύμπῳ (*Cities and Bish. of Phr.*, ii., p. 471), or more formally after the analogy of *C.I.G.* 2686 (οἰκήσει μὲν Μειλήσιος, φύσει δὲ Ἰασεύς). Josephus, *Ant.*, xx., 7, 2, speaks of Simon resident in Caesareia Stratonis as Ἰουδαῖον, Κύπριον δὲ γένος.

The form ἀπὸ Ὀξυρύγχεως, etc., is used in the Egyptian Papyri apparently in the sense of "belonging to Oxyrynchos, etc.," without any implication that the person was not resident there; but in this expression the critical word γένος is omitted: examples are numerous, *e.g.*, Ἀλοίνης, Κώμονος, Διονυσίου, τῶν ἀπὸ Ὀξυρύγχων πόλεως, Grenfell and Hunt, *Oxyr.* No. 48, 49.

The form τῶν ἀπὸ is also used in a way different from the last example, equivalent to ἐκ τῶν, *e.g.*, ὑπὸ Νεφέριτος τῶν ἀπὸ Μέμφεως, *Greek Papyri Br. Mus.* p. 32 (Nepheris was resident in Memphis); compare also Κάστορος . . . τῶν ἀπὸ κώμης Ἀκώρεως καταγεινομέν[ου][1] ἐν κώμῃ Μνάχει, *Amherst Papyri*, 88. In the second case Castor was not a resident in his proper village: in the former case it is possible that the formula is used in a papyrus of the Serapeum, because Nepheris was at the moment at the Serapeum outside of Memphis. But I do not venture to make any statement about Egyptian usage. Literary usage certainly has a distinguishing sense for τῶν ἀπὸ, *e.g.*, Σεβῆρος τῶν ἀπὸ τῆς ἄνωθεν Φρυγίας, Aristides, i., p. 505 (Dindorf): this Roman officer of high rank belonged to a Jewish family of Upper Phrygia and also of Ancyra, but he was not a resident in

---

[1] ωι in pap., corrected to [ου] by the editors: the writer made a grammatical blunder, which ought not to be improved by editors.

Upper Phrygia, for we know his career of Roman service (Waddington, *Fastes*, p. 218); in fact, considering the customs that ruled at the period in question, he was probably not even educated in Upper Phrygia, but in Italy, as he was able to enter the senatorial career when a youth.

The expression τῶν ἀπὸ is also used in the sense of "descended from a person," *e.g.*, τῶν ἀπ' Ἄρδυος Ἡρακλειδῶν (*Bull. Corr. Hell.*, 1892, p. 218), "of the Heracleids descended from Ardys," the Lydian king.

Fränkel, *Inschr. Perg.*, i., p. 170, takes the phrase appended to a royal letter, Ἀθηναγόρας ἐκ Περγάμου, as meaning that Athenagoras the scribe was not a Pergamenian citizen, but a resident only. But the meaning is, "Athenagoras (was the scribe: the letter was written) from Pergamos".

II.
THE OLDEST WRITTEN GOSPEL

II.

THE OLDEST WRITTEN GOSPEL

IN reviewing Professor Harnack's study of *Luke the Physician* we found that the best part of a very notable book was the comparison of the sections which are common to Luke and Mark, and the analysis of the relation between those two writers. In this detailed comparison the Author could not confine himself to considerations of words (that vice of the nineteenth century); he was obliged constantly to take into consideration the things of real life; and we observed in this case, as often before, that Lukan criticism keeps right only when the study of words is constantly controlled and directed by the observation of facts and realities.

The problem before the Author was to determine the principles on which Luke had dealt with the narrative of his authority, Mark. This task, which would have been impossible if the authority had perished, was facilitated by the fact that the same original document which Luke employed in those sections lies now before us as the Gospel of Mark; and it is possible to see exactly what changes Luke introduced, and to determine what reasons and principles guided him in making certain modifications in the narrative of Mark. As a whole, the result of the Author's examination was that Luke reproduces the facts accurately, that he to a certain degree changes the words in the interests of literary style, but that even these verbal changes are generally confined to single words or short phrases; and that there is a notable absence of all attempt to introduce new meaning into Mark's narrative or to intrude into the record ideas belonging to the age when Luke was writing. Luke improves the language of Mark, where he follows him; but represents his meaning with impartial and remarkable fidelity. Where he desires in his Gospel to give more information than Mark gives, he generally does it in distinct sections, based evidently on other authorities, written or oral.[1] And the fair presumption is that he represents those other authorities with the same perfect fidelity as he shows in the case of Mark.

We found ourselves compelled to differ from the Author chiefly in two respects. In the first place, there were other parts of his work in which he seemed to be too much under the influence of purely verbal methods, a kind of reasoning of which we entertain a profound distrust, and one which has led to many errors in many departments of literature; purely literary considerations of language and style often afford valuable suggestions and start new trains of thought, but they have never produced any results that can be relied on permanently, except when they are constantly guided and tested and controlled by more objective and real methods. The plan of the Author's new book, which forms the subject of the present article, leaves little or no room for this fault.[2]

In the second place, the Author seemed to us occasionally to have not quite freed himself from certain prepossessions

[1] We were, however, disposed to believe (differing herein from the Author) that occasionally Luke modified or completed a statement of Mark by knowledge gained from some other source (see p. 58); though these modifications do not amount to changes of essential facts.

[2] *Sprüche und Reden Jesu, die zweite Quelle des Matthaeus und des Lukas*: Leipzig, Hinrichs, 1907. *Beiträge zur Einleitung in das Neue Testament, II. Heft*. Since the present article was first published, a translation by Rev. J. R. Wilkinson, M.A., has appeared (Williams & Norgate, 1908).

and assumptions which ruled the hard and unilluminative criticism of the later nineteenth century. That that criticism was needed as a protest against older dogmatism and previous assumptions, I should be the last to deny, and have always freely admitted; but it was only on the destructive side that it was sound; its attempts at reconstruction were valueless and misleading, because the negative presumptions from which it started vitiated all its positive inferences.

In the Author's new book, *Sayings and Speeches of Jesus*, forming the second part of his *Contributions to the Introduction to the New Testament*, the method of detailed comparison, which ruled in the best portion of his *Luke the Physician*, is carried out even more completely, and forms the basis of the whole study. Hence I find myself in cordial agreement with the method and the results to a much greater degree than in the previous case. The main result, that the lost Common Source of Luke and Matthew was a work earlier than Mark, appears to me to be firmly established, and to lead straight to conclusions of the highest importance. Although those conclusions are not in harmony with the Author's opinions, they seem to me to spring inevitably from his main line of argument.

That the first, and in many respects the most important, authority on which Matthew as well as Luke relied was the Gospel of Mark, practically in the form in which we possess it, is now generally admitted. In studying the relation of Luke to this Source, the Author did not require to take into account Matthew's version of the same Source, because Luke was wholly independent of Matthew, and the Source still lies before us. But in the case of the second Common Source of Luke and Matthew, the problem is a far more complicated and difficult one. The Source has been lost, and it is only through the comparison of Luke and Matthew that we can recover an outline of its contents and character, and to a certain extent reconstruct the lost original document. This original is for brevity's sake referred to as Q; and on pp. 88-102 the Author prints all of it that he believes to be recoverable with certainty or high probability. As he says himself, it is necessary to fall back occasionally on conjecture and hypothesis, as the evidence does not justify perfect confidence.

In the course of this article we shall diverge slightly from the Author's custom, and shall use the symbol Q to denote the restored form of the lost Source, as given by him, pp. 88-102, while we shall refer to the Source in its complete and original form (which was indubitably longer, perhaps much longer, than the Author's restoration), by some circumlocution, such as "the lost Common Source" or "the Collection of Sayings" (a name used by the Author, but not in our view an adequate name, though it perhaps rests on ancient authority).

The original of Q was written in Aramaic; but both Luke and Matthew used the same Greek translation, and therefore throughout the Author's work Q denotes a certain Greek book, and not the older Aramaic original. The question is mentioned whether Luke or Matthew may occasionally have gone behind the Greek form Q and consulted the Aramaic original for some details; but the Author is confident that such a procedure, if it ever happened, was extremely rare, and that generally Q alone may safely be assumed as the single and final source of a certain portion of Luke and Matthew, about one-sixth of the former and two-elevenths of the latter. Perhaps Aramaic scholars might differ from the Author on this question: it is understood that one well-known English scholar, who has always taken a very different view, still adheres to his own opinion. But at least there can hardly be any doubt that a Greek translation did exist, and was used by both Luke and Matthew, whether or not they controlled it by consulting the Aramaic in addition. And the Author seems also to have established his theory of Q to the extent that his restoration can be relied on as giving a fair amount of the original document in a trustworthy form and as permitting certain positive inferences, but not negative inferences founded on the failure of any particular incident in his restoration of Q. There is much probability that in some cases the lost Common Source was much longer than the restored Q.

Incidentally, in this study of the two largest Sources which Luke and Matthew made use of, one must be strongly impressed with the utter impossibility of recovering from any single author alone the authorities which he transcribed. Let any one take Luke's Gospel by itself, or Matthew's Gospel by itself, and examine verse by verse the parts that come from Q and from Mark respectively. He must conclude that the problem of analysing either the Third or the First Gospel separately and distinguishing the Q-parts, the Mark-parts, and the parts taken neither from Q nor from Mark, would have been quite insoluble without extraneous help.

And, more than this, if Mark were lost, while both Luke and Matthew were preserved, it would of course be easy to distinguish the common Matthaeo-Lukan parts from the parts peculiar to each; but it would be utterly impossible to analyse that common Matthaeo-Lukan Gospel into its two parts, the Markan and the non-Markan. Only the existence of Mark makes it possible to tell what is

Markan and what is non-Markan. Yet take Q by itself, and read it apart from Mark, and the least observant scholar must be struck by the difference of character, style, language, and point of view.

Further, if one took Luke's Gospel by itself, and proceeded according to some definite peculiarity, such as, for example, the name of the Holy City, starting from the principle that the passages in which the Hebrew form Jerusalem was used were founded on a different original Source from those parts in which the Greek form Hierosolyma was used, how misleading and absurd would be the results of such an hypothesis! So in the Acts, the old "critical" (or rather uncritical) idea that the use of the names Paul and Saul indicated two different Sources has probably been abandoned by even the most unenlightened and unprogressive of modern scholars. It has long been proved conclusively that Luke had a definite purpose in distinguishing the names Paul and Saul, and employed sometimes the one, sometimes the other, for the sake of historical effect. So, also, he had a clear purpose of his own in distinguishing the names Jerusalem and Hierosolyma, and he actually alters Mark's Hierosolyma into Jerusalem, in order to carry out his own peculiar purpose (see above, p. 51 ff.).

The futility of various other similar criteria might be easily shown, if it were worth while; but we pass on, only pausing for a moment to ask whether in the analysis of the Pentateuch too much has not been made of the distinction between the two names of God, Elohim and Jehovah or Yahwe. Even admitting (as we do fully) that different older Sources lie behind the extant form of the Pentateuch, is it not possible that there may be some purpose guiding the choice of the final compiler or author in his use of the two names? I always bear in mind the warning words which Robertson Smith often emphatically used in conversation, that, while the diverse Sources of the Pentateuch could on the whole and in the rough be distinguished, it must always be utterly impossible to attain certainty about the precise points and lines of cleavage in the existing text (a warning which has been wholly forgotten by some scholars, who since his death claim to speak for him and to present his views on current questions to the public).

A general outline of this pre-Lukan and pre-Matthaean Common Source, then, can be recovered from the agreement of the non-Markan parts of Luke and Matthew; but, of course, there remain two important questions to be determined before we can regard the resultant group of literary fragments as a full and trustworthy representative of that old book.

In the first place, did Luke and Matthew take the whole of the lost Common Source and incorporate it in their respective Gospels? Were there not parts of that book which Luke alone or Matthew alone extracted, and for which therefore we have only one authority? It seems to us probable,[1] and even practically certain, that there was a good deal which only one of them incorporated in his Gospel: Luke treats the book with great freedom, and puts in different parts of his Gospel scraps of it which Matthew places side by side as continuous exposition. Such freedom seems quite irreconcilable with the idea that they agreed in utilising the entire book. This part of the Common Source (which we believe to have been considerable) is for the most part hopelessly lost to us. We may conjecture that certain

---

[1] The Author holds the same opinion.

paragraphs or sentences of Matthew alone or of Luke alone were taken from the lost Source; and in such cases arguments from language or style or thought might be fairly brought in to support the conjecture. But such conjectures can never be ranked on the same level as the agreement of Matthew and Luke; and they do not apply to any large continuous part of the book. Yet the attempt ought to be made, and will certainly be often made, to specify and collect those parts of the lost Sources that were used only by one Evangelist. The Author expressly recognises that this is a work which awaits and will reward patient investigation (pp. 2, 121).

Further, are there not passages in which the Source coincided in subject with Mark, and the latter seemed to Luke and Matthew to be preferable—not necessarily as divergent, but as more complete or better expressed? Was it the case—as it would be if the Author's restoration of Q were even approximately complete—that the lost Source never, or hardly ever, covered a part of the same ground as Mark? There seems an overwhelming probability that two such books must have agreed oftener than appears in the Author's restoration. It is clear that they covered the same ground as regards the relations of Jesus with John the Baptist and as regards the Temptation, but covered it in very different ways. In the case of the Temptation, for example, Mark restricts himself to a brief sentence; and both Luke and Matthew here neglect Mark and follow Q. Now suppose it had happened that the lost Common Source had been preserved, but that Mark had perished and we were attempting to restore his Gospel from the agreement of Luke and Matthew, some critics would certainl maintainy that Mark had never heard of the Temptation. As it is, we can see that there is no inconsistency or disagreement on this point between Mark and Q ; but the latter is far more detailed and complete. Were there not many cases in which the sharp and clear narrative of Mark was preferred by the two later Synoptics to a brief allusion in the lost Common Source? This seems to us inevitably to have been the case; and all these parts of Q, which were distinctly inferior to Mark in historical import and weight, are now hopelessly lost.

The consequence of this loss has been that Q has the appearance of being almost wholly confined to Sayings and Speeches of Jesus. This appearance we must consider to be untrue to the real character of the original lost Source. It is clear even from the agreement of Luke and Matthew that Q was not quite free from narrative: the parts relating to John the Baptist and the Temptation and the Centurion of Capernaum contain some narrative; several sections in the Author's Q, 3, 18, 22, 29, 30, 54, and others, must obviously have been accompanied by some narrative, however brief. In many others it is inconceivable that a first-hand authority (as the Author considers the writer of Q to have been) could have sent down to posterity, or published for his contemporaries, such a disjointed and disconnected scrap as that which can be got from the agreement of Matthew and Luke.

We must, therefore, conclude that there was more narrative in the lost original document than appears now in Q, and that sections 1, 2, 13, 14 [1] of the Author's restoration give a truer conception of its character than most of the other sections. It was not a mere collection of sayings, but a narrative, noted down by a person whose interest lay mainly in the sayings and the teaching of Jesus, and who made the

[1] The Baptist, the Temptation, the Centurion.

narrative subsidiary to the speeches. This person wrote, not with the purpose of composing a biography, but from interest in the character and the teaching of a remarkable personality, recording what He said, and employing narrative mainly in order to make the recorded words more significant and more instructive. In the account of the Temptation it is evident that the circumstances and the situation must be described in order to make the words intelligible to the reader.

These conclusions, to which we seem to be involuntarily driven by the facts, are quite consistent with the Author's views, though they perhaps modify in some degree the general impression which he gives of the lost Common Source. The opinion which on the whole he is disposed to hold is that this Source was the work of the Apostle Matthew, being the collection of Logia which Matthew (as Papias says) composed. The Author fully concedes that Papias understood this collection of Logia to be simply the First Gospel (p. 172); but he tends to the view that Papias in this matter misunderstood his authority, that Matthew merely gathered together a collection of sayings, and that both Luke and the writer of the First Gospel made use of the collection.

The question here rises, how do the two extant Gospels stand related to the original Source? Do they represent it fairly, and which of them reproduces it most accurately?

The Author shows repeatedly, both as regards the Markan portions and as regards Q, that while Luke sometimes gave more emphatic expression to the ideas of his Sources, he did not add anything of consequence to them on his own authority. In fact, as has been previously pointed out,[1] the

---

[1] See above, pp. 47, 4, 32.

Author's results from his detailed examination of Luke, sentence by sentence and paragraph by paragraph, stand in the most marked contrast with his general reflections upon Luke's character as a historian. In both the Author's volumes Luke bears the detailed test even better than Matthew; the Author declares that while Matthew on the whole preserves the actual words of the Sources more exactly than Luke, he in certain rare cases adds something of his own to them, whereas he finds no case where Luke adds to the Source any expression betraying the spirit and ideas of the later time when he was composing his Gospel. But while the Author's detailed test gives this result, he strongly condemns in general Luke's incapacity, inaccuracy and untrustworthiness as a historian.

As to the date when this collection of Sayings was gathered together, the Author expresses a definite opinion. He considers that the book of Sayings and Speeches was composed before the destruction of Jerusalem in A.D. 70, and before the Gospel of Mark. Otherwise he leaves the question of date an open one, except that he will not allow it to be much earlier than Mark. This he infers from the fact that the Gospel of Mark is wholly independent of and unconnected with the collection of Sayings; he argues that if this collection had been long in circulation before Mark wrote, it would be impossible that Mark should not have known it and used it (p. 172).

But, while the Author rightly perceives that this lost Source is older than Mark, his train of reasoning seems inconclusive and unconvincing. It involves one big assumption, *viz.*, that Mark desired to make his work supersede that older book. Now, if we follow the authority of Papias that Mark wrote the "Gospel according to Peter," there seems not the slightest reason to think that he would desire to supersede the older narrative, or to intermingle with Peter's narrative the account given by another (whether Matthew or any one else), or that he would feel himself bound to introduce speeches and sayings from another Source into the narrative as he gathered it from Peter. It is perfectly natural and probable that he may have known the old book of "Sayings and Speeches," and yet composed a narrative according to Peter, wishing not to supersede but to complete the older work. Still we are not eager to maintain that Mark was acquainted with the collection of Sayings. That lies in the region of possibilities, not of scientific investigation.

At this point we meet one of the Author's prepossessions, which we cannot sympathise with. He holds that the type of a Gospel—*viz.*, the principle that its central topic and guiding motive must be the death and resurrection of the Lord—was fixed by Mark; "being required by the needs of a catechetical apologetic" (p. 174). We must differ *toto caelo* from this assumption and from the vast consequences that follow from it. The type of the Gospel was fixed by the facts, and not by the accident of Mark's composing a Gospel. This type dominated the whole situation, and guided the thought and word of the Apostles from the moment when they began to understand the facts, *i.e.*, from the first Pentecost. In this type of the Gospel, as it quickly formed itself out of the actual events, the death of Christ was the essential and critical factor; and on this factor the whole narrative turns. That was the case with the speeches of Peter and of Stephen at the very beginning —and, as we take it, with every exposition of Christian truth thereafter, except when from time to time a "new theology" arose and lingered for a short time, only to pass away, often finding its grave in the mind in which it originated.

But the Author, on the contrary, is obliged, by his assumption that Mark fixed the type of the Gospel, to hold that the picture of the first Church, as given in the Acts, is unhistorical, and that the speeches of Peter and Stephen are merely the free compositions of Luke, expressing his own ideas of what they ought to have said, an incipient Paulinism. So he is in consistency bound to maintain, and so he does maintain, even in his latest expression in *Lukas der Artzt*.[1] And, on the same principle, he holds (p. 171) that the same cause, Paulinism, exerted a strong influence in moulding the form of Mark's Gospel. In a word, this view practically implies that Paul originated the recognised type of Gospel, that pre-Pauline Christianity was of an essentially different character, and that in that earliest period any so-called germs of Paulinism, *i.e.*, any stress laid on the efficacy and power of the Saviour's death, must be regarded as an anachronism and an impossibility. The nature and origin of Paul's teaching is here involved; and I find myself absolutely at variance with the Author. To me it appears that the facts, which determined the type of the Gospel, imposed it on the minds of the Apostles, generally, and that Luke's report of those early speeches is historical and trustworthy; and I am utterly sceptical as to the possibility that Mark, or any other man, could have fixed immutably and permanently (as the Author maintains, p. 174) the type of all subsequent Gospels.

But, it will be objected, here in Q is a Gospel which is utterly different from the established type, which never mentions the death of Christ or bases the efficacy of Christ's

---

[1] He often tacitly assumes it. See above. p. 22.

teaching on His death—a Gospel which the Author, mainly on the ground of this character, holds to be earlier than Mark's Gospel, but not very much earlier.

This is an important argument, which needs and will reward careful consideration. It involves two points, (1) Is it true that, as the Author maintains, the lost Common Source took no notice of the death of Christ? (2) If that was the case, when was that Common Source written?

It is, of course, correct procedure on the Author's part to restrict the scope of Q in the first instance to the parts which can be restored with approximate certainty from the agreement of Matthew and Luke, and to set aside rigorously all that does not rest on this assured basis—though even thus there are some places where, as he says, it is impossible entirely to avoid conjectural work. But in deducing from this restoration the character of the lost Source, one must remember that this restored Q is incomplete, and one must draw no inferences of a purely negative character, *i.e.*, one must never infer that there was in the lost Source no mention of any particular event or group of events merely on the negative evidence that in the restored Q no mention occurs of the event or group of events. To justify such an inference it is necessary to show that Q is positively inconsistent with the supposition that the event or group of events was known to the writer of the lost Source.

Accordingly, to find that there is in Q (as determined by the agreement of Matthew and Luke) no mention of Christ's death, does not afford sufficient proof that His death was not mentioned in the lost Common Source. It would, as far as this reason goes, be quite possible that this Source (which on the narrative side is scanty and confessedly poorer than Mark) was in the conclusion so distinctly inferior to Mark that the latter (combined to some extent with other Sources) was preferred by both Matthew and Luke; and it might even be possible to speculate whether this Source was not used by one of the two alone in some parts.

But there is stronger ground for the Author's view: the teaching of Q is inconsistent with the idea that the writer of the lost Source regarded the death of Jesus as the fundamental fact in the Gospel. One acquires the impression throughout that Jesus was to him the great Teacher, not that He was the Redeemer by His death: Jesus was to him the Son of God, the King who reveals the Kingdom of Heaven. In the Teaching of Jesus, the Kingdom of God stood out prominently, and its nature, with the conditions of entering it, were emphatically stated: the sons of the Kingdom, who had the right of birth, *i.e.*, the Jews, were to be rejected, and the Gentiles from all the world were to find a home with Abraham and Isaac in the Kingdom of God (sections 42, 13, 30); it was not a Kingdom of this world, it was a process of development and growth in the mind of the individual (section 40): hence, to speak against the Holy Spirit (which works this process in the mind of man) is the fatal and unpardonable sin (section 34*b*, 29): in this it is already implied, as is said in Luke xvii. 21, that "the Kingdom of God is within you". The way of salvation, *i.e.*, the Kingdom of God, does not lie outside of, or apart from, common life, but in the ordinary life of man (*i.e.*, it is the spirit in which that life is lived); and every man has the opportunity of being justified by the spirit of wisdom (section 15, 12). The revelation by the Son is the only and necessary way by which man can attain to the knowledge of God (section 25); this way of salvation is a difficult path with a single narrow entrance (section 41); it was unknown to many prophets, though now shown publicly to those who saw and heard Him (section 26); it is hidden from the wise and the educated, but revealed to infants (section 25); the Kingdom of God has come near those cities whither the true teachers and Apostles go (section 22, 16); there is need for many workers in this harvesting of the world (section 18).

In this Teaching there lies implicit the Gospel of Christ, but the foundation on which alone (according to the universal Christian Gospel from Peter and Stephen onwards) the Kingdom of Heaven can be built up, is wanting, for there is no allusion to the death of Christ, which gives the needed driving force and the power. The central and determining factor which makes the Christian religion is wanting, and the want of it was not felt by the writer. Jesus meant to him something markedly different from what He is in all the Gospels and in the whole New Testament outside of Q.

The question then is, When could such Teaching as this be written down in a book? The Author replies that it was written down shortly before Mark's Gospel, but after Peter and Stephen and Paul had been preaching the Gospel of the death of Christ. The type of the Christian Gospel had not then been fixed by Mark; and, in the Author's view, apparently, the Gospel might be anything that any writer pleased until Mark had shown what a Gospel ought to be, after which no writer could do anything except follow the type as fixed once for all, by Mark. He apparently believes that the other Twelve Apostles preached anything they found good in the way of teaching from the beginning down till Mark's publication; no one perceived what was the meaning and power of Christ's death until Mark's Gospel, in accordance with apologetic needs, fixed the type.

The Author's theory mistakes literature for life, and

regards the chance of Mark's publication as determining the course of subsequent Christianity. He ignores the facts (as we hold) that Mark was only an accidental agent, who wrote what the development of Christian teaching forced him to write; that it was not apologetic needs, but the force of inner life and growth, which gave form to the Gospel; and that the Gospel existed before Mark and independent of Mark. He even thinks that Mark, if he had known Q, would have given a different character to his own Gospel.

It is impossible that any of the disciples could about thirty years after the Crucifixion picture Jesus simply as the great living Teacher, or could set forth the way of salvation as being through the true knowledge which is revealed only by the Son of God, and yet never in any way allude to His death as being an essential factor in the process of salvation. The disciples realised immediately after the Crucifixion that they had never rightly understood the teaching of Jesus in His lifetime, because they had missed that cardinal fact of His death. Here we have an account which sets before us Jesus as the Saviour without alluding to the cardinal fact. The writer did not know that fact, which so radically changed the minds of all. Had he known it, he could not have been silent about it.

The Author lends plausibility to his view by denying all credibility to those parts of the Gospels and the Acts which throw light on the feelings and thoughts of the disciples during the period between the Resurrection and the writing of Mark's Gospel. In his view the course of early Christian history was quite different from what it is described to us; a false Pauline-Markan colour has been painted over it all, and the disciples understood everything quite differently until Paul through Mark taught them otherwise.

This is the only way to give a reasonable character to the Author's dating of Q. Only those who are prepared to go so far can accept his view. But it seems inconsistent and incredible that the period of Christ's life and the post-Markan period should have been pictured to us in such a fairly trustworthy form as the Author allows, while the intervening thirty or forty years is so totally misrepresented. This is not a reasonable or natural view; and no attempt is made to put it on a reasonable basis. The assumption is made that the first half of the second book of Luke's history is utterly untrustworthy; and an unattested and unsupported historical sketch is founded on the assumption. Here and everywhere in the study of the New Testament we see the evil consequences of depreciating the trustworthiness of Luke.

One other explanation can be suggested which would make the Author's date for Q conceivable; and that is that the writer of the lost Source in the first part of his work described the mind and belief of the disciples as they were while Christ was still living, and then in the last part described the change that was produced in them after the death of Christ had revealed to them the real truth. But such an artificial explanation cannot for a moment be entertained. The Author does not even think it worthy of notice, but tacitly rejects it and insists on the simplicity of the lost Source. This explanation is utterly inconsistent with the possibilities of the situation. It supposes a straining after dramatic effect which cannot be reconciled either with the character of early Christianity or with the habits and established canons of ancient literature.

We conclude, then, that the date assigned by the Author is impossible in itself and inconsistent with his own views. The lost Source cannot be placed either between Mark and

Luke, or a little before Mark. It cannot be placed later than the time when the disciples began, at the first Pentecost, to understand the true nature of the Gospel, and Peter began to declare it publicly, establishing it on the firm foundation of the sacrifice of Christ's death.

A date between the death of Christ and the first Pentecost is equally impossible; and is not likely even to be suggested by any one. In that period of gloom and despair, who would sit down to compose a Gospel in the tone of Q?

There is only one possibility. The lost Common Source of Luke and Matthew (to which, as the Author says, Luke attached even higher value than he did to Mark) was written while Christ was still living. It gives us the view which one of His disciples entertained of Him and His teaching during His lifetime, and may be regarded as authoritative for the view of the disciples generally. This extremely early date was what gave the lost Source the high value that it had in the estimation of Matthew and Luke, and yet justified the freedom with which they handled it and modified it by addition and explanation (for the Author's comparison of the passages as they appear in Luke and Matthew shows that the lost Common Source was very freely treated by them). On the one hand, it was a document practically contemporary with the facts, and it registered the impression made on eye-witnesses by the words and acts of Christ. On the other hand, it was written before those words and acts had begun to be properly understood by even the most intelligent eye-witnesses. So, for example, John says (ii. 22) that "when He was risen from the dead, His disciples remembered that He had said this unto them," and they then comprehended the reference to His death which at the time they had not understood.

The same tone is observable frequently in the Synoptic Gospels; so, for example, in Matthew xvi. 21 f.: "From that time began Jesus to show unto His disciples how that He must . . . suffer many things . . . and be killed and the third day be raised up. And Peter . . . began to rebuke Him, saying, Be it far from Thee, Lord; this shall never be unto Thee. But He turned and said unto Peter, Get thee behind Me, Satan; thou art a stumbling-block unto Me: for thou mindest not the things of God, but the things of men."

This is found also in Mark; but Luke omitted the reference to Peter, apparently disliking the harshness of the language.

Then there immediately follows in Matthew a passage strongly reminiscent of Q as restored by the Author: compare xvi. 24 with Q section 46, and xvi. 25 with Q section 57.[1] In fact, xvi. 24, 25, are almost a repetition of x. 38, 39, but the former belongs to the Markan portion of Luke and Matthew, the latter belongs to Q.

Luke ix. 44 f.: "While all were marvelling at all the things which He did, He said unto His disciples, Let these words sink into your ears; for the Son of Man shall be delivered up into the hands of men. But they understood not this saying, and it was concealed from them, that they should not perceive it: and they were afraid to ask Him about this saying." This also is common to Mark ix. 31, 32, and Matthew xvii. 23, but the latter gives only the words of Jesus, without remarking on the ignorance of the disciples.

---

[1] Q 46 is Matthew x. 38, Luke xiv. 27; Q 57 is Matthew x. 39, Luke xvii. 33.

Luke ix. 54-56 mentions the rebuke to James and John on the way towards Jerusalem for their suggestion, which was so incongruous with the spirit of Christ and the occasion. This is Lukan only.

Luke xviii. 31-34: "He took unto Him the twelve and said unto them, Behold we go up to Jerusalem, and all the things that are written by the prophets shall be accomplished unto the Son of Man. For He shall be delivered up . . . and the third day He shall rise again. And they understood none of these things; and this saying was hid from them, and they perceived not the things that were said." Matthew xx. 17-19 and Mark x. 32-34 mention that Jesus revealed the coming facts to the twelve disciples, but do not remark on their failure to understand.

The Author, if we do not misunderstand him, takes a different view of these and similar passages: he regards them apparently as being of distinctly later origin, barely of apostolic period, but rather representing the reflections and moralising of a later generation with regard to the simpler ideas entertained by ruder minds in an earlier time, before the later views about the death of Christ and its meaning had established themselves: see especially below, pp. 240-2.

We would not affirm that the writers of the canonical Gospels never added such reflections; but that tone and attitude of mind seems to us to have originated in the period immediately following the Crucifixion, and to be the inevitable accompaniment or expression of the gradual realisation by the disciples of their new knowledge that the death of Christ was a necessary and fundamental part of His Gospel. In our view, the utmost that can be attributed to any of the evangelists is that he gave more sharp and emphatic form to those reflections; we cannot allow that he created them.

There seems no other supposition but this which would satisfactorily explain the character of Q. On this view everything in it becomes clear. According to this view Jesus stood forth in His lifetime as the great Teacher, because in that way alone He had as yet become known even to the most faithful and devoted of His followers. The way of salvation was the way of right wisdom: knowledge was what Jesus revealed, *viz.*, the knowledge of God the Father. But Jesus alone could impart this knowledge. As He said, "I thank Thee, O Father, Lord of heaven and earth, that Thou didst hide these things from the wise and understanding, and didst reveal them unto babes. . . . All things have been delivered unto Me of My Father; and no one knoweth the Father save the Son and he to whomsoever the Son willeth to reveal Him." Such is the original form (Q), which the Author specifies as lying behind Matthew xi. 25-27 and Luke x. 21-22. He regards the omitted part of the last sentence as an interpolation (see especially pp. 204-6).

The two sentences which immediately follow this passage in Matthew xi. 28-30 are regarded by the Author as probably truly words of Jesus, taken, however, not from Q but rather from some other trustworthy Source and placed wrongly in this situation by Matthew. The passage is the familiar and frequently quoted one: "Come unto Me, all ye that labour and are heavily laden, and I will give you rest. Take My yoke upon you and learn of Me; for I am meek and lowly in heart; and ye shall find rest unto your souls. For My yoke is easy, and My burden is light." The Author sees and explains admirably the close relationship of thought and meaning between these two passages. The knowledge of God in the one case is the intellectual aspect of that which in the other case is called in its moral aspect the yoke or burden of duty; and Jesus describes Himself as at once the conveyer of the instruction and the imposer of the yoke, "take My yoke upon you and learn of Me". This is merely an enforcement in the imperative mood of the truth stated as a fact in the preceding verses. Thus the whole passage runs continuously in perfect sequence.

But the failure in Luke of any parallel to Matthew xi. 28-30 constitutes an argument so serious as to convince the Author that Luke did not find those last three verses in the lost Common Source, for it is not easy to understand how he should have omitted an expression which is so harmonious with the tone and spirit of his Gospel. It is, of course, always an uncertain argument to found any inference on the fact that some saying or event was omitted by Luke out of the vast number from which he had to select: he certainly omitted much that we should have been glad to have. But selection was necessary, and no two persons will select in exactly the same way: one will mourn the omission of something which the other suffered to be crowded out. Yet there is probably no other case where a deliberate omission by Luke seems so strange as this; and hence many will agree with the Author that Matthew took these three verses from some other Source and placed them here on account of their intrinsic suitability.

We cannot, however, agree with him when he seeks to strengthen this argument by the consideration that the verses common to Luke and Matthew are a statement in the indicative, while the addition peculiar to Matthew is an invitation in the imperative, and that there is too much change between the situation in the two parts. This reasoning is founded on the assumption, which the Author makes throughout, that what is early in the Gospels is necessarily simpler and more single in tone than what is later. Jesus was a complex character, and His Teaching had many sides; and we ought to find traces of this complexity in the very earliest faithful presentation of Him. But this is a point which is too important for us to enter upon at present. At present I would only point out the really close philosophic connection of the two parts in Matthew. The first part, xi. 25-27 (Luke x. 21-22), is the statement that right knowledge of the Divine nature can be acquired by man only through direct revelation from Jesus. The second part invites man to come to Jesus and acquire this knowledge, declares His readiness to reveal the knowledge, mentions that man in coming must co-operate by "taking on him the yoke of Jesus," and adds that the yoke is easy. In the two parts of Matthew's saying we have in embryo the whole philosophy of history and the history of religious development as Paul understood it.[1]

The Author rightly finds a corroboration of his opinion that Matthew xi. 28-30 is truly a word of Jesus in 2 Corinthians x. 1 : " I entreat you by the meekness and gentleness of Christ, I who in your presence am lowly among you".[2] We should also be disposed to think that the expressions used in Acts xv. 10-11, 28, rose to the mind of Peter and the Apostles from recollection of the Saying contained in this

[1] *Cities of St. Paul*, pp. 10-15.
[2] In the writer's *Cities of St. Paul*, p. 38 f., it is argued from this passage, together with Ephesians iv. 1, 2, and Colossians iii. 12 (juxtaposition of πραΰς and ταπεινός, or πραΰτης and ταπεινοφροσύνη), that Paul knew this Saying (whether from the Collection of Sayings or from oral information).

passage of Matthew.[1] Peter in his speech to the Council said, "Why tempt ye God that ye should put a yoke upon the neck of the disciples, which neither we nor our fathers were able to bear? But we believe that we should be saved through the grace of the Lord Jesus in like manner as they." And the Decree of the Council ordained, "it seemed good . . . to lay upon you no greater burden than these necessary things". Here the yoke and burden of the Jewish Law is contrasted with the saving grace of Jesus; and the Author points out that the yoke and burden which is meant in the passage of Q just quoted is that which the Pharisees imposed.[2] That the Author is right becomes evident where this passage is combined with Matthew xxiii. 4 (identical in force with Luke xi. 46), which is part of Q section 33, "the Pharisees bind heavy burdens . . . and lay them on men's shoulders". The heavy burden was the teaching of the Pharisees and of the Law; but the Teaching of Jesus imposed a light burden and an easy yoke.

But it is hardly necessary to go searching with the Author for arguments and external proofs that the words of Matthew xi. 28-30 were in real truth spoken by Jesus, and not invented by a later fancy. The practically universal consent of all subsequent thought has recognised those verses as among the most characteristic, the most exquisite, and the most perfectly adapted to the needs of mankind, that have been preserved to us in the Gospels. No proof can be so strong as that consent, *Securus iudicat orbis terrarum.* There was no second Christ to speak those words.

[1] Whether from their own recollection of the words which they had heard or from their knowledge of the book of the Sayings, or from both.
[2] The Author does not mention this analogy; and on his view of the late date and spurious character of the Decree, he would explain it in a very different way.

Nor need we restrict their intention so narrowly as the Author seems to do. They are far wider in application than he allows—as wide as the burden of every trial and every sorrow that men know; but they certainly include, as he says, the contrast between the burden of Pharisaic law and the freedom of Christ's teaching; they anticipate the controversy between Paul and the Judaising party; and they lead up to the Epistle to the Galatians. And what a difference in temper and spirit is there between the Saying of Jesus and the Epistle of Paul, great as the latter is: all the difference between the Divine and the human.

It is clearly apparent that Luke treated the text of Q with considerable freedom, and that the agreement of Matthew and Luke is in many places confined to small sayings, which might possibly have come to them from independent sources. In this respect there is a decided contrast with the triple agreement (of Matthew and Luke with Mark), where the likeness generally extends over considerable passages, sometimes over long continuous stretches of narrative. This difference has led some scholars[1] to doubt the existence of any real single written authority Q behind this double agreement (of Matthew and Luke, independent of Mark). They would rather incline either to a verdict of "Not Proven," or to a definite opinion that the double agreement rests on strong general likeness in a widespread oral tradition or in several different documents.

The Author's answer to this is given in one of the most striking passages in the whole work, a passage conceived in a singularly lofty spirit of sympathetic insight and of the

---

[1] Notably my friend, Rev. Willoughby C. Allen, in his edition of the first Gospel.

highest kind of "Higher Criticism," on p. 162 ff. (though in it there are passages which do not convince me):—

"The proof that Q is essentially a homogeneous and an ancient source is ultimately based upon the nature of its description of the personality of our Lord."[1] We see that there was an ancient written Common Source, because Q presents to us so remarkable, individual and unique a conception of Jesus. This conception is of inestimable value. Throughout all subsequent time the value has been acknowledged in every attempt made to sum up His personality. "The portrait of Jesus as given in the sayings of Q has remained in the foreground."[1]

The reason why Luke treats with greater freedom that old Common Source is complex. Two causes can be specified forthwith; and there probably are more. In the first place, a book in which the narrative was slight and the writer's interest was directed almost entirely to recording the sayings and teaching of his hero could not be adapted to a narrative form without some freedom. Secondly, in the teaching of Christ the same subjects and topics were, beyond all doubt, insisted on repeatedly. John gives in different situations a fuller discussion of topics which are briefly mentioned in the Synoptic Gospels. This is a subject which would require and reward full treatment.

The individualised conception of the Saviour's personality, which the Author rightly emphasises so strongly, proves also that it is impossible to regard Q or the original Common Source as a practical catechetic manual, drawn up about A.D. 60-70 for the use of teachers and pupils in the Christian doc-

---

[1] The translation is Mr. Wilkinson's, which I purposely adopt, partly to exemplify its excellence, partly to avoid any risk of colouring the Author's words to suit my point.

trine—which is the view taken by esteemed friends, especially by Dr. Sanday. In such a manual or handbook how can we expect to find a human being, portrayed in such markedly original traits, so unlike the conception that was current in all other early Christian documents? The compilation of a catechetical manual at any period must not be assumed without definite proof that the character of that period is clearly marked in the compilation. Now the Author rightly emphasises repeatedly as characteristic of Q that it has no Christological-apologetic interest, that it was not compiled in the interest of Christological apologetics, and that it follows no apologetic-Christological aims.[1] In the assumed period, A.D. 60-70, when Christianity was a missionary religion, already for a long time subject to attack and supported by defensive statements and teaching, such a document as this is wholly out of place and inconceivable. We have in it the contemporary notes of a person in immediate personal contact with Jesus, fascinated by His personality as a living man and as a great Teacher and Prophet, not thinking of His death and of what was to ensue thereon. When we desire to realise the character of the living man Jesus, we must go to contemporary record. It would be vain to seek for Him in the grave of a catechetical manual.

In conclusion, it is perhaps right to refer to an argument which will weigh with many minds against the date which we assign for the composition of the lost Common Source of Luke and Matthew. It is a widespread assumption that the earliest Christians did not commit to writing any record of the life or the words of the Saviour; and that it was only at a later date, after at least the first Epistles of Paul had been written, and when the disciples had ceased to expect

[1] See pp. 163 and 167.

the immediate Coming of the Lord and the end of the world, that they began to think of composing accounts of the events and teaching in which their faith originated. If you ask for reasons to support this assumption, there are none that seem to have even the slightest value. It is a pure prepossession, which has lasted from the time when everybody believed that the art of writing was a late invention; that the custom of writing spread gradually and slowly, and was in ancient times (as in mediæval) rare and unusual; and that the composition of every document ought always to be assigned on principle to the latest possible date. This is a prejudice which has been decisively disproved by recent discovery. The art of writing is very old. The knowledge of writing was far more generally diffused in the east Mediterranean lands in ancient times than it was in mediæval Europe; and the strong presumption is that every important event in the early Imperial period was described in informal or even formal documents, often by several persons, at the time that it occurred.

Protestantism first supplied the driving force to popularise reading and writing among the mass of the people in modern times, and from the Protestant countries the custom spread; but still it is only in a few countries that the familiar use of writing in everyday life is so widely diffused as it was in the most civilised regions of the Mediterranean world about the time of Christ. The whole burden of proof lies with those who maintain that the earliest Christians committed no record to writing, for that view is quite out of harmony with the facts and tone of society in that period and region.[1]

[1] The reasons for this opinion are stated more fully in the first chapter of the *Letters to the Seven Churches*, though even there they are merely given in outline.

There is one word which the Author sometimes uses in a way which does not convince me—the word "legend". Wherever it occurs it is a sign of the same old evil which has long been blocking progress—the hard, unsympathetic, self-satisfied, unresponsive and contemptuous attitude in cases where the East perplexes the West, where the first century eludes the comprehension of the nineteenth. In all such cases the nineteenth century way of thought, its refuge from the duty of learning to understand what lay outside of it and beyond its narrow view, was to condemn as "legend" what it could not understand. The word "legend" was used in an unintelligent and irrational way. The typical nineteenth century scholar did not begin by properly conceiving what is the nature of "legend". He started with a certain fixed standard of instinctive and unreasoning dislike: whatever he could not comprehend, he condemned as "legend". The honest and scientific method in such cases would have been to say simply, "this I do not understand"; it would have been human and pardonable to add, "since I do not understand it, I am suspicious of it". That the four Gospels, of which even the earliest is long posterior to the events it records and was not written by an eye-witness, are free from "legend" I personally do not maintain; but that much which has been called legend is of an altogether different character and has nothing about it of the nature of legend, I feel firmly convinced. That the domain ascribed to "legend" in the Gospels by modern scholars has been much diminished in recent years is patent to all. It is much to be desired that those who use the term "legend" in this connection should begin by understanding clearly what legend is. Even admitting that some statement or narrative in a Gospel is not trustworthy, it does not follow that this statement is legend: it may have originated in some other way. The Author is not free even now from this loose and unscientific way of labelling what he dislikes as "legend". But this topic is too big to discuss at the end of an article.

III.

ASIA MINOR: THE COUNTRY AND
ITS RELIGION

III.

ASIA MINOR: THE COUNTRY AND ITS RELIGION

IF geography be regarded as the study of the influence which the physical features and situation of a country exert on the people who live in it, then in no country can geography be studied better than in Asia Minor. The physical features of the country are strongly marked; its situation is peculiar and unique; its history can be observed over a long series of centuries, and amid its infinite variety there is always a strongly marked unity, with certain clear principles of evolution, standing in obvious relation to the geographical surroundings.

In the first place, the Anatolian peninsula stretches like a bridge between Asia and Europe. Owing to the great barrier of the Caspian, the Caucasus and the Black Sea, all migrations between Asia and Europe must either keep the northern side, through Siberia and Russia, or the southern, along the Anatolian road. A few of the invasions of Europe by Asiatic peoples have taken the northern path; but, generally, westward moving migration and invasion have followed the southern road through Anatolia, and all westward movement of civilisation which did not travel on shipboard took the same path.

Of the many invasions in which Europe has retaliated and sent her armies eastward over Asia, only one of any importance has passed north of the Caspian, and that is the great movement now going on, whereby Russia is throwing her armies, her railways and her peoples over Asia to the shores of the Pacific. Otherwise, all movements eastward from Europe in so far as they did not go by sea—the movements of armies, of pilgrims and Crusaders, of state messengers, of merchants and trade—have followed the lines that lead eastwards over Anatolia.

In the second place, Anatolia is a bridge with lofty parapets. The roads traverse the high, hollow, central plateau, closed in by loftier mountain ridges which separate that open plateau from the sea. The parapet on the south is the vast ridge of Taurus, stretching back from the western sea into the main central mass of the great Asiatic continent, only at a few points traversable by migrations or by armies, or by the rivers that drain the plateau and flow south in deep chasms cut through the heart of the mountains. I do not mean that Taurus was ever absolutely untraversable. Men can traverse any mountains, and there are ridges far more difficult than Taurus. But (except for hardy and resolute travellers) it is practically impassable in unfavourable weather, and during the months when it is liable to be covered with snow;[1] and at all times elaborate preparation and provision must be made for the crossing of a body of men, for Taurus is not a single narrow ridge, but a broad, lofty and much broken plateau, and the passes that traverse it are seventy or more miles long. Thus in practice the roadways were few, and migrations were confined to known lines.

The mountains which form the parapet on the north, though not so strikingly continuous, and at no period in history called by one single name, are really almost as serious

---

[1] Of the feeling of the ancients that not merely the mountain-passes, but the roads across the open plateau, were closed to travellers during the long winter, examples are quoted in *Pauline and other Studies*, p. 385 f. See p. 139.

PLATE I.

The Pass leading to Dorylaion (from the window of a Railway Carriage).

PLATE II.

To face p. 106.   The Central Trade Route : Sources of the Maeander.

a barrier confining the tides of movement to the main Anatolian east and west roadway.

You enter the roadway at one or other of a few points, where alone entrance is easy, and you are driven on, eastwards or westwards, according to the temporary direction of the tide. If you come from the west, you enter with Godfrey and the Crusaders at Dorylaion, or with Alexander the Great at Celænæ.[1] Until a few years ago you entered the bridge on horseback or on foot; now you enter in a railway carriage.

Plate I. illustrates the way from the coast to Dorylaion, the great military road of the Byzantine Empire. The spot chosen is where this road passes through a narrow gorge between two walls of rock, which leave room only for the little Black-Water (Kara-Su), a tributary of the Sangarius. The road has been in great part cut or tunnelled in the rock. The view is taken from a window of the German railway train passing through the gorge.

Plate II. shows a scene on the other chief line of approach to the Plateau, the great Central Trade Route, which led up the Mæander and the Lycus, past the salt lake Anava (or Sanaos) and Apameia-Celænæ. This view, with its open quiet scenery and gently sloping hills, when compared with Plate I., shows well the contrast between the easy character of the one great approach which nature has made to the Plateau and the difficulties that encumber all other approaches.

The scene is the single head-source of the Mæander river in all its Apamean branches, Marsyas, Mæander, Obrimas

---

[1] Dorylaion, the modern Eski-Sheher, junction of the German railway lines to Angora and to Konia (ultimately to Syria, Mecca and Bagdad). Celænæ, the Seleucid and Roman Apameia, present terminus of the Ottoman Railway from Smyrna: it was one of the most important points on the great Eastern Trade Route in Hellenistic and Roman times.

and Therma. It lies in the high valley of Aurokra above Celænæ on the east. The Ottoman railway has not yet reached it, but will soon do so.

The fountain gushes out from the rocks on the east side of the valley of Aurokra, and runs down a mile or two to the west side of the plain, where its waters collect in a marshy lake against the hills that divide the Aurokra valley from Celænæ. The water of the lake runs off under the hills through two holes (which can be clearly seen when the light falls in the proper direction by any one standing on the hills above), and emerges on the other side of the hills at a much lower level in the fountains of the four streams of Celænæ, which combine to form the river Mæander.[1]

The head-source, in Plate II., was called the fountain Aurokrene or Aulokrene; and the latter name, which seemed in Greek to give the meaning Flute-Fountain, affected the form of the legends, which connected themselves with this magnificent spring.[2] Hardly even in Greece itself is there a spot more sacred in folk-lore and religion. Here Athena threw aside her flute, and Marsyas picked it up. Here Marsyas contended with Apollo in music, and on one of the plane-trees beside the spring he was hung up to be flayed. In the plain below Lityerses was slain by the sickles of the reapers. The physical features of the plain are so striking that we need not wonder to find so many legends attached to it. The myth implies as its scene a place where there

[1] There is a fifth stream, Orgas, which rises some miles south-west of Celænæ in a different range of hills. The whole series of fountains and names is described in *Cities and Bishoprics of Phrygia*, chap. xi.

[2] The name *fontes Rocreni* occurs in Livy, xxxviii., and marks the line of the robber-raid of the Consul Manlius from Pisidia to Galatia. The initial vowel has been lost in this form.

To face p. 108.

The Falls at Hierapolis on the Central Trade Route.

abounded the reeds, from which the earliest and simplest kind of flute was made. The lake of Aurokra is in great part a reedy marsh, though the water lies deep against the western hills.

On this same road, the white cliffs of Hierapolis (shown in the Frontispiece) strike the traveller's eye for many miles of his way through the Mæander and the Lycus valleys. They are almost literally petrified water, being the white deposit which the water of the hot springs has left as it tumbles down over the steep cliffs to the level plain of the Lycus. In the photograph it is quite impossible to distinguish the flowing water from the petrified incrustation. The form and colour are so exactly the same that even the traveller's eye, if he stands a little back from the falls, is deceived.

After reaching the Plateau by one of the few entrances, you move on eastwards, and pass off the bridge by one or other of a few well-marked exits. If you come from Asia, you follow the same inevitable paths; nothing differs except the direction of your motion and the tides or the motives that impel you.

Thus the history of Anatolia has been one of startling vicissitudes, of constant variety, of rapid changes in population, in government, in the trend of development; and yet the unity amid the variety is so easy to comprehend that it may fairly be called unmistakable. The development has always lain in the action and collision of forces moving eastwards or westwards; it has rarely been complicated by side influences

III. *Asia Minor:*

coming in from the sea on the north or on the south;[1] it has been simply the series of phases in the immemorial conflict between Europe and Asia. The central point of that never-ending battle varies from age to age. At one time the Greeks gather to a siege of Troy; at another the Arabs or the Egyptian Memluks storm the walls of Tarsus, defended by Greek fire or by Crusaders' axes and lances, or by that small fraction of the Armenian kingdom of Cilicia who could be induced to forget their mutual quarrels about points of ritual and unite to save their own families against the slaughterers from the East; at another the Arabs are being beaten back repeatedly from the ramparts of Constantinople, or the Turks are pouring in through a breach. As you cast your eyes back over the past, you see Crœsus crossing the Halys to destroy a great kingdom, or you watch the younger Cyrus the Persian leading 10,000 Greeks from Sardis to Mesopotamia, to show them how easily a vast Persian army might be scattered by a few trained and disciplined troops. You may see, on New Year's Day in A.D. 1148, Louis VII. with his French Crusaders, fording hand-in-hand the unfordable Mæander, and scattering before their first charge the Turkish army drawn up on the further bank to prevent their crossing;[2] or Manuel with his splendid army of mail-clad warriors, European and Byzantine, jammed against their baggage train in that open pass west of Pisidian Antioch, and slaughtered at will by the Turks charging down from the

[1] The influence of the old Ionian colony of Sinope (cp. Strab, p. 540) and probably also of the old Ionian colony of Tarsus (cp. *Cities of St. Paul*, p. 113 ff.) may be quoted as to some degree exceptions.

[2] This brilliant feat of arms is wrongly attributed by Gibbon to Conrad, the German Emperor, who also took part in the second crusade. On the scene, see *Cities and Bishoprics of Phrygia*, vol. i., p. 162.

higher ground on the north.¹ If you want to see what happened when an army abandoned the few recognised paths, cast your eyes on the soldiers of the First Crusade, wandering and perishing amid the mountains of Anti-Taurus, or Frederick Barbarossa's German Crusaders struggling over the central Taurus, fed by an Armenian prince in his stronghold among the mountains, and Barbarossa himself disappearing under the waters of the Calycadnus so suddenly that his people could not believe he was dead, and long imagined that he was only waiting the proper moment to reappear in his German home. All are but small skirmishes in the great battle of East and West.

To illustrate this principle fully would be to write the history of the Anatolian peninsula. In every age, in every war, in every crisis, the opposing forces may be recognised as respectively Eastern and Western. Often, where two rivals contend for the succession to a throne or a tent, one may be recognised as champion of the East, and the other, as his opponent, attracts the support of the West; and probably that was the general rule in such contests, though we are not always well enough informed of the facts. But the writer's *Historical Geography of Asia Minor*, which has had the honour of being published by the Royal Geographical Society, illustrates on page after page the infinitely varied forms in which the principle has worked itself out in history (though, from its extreme brevity, it gives only the dry bones of history, into which the reader must breathe life for himself); and we pass from it. I may only be permitted to say, in passing, that the experience and study of twelve years since that book was written have amply

---

[1] *Studies in the History and Art of the Eastern Roman Provinces*, p. 235 ff.

confirmed the general scheme of topographical history contained in it, and also furnished both many corroborations of details in the application of the general rules and many improvements or corrections in other details. I do not know which have given me personally greater pleasure; it is pleasant to find that one's instinct or reasoning has been right, but it is almost more pleasant to find that a mistake has been put right and a stumbling-block cleared away. The corroboration gives one confidence to go on in the path of investigation; but the correction opens a door, and often reveals a new chapter in the political or historical geography of the country. Moreover, most of the corrections have come from investigators whom I might almost venture to call pupils of my own, because they made their first essays in my company or with my advice; and it is always a peculiar pleasure to learn from men whose early steps one has helped in some small degree to direct.

One of the omissions in that book was that the importance of the mountain barriers on the north and south was not sufficiently worked out, and thus several chapters of history passed unobserved. To this subject my studies have recently been directed, and they have been illuminated by explorations which, after a long interval of ten years, I was enabled to resume by a concurrence of favourable circumstances. One point in this wide subject may detain us for a few moments.

The great mountain wall of Taurus, on the southern side of the plateau, has always been the most effectual boundary-line in the Anatolian peninsula; and this in spite of the fact that the plateau has rarely been the seat of a capital, but has generally been subject to one of the great empires of the East or the West. Many causes of course contributed to

To face p. 112. The City, Rock and Castle of Afion-Kara Hissar. *See p. 137.*

give Taurus this importance as a dividing-line; but we here simply assume the fact without analysing the contributory causes.[1]

The ancient records often express the bounds of nations or of spheres of influence by the phrases "within" or "beyond the Taurus". Taurus was the dividing-line between east and west. Even at the present day, when the whole of Anatolia outside the walls of Smyrna and the railway-lines is in a sense distinctly Oriental, one feels that, after crossing Taurus by the pass of the Cilician Gates and descending south and east into Cilicia, one has passed a line of demarcation and is surrounded by a more Oriental spirit. Cilicia, as the Romans long arranged it, is more a part of Syria than of Asia Minor. In it you detect at once the impression of the Arab and the Ansarieh; you hear yourself addressed no longer as Tchelebi, which was practically universal as a title of respect before you crossed Taurus: the people now style you Hawaja, as in Syria or Egypt. That single detail is significant of the changed atmosphere that rules beyond the Taurus.

In my *Historical Geography* the contrast between the Ægean coastlands and the rest of the great peninsula is described, the former being, as it were, a part of Greece, full of the light and the variety and the joyous brightness of the Greek lands; the rest, including the whole plateau, being, alike in geographical character and in spirit, part of Asia, impressive in its immobility, monotony and subdued tone.

---

[1] For example, one may mention the difference of climate between the plateau north of Taurus (with its long hard winter) and the hot coastlands of Cilicia. My friend Mr. Hogarth emphasised this very rightly in the discussion which ensued after the paper was read. Taurus was a boundary, not simply because it was Taurus, but because of all the many physical facts that combined to give it importance. (See p. 139.)

But one feels inclined to draw a further distinction, and to describe the west coast as Greek, the plateau within Taurus as the Debatable Land, and the country beyond Taurus as Eastern and Asiatic. Yet the moment that one has uttered the words one feels that they are inaccurate. More than any other city, Tarsus impresses one as the meeting-place of East and West. And in history what variety is there in the lot of Cilicia and in the kind of division which Taurus marks!

In the long wars between the Byzantine (or rather the Roman) Empire and the Saracens, Taurus with Anti-Taurus divided the Romans from the Arabs for centuries, Tarsus on the south-west and Melitene on the north-east being the frontier fortresses on the Arab side. The Arabs twice attempted to advance their frontier from Tarsus over Taurus and to hold Tyana; but both the Caliphs Harun-al-Rashid and Al-Mamun, each of whom built a mosque and stationed a garrison in Tyana, found it necessary to draw back to Tarsus before two years had elapsed.

For a longer period the Arabs held Cæsareia, in their advance from Melitene; but that also they failed to hold permanently. They could never establish themselves beyond Taurus. They crossed that mountain barrier in their annual raids, often in two raids per annum; they captured almost every city in the whole land; they thrice besieged Constantinople; and yet through three long centuries of such war they never held a foot of land beyond Taurus outside the range of their weapons at the moment. They conquered and they passed, and the people of the land recovered from every blow with marvellous rapidity. In all history there is probably no other proof so striking of the elasticity and recuperative power that belongs to the well-knit society of an organised people, welded together by a long-established system of reasoned law and by a common religion. Roman society was too compact for the Arabs to conquer—a hundred battles and a hundred defeats had no serious effect on it. The lower civilisation of a loosely knit Oriental despotism could make no permanent impression on the fabric that Roman organising genius had created.

But, if the Roman social fabric survived the sufferings of those terrible centuries, when Arab raids were to be dreaded every year, the suffering was terrible. The Roman civilisation had weakened the stamina of the nation, and a long continuance of peace had made the general population feeble, unwarlike, perfectly content to be defended by a professional army, which had become almost a caste. When a civilised people has lost the fighting strength, which must in the last resort be its defence against the attack of barbarism, it is always in danger. A large population of traders and artisans, clergy and schoolmasters, and other peaceful persons, was powerless before a small force of hardy barbarians, accustomed to weapons from infancy, regarding war as the one business of life and the chief duty of religion. Hence the Arab raiders could go where they pleased, ravage almost any city they chose, and easily avoid the slower regular armies of Roman trained soldiers; but they could hold nothing permanently beyond the line of Taurus.

The professional army might have found it an easier task to defend the line of Mount Taurus and keep the Mohammedan wolves from the Roman sheepfold, if the great pass of the Cilician Gates had been the only way of crossing Taurus from Cilicia. That pass, an easy road for the most part to traverse, is also a very easy one to defend at many points by even a small force. In Byzantine time it was strongly garrisoned, and a line of beacons flashed the news to Constantinople as soon as the Arabs were moving against it. But the long-continued peace and prosperity of the Roman Empire had opened other roads. Taurus had never been an absolutely impassable barrier, and under the Roman peace many cities had grown and prospered in its highest grounds, where now no dwelling is known except a few black tents of nomads in the summer. Those cities, rich and prosperous, had improved the roads, and made it easy for the light raiding armies of the Arabs to cross the mountains.

If, at a later time, the more barbarous Turk achieved what the more polished and fiery Arabs had failed to do, the Turkish triumph exemplified the only way in which, apart from practical extermination, barbarism can conquer a civilised and organised society, *viz.*, by breaking up the fabric and constitution of society and reducing it once more to an aggregation of disconnected atoms. The Turkish conquest was not achieved through pitched battles and victories; it was gained by the nomad tribes which spread over the land, destroyed the bonds of communication which held society together, and reduced the country from the settled to the nomadic stage. The Turkish conquest meant the nomadisation of the country.

But the number of questions which open on every side when one begins to discuss that great subject of the degeneration from Roman organisation to the nomadic stage in Asiatic Turkey is endless; and we must return to our immediate topic, *viz.*, the effect of the Taurus range as a division between races, as a defence of a settled people against invasion, and as a limiting wall to determine the lines of migration or of ecclesiastical organisation.

If Taurus divided Arab and Roman, Mohammedan and Christian, in the time of the Saracen wars (641-965), it was

PLATE V.

The Rock and Castle of Sivri-Hissar.

PLATE VI.

To face p. 116.   Roman Milestone on the Syrian Route.   *See p.* 138.

again the boundary between Christian and Mohammedan in the early Turkish period for about four centuries beginning from 1071 A.D. The Turks came in from Central Asia over Armenia, and held the central Anatolian plateau for centuries before they gained possession of Cilicia; they captured Constantinople and advanced to Belgrad before they captured Tarsus. Christian powers — Byzantines, Latin Crusaders and Armenian princes—quarrelled with one another for possession of Cilicia. Taurus saved the land by the sea from Turkish armies; but there was no such barrier on the Syrian side,[1] and the Memluk sultans of Egypt destroyed the Christian kingdom of Cilicia. Here again the nomad Turkmen tribes, gradually spreading across Taurus and over the plains, were the true conquerors, sapping and destroying the links that held together society in the country.

Thus the effect of the Taurus as a division between nations, as well as in directing and limiting the march of armies, might in itself furnish a great subject.

Only in one case is there a district of any importance in the Anatolian peninsula which lies outside of our classification into central plateau, mountain-rim and coast valleys. There is one secondary valley on the north, where there intervenes between the plateau-rim and the sea a second mountain-ridge. Between these two parallel ridges there stretches east and west a valley of considerable importance, forming the most fertile part of the ancient country of Paphlagonia. That valley has a history which stands entirely apart from the history of either the plateau on the one hand or of the sea-coast cities on the other. Just as you might sail and explore along the coast, and travel extensively

---

[1] The ridge of Amanus, which bounds Cilicia on the east, is easily crossed by passes about 2,000 ft. high or less.

in the northern parts of the plateau itself, yet never enter the great Paphlagonian valley, so you might write a minute study of the history of the coast and of the plateau, and hardly ever have occasion to mention the intermediate valley. And yet the valley had a great history. It contained some powerful cities. The wars of the Mithridatic dynasty of kings against the Romans and the states of the West, for the most part, were fought or manœuvred along that valley. Some of the most obscure campaigns in the long wars between the kings of the Romans and the Saracen invaders seem to have taken place in the valley, and those campaigns are so obscure because the ordinary data for interpreting the evidence by the conditions of the plateau or the coast fail us for the intermediate Paphlagonian valley. Its cities became even more important, in comparison to the rest of the country, during the earlier stages of the Turkish period, and are often mentioned.

But that long history of the Paphlagonian valley has never been written.[1] Its many ancient towns are for the most part unknown even by name. Perhaps the task cannot be achieved, because recorded history has kept to the leading paths, and neglected the secondary roads; but if the task is attempted it demands a special historian, who is prepared to explore and study it by itself and for itself.

Once you have reached the plateau it is, as a rule, possible to make a road almost anywhere. Yet even there there are certain gates towards which many roads must converge, and through which they must pass. Two zones of mountains, whose old names are unknown, and which are almost name-

[1] M. Theodore Reinach has done all that is possible without long and methodical exploration to illuminate the bearing of this valley on the Mithridatic history; but want of personal knowledge of the localities makes the geographical side of his excellent study necessarily inadequate.

less in modern times, run north and south across central Phrygia, and roads must keep either to the north or the south of them. All travellers from Ephesus to the East passed by the southern end of those mountains; but travellers from Smyrna and northern Lydia generally went by the northern end. The routes may be distinguished as the "Central Trade Route" and the "Royal Road".[1] The two modern railways from Smyrna follow the ancient lines.

The lofty ridge which comes up from the west from Trojan Ida, called Temnos and Dindymos in parts of its course, approaches very close to those central Phrygian mountains; and a narrow glen, down which flows a tributary of the Mæander, divides them. That glen forms a funnel, up or down which roads and travellers going in very diverse directions must necessarily pass. For about ten or twelve miles persons going from south to north travel side by side with others who are going from east to west. Their roads all converge to one end of the glen, and diverge again at the other.

Until that glen was noted on the map, and its importance observed, the march of the Ten Thousand, which Xenophon has described, was an insoluble riddle. In my earlier years of exploration, having only the vague, featureless and inaccurate old maps, I found the glen a sore trial and puzzle. Filled with the desire to be constantly traversing new routes and to avoid repetition, I found myself in the most annoying way doing the treadmill up and down the steep ascent. In one year, when thoroughly on my guard against it and resolved to avoid it, I traversed it three times.

But this repetition only gave proper emphasis to its importance. Then it became obvious that the Ten Thousand,

[1] On the two routes see "Roads and Travel" (Hastings' *Dict. Bib.*, v., 390).

who had marched from Sardis towards the southern end of the central Phrygian mountains, as if to follow the southern route, and had turned backwards towards the north-west, must have traversed the glen and gone round the northern end of the mountains. No other way was possible, and when this observation was applied, it was easy to follow the march of the Ten Thousand all over Phrygia, and to say at any point that Xenophon's foot must have trod within a few hundred yards of where we stood. At the south-western entrance to the glen stands Keramon Agora, the Market of Tiles, that "peopled city"; and after leaving its north-eastern exit, the eastward bound army soon found itself in the broad plain of Kaystros.

Communication on the coasts, of course, took place mostly by ship, and lies outside our present subject, except in so far as it affected or was affected by land conditions. Since the mountains touched the sea at various points, and the coast road was tedious and difficult, communication was thrown more and more completely on to shipboard, and was therefore for centuries entirely in the hands of the Greeks. Hence the coast towns, as far east as Tarsus and Trapezus, were strongly affected by Greek influence, and often even transformed into cities of the Greek type, with free institutions and constitutional government by elected magistrates according to published law.

Moreover, the sea was dangerous and difficult. On the north coast, the Black Sea was the most uncertain and treacherous known to the Greeks: at no period of the year could the weather be counted on; in the most settled summer weather a tempest might occur. Far back, in the beginning of Greek history, we can dimly trace the immense influence exerted on the Greek mind by the first experience of that

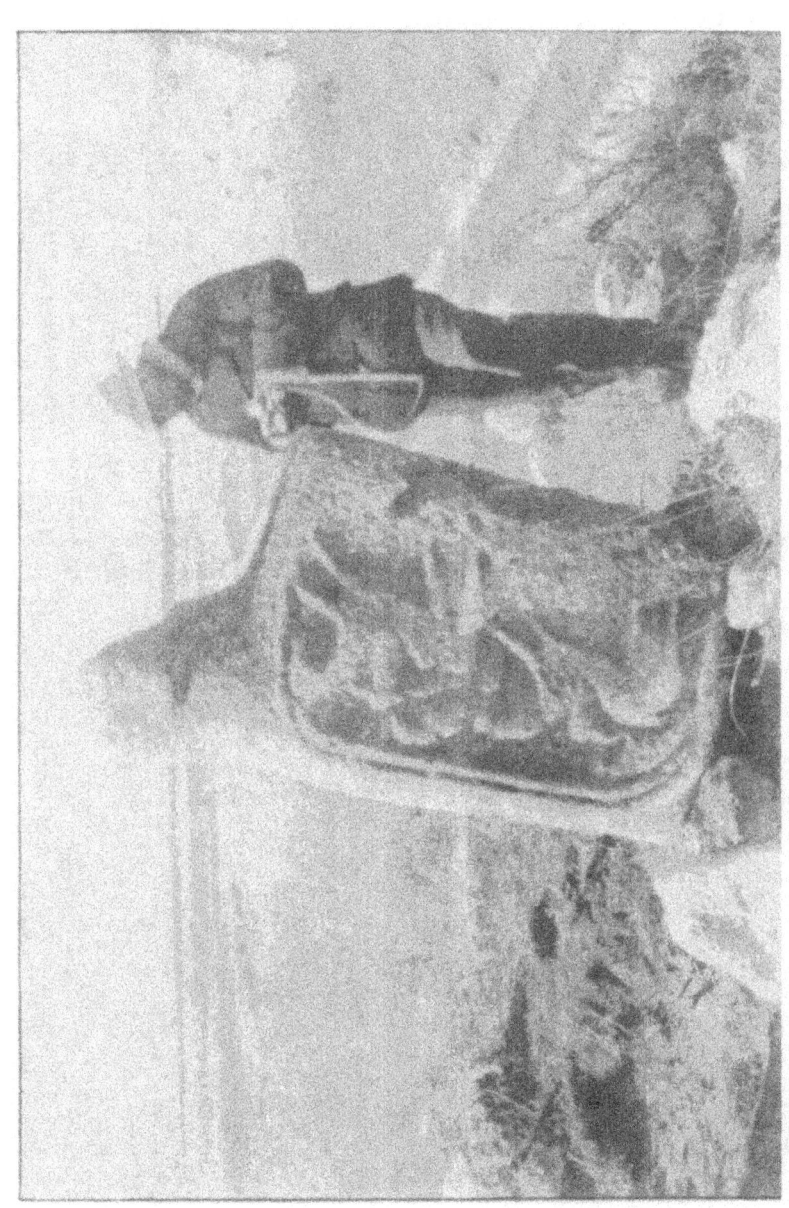

November weather in Phrygia: Archaic Grave Monument, Sheep with Sculptured Hunting Scene on both sides.

To face p. 120.   See p. 139.

sea with its dangers and its wonders. It is not too much to say, though here we can only make the strong statement and pass on, that the discovery of the Black Sea played as important a part in forming and training the Greek mind, in determining its bent, in moulding its literary expression, as the discovery of America has played in the modern world.

But the life of a country is always mirrored and idealised in its religion; and the religion of the coast cities must necessarily have been moulded a great deal by their dependence on the sea. This we can observe well on the north coast. The Ruler of the Sea, Achilles Pontarches, was the great deity of the north coast cities; an association of cities was allied in his worship, and the high priest was called by the same name as the god, the Pontarch. The god had his chosen home in an island, opposite the mouths of the Danube, where he dwelt with Helena, the island which occasionally appeared before the storm-tossed sailor as a haven of quiet. But he was reverenced also in the cities whose prosperity depended on his favour, and whose sailors made their vows to him before they sailed and paid them after their safe return. He was worshipped in all the cities in South Russia and the Crimea, as well as on the Asia Minor coasts; but probably his chief seat was in Sinope, that great harbour of the early time, on the promontory that juts out far into the sea. And when a new form of religion required a new expression of the old religious fact, a Christian saint was substituted for the pagan Pontarch Achilles; and St. Phocas of Sinope became the sailors' god, or at least their patron and protector.

The severance of the north coast from the plateau is thus as strongly marked in religion as in history. It would not, however, be true to say that the severance in religion was absolute. The mountain-ridges which barred and hemmed in ordinary communication offered no insuperable barrier to the spread of religion. The strange fervid cults of the plateau proved as impressive on the coastlands as they did in the European lands to which they spread in wave after wave. Any divergence in the religion of the coast from that of the plateau took the form of additions—such as the cult of Achilles Pontarches—to a common religious stock.

On the south coast less is known of maritime religious foundations. The existing records show little except gods of the common Anatolian type. Yet there must have been others. Especially at Myra in Lycia we may look for some special sailors' cult. Myra was the harbour for the direct over-sea communication with Syria and with Egypt.[1] This communication was not old—the early ships never ventured to desert the coast and strike boldly out to sea. But at least as early as the first century of our era vessels sailed from Myra straight across to the Syrian and Egyptian coasts; and the large ships which carried the Egyptian corn to the Roman granaries habitually tried to run straight across from Alexandria to Myra. Westerly winds blow with wonderful uniformity in the Levant, and those ships could commonly trust to a good run due north to the Lycian coast. But if the west wind blew too strong, the ship would make too much leeway, and find itself unable to clear the western end of Cyprus; and then it was obliged to run to the Syrian coast and keep round the east and the north of Cyprus. In such circumstances the blessing of the god of Myra would be sought with special devotion; and, though this cult is not proven in its pagan form, which as we have seen was only of quite late

---

[1] *St. Paul the Traveller*, p. 298 f.; " Roads and Travel in N.T. Times " in Hastings' *Dictionary of the Bible*, v., p. 381.

origin, the Christian cult which took its place is well known. St. Nicholas of Myra played the same part among the sailors of the Levant as St. Phocas of Sinope did among those of the Black Sea.

Phocas was a martyr of the reign of Trajan. Nicholas was Bishop of Myra more than three centuries later. The Christian form evidently established itself earlier on the north coast than on the south, and this is in strict accord with other evidence, which shows that the new religion had taken deep root in the northern coastlands by the time of Trajan, whereas on the south it was very much later in attaining such strength.

But it is not merely armies, or migrations of peoples, which have swept eastwards or westwards across Anatolia. Art and knowledge, new thoughts and new religions have trod the same path in either direction; they, too, move westwards or eastwards across the bridge, rarely northwards or southwards. Such movements, though less imposing and romantic than the march of armies and the combat of heroes, may justifiably detain our attention longer, precisely because they are less striking and more easily escape notice.

There are some apparent exceptions, which, however, vanish under more careful scrutiny, and therefore only help to emphasise the general principle. One example may here be given. The present writer is responsible for the theory (published in 1882) that the Greek alphabet, after travelling by ship with the Ionian merchants to Sinope, penetrated thence southwards across the mountains into the central plateau, where we find it in use east of the Halys about the seventh century B.C. But after further study he retracted this theory, and argued that the Greek alphabet was carried up eastwards from the west coast, in the ordinary course of trade and political relations; and dated that communication by the recorded fact that a king of Phrygia was married to a daughter of Agamemnon, King of Æolic Cyme, about 700 B.C.[1] Historic tradition remembered that dynastic fact—a striking example of the way in which a royal family embodies and represents the history of its nation; and the union of the two royal families stands to us for the intercommunication between the active Greek cities of the west coast and the peoples of the plateau, in the course of which the alphabet and many other ideas passed eastwards or westwards. That second theory may now be regarded as the accepted view. Even those English scholars who accept no historical theory, unless it is printed in German, may accept this view with easy minds, because it has been rediscovered independently by a learned and able young German professor, A. Koerte, who, travelling in Anatolia about five years after the second view had been published and republished in the *Journal of Hellenic Studies*, soon found out and made known the truth, gently rebuking the error of the English scholar who had advanced the first theory.

Such movements of thought and religion are complicated by another factor, the influence of the land. Those movements did not merely sweep across the country like armies from one side or the other; sometimes they originated in the country; sometimes they were modified, profoundly or slightly, as the case might be, in their passage. An army may march across the country, gaining no material strength, but merely losing part of its force, and exercising no influence on the population except to impoverish it—although some-

[1] *Journal of Hell. Stud.*, 1889, p. 186 f.

PLATE VIII.

The Tomb of Midas the King: a Phrygian Holy Place.   *See p.* 139.

PLATE XVIII.

Part of a Monastery above Bin-Bir-Kilisse, showing short zones of brick used as ornament in a stone building.

To face p. 124.   *See p.* 161.

times even an army may learn something in its long travels, and those who return to their own land may, like the remnant of the Crusaders, come back wiser and better able to understand the world than when they started. On the other hand, an idea moves over the land by passing from mind to mind; it is sensitive and living as it moves.

This geographical influence, the power of the country on the minds of men, may take one of two forms. In the first place, it may arise out of the situation of Anatolia as a bridge and meeting-place between Eastern and Western ideas. When the thoughts and knowledge of two diverse peoples meet, either in alliance or in hostility, the result is not to be represented as a simple addition. Ideas are not like dead matter to be placed side by side: they unite and are productive, or they die; but they cannot remain inert and unvarying. The result of their meeting may be, and commonly is, more like a process of multiplication; occasionally, it is a process of division or destruction. For example, the invention of the art of coinage is attributed to Asia Minor by Herodotus; and modern opinion agrees unanimously with him.[1] In the great highway of commerce and intercourse it was natural that this idea of a common measure of value, guaranteed by a trustworthy authority, should be struck out. Along with this invention we may refer to the speculation of M. Radet[2]—in one of the most brilliant pages of his striking work on Lydia—that the organisation of trade and caravans and bazaars, the typical Oriental method of commerce, belongs to the same country.

---

[1] It is generally attributed to Lydia; Professor P. Gardner has recently maintained that it should be attributed to the Ionian Greek cities.

[2] Criticised and accepted with some modification in the writer's *Cities and Bishoprics of Phrygia*, vol. ii., p. 416.

Similarly, the development and improvement in practical working of many ideas springs from the intercourse and jostling of many men and many minds along the great bridge. The simplification of chronological reckoning by the use of a definite era, so that a date can be expressed by a single number, may belong to Asia Minor; it became common, and probably it originated, in the adapting of Greek ideas to a wider sphere of practical life, which occurred after Greece went forth under Alexander the Great to conquer the East, when it settled down under his successors to the great practical problem of how to rule the conquered world. The cumbrous method of dating by the annual magistrates of the city, which commended itself to the patriotism and pride of the Greek citizen in Greece, became too obviously unworkable in the wider sphere of the Hellenised East. In no part of the ancient world is the custom of expressing dates by counting from a fixed era more firmly established in common everyday use than in one district of Asia Minor, embracing the eastern part of Lydia and the western half of Phrygia.

But, in the second place, there is a growing opinion among the most recent investigators—an opinion strongly held by the present writer—that Anatolia was not merely an intermediary, developing foreign ideas in a practical way, but also played a not unimportant part as an originator. We are inevitably forced back to a time when Anatolia was not merely a bridge between opposite lands and great peoples, but was itself the centre of a great empire exerting an influence on the outer world. The empire is closely connected with the most fascinating and the most obscure historical problems which are at the present time under discussion. Every step that is being made in the rediscovery of the early

Greek world, and the history of early intercourse in the Eastern Mediterranean lands, constitutes at the same time indirectly an advance in the history of the ancient Anatolian world, even though the discoverer is not conscious of the side light which he is throwing on that subject. Twenty years ago that Anatolian Empire was not even dreamed about by any one; even yet it is almost an unknown quantity, which is to be estimated from its effects more than from direct evidence about its actual nature. But the direct evidence is slowly being discovered—very slowly, because there is no organised effort being made to discover it, but mere sporadic experiments by occasional travellers, generally inexperienced, who, as soon as they acquire experience and become skilled and interested in the investigation, are drafted off to other spheres of life. But still discovery, though slow, does progress; and what ten years ago was reckoned by many only a dream, is now admittedly a real factor in history, which has an acknowledged place in every modern discussion of the early Mediterranean world, and which, after ten or twenty years, will occupy far greater space than it does now.[1]

An ancient system of writing in hieroglyphics, different from any other known system of expressing thought by visible and permanent symbols, is known in Asia Minor through a long process of development, and is dimly traceable as an influence on other countries.[2] Characteristic

[1] Five years after the forecast in the text was printed, it was justified by Dr. Winckler's excavations at Boghaz-Keui, which within a few weeks after their inception demonstrated the existence of this ancient Anatolian Empire. The excavations were made in the city which already in 1882 the writer described in the following terms: "There can be no doubt that this was the capital, or at least one of the strongest cities, of a genuinely oriental power which ruled over a wide country" (*Journal of the Royal Asiatic Society*, 1882, p. 4).

[2] See below, p.159.

Anatolian artistic forms have been studied and specified by several investigators, though still they are chiefly traceable as the unknown factor needed to explain the development of the East Mediterranean world.

Most certain and most typical of Anatolia is its religion, the influence of which on the Greek and Roman world is the one form in which Anatolian influence has been long recognised by modern scholars. This they could hardly fail to do, seeing that the ancients themselves acknowledge it, describe it, and inveigh against it; but still it was left to comparatively recent scholars to show how far-reaching and long-continued that influence was; and among those scholars the most acute and able has probably been Mr. P. Foucart, formerly Director of the French School of Athens,[1] who writes of Anatolian religion entirely from the Greek point of view as being an outrage on the Greek spirit, saved from being abominable only by becoming sometimes ridiculous in its fervour. But at least he established the fact that this influence spread in wave after wave of a sort of religious revivalism over the classical world, mostly among the uneducated classes, but still often affecting the population so profoundly as to receive State recognition or require State regulation and even coercion. For good or for evil, it was at least enormously powerful.

In all these departments, writing, art, religion (and doubtless others might be added), there is perceptible a connection with the geographical character of the country. Elsewhere I have argued[2] that the hieroglyphics must have been originated on the great central plains; and I believe that an important part in the domestication of certain animals must be as-

---

[1] Foucart, *Les Associations Religieuses chez les Grecs*, 1873.
[2] *Cities and Bishoprics of Phrygia*, vol. i., p. xv.

PLATE IX.

To face p. 128.   The Grave of a Phrygian Chief.   *See p.* 139.

signed to the same localities. The soil of those now desert plains is generally highly fertile. Only the application of water and skill is needed to make them very fruitful; and the ruins of large and rich cities are found where now the country is absolutely barren, and where it is barely possible for a few families to support life owing to the scarcity of water. In the most arid parts of the plateau one observes the remains of great engineering works designed to store water. On the edge of the mountains, where the torrents at the present day carry down a great mass of water during rain and are dry again an hour after the rain has ceased, the beds were formerly blocked by a series of embankments each of which held up a body of water and the soil borne down by the water; but all are now broken and useless. I have seen numberless cisterns, some small, some very large, most of them now always dry; and I have traced for part of its course a very large artificial stream winding round the edges of the Taurus and carrying its water to form a marsh many miles away from its source, because no one now cultivates the land. I made a cutting across the top of a large broad embankment, fully fifty feet high in the middle, and about a quarter of a mile in length, which crosses a depression in the plain near Khadyn-Khan: it is evidently a dam intended to store up water; but, though it is still as perfect apparently as ever, it holds up none, because the means of conducting the water to it from the hills are ruined. Villagers have brought to me lengths of large terra-cotta channels, which they dug up on the side of a gentle elevation in the centre of the Axylon, many miles away from any source. One who is on the outlook will find everywhere numberless examples of skilful works like these; and I have been told by engineers of far more wonderful feats of engineering which I hesitate to describe in the terms of my informants, until I can vouch for them by personal examination.

All such works have a religious side, because they were not carried out through the initiative of the ignorant peasantry. The arts that were needed to make those wide plains productive and useful to man were all embodied and taught in the religion of the country. The domesticated animals were all sacred, and the treatment of them was prescribed as part of religious ritual.[1]

As might be expected, therefore, it is in religion that the direct influence of geographical features is most obvious. Ancient religion was far more intimately and universally associated with social and family life than is the case with modern European nations. Religion had made and ordered all social relationships. The individual was bound in the ties of religion from his cradle to his grave. Every act of his life, good or bad, joyous or mournful, moral (to our conceptions) or immoral, was equally presided over by a divinity, and, as it were, done under the divine sanction. The early religion of Anatolia was therefore the outcome of the whole circumstances and environment that acted on the people.

One feature in the Anatolian religion rises before us prominent and impressive at the first glance. The ordinary and familiar idea is that God is the Father of all mankind and all life. Such is the almost universal European and Semitic conception. But it was the motherhood of the divine nature that was the great feature in the Anatolian worship.[2] The male element in the divine nature was recog-

---

[1] *The Religion of Greece and Asia Minor*, p. 114 f., in Hastings' *Dictionary of the Bible*, vol. v.

[2] The same idea is widely spread, and found in many primitive forms of religion; but on this subject it is not within the scope of this paper to enter.

nised only as an occasional and subsidiary actor in the drama of nature and of life. The life of man came from the Great Mother; the heroes of the land were the sons of the goddess, and at death they returned to the mother who bore them.

In the social customs of Anatolia, even after it was overspread by Greek manners and Greek ideas, many traces remain of that primitive idea. Descent was sometimes reckoned through the mother; women magistrates are frequently found even in the Hellenised cities of the land. And in its history the same impression remains: it is everywhere the most pathetic of histories. Not vigour and initiative, but receptivity and impressibility, swayed the spirit of the people, marked their fate, and breathed through the atmosphere that surrounded them—a continuous, barely perceptible force acting on every new people, and subtly influencing every new religion, that came into the land. For example, the earliest known trace of the veneration of the Virgin Mary in the Christian religion is in a Phrygian inscription of the second century; and the earliest example of a holy place consecrated to the Mother of God as already an almost divine personality is at Ephesus early in the fifth century.[1]

On the great level plains of the central plateau the spirit of man seems separated from the world by the mountains, and thrown back on its own nature; but it is not confined, for the idea of confinement is absolutely alien to that wide expanse, where the sole limit to the range of the human eye seems to be its own weakness of vision, where a remote mountain-peak only emphasises the sense of vastness because it furnishes a standard by which to estimate distance. The great eye of heaven, unwearying, unpitying, inexorable, watches you from its rising over the level horizon till it sinks below the same

---

[1] This subject is treated more fully in *Pauline and other Studies*, p. 125-159.

level again. There is a sense of rest, of inevitable acquiescence in the Infinite, all-pervasive and compelling Power which surrounds you. The sense of individuality and personal power grows weak and shrinks away, not daring to show itself in the human consciousness. The phases of the year co-operate in this effect, with a long severe winter and a shorter but hot summer. Where water pours forth in one of the many great springs which give birth to strong-flowing rivers, the country is a garden; but otherwise the fertile soil is dependent entirely on the chances of an uncertain rainfall. The north wind tempers the heat, and the harvester trusts to it entirely to winnow his grain on the threshing-floor. Everything impresses on the mind the utter insignificance of man and his absolute dependence on the Divine power. The peasant of the present day still—as doubtless his remote ancestors did 2,000 years before Christ—calls almost every great life-giving spring Huda-verdi, "God hath given".

But the Divine power that was so evident was not the stern, inexorable power of the hard desert. The people saw the nature of the land, rich and full of good things to those who accepted the divinely revealed method, and cared for the holy soil and the sacred animals, as the goddess, their mother and patron, required. St. Paul, with his usual unerring insight into the character of his audience, spoke to the rude Lycaonian peasants about the God "who did good, and gave rain from heaven, and fruitful seasons, filling the heart with food and gladness".

For the student of that country and history, it is always and everywhere necessary to go back to that religion, to recognise it as the originator of all national life and of all social forms, and as a continuous force acting throughout the later development of the country.

To face p. 132.   Broken Remains of the Grave of a Phrygian Chief: Leontos-Kephalai.   *See p.* 139.

In the exploration of the city of Ephesus an example may be found of the use that might be made of this principle. Mr. Wood spent six years searching for the site of the Temple of Artemis, and at last he found it exactly where it ought to be, beside the little hill on the top of which was built the great church of St. John Theologos, and on the lowest slope of which is the splendid mosque of Isa Bey. The church was the largest built by the Emperor Justinian,[1] that greatest of builders with the single exception of the Emperor Hadrian.

The historical process is obvious, since Mr. Wood's discovery disclosed it. The Christian religion when it became dominant had to claim for itself the sanctity attaching to the ancient site. It did so by building that great church overlooking the temple. But Christianity in its turn gave place to Mohammedanism, and again this new religion made itself heir to the religious associations and holiness of the locality by constructing between the two older religious sites one of the largest and most splendid mosques in the whole country.

The history of Ephesus is an extraordinary series of vicissitudes, but the religious centre is always the same. The Greek city was at a distance from the religious centre; it aimed at commercial or military advantages, and its site was changed more than once as the sea-coast receded. The holy place was the governing centre of the plain before the Greeks came; its priests watched the Greek cities grow and change and decay. The outward form of the religion was altered, but the old belief was not extirpated, and it took new root in the heart of the conquering religion, so that in the fifth century we find the legend of the Virgin Mother of God firmly established among the Christians of Ephesus, though

---

[1] St. Sophia in Constantinople was larger; but it was not founded by Justinian.

it was not strong enough to obliterate the historical fact that the Holy Theologian had lived many years and died in the city. But the belief in the old holy place was a force always attracting the population thither, and growing stronger as the standard of education in the Eastern Church degenerated, and at last proving irresistible. Thus the centre of population was moved back to the old centre of religion. The old Asiatic paganism had proved too strong alike for the Greek trade and education and for the Christian teaching. The Greek spirit had come, and lived for twelve hundred years, and died of weakness, but the old beliefs continued as strong as ever. The old goddess had not merely her home in the open plain among the haunts of men; she was the goddess of wild nature and nursing mother of all wild animals, and she had her other home among the mountains on the south of the plain. And so among the Christians the home of the Virgin Mother of God was discovered and made a centre of worship and pilgrimage near the old mountain house of the Goddess-Mother.

An apparent exception to the principle that the great movements of history and thought must either keep to the coast-lines or to the central bridge, and that no great movement on the central plateau ever springs from the northern or the southern coast, is presented by the enterprise which carried the first Christian mission from Perga on the Pamphylian coast to Pisidian Antioch and the neighbouring towns on the central bridge. The theologians have disputed, and will doubtless dispute to the end of time, about that sudden transition; but the geographer and the historian who study facts instead of starting from theories can never hesitate as to this great fact. The first mission movement began to work its way westward along the sea-route by Cyprus and the

Pamphylian coast; but at this point it deserted the coast-route and transferred itself to the far more fruitful and important land-route over the central bridge. The important movements of thought had almost always taken the land-route, for the coast-route affords only narrow and limited opportunities along its course. It was easy for the pioneers of new ideas to carry them by sea from the Syrian shore to Athens or to Rome; but by the way they as a rule made no impression and left no seed. On the other hand, along the land-route new religious movements worked their way by conquering the cities and the peoples through which they passed: they planted themselves firmly at each stage, and each step was the preparation and the basis for a further step.

Of the many movements of thought that have occurred along the great bridge, the only one which can be traced in any detail is that by which Christianity was diffused over the country and into Europe; and it would be an instructive example of the principles which have just been laid down to study the geographical lines of that important movement. But it would need a separate article to do so even in the briefest outline. One may only say here that the current conception, which indicates the spread of that movement by a series of lines radiating from Syria across Asia Minor to the north, north-west, and west, is entirely incorrect. The movement of thought was along the great bridge, by the road on the southern side of the plateau, direct west from Syria to Ephesus, and then back again in return waves along the north coast by sea, and along the northern roads over the plateau by land. And probably the older movements, about whose diffusion we have no information, exemplified equally the same geographical laws.

In conclusion, two noteworthy features of the old religion may be noticed and illustrated.

In the first place, the Divine power that resided in, or brooded over, or sat in state upon[1] prominent peaks and lofty mountains was everywhere an object of popular veneration. Elsewhere the writer has repeatedly alluded to this subject,[2] and described how certain striking peaks, which seem to dominate the landscape, and to watch over and guide and measure the traveller's course, became objects of worship—partly in the higher view as abodes or seats of the Divine might (which was distinct from the mountain, a formless guiding power, present anywhere and everywhere to its worshippers), partly in the lower view as themselves Divine things, Gods to be worshipped. The two views were both potentially present in the primitive conception, which had not yet been fully thought out; and the future was to determine whether the early conception should be developed to the higher stage or degraded to the lower.

Besides the evident value of peaks to the traveller's and the trader's eye, there are many other considerations which must have given importance to them. Some of these we can trace practically in the Byzantine time, and can apply with suitable modifications to the earliest ages. In the rude warfare of the Byzantine period it must be observed that it was no longer possible or safe to trust to the kind of military strength that depended on artificial fortifications, on well-trained officers, on a disciplined and obedient soldiery, and on constant watchfulness and forethought in the highest ranks of the service. The Byzantine service had degenerated, and was not kept in a state of preparedness and good discip-

---

[1] See below, p. 160.
[2] See especially the *Cities of St. Paul*, p. 389.

PLATE XI.

Rock-tomb in Phrygia: Roman period: Christian Arcosolia of later period in the rock beneath.

To face p. 136. *See p.* 139.

line. The Oriental invaders were always ill-organised, and relied mainly on sudden, unexpected attacks on a peaceful country. In those circumstances it was inevitable that the old Hellenistic and Roman style of fortified cities, close to the roads and convenient for trade and administration, should give place to fortresses perched high on peaks as nearly inaccessible as possible. These were safe refuges against sudden attack, and the population could retreat to them when beacons on peaks beside the Eastern roads gave warning that a raiding army was crossing the Taurus. They could not have been defended against a long regular siege owing to deficiency in the water-supply, but a regular siege was not to be feared from the raiders of the East.

Thus the circumstances of the great war against Sassanian and Arab power tended inevitably to make the minds of the Anatolian population dwell upon the importance and the saving power of lofty peaks; while their religion prompted them to plant churches and monasteries as well as castles on them, and led them first to wish, thereafter to believe, that the saints who championed and marshalled the local defence dwelt permanently on these high hills.[1] The same applies in some degree to the earliest times.

As examples of those lofty, fortified rocks, which are so numerous in Asia Minor, take Plates IV. and V. In the former is shown the rock of Kara-Hissar, the Black Fortress,[2] the ancient Akroênos, where was won in A.D. 739 the first great victory in a pitched battle that cheered the Byzantine Empire in the task of repelling the Arab con-

---

[1] On this subject see the following paper, "The Orthodox Church in the Byzantine Empire".

[2] Kara here means "black" rather in the moral sense of terrible, grim, strong, than as the colour.

querors.[1] It seems to have been known afterwards as Nikopolis, the City of Victory, and became a bishopric in the eighth century. It is now one of the chief cities of the Plateau, and is distinguished from many other towns of the same name by the epithet Afion, from the opium which is extensively cultivated in the plain adjoining.

Here is the meeting (not allowed at present to be practically utilised as a junction) between the German Railway from the Bosphorus to Konia, and perhaps ultimately to Bagdad, and the French Railway from Smyrna to Philadelphia, Ushak and Kara-Hissar.

Plate V. shows the city now called Sivri-Hissar, Pointed Fortress, one of the centres of the angora-wool trade, the ancient Justinianopolis, one of the great fortresses on the Byzantine Military Road by which Justinian tried to protect the land of Anatolia. Its double peak is one of the most noteworthy points for surveyors : I have taken readings to it from very distant points in the Phrygian mountains (one being the highest point of the Midas-city).

In the second place, almost every seat of ancient life carries veneration and often religious awe with it : frequently it is regarded as the seat of Divine power, and a sacred place. To illustrate this in detail is the work of a large book. It has been referred to briefly in a paper on the " Permanence of Religious Awe in Asia Minor ".[2] Some of the annexed Plates may serve to illustrate it.

Plate VI. shows a Roman milestone standing in its original position on the great Central Trade Route, about a mile west of the important Roman station of Psebila or Pegella (afterwards renamed Verinopolis from the Empress Verina

---

[1] *Studies in the History of the Eastern Provinces*, p. 288.
[2] *Pauline and other Studies*, p. 163 ff.

in the end of the fifth century), where was a knot of five great roads, (1) the road from Constantinople, Dorylaion and Amorion, (2) the Trade Route from the West, (3) the road connecting the two great Galatian provincial centres Ancyra and Iconium, (4) the Trade Route from Cæsarea and the East, (5) the Syrian road through the Cilician Gates.

Plates VII.-XI. show a few of the most noteworthy monuments of Phrygia. In VII. an archaic sheep, once used as a sepulchral monument, is seen: a pair of hunters on horseback are sculptured on the side of the unformed mass, and on the other side three ibexes of a species still common in Anatolia. The custom of representing animals on the sides of the statues of other animals was common in the early Anatolian or "Hittite" period. The human figure who stands by, dressed in early November as for the Arctic regions, affords a practical proof of the severity of the climate on the Plateau.[1]

The Tomb of Midas the King appears in Plate VIII., the type and best example of a large class of Phrygian sepulchral monuments (which were at the same time shrines of the deified dead). The quaint delicate work and the romantic surroundings make this one of the most beautiful monuments known to modern times; and its historical interest even surpasses its beauty. The two inscriptions, in letters of gigantic size and archaic Greek form, make the nature of the monument certain; though some scholars dispute it.

Plate IX. gives another grave-monument of an ancient Phrygian chief, without inscription and probably older than the introduction of Greek writing into Phrygia. The analogy to the famous Lion-Gate at Mycenæ lends special interest to this great tomb. Over the little door leading

[1] See above, p. 106, and *Pauline and other Studies*, p. 385 f.

into the plain and small grave-chamber, where the dead was simply laid on a low couch of rock, stands a column supporting a very heavy architrave at the top of the rock. Two lionesses with a cub beneath each rest their forepaws on the top of the door.

In Plate X. the broken remains of an even greater monument, close to the last, are seen. The head of the lion on the left measures seven feet and a half across. It is exeecuted in singularly life-like vigorous style, and the complete monument, with three great heads of lions like this, must have been wonderfully effective. The town or village beside it was in the fifth century and later called from this monument Leontoskephalai. It is about six hours north of Afion-Kara-Hissar and five hours south of the Midas Tomb.

Plate XI. shows a sepulchral monument of the Roman period, in quite Greek style. The family tomb is here conceived as the temple of the deified dead, who lay in chambers cut in the rock. Before the doors is the portico, supported by two Doric columns, closely imitating the front of a Greek temple.

Plate XII. shows the site of the ancient Antioch of Pisidia, the southern capital of the Province Galatia, with the snowy Sultan Dagh behind. The site lies in the middle distance, on the left-hand side of a break in the ridge of front hills. Through that break the river Anthios flows in a deep narrow gorge, close under the city walls. The ridge continues to the right of the gorge, rising much higher than on the Antiochian side. The faint, hardly distinguishable remains contrast with the numerous buildings of Deghile (Plate XIII.).

PLATE XII.

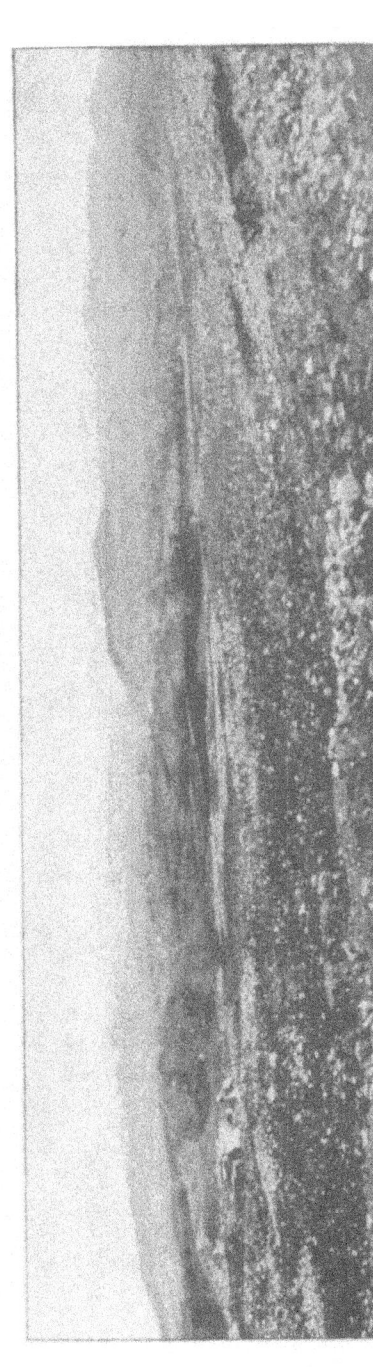

Pisidian Antioch, with the snow-clad Sultan-Dagh (the City is situated on the left part of the front ridge: the gorge of the Anthios, dividing the site from the higher part of the front ridge, is in the centre of the picture). *See p.* 140.

PLATE XIII.

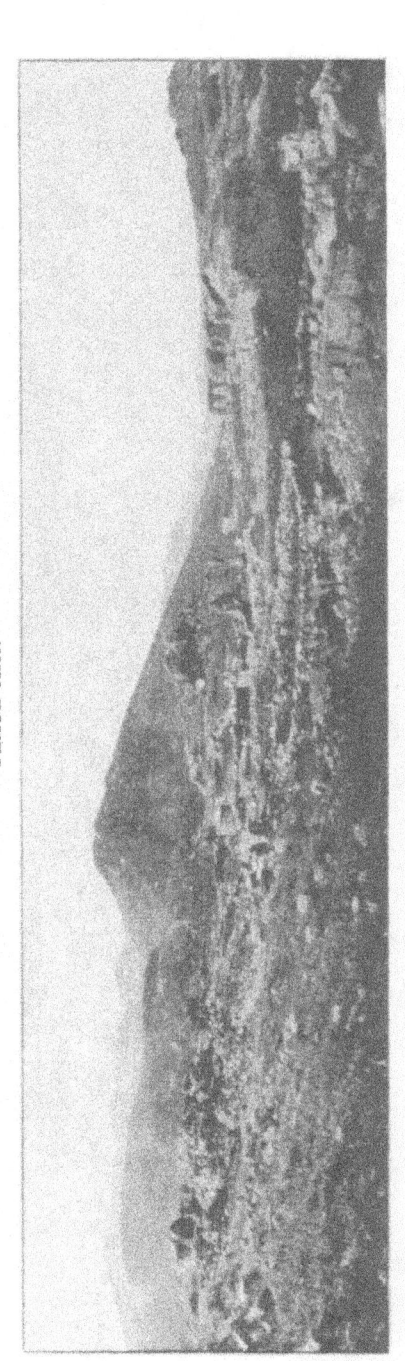

General View of the Ruins at Deghile: the Monastery-town above Barata.

To face p. 140. *See p.* 161.

IV.

THE ORTHODOX CHURCH IN THE BYZANTINE EMPIRE

ADDRESS ON BEHALF OF SECTION VI. (CHURCH HISTORY)
DELIVERED TO THE FINAL GENERAL MEETING
OF THE CONGRESS OF HISTORICAL
SCIENCES, BERLIN, 1908.

IV.

THE ORTHODOX CHURCH IN THE BYZANTINE EMPIRE [1]

I WILL not fill up the last minutes of the Congress with minute details of the subject about which I have to speak. Rather, I shall attempt to show it amid its surroundings as one aspect of the immemorial struggle between the East and the West. In the electric contact between Asia and Europe has been generated the greatest motive power throughout history; the impulse is constantly varying in character from age to age, yet the principle is fundamentally the same.

In the lands of the Aegean and the Levant the cardinal fact of history has always been and is now the struggle of Hellenism to make itself dominant. On the coasts and islands it rules almost by right of nature; and it is constantly striving to force its way inland. As a motive force in the Levant world it gained strength and direction by being moulded into the Roman organisation; and the Roman Empire was in the East the Hellenic Empire, an invigorated Hellenism, which lost the charm, the delicacy, the purity and the aloofness of the unalloyed Greek spirit, but gained practical and penetrating power.

In one of his most remarkable papers, written in later life,

[1] Address on behalf of Section VI. (Church History) delivered to the final general meeting of the Congress of Historical Sciences, Berlin, 12th August, 1908. It was shortened in delivery by the omission of many sentences or clauses.

when his genius and historic insight were brightest and most piercing, because they were guided by longer experience and by a width of knowledge almost beyond the right of mankind, Mommsen has described how the Roman Empire, at the moment when it seemed no longer capable of maintaining itself, was restored to vigour by the incorporation of a new idea into its constitution, and became the Christian Empire. This was only one out of many cases in which by a single article Mommsen either permanently changed thought regarding an old branch of study or created an entirely new one. He has made it impossible for any scholar ever again to say much of what used to be repeated parrot-like by generation after generation of writers about the relation of the Church to the Roman State,[1] and he has made it urgently necessary that the history of the Roman Empire should be rewritten from a new point of view.

The new Christian Empire lasted as a power patent to the eyes of all the world for more than eleven hundred years. What was the idea, what the new factor in organisation that recreated and rejuvenated the dying Roman Empire? It was the Church, the Church as an organised unity, the Church as a belief, and the Church as a body of ritual.

In this connection we are struck with a certain difference between the Latin Church and the Greek. The Latin Church has often been able to maintain its hold on discordant nations: many peoples have remained faithful to the belief and the authority of the Roman Church, while preserving their independence, their separation, and their

---

[1] *Der Religionsfrevel nach röm. Recht.* The legal aspect is restated in his *Strafrecht* from a different point of view, and in some details perhaps more correctly; but the older paper takes a far wider outlook and a more illuminative view than the legal book, which, though published later, stands nearer the ordinary point of survey, because it is narrower in its range of interest.

mutual hostility. But the Latin Church could not hold together the Western Empire. It never identified itself with the Empire. It represented a higher unity than the Roman Empire: so far as it lowered itself to stand on the same level as the Empire, it was a rival and an enemy rather than an ally of the Empire.

But the Orthodox Church in the East cast in its lot with the Roman Empire; it was conterminous with, and never permanently wider than the Empire. It did not long attempt to stand on a higher level than the State and the people. It has not been an educating and elevating and purifying power. It has been content, on the whole, in spite of some notable and honourable exceptions, to accept the world as it was; and it has been too easily satisfied with mere allegiance and apparent loyalty to the State among all its adherents. It was the faithful ally of the emperors. In the controversies of the fifth century it elected to side with the uneducated masses against the higher thought; and in an Œcumenical Council, at which the law of the whole Christian world should be determined, it admitted to its deliberations a bishop who could not sign his name because he did not know letters. But on this lower level it stood closer to the mass of the people. It lived among them. It moved the common average man with more penetrating power than a loftier religion could have done. Accordingly the Orthodox Church was fitted to be the soul and life of the Empire, to maintain the Imperial unity, to give form and direction to every manifestation of national vigour.

Practically the whole of Byzantine art that has lived is ecclesiastical, being concerned with the building and the adornment of churches, and of the residences of officials in Church and State. The subjects of its painting became more and more exclusively sacred. Art itself was frowned upon; and the controversy between Iconodouloi and Iconoclastai was to a certain extent a contest as to whether Art should not be expelled even from churches. Of Byzantine literature, if you take away what is directly or indirectly concerned with or originating out of the Church, how little remains! To letters the Orthodox Greek Church has never been very favourable. It has never played the part in preserving the ancient classical literature that the Latin Church has played.

Yet it has always clung to the Hellenic language as tenaciously as it has allied itself with the Hellenised Empire, to which it had given new life; but it did so rather on political and social and religious grounds than from literary sympathy. Greek was necessarily the language of Hellenic civilisation and order; and it was the language of the sacred books. Accordingly the Church destroyed the native languages of Asia Minor,[1] and imposed the Greek speech on the entire population, though it could not do this completely in Syria or in Egypt. As it identified itself with the Imperial rule in the State, so it identified itself with Hellenism as a force in society; but its Hellenism was a degenerate representative of the old classical Hellenism, hardened and narrowed in its interests, but intense, powerful, strongly alive, resolute to make the single language, the Hellenic speech, dominant throughout the Church, yet able in the last resort, to abandon for the moment, under the pressure of necessity, or of overpowering national feeling, even the Hellenic speech, and to leave only the cultus and the hierarchy and the ritual

[1] That Christianity, and not the older Greek or Roman civilisation, destroyed the native languages and imposed Greek on the peoples of Asia Minor, has often been maintained by the writer. Professor Holl has published a convincing argument to this effect in *Hermes*, 1908, p. 240 ff.

of the One true Church as the sole living unity in the Empire.

The rise of every national movement that sought to develop itself within the Empire was consecrated and vitalised by the formation of a new Church. In some cases, as in the Armenian schism, or in the severance between the two great sections of the original Catholic and Imperial Church, *viz*., the Latin and the Greek, there was some difference of dogma, of creed, or of ritual. But these differences were, in the historian's view, not the essential features in the quarrels that ensued between the opposing sections of the Church. Those differences of creed were only the insignia emblazoned on the standards of forces which were already arrayed against one another by national and other deep-lying causes of hostility. Accordingly in the severance between Slavic and Hellenic nationalities, in the bitter hatred that has often raged between Slav and Hellene, there is practically no difference of creed or ritual; there is only a difference of ecclesiastical organisation. The separate nationality formed for itself a separate ecclesiastical system, and the two powers, which in truth represented two hostile races and two different systems of civilisation and thought and ideals, regarded one another as rival Churches. Where the historian sees Hellenism in conflict with Slavic society, the combatants hate each other as ecclesiastical foes, orthodox on the one hand, schismatic on the other.

Before our eyes, in this present generation, there has occurred one of these great national and social struggles, a struggle still undetermined, between the Bulgarian and the Hellenic nationality. When the Bulgarian national feeling was growing sufficiently definite to take separate form and to disengage itself from the vague formless mass of the

Christian subjects of Turkey, it expressed itself first by demanding and in the year 1870 attaining separate ecclesiastical standing as the Church of the Exarchate. Since that time the war to determine the bounds between the spheres of Hellenism and of Bulgarian nationality has been waged under the form of a struggle between the adherents of the Patriarchate and of the Exarchate. We at a distance hardly comprehend how completely the ecclesiastical question overpowers all else in the popular estimation. It is not blood, not language, that determines the mind of the masses; it is religion and the Church. The Bulgarian born and bred, who is Mohammedan by religion, sides with the Turks; the Bulgarian who is of the Patriarchate chooses Hellenism, and in ordinary course (if the natural tendency of history is not forcibly disturbed) his descendants will ultimately become Hellenes in language also; only in the Exarchate is the Bulgarian nationality supreme and lasting. Religion and the Church is the determining principle for the individual.

In the islands and in Asia Minor you find the same condition. The Church is the one bond to hold together in feeling, aspirations and patriotism the scattered Hellenes. When we began to travel in the country thirty years ago, there were many cities and villages where the Orthodox Church claimed the adherence of considerable bodies of population, yet where the Greek language was neither spoken nor understood. These people had no common blood: they were Isaurians, or Cappadocians, or Lycaonians, men of Pontus or Bithynia or Phrygia. But they were one people in virtue of their one Church; they knew themselves to be Hellenes, because they belonged to the Church of the Hellenes. The memory of their past lived among these Hellenes, and as that memory grew stronger it awoke their ancient tongue to life; and now their children all speak the language of the Eastern Roman Empire, and look forward to the reawakening of the Christian[1] unity as a practical factor in the development of the country. That old Roman Empire is not dead, but sleeping. It will die only when Hellenism ceases in the Aegean lands, and when the Church is no longer a living force among their population.

We see, then, what a power among men this Orthodox Church has been and still is—not a lovable power, not a beneficent power, but stern, unchanging, not exactly hostile to, but certainly careless of, literature and art and civilisation, sufficient for itself, self-contained and self-centred. The historian must regard with interest this marvellous phenomenon, and he must try to understand it as it appears in the centuries.

I set before you a problem and a question. I do not attempt to answer it. It is not my province or my work to propose theories; but to ask questions, to state problems, and to observe and register facts, looking at them in the light of these questions. And during the last seven years, it has fallen to my lot to study closely the monuments, the hieratic architecture and the epitaphs which reveal something of the development of the Orthodox Church in the region of Lycaonia. I have had to copy many hundreds of Christian inscriptions ranging from the gravestone of a bishop of the third century to an epitaph dated under the Seljuk Turks in the years 1160-1169. It would be pedantic and impossible on this occasion to attempt even an outline

---

[1] It is the only "Christian" Empire to the Hellenes, who call no man Christian unless he is a member of the Orthodox Church. The old distinction between Hellenes and Barbaroi is now expressed as a classification into "Christians" or Orthodox and all others.

of the results which follow from the study of these epitaphs, and of the "thousand-and-one churches"[1] in which the piety of the inhabitants found expression. I shall restrict myself to a few general statements, taking first the inscriptions as beginning earlier than the oldest surviving church-building.

The inscriptions are almost all engraved upon the tombstones of the ordinary population of a provincial district. Even the bishops who are mentioned must, as a rule, be regarded as mere village-bishops ($\chi\omega\rho\epsilon\pi i\sigma\kappa\sigma\pi\sigma\iota$). Similarly, the ecclesiastical buildings belong not to capitals of provinces or to great cities, but to villages and unimportant towns, where there was little education but a high standard of material comfort. Those of which I to-day speak lie in and around the humble and almost unknown town of Barata. But in the humbleness of its range lies the real value of this evidence. It reveals to us the lower and the middle class of society; it sets before us the commonplace individuals who composed the Imperial State.

The epitaphs help to fill up a gap in the information which literary authorities furnish about the Christian Empire. Those authorities give their attention to emperors and courtiers and generals, to the capital of the Empire with its mob and its splendours, to bishops and church leaders, to Œcumenical Councils and the rise of heresies. But the world is made up of ordinary, commonplace men. The leaders cannot exist, unless there is a people to be led. There are indeed scattered about in the literary authorities certain pieces of evidence about the common world; and there are more in the private correspondence of writers and great men.

---

[1] This name (Bin-Bir-Kilisse) is the descriptive appellation given by outsiders to the modern village which occupies part of the site of the ancient Barata, but not used by the villagers themselves (who call their home Maden-Sheher).

But this evidence has never been collected.¹ It is to the humbler epitaphs that we must look for aid in attempting to estimate the influence which the Church exerted on the mass of the people, and to appreciate the standard of education and life which it produced among the general population, especially in small towns and villages.

The Lycaonian gravestones will give at least the beginning of the material for answering the questions which are thus raised. Though a few of the epitaphs are earlier and a moderate number are later, yet the great mass of them belong to the fourth and fifth centuries (especially the period A.D. 330-450). They set before us, on the whole, the Church as it was in Asia Minor from the time of Constantine to that of Theodosius, the Church of Basil of Cæsarea, Gregory of Nazianzus, Gregory of Nyssa, and Amphilochius of Iconium—a great period in ecclesiastical history. I am convinced that some passages in the literature and many in the letters written by the contemporary leaders of the Church will acquire a new and fuller meaning and more living realism through comparison with these memorials of their humble followers.

To take just one example. When Gregory of Nyssa wished about A.D. 380-390 to build a memorial chapel, he wrote to Amphilochius at Iconium begging him to furnish workmen capable of executing the work, and he wrote afterwards a very full description of the cruciform church which he hoped to build. We have now abundant evidence that the cruciform was in those regions the accepted type for memorial churches. We find in the country subject to the

---

[1] In a paper printed in *Pauline and other Studies*, pp. 369-406, a beginning is made in a small way to exemplify the value of the material for social history in the letters of Basil. See also Holl, *Hermes*, 1908, p. 240.

metropolitan bishop of Iconium a quite unexpected number of churches in almost every form known to Byzantine architecture. And we see in the graves throughout the country north and north-east from Iconium a marked inferiority in the technique of sculptor and architect, and an equally marked superiority throughout the hill-country that lies near Iconium on the south and south-west. The fashionable type of ornament on the gravestones of this latter region is architectural, as if architecture were the dominant art in the district.[1] It was, therefore, natural that the Bishop of Nyssa should have recourse to Iconium for artisans able to build and to adorn the church which he had in mind.

The picture of the Lycaonian Church that we put together from these humble memorials is, on the whole, a very favourable one. The Church was still the educator of the people. The Presbyteros is set before us in simple, striking terms as the helper of the orphan, the widow, the poor and the stranger.[2] We have little or no trace of alliance with the State: we have the Church of the people, creator of charitable and hospitable institutions, the Church as it was in the mind and the aspirations of Basil.

We find Lycaonia a Christian land in the fourth century.[3] It is the one province of Asia Minor whose ecclesiastical organisation can be traced already perfect and complete in the councils of the fourth century. This organisation, therefore, must be in great part older than the persecution of Diocletian. From the writings of Basil of Cæsarea we learn that as early as A.D. 370 a city church in Cappadocia was

[1] On the Isaurian masons see an important paper by Professor Holl in *Hermes*, 1908, p. 242, and in this volume XII., No. 10-12.
[2] See below, p. 352.
[3] The few pagan inscriptions of the period belong, some certainly, some probably, to the engineered anti-Christian movement under Diocletian and Maximin, on which see *Pauline and other Studies*, p. 106 ff.

already regarded as only one part of a great surrounding complex of buildings for public utility, which formed a centre for social and public convenience. The church was already fully marked as the focus of city life.

This conception of the church building in its relation to the life of the city is much older than Basil's time. It is the original idea of the early Christian world, when the Universal Church, in competition with the Emperor and Father of the State, raised its claim to be the parent and guide of the people. Such a Christian ecclesiastical establishment took the place of the ancient Anatolian *hieron* as the centre of social and municipal life. The Greek conception of a free people governing itself without priestly interference was dying out, and the Asiatic conception of a religion governing in theocratic fashion the entire life and conduct of men was reviving. The early Christian inscriptions of Lycaonia show this old idea as it affected the people before Basil.

I will mention here only one inscription, the epitaph of a bishop who administered the see of Laodicea about A.D. 315 to 340, a Roman soldier, with the Roman triple name, a man of good family and wealth and position (like so many of those who played a prominent part[1] in the history of Christianity in Asia Minor). In his epitaph he tells how he rebuilt the church of the city, which evidently had been destroyed during the persecution of Diocletian. The bishop enumerates the whole architectural equipment which he had built,[2] and which he evidently considered as indispensable in a proper ecclesiastical establishment—"rebuilding the whole church from its foundations and all the equipment around it,

[1] *Studies in the History and Art of the Eastern Provinces*, p. 372 f.; *Pauline and other Studies*, p. 375.

[2] The inscription is published by the discoverer, Mr. Calder, Christ Church, Oxford, in the *Expositor*, November, 1908. See below, p. 339.

viz., stoai and tetrastoa and paintings and screens of woodwork and a water-tank and an entrance gateway, together with all the mason-work, and, in a word, putting everything in place". While we cannot suppose that the old church, which had evidently been destroyed to the ground under Diocletian, was as magnificent in its equipment as the new one, we can safely infer from this document that the same idea of a social as well as a religious centre had been embodied in it originally, and that the whole establishment was restored. This idea is apparently presumed in the inscription, as natural and self-evident.

Some years later the same idea was embodied in Basil's great foundation at Cæsarea of Cappadocia—which included an almshouse, a place of entertainment for strangers, both those who were on a journey and those who required medical treatment on account of sickness, and so established a means of giving these men the comfort they wanted—doctors, means of conveyance and escort.[1] The church, which formed part of this establishment, was the indispensable centre for the whole series of constructions.

Even the cistern or water-tank at Laodicea was intended, not as a baptistery for hieratic purposes, but simply to afford a supply of water for public convenience: this is proved by the cisterns at many establishments similar in character but smaller in scale, which we have found elsewhere in Lycaonia. In that waterless region a permanent water-supply was indispensable for comfort; and as running water can very rarely be supplied, a tank or cistern for storage was used instead of the fountain, which would have been employed in a district where flowing sources were abundant. But at Laodicea, under the hills, the tank held running water.

---

[1] *Pauline and other Studies*, p. 385; Basil, *Epist.* xcvi.

Those who are interested to trace the continuity of religious custom will not fail to observe that the "Brotherhoods" of the early Turkish time,[1] and the Bektash Dervish establishments (which have lasted down to the present day), fulfil under Mohammedan forms many of the purposes which Basil aimed at in his great foundation. And the fountains in the courtyard of every mosque and Dervish tekke, though primarily intended for the religious ablution before prayer, are used for general purposes of public utility. If we could trace the character of the ancient Anatolian *hiera*, we should probably find in them the type of Basil's establishment.

As to the surviving church-buildings, the most important among many remarkable groups is a series which we had the advantage of studying and excavating in company with Miss Bell in 1907, and by ourselves in 1908 in some small supplementary work—about seventy churches in and around the Lycaonian city of Barata, fifty miles south-east of Ikonion, and subject from A.D. 372 onwards to the metropolitan of that city. These churches form a definite group, possessing a certain unity, revealing to us the history of a small Lycaonian city from the fifth to the twelfth century. The memorials of city life were no longer recorded in inscriptions and the other monuments of the old Greek cities: they stand before us in the churches built by the piety or the sense of public duty of the people, often by the piety of individuals similar to the bishop of Laodicea.

Churches have to be studied by historians as the one form in which the public spirit and patriotism of the Byzantine cities sought expression. The Church was the focus of the national life, and the ecclesiastical buildings mirrored the

[1] On these Brotherhoods see the *Cities and Bishoprics of Phrygia*, vol. i., p. 96.

fortunes and the sufferings of the people. Such buildings were generally constructed as the payment of a vow; and in the inscriptions which often recorded the name of the builder the opening formula was gradually established, "through the vow of . . . "

To take one example: the outstanding fact with regard to the Byzantine Empire as a whole and with regard especially to Asia Minor, is that they were exposed to the full force of the attack which the barbarism of Asia was constantly making on the Roman Empire and the Hellenic civilisation.[1] The Church of Anatolia, if we rightly estimate its character, could not remain insensible to the great national struggle against the Sassanian and Arab invaders, that dread, ever-present danger. Accordingly, we find that one of the churches at Barata was the *memorion* of a citizen who "died in the war," another of one who "endured many wounds," and a third was built as the memorial of a general who had led the Byzantine armies: his name is not given, but only his position in the Empire, for he was doubtless the only native of this obscure town that ever attained that high rank in the army, and hence he is called simply "the Domestikos". The largest and probably the most magnificent church in the town was decorated with paintings executed by certain artists, who are named, under the direction of Indakos, monk, presbyter and eponymous tribune; and a fifth church was dedicated according to the vow of Mammas the tribune. When we see that churches form the angle of the fortifications of the city, that monasteries make part of the walls, that a small church crowns many a little hill near the line of the walls as well as every high peak of the mountains farther away, we realise that the Byzantine Church mar-

[1] *Studies in the History of the Eastern Provinces*, p. 287.

rallied and inspired the Hellenes of the later Empire to defend Hellenism against barbarism, and that the tribunes who built those churches were at once ecclesiastical, municipal and, after a fashion, military officers.

That this Church militant was an effective military leader cannot for a moment be supposed. There was a vast difference between the military orders of European chivalry, the Templars or the Knights of St. John, and these monks and tribunes of places like Barata. But, in the temporary decay of the Eastern Empire, the Church did undertake the guidance of local efforts at defence, which the Emperors had abandoned; and thus the life of the nation came to be more and more completely summed up in the Church. And when the Empire revived in the ninth century, it could not recover the hold which it had formerly possessed on the national loyalty. The Church had entirely supplanted it in the minds of the people.

Hitherto we have been too much disposed to think that, because the regular army of the Empire was professional and the soldiers of the later Roman period were almost a caste and not a truly national army, no power of resistance and self-defence was developed in the districts that were most exposed to Arab attack. But the churches of Barata tell a different tale, and their evidence is confirmed at a later period by the example of Philadelphia,[1] which maintained itself by the energy of its own citizens, unaided and even disowned by the Empire, against the victorious Turks for a century. Where the people had the army to depend on, they trusted to it; but where, as in Barata and Philadelphia, they were left open to the constant attacks of the enemy without military protection, they trusted to them-

[1] *Letters to the Seven Churches*, pp. 400, 412.

selves and the Saints, but chiefly the Saints. It was Michael commander of the hosts of heaven, and the other Saints on every prominent point of the city and every peak of the mountain, who marshalled and stimulated the defensive efforts of the people of Barata.[1]

Here, again, we see how close the Imperial Church stood to the life of the people. But this nearness was bought at a heavy price, and much of the character of the Orthodox Church was sacrificed to attain it. If we take the succession of the ecclesiastical buildings at Barata, ranging from the fifth to the tenth or the eleventh century, we can trace in them, especially through their dedications, the change of feeling: we see the degeneration of the Imperial Church to the popular level of thought and religion, the revival of the old pagan religion of Asia Minor, and the resuscitation of the ancient gods under Christian names.

An example, the most striking out of many, occurs on the summit of the mountain that overhangs Barata on the south. Standing on that lofty peak, an island in the Lycaonian plain, 7,000 feet above sea level, one remembers the ancient idea, nowhere stronger than in Anatolia, that all lofty peaks were the chosen home of Divine power, and feels certain that this was a "High Place" of the old paganism. The proof is at hand. Although in the change of religion the old sanctuary has been destroyed, and a monastery, a church and a memorial chapel (which bears the name of Leo) cover almost the entire summit, and conceal the earlier features of the place, yet the traces of the original "High Place" are not entirely obliterated.

[1] On the circumstances and needs of local defence which tended to encourage among the people this belief in the saving power of high peaks and the abode of their Saints and champions on high hills, see above, p. 136.

PLATE XIV.

Church and Memorial Chapel of Leo on the Summit of the Kara-Dagh.

PLATE XV.

Church on the Summit of the Kara-Dagh: Apse and South-east Corner.

To face p. 158.

In the rocks that support the church on the north side is a passage, partly natural, partly artificial, now to some extent narrowed by walls of the Byzantine period. On the rock walls of this passage, perhaps formerly hidden by Byzantine building, are two inscriptions in the ancient hieroglyphics, which are now generally called Hittite, but which were probably Anatolian in origin. These put the ancient holy character of the locality beyond all question. We have here the first known example of a Hittite "High Place" not entirely destroyed; and we see that its ancient sanctity was preserved in a Christianised form by the Byzantine Church.

This group of monuments, discovered by Miss Gertrude Bell in May, 1907, after so many travellers had visited this ancient city, is one of the best known examples of the general principle which has often been stated—that religious awe in Anatolia clung permanently to the same localities.[1] There can be no doubt that the church and monastery were placed here because of the old sacred character. The new religion was obliged to satisfy the religious instincts of the population, which reverenced this ancient seat of worship. The church and monastery have every appearance of being comparatively early: at latest the sixth century is the date to which they should be assigned. The Byzantine type of architecture with dome standing within a square tower was already fully developed when the church was built; hence one would not be able to date the foundation too early.

The series of monuments on the highest summit of the mountain would, even if they stood alone, furnish a complete proof of the very early origin of civilisation at this site. But it was our good fortune to find a second almost more striking confirmation of the Hittite occupation. On the

[1] See especially *Pauline and other Studies*, p. 163 ff.

north-west side an outlying hill, called Kizil Dagh, about eight miles from the city, was made into a fortress to defend the approach to the central city. The early Anatolian or Hittite character of this fortress is shown by its style, and by three hieroglyphic inscriptions, one on a sort of altar at a gate in the west wall, and two on a "Holy Place," a pinnacle of rock forty feet high, roughly carved into the shape of a seat or throne with high back, below the west wall of the fort. On the throne is incised a figure of the god, sitting, holding a sceptre in the left hand and a cup in the right.[1] He wears magnificent robes and rests his feet on a footstool. He is the god who presides over and guards the city of the mountain, with its bounteous vineyards, its fruit trees, its riches, and its cool, delightful climate in summer. The discovery of this throne would have gladdened the heart of a scholar, who died too young (the late Dr. Reichel), who wrote from very slender materials a most suggestive paper on the importance of the throne in early Anatolian religion. Since his death his views have been confirmed by the discovery of several monuments which prove that a throne played a very important part in the equipment of the primitive cultus in Anatolia. This "High Place" remains unharmed by any destroying hand, except that of time and weather. Its ancient sanctity was forgotten by the Orthodox Church; and the features of the locality are unchanged since it was the place of worship for the garrison of the old fortress.

The name of the same priest-king, Tarkuattes, appears in the inscriptions on both these Hittite sites, as Professor Sayce informs me. This priest-king must have been the

[1] Professor Sayce tells me that he interprets differently the symbol which I took for a cup; but this is immaterial for our present purpose. He regards the seated figure as that of the priest-king; but in that case, according to the usual practice, the priest wears the dress and plays the part of the god.

PLATE XVI.

The Throne of the Anatolian God: with Two Hieroglyphic Inscriptions and a Relief.

PLATE XVII.

Church No. 29 at Bin-Bir-Kilisse: Double-arched West Doorway seen from the inside: on the left is the Wall of the South Chamber of Narthex.

To face p. 160.

dynast either of Barata or of some remoter city to which Barata was subject, and the former seems far the more probable supposition.

We observe three periods in the development of the churches of Barata and the vicinity. During the fifth to the seventh century, we have churches in the lower city, and a group of monasteries high on the hills above the city. From A.D. 700-850 we trace the destruction of the lower city by the Arabs, and the formation of the principal group of monasteries into a fortified town. Between 850 and 1070 occurred the revival of the lower city, as the Arabs were repelled and the danger which had driven the people of Barata into the safe obscurity of the mountains diminished and came to an end. Then the people began to rebuild in the lower ground the ancient city, which now lies a ruined town of the period 850-1070. Several of the largest churches which had fallen into ruins were then restored and remodelled; and it is still possible to trace the changes which were made in order to repair as quickly as possible the shell of the old buildings. Some of the smaller churches perhaps remained standing, having survived the destruction wrought by the Arabs and perhaps by earthquakes. But the majority of the churches which the traveller surveys were probably built from the foundations in the ninth or tenth century. The city was now of smaller extent, and at least one church seems to have been left unrepaired on the western side of the town.

A deterioration in the builder's art is now manifest. The churches were built on good old plans; but the work was carried out rudely and probably in great haste; yet the haste is rather that of carelessness than of urgent need. There are no signs of loving desire to make the work as good and rich as possible. We cannot, indeed, say how far colour may have been employed to supplement the strictly architectural work; but the style is indisputably rather mean in character. The late churches produce the general impression of a degenerating people, a dying civilisation, an epoch of ignorance, and an Empire going to ruin.

Yet, with all their faults, even these late buildings retain for the most part a certain dignity and an effective simplicity. The tradition of the old Byzantine architecture was preserved in this sequestered nook, so long as the Imperial government maintained itself. It was only when the Empire shrank to narrower limits, and Lycaonia was left to the Turks, that the dignity of the Imperial Church was lost, and its places of worship show themselves plainly to be the meeting-places of a servile population.

What was good in the late architecture was traditional, surviving from an older time. What was bad in it was contributed by the age when the work was executed. The decay of true architectural feeling corresponded to decay in the civilisation of the period. The people were dominated by ecclesiastical interests. Monasteries multiplied all over the mountain; and much of the land must have belonged to these foundations, and so been withdrawn from the service of the State. Patriotism could not survive in such an atmosphere; and there is no reason to think that the Imperial government either tried or deserved to rouse a national and loyal spirit, for it was becoming steadily more oriental, more despotic and more rigid. But the major part of the blame for the national decay must be laid on the Orthodox Church. The nation had been delivered over to its care. It had long been supreme and its authority unquestioned. The result was that art and learning and education were dead, and the monasteries were left. The Orthodox Church had allied itself with autocracy against the people, and with the superstitious mob against the heretics and the thinkers. Its triumph meant the ruin of the nation and the degradation of higher morality and intellect and Christianity and art. In our excavations, never deep, we never found any article worth picking up off the ground.

The city lived on its past. All that was good in it was inherited. The mountains of Barata, now called Kara-Dagh, the Black-Mountain, must have been in ancient time the summer sanatorium of the Lycaonian plain. Owing to their height the climate is delightful. The soil is very fertile, and, being volcanic, is specially suited for vines. Many kinds of fruit trees also were cultivated. Water is not plentiful, but there are several springs of remarkably good water. The needs of agriculture and viticulture were met by a wonderfully elaborate system of storing the rain and the melted snows of winter. The mountain had been won for the use of man by long labour and by great skill.[1] The inheritance from past civilisation, the traditional agriculture and industry, was preserved just so far as to maintain the works of former time; and a high standard of material comfort still reigned in the mountain. The delightful air could not be ruined. The water supply, bountifully provided in early time, was cared for and maintained in good order. The vines grew generously on the volcanic soil of the hillsides. Whatever else failed, the wine-presses, which we found in numbers, were still trodden, the harvests were still reaped, and the fruit still gathered from the trees.

The site of this ancient city is now the most inhospitable to travellers in the whole of Lycaonia. There is no water

[1] On this subject see the following paper.

except filthy half-poisonous puddles stored in the ancient cisterns, and he who drinks runs the risk of death. The vines have almost entirely disappeared, the orchards remain only in a few trees run wild. There is hardly any cultivation. The water runs rapidly off the steep slopes of the mountain, and is of no benefit to agriculture except in the lowest part of the little sheltered valley where the city was built. The wealth, the abundance of crops, the fertility of the soil, the vines that grew rich on the sides of these volcanic hills, the water stored up by a series of dams in every ravine and channel, the drinking water brought to the city from fountains at a distance—all these were produced by the labour of men, guided and ordered by the wisdom of the Divine power. It was not through the high education of the individual that those great results in engineering and agriculture and the use of the earth generally were gained. It was through the guiding power of their religion. The Goddess herself, the Mother Earth, taught her children; as she gave them birth and life and nourishment, so she showed them how to use the things that she tendered to the use of man. The religion was agricultural and economic; and its rules and practices were the annual cycle of events in the industrial year.[1]

In this way that ancient religion acquired an extraordinarily strong hold on the simple minds of a little-educated population. In their religion lay their sole education; but it prescribed to them all the wisdom and the conduct that they needed for a prosperous agricultural life. The hold which it possessed on their minds lasted through the centuries that followed, when new rulers and strange religions became dominant in the land. The old holy places, perhaps also

[1] On this see the following paper.

PLATE XIX.

Church No. 32 at Deghile, looking from S.E.: North Arcades of the Nave: Chamber, South Extension of Narthex, on the left: Monastery Halls behind on left.

PLATE XX.

Church No. 5 at Bin-Bir-Kilisse, Apse and South Arcades of the Nave.

To face p. 164. *See pp.* 155-161.

the old religious customs to some extent, imposed themselves on the Christians of the Byzantine time ; and it is not easy to see any great or deep difference between the Byzantine saints and the Divine figures who surrounded the principal deity in the early religion.

Such was the heritage which fell to the lot of the Christian population of Barata. They were heirs to a prosperity gained by industry and knowledge and science. They were heirs also to a religious belief deep engrained in their hearts through generations, a reverence for the religion to whose teaching they owed the beginning and the foundations of their prosperity: they owed to it also the conservation of their prosperity, for those numerous engineering works had to be kept in good repair, and we must suppose that this duty also was part of the ritual of the early religion. The deity who taught them became an inalienable part of the national mind and temperament; and the Christians could not get free from their heritage of belief and reverence,[1] nor would it have been right to force them to throw off all their inherited ideas, fixed in their nature through countless generations.

When the churches and the epitaphs engraved on many of them are regarded in chronological order, it is apparent that they show a reversion to the simplest ancient belief about the grave. Just as the ancient grave was a temple, the home of the dead, who is a god identified with and partly merged in the supreme deity, so in this late Christian period the church is, so to say, the sepulchral monument. The one great religious duty, alike in this late time and in the oldest period, was to prepare a grave, and the grave was a sanctuary. No trace remained, so far as we can observe, of the idea that

[1] See *Pauline and other Studies*, p. 136 ff.

the church was a place of instruction in moral duty and religious thought; the church was in itself holy, and it was a duty supreme above every other—so far as remains show—to build a grave-church.

The history of this city thus seems to end where it began; and yet through all the degradation the Orthodox Church is not dead. It still maintains the Hellenic unity.

The Imperial Church lives, and while it lives the Imperial unity is not dead, but only asleep. It is like the old German Kaiser Barbarossa, who led his army of the great Crusade from the Hellespont to Cilicia, triumphing over every difficulty with marvellous skill and tenacity of purpose, to disappear from the eyes of men in the waters of the Calycadnos: but the creative imagination of popular belief knew that he is not dead, that he waits the moment and the signal to reappear among men. So it is with Hellenism as a world-power. It may revive: the Church has always to be reckoned with as a possibility in the future. Asia has in store as great issues and as great surprises for the western world in the future as she has often produced in the past.

And since I have mentioned the Kaiser of romance and the Crusade that he led across Asia Minor, I may venture, in the last words addressed to the Historical Congress in the German Capital, to recall the new German Crusade which is conducting another march across the same land. It is no more an army of mail-clad warriors. It is an army of engineers and workmen. At Dorylaion, where the first Crusade fought its first great battle, at Ikonion, where Barbarossa gained his greatest victory, you find now large German workshops and German hotels. This new Crusade moves more slowly than the army of Barbarossa; but it moves more surely. It has surmounted difficulties as great as those which

Kaiser Friederich met. It has yet other even greater difficulties to encounter. It has to accommodate its organisation to the people of the land, and give form to itself as part of the national resources.

The historian must regard with the keenest attention this great historical development. He must admire the forethought and the patient tenacity with which every obstacle is provided for and overcome, and he watches with interest how the arrangement with the Orthodox Church and the power of the new Hellenism will be concluded. For myself, as I have loved on many journeys to trace step by step the victorious march of the old German Kaiser, and as I have with keenest interest and growing admiration watched every stage from the beginning of this new Crusade, so I look forward to observing on what terms and in what spirit the new Crusaders will meet—as they must inevitably at some time meet —the force of the old Imperial Church.

NOTE.—I take this opportunity of supplying an omission in my *Cities of St. Paul*, due to lapse of memory in finishing the book amid the many pressing duties in the opening month of University classes, October, 1907.

On the native religion of Lystra the published monuments throw no light. They refer only to the religion of the Roman Colonia, mentioning the worship of Ares and of the Emperor. Fig. 5, p. 216, sets before us one aspect of the native religion. It is a very small relief, about eighteen inches high; the surface is much broken, and the work, even if it had been well preserved, is of the rudest character. Photographs of the worn flat surface taken in 1901 and 1907 are too faint for reproduction. The stone sets before us the local god, protector of the flocks, which must have been a chief source of the city's prosperity. The river valleys beside the city are rich arable land, but most of the territory consists of low undulating hilly ground suited for pasturage. There is therefore a sheep beside the platform on which the god stands. He is marked by the lustral branch in his right hand as the god of purification—an important and constant feature of the Anatolian god. His left hand reaches down towards an altar in the shape of a table (compare the shape of the Hittite Lycaonian altar, frontispiece to my *Studies in the History of the Eastern Provinces*); but this part is so broken that the action is uncertain. The nature of the Anatolian god, as revealer to men of the ritual that should be observed on his own altar, is described in the *Letters to the Seven Churches*, p. 64.

The inscription states the name of the god and the occasion of the dedication. It began with the word "consecrated," now lost. "[Aur.?] Neon C . . . . onianos, son of Dionysius, [consecrated] the (statue of) Apollo to the Tribe (called) Holy Thiasos, a vow".

The Thiasos was the company of worshippers of the god; and the fact that it was one of the city Tribes is highly important. It was, doubtless, a Tribe large in numbers, including most of the native population. The dedicator bears a Hellenic (perhaps also a Roman) name, and he applies a Hellenic name to the god. He therefore belonged to the Hellenes, who were a part of the Lystran population (as, *e.g.*, Timothy's father). The god is here assimilated to Apollo as the sheep god, and the god of purification; but the identification with Zeus as the supreme god was equally suitable. A similar conception of the divine nature on the plateau of Asia Minor is elsewhere called Zeus Galaktinos, the milk-god. He is the Zeus-before-the-city of Lystra.

V.

THE PEASANT GOD:
THE CREATION, DESTRUCTION AND RESTORATION OF AGRICULTURE IN ASIA MINOR

V.

THE PEASANT GOD:

THE CREATION, DESTRUCTION AND RESTORATION OF AGRICULTURE IN ASIA MINOR [1]

[The following words, published a year after this article appeared in the *Contemporary Review*, express the central thought of my article so exactly from a totally different point of view, that I may be permitted to quote them as a motto:—
THUS THE MEN OF INSPIRATION OF THE FOURTEENTH CENTURY, THE CHAUCERS AND THE LANGLANDS, SAW IN THE TYPICAL AGRICULTURAL LABOURER THE GREAT MORAL FIGURE OF THEIR WORLD.—Rd. Heath in *Contemp. Rev.*, Jan., 1907, p. 84.]

WHERE the mountains of Taurus rise sharp and high from the southern edge of the level plains of the great central plateau of Asia Minor, and near the point—vague and never strictly defined on that flat, featureless land—where Lycaonia and Cappadocia meet, there is a narrow well-wooded glen which runs up two or three miles southwards into the mountains. It ends in a theatre-shaped hollow, at the back of which the rocky sides of Taurus tower almost perpendicularly for some thousands of feet. At the foot of the cliffs is the source of a stream which gushes forth in many springs from the rock with a loud noise that almost drowns the human voice. Strangers find it difficult there to converse with one another, and the speaker has to put his mouth near the ear of his auditor. The people of the tiny village of Ibriz, near the head of the glen, when they come to the

[1] This paper is the enlargement of a lecture delivered before the Geographical Section of the British Association at York, August, 1906.

springs, talk in a high-pitched voice, which is heard across the continuous, monotonous roar of the tumbling water.

A river flows rapidly down the steep glen from the source, and out into the plain, where it transforms this tract of the arid, bare, burnt-up plateau into a garden, as rills of its water are diverted into hundreds of little irrigation channels. It turns north-west and west, watched over by a great ruined castle perched high on a hill two miles north of the mouth of the glen, a hill at the western end of a long spur of Taurus. This is the "strong Castle of Hirakla," as the Arabs called it, Herakleia of the Greeks, which is described by an Arab poet, detained or imprisoned in the Byzantine country, as one of the obstacles that intervene between him and his lady; "O thou who art separated from me by the Roman mountains and their steeps, by the twin fords of the Sarus, by the Pass (*i.e.*, the Cilician Gates) which interrupts the way, by Tyana of the frontier, and by Hirakla". Past this great castle (which, lying off the ordinary road, was never noticed by any traveller, until in 1891 my wife and I crossed the hills late one evening and passed close under its walls) the river flows on five miles, traverses the wretched town of mud-hovels called Eregli,[1] which has replaced the old city and bishopric —at last about 1060-64 glorified into an archbishopric—of Kybistra, then turns south of west, and after a few miles more flows into the White Lake, Ak-Giol, a considerable

[1] Eregli is now reviving, as it is practically the terminus (for the time) of the Bagdad Railway: the actual rail-head is out in the plain at Bulgurlar, a Turkmen hamlet, five kilometres beyond Eregli, and is likely to remain so for some time [1906: it remains to be seen whether the agreement concluded in 1908 between the Porte and the association of German Banks which is pushing the Bagdad Railway will soon begin to be carried into effect. Advance beyond Bulgurlar implies an energetic effort to carry the railway over or through the Taurus. Bulgurlar is the point where the connection with Tyana, Nigde, Kaisari and the north-east generally, is most convenient.]

body of water in some seasons, in others dwindling to a large pond bordered by great marshes. The lake at its south-western end approaches the Taurus mountains, and when the water is high empties itself through a short channel into a great circular hole under the rock wall of Taurus, and thus is received back into the divine mountain from which it came.

The river shadows forth in its course the life of man, as the old Anatolian religion conceived it; from God it comes, and to God it returns in the end. Nature, as that religion understood it, was in all its various phenomena expressing over and over again the one great truth—the life of God is the life of nature and the life of man.

The source of this river is still called, like others of the most strikingly beneficent springs of Asia Minor, by the expressive name "God has given," Huda-verdi. Never was a case in which the gift of God was more clearly declared, or the immediate presence and permanent beneficence of God more manifest. The river is given to transform this corner of the dry land into a fertile garden, and as soon as its work is done, it is received back into the rich bosom of the Great Mother Earth.

It has never been my good fortune to see the phenomenon of the disappearance of the river beneath the mountains at its end. The lake has been too low on the two occasions when I have passed that way. The main road from the west by Iconium to the Cilician Gates and Syria crosses the last part of the river channel by a rickety wooden bridge.[1] The great hole in the ground at the foot of the mountains gaped close beside us. Tombs cut in the rock walls attested the desire of the ancient population to lie in death at this

[1] The bridge may have been improved since we last saw it in 1891.

holy place. But the stream was dry, the graves were empty, and the country here was uninhabited and desert.

On the rock near the sources of Huda-verdi, on a large space prepared to receive it,[1] the ancient religion expressed by the most striking monument in all Anatolia the truth of life, as it was shown manifestly in this holy place. There on the rock stands the king of the land, as the representative of the whole people. He is dressed in magnificent embroidered robes; he is wealthy, great and tall (about nine feet in height), fit representative of a rich and prosperous population; and he stands with hands raised in front of his face, adoring the present god. The god is a gigantic figure, nearly twice as large as the king. He holds in his hands the gifts which he offers to men, the corn and the grapes. At his feet is an implement, which seems to represent a small rude plough. He is dressed in a short tunic, simple and unadorned, girt with a broad girdle, with bare knees, his feet covered with thick-soled boots which reach up the leg far enough to protect the ankles and the lower part of the calves. The upper part of the boots consists of two flaps at back and front, and the fastening is by a string which is twisted a good many times round to hold the flaps together and keep the boots in place. Everything is of the plainest kind. The god wears the minimum of clothing, and that of the simplest. The belt is worked in zones of simple line-pattern, chiefly zig-zag; in that country some simple kind of ornamentation is and was almost universally used; even "the coarsest sacks bear ornamental patterns, and the very paper in which

---

[1] A second monument of the same character and showing the same subject, in poorer preservation, was discovered by Mrs. Doughty Wylie in 1906. It is about 300 feet higher up the mountain side, and on a shelf of the steep hillside close to it stands a Byzantine church, an interesting proof that the pre-Christianity sanctity lasted through the Christian times: see p. 158.

PLATE XXI.

The Peasant-God at Ibriz.

To face p. 174.

shopkeepers wrap their parcels is often adorned with coloured patterns ".[1]

The peasant from the neighbouring village who conducts the travellers to the Huda-verdi source wears clothing almost exactly the same in style as the god's, the tunic, the boots and the belt. Little has changed here. Your guide proves to you the nature of the god. He is the peasant-god, the toiling, simple agriculturist, living by the work of his hands, and making wealth and prosperity for the country and its kings and great men. The kings have come and gone, nothing remains of them and their work. The peasant is eternal and unchangeable. You feel that there was a large foundation of truth and wisdom in the religion which so correctly gauged the relative importance of the king and the peasant, and anticipated Carlyle in his philosophy of clothes, giving the outward distinction of show and dress to the king, an ephemeral personage, and assigning to the peasant the real distinction of work and of service to mankind and of the gifts which he bestows on the world, the corn and the wine.

One part of the clothing differs. The head-dress marks the god. He wears authority on his head, just as St. Paul, in his first letter to the Corinthians xi. 10, says that the veil on her head is the authority of the woman; with the veil on she is in an Oriental land supreme wherever she goes; without the veil she is a thing of nought, whom any one may insult with impunity.[2] The god shown in the sculpture at

[1] Miss Ramsay in *Studies in the Art and History of the Eastern Roman Provinces* (Hodder & Stoughton, 1906), p. 21.

[2] I speak of the typical Oriental feeling, where it has not been affected by knowledge of European customs. Where European ladies have been known, they are treated respectfully (in some cases with very marked respect in Turkey); but the earlier missionaries in Turkey found the situation often very difficult.

Ibriz has a high pointed tiara with two horns projecting in front, the mystic sense and power of which we cannot now interpret in their full import.

But why is the divine power described on the rock beside Huda-verdi as the toiling peasant, and not as the joyous river-god, or as the Goddess-Mother of all life, the Earth herself, who from her bosom gives forth this bounteous gift to the world in its need? The mind of Greece, at such a spot as this, would have been filled with the gladness of the loud-laughing water and the promise of fertility and growth and prosperous husbandry. The Anatolian mind was generally filled with the thought of the divine Mother, the giver of all things, the ultimate source of all life; and surely here, if anywhere, her bounty and graciousness are conspicuous. In her life the god is a mere accidental and secondary personage. Yet here on the rock the dominant thought is about the work of men, symbolised by the toiling god, subduer of the waste and unprofitable places. Not the free gift of the divine nature, but the labour that must be applied by man to make that gift profitable, stands graven on that great monument. The primary personage of the divine nature, the goddess, is away in the background, and the secondary personage, the god, monopolises the scene.

Now it is the law of the world that, while the divine power gives rain and fruitful seasons, there is an annual cycle of work by the hands of man which must be applied to plough, to sow and to reap. But that work is always understood as the ordinary course of life; it is not a toil, but a pleasure; it is the mere effort of raising to the lips the food which the god has bestowed; it constitutes the permanent enjoyment of the bounty of God, extending over the year and the whole life. The man who regards the regular operations of husbandry as toil and labour, undertaken solely with a view to the distant harvest, is not a true agriculturist. The true agriculturist is he who takes the work of the year as the cycle of a happy life, and does each part of the year's duties with a heart full of gratitude to the God who has permitted him to do this duty. So far as this aspect of labour is concerned, the rock-sculpture of Ibriz might be expected to portray the pure bounty of the beneficent god, who pours forth the life-giving and wealth-producing water for the happiness of man. A deeper thought lay in the mind of the sculptor who portrayed that scene on the rock at Ibriz. This is the religious problem of the sculpture; and the answer to this problem lays open a far deeper view into the heart of the old Anatolian religion than the writer ever before was able to attain.

The early religion of Anatolia, often called the Phrygian religion—a name which is historically incorrect, for the Phrygians were a mere body of intruders from Europe, who adopted the religion of the land into which they had come as strangers somewhere about a thousand years before Christ, that ancient religion which was supreme in the country in the second and third millenniums B.C., and the date of whose origin cannot even be guessed at [1]—embodied in a series of rules and ceremonial practices the past experience and accumulated wisdom of the race. In regard to agriculture, the domestication and breeding of animals, the cultivation of valuable trees like the olive and the vine, sanitation, the rights of society as against the individual, the law of property and boundaries, the right of free intercourse and markets, in short, the whole life of society, the customs which had been approved as salutary by the collective and growing

[1] " Religion of Asia Minor " in Hastings' *Dict. Bib.*, V., p. 110 ff.

wisdom of the race, were taught as obligatory rules and enforced by religious authority: the offender who trespassed against any of those rules was chastised by the god. The divine power tenders to the use of man all its gifts; but they must be won by knowledge and by work. The knowledge, learned slowly by the experience of generations, was regarded in the religion as revealed by the goddess, the Great Mother of all life, who bore and nourished, warned and taught, directed and chastised, all her people, and in the end receives them all back to her kindly bosom. Her religion set forth in a body of wise rules and precepts all the knowledge which was needed in ordinary circumstances. Her people had only to obey and to be faithful. In exceptional circumstances the Great Mother was ready to give special advice through her prophets and in dreams. She punished inexorably all infractions of her law, by misfortune, by sickness, and above all by fever, that strange malady which burns up the strength and the life by direct effort of the divine power without any definite or visible affection of any part of the body. Such was the penalty inflicted on every individual transgressor of the law; and confessions of guilt, with warnings as to the penalties that followed guilt, were inscribed on tablets and put up publicly at the temples of the goddess,[1] where the traveller of the present day may read them and publish them to a wider public than was dreamed of by the first authors. Not merely was the individual punished. The community as a whole was punished by the loss of prosperity, of security and ultimately of its very existence, if the law was persistently broken; and to safeguard it the religious sanction was strict and inexorable.

[1] Many examples in *Cities and Bishoprics of Phrygia*, i., pp. 134 ff., 147 ff.

Now in the beginning it was the labour of generations of the working peasants that redeemed the soil from its original unproductiveness; and this god on the rock at Ibriz stands for the work that had given the soil to agriculture. There is no question in Anatolia of a natural soil which has simply to be cultivated in order to produce. The soil originally was waste and valueless. A vast amount of toil and skill had to be applied before the land could begin to be cultivated. The rock-sculpture bears witness to one of those great engineering works that lie away back at the beginning of agriculture and history. All over the Eastern Mediterranean lands—probably round the Central and Western Mediterranean also, if we had any records—the reclamation of the soil from waste to fertility was regarded as the work of a toiling god, bound to service under a stern master or king, who has in some way got a hold over him and can compel him to a labour in itself ungrateful and performed only under compulsion. Hercules was the commonest name for that toiling god. Hercules drained the marsh of Lerna with its fifty heads of water, and gave to men the richest part of the valley of Argos. Hercules cut the passage through the mountains by which the lake imprisoned in the land-locked vale of Stymphalos was enabled to flow away and the fertile soil was made available for the happy husbandman.

It was the forethought and knowledge displayed in those great engineering works that seemed to the ancient mind to be divine. The god condescended to work as a toiling peasant and won for the use of men this far-off good, which human skill alone could not have foreseen, and thus he gave to man in free gift the soil out of which should come the corn and the wine. But to understand all that is implied in this, one has to look at the country as it is at the present day, when it has to a large extent gone back to the state of nature and of waste land. How has this come about, and what is the cure?

Elsewhere the present writer has described the character of the Mohammedan conquest of Asia Minor.[1] The Saracens, a congeries of various Asiatic races, led by the Arabs, attempted it, and failed completely. During three centuries of war they never permanently held any land beyond Taurus except what their armies actually covered.[2] The Turks, first the Seljuk Turks and afterwards the Osmanli, achieved what the Saracens could not do; and they succeeded only by breaking up the fabric of the superior society and reducing it to disconnected atoms. This was not done consciously or intentionally. The Turks did not wish to destroy the industry and wealth of the country; the intention of the Sultans was to profit by its prosperity. The ruin was the work of the Nomads, who followed close after the irruption of the Turkish armies.

The distinction between those Nomads—Turkmen, Yuruk, Avshahr, etc., as the traveller still sees them—and the Turks proper, who now call themselves Osmanli, was as evident to the Byzantine authorities in the twelfth century as it is to-day, or was fifty years ago. But the real nature of the distinction and the origin of the various tribes are obscure, and so far as I know uninvestigated. Those tribes are described under the names of Nomads or Turkmens by Anna Comnena, Nicetas of Khonai and Joannes Cinnamus. They evidently followed close on the first Turkish armies of invasion; and their relation to the soldiers of those armies is

---

[1] See especially a paper on the war of Moslem and Christian for the possession of Asia Minor, in *Studies in the History and Art of the Eastern Roman Provinces*, p. 281 ff.

[2] See in the present volume, p. 116.

difficult to determine. That is one of the many questions which await the historian of the Turkish conquest of Asia Minor. Were those Nomads the offspring of the first invaders in A.D. 1070, who maintained in Asia Minor their national way of life as they had led it in Central Asia, while the Turks of the cities were a people mixed of the old population turned Moslem with part of the invading armies?

The story of the Seljuk conquest has still to be written; for Gibbon's generalisations are brilliant and unsatisfactory, while Sir H. Howorth's excellent essay is just sufficient to make us long for a detailed study according to localities. It is abundantly clear that, after their first inroads and their first great victory at Manzikert, the loose and ill-organised Turkish armies were not able to meet in fair fight and on even terms a Byzantine army, if the latter was led with any degree of prudence and skill.[1] Yet the Roman civilisation, which had resisted three centuries of constant Arab raids and numerous Arab victories, died out before the undisciplined Seljuk power. It was the Nomads who destroyed it against the wishes and intentions of the Seljuk government, whose enemies they very quickly became.

The Nomads remain now generally quite apart from the Osmanli or Turks, though the Osmanli were a mere Nomad tribe as late as A.D. 1300; and they continued practically independent of the Turkish rule until late in the nineteenth century, some of them till the twentieth century. I have in my own short experience come in contact with several

[1] I speak only of the Seljuks, not of the Osmanli or Ottoman Turks, whose Janissaries were more dangerous than the best forces in Europe; but the Janissaries were the tax levied in brain and muscle on the Christians. The Seljuk victories were gained in the decay of the empire; but John Comnenus prepared a revival of Byzantine power, which was wasted by the rash folly of Manuel in the Pisidian rout (*Studies in the History of the Eastern Provinces*, p. 235).

examples of the recent subjugation of tribes whom travellers a little older describe as independent. One case only out of several that have come under my own notice may be described.

In the Ouzoun Yaila, the long high-lying plains between the south-eastern affluents of the Halys and the most westerly affluents of the Euphrates (especially the Tokhma-Su), the nomad Avshahr were supreme and free until about 1866. Then great numbers of Circassian refugees entered Turkey, at the invitation of the Government, fleeing from their homes which had been conquered by Russia. The first act in the new drama was that the Turkish officials, charged with the duty of settling the immigrants in this sparsely populated land, plundered those wretched and poverty-stricken refugees of everything that they had brought with them. The next was to let them fight with the former inhabitants for land—a fight that has been going on in a smouldering way ever since. A large body of Circassians was brought to the borders of the Ouzoun Yaila, and encouraged to take possession of the land. A regular war ensued. The ill-armed Avshahr were defeated and driven into the mountains of the Anti-Taurus; and the plains of the Ouzoun Yaila are now inhabited by Circassians.

Those Nomads, the real conquerors of the land of Anatolia, are still in some respects the most interesting people in the country, though great efforts have been made in the last fifteen or twenty years to force them to settle down by seizing their beasts of burden and preventing their customary annual migrations. Much suffering has been caused to the present generation, and much injustice has been done to individuals; but it must be allowed that the migrations were not compatible with order and industry. The process has been an interesting one to watch. Every year I notice new villages, where formerly were only nomad encampments. The Peasant-God is slowly beginning to work. It is a hard task, unwillingly undertaken, at the command of a stern taskmaster. The life of the nomad, a perpetual holiday, has to be exchanged for this toil of reclamation; and it will be a slow and painful process to bring back the land into its former state of high cultivation. These amateur agriculturists have no agricultural tradition, no store of knowledge and method accumulated through generations and centuries, few implements and no practice in using them. The women mainly do the work. If a modern artist arises to express in sculpture or painting the history of the re-creation of agriculture, he will have to change the sex of the deity who stands for the toil expended by mankind in this transformation.[1] It is no longer the goddess who teaches and gives counsel and practises the household arts, and the god who does the field labour. The woman works in the field, and there are no household arts. It was pathetic, when we spent some nights in nomad Kurd encampments on the central Anatolian plains, to see the envy and admiration with which the women looked at and handled the few needles and simple articles for the household and the toilet which my wife had with her. As the nomads do not seclude their women, I was a witness of some interesting scenes and phases of feminine nature. We were specially struck with what one might almost call the rage of envy with which one handsome young woman looked on and refused to touch; never have I seen such

---

[1] I speak only of the Turkish and Nomad population. The Circassian women are not so hard-worked, though Turkish custom is affecting the immigrants. Among the Christians the women do the house-work and practise the household arts and go out dressed in their best clothes on Sundays and holidays, and are free from all but the lighter field-labour. So also among the Albanians so far as I have seen them.

rebelliousness against the tyranny of fate as glittered in her eyes. She wanted the things for herself: she would not admire them when they belonged to another. No wonder that the son of a Kurdish Bey in a village of the Anti-Taurus once said to us, "all our men are thieves". Thus the various races of Nomads stand opposed to the settled Mohammedan population of the towns and villages at the present day.

The picture which the Byzantine writers set before us of the conquest by the nomads has been briefly described elsewhere by the writer;[1] "the nomad Turkmens spread over the face of the land; the soil passed out of cultivation; the population decreased; the old Christian cities (which had not lost their former industries) were isolated from each other by a sea of wandering tribes; intercourse, and consequently trade and manufactures, were to a great extent destroyed. . . . Thus was accomplished the degeneration from civilised to barbarian society, a process which it would be instructive to study in detail, but which can be summed up in one word, the nomadisation of Asia Minor." The detailed study which is hinted at in the last sentence would be the work of a lifetime; but a sketch of the process, so far as during ten years of further study it has become clearer to me, may here be given.

It is almost literally the case that the flood of nomadism drowned out the old civilised society and submerged the land. The process was gradual. The cities were first of all isolated from one another. They remained as islands in the sea of nomadism, they were still inhabited by a manufacturing and

---

[1] *Impressions of Turkey*, p. 103 (with some verbal changes). The progress of the Nomads in the western regions of Asia Minor is described in *Cities and Bishoprics of Phrygia*, i., pp. 16 f., 27 ff., 299 ff.; ii., pp. 372 f., 447, 598, 695.

trading population, which the Seljuk Turks allowed and even encouraged. But trade implies communication, facilities for travel, opportunities for exchange. In a civilised society like that of the Roman Empire no city had been self-sufficient, all had depended on one another. The life-blood of a civilised State must circulate freely through the whole body. If the circulation is impeded, the body languishes and dies.

That was now the case in Anatolia. The cities were isolated from one another by the "estranging sea" of nomadism. Across this sea, slowly and always exposed to the attacks of the nomads, especially of course at night, voyaged caravans, seeking to maintain the necessary circulation of the life-blood, the communication between city and city. To make these voyages safer the Seljuk Sultans built many great khans along the principal roads that radiated from their capital, Konia; and those buildings, in many cases magnificent both in scale and in architecture, rank among the most impressive features of modern Anatolia, and deserve notice, along with the beautiful mosques, colleges (*medressé*) and tombs, as evidence of the remarkable development of architectural art in the Seljuk period.

Some recent German travellers have described those great khans as a proof of the high level of civilisation on which the Seljuk State stood. One of the latest of them expresses the opinion that the Seljuk khans have taken the place of similar large Roman and Byzantine buildings, and conserve in their plan, which is everywhere practically the same, the accepted method of those older hotels on the Roman roads. There is a large element of truth in part of this opinion, but part needs serious modification. As those same travellers remark, the large Seljuk khans resemble fortresses, with their massive walls, unbroken by any opening except slits which are loopholes rather than windows, and their single, well-protected entrance. If there were similar buildings along the Roman roads, how comes it that not a trace has ever been found of them? The truth is, that such buildings were not wanted where travelling was fairly safe, as it was in the Roman Empire. The inns and *mansiones* of the Empire were buildings of a humbler and less lasting character. Fortresses were not needed. Private enterprise was sufficient to maintain hotels or inns adequate to the needs of travellers. All that is known of them suggests that they were of a humble character, squalid, dirty and vicious,[1] and that wealthier travellers avoided them and took their own equipment. In a few cases, on the summit of high passes across the mountains, buildings of a more permanent kind were needed, as, *e.g.*, at the summit of the great Taurus pass just above the Cilician Gates; and it is noteworthy that at this point was the ancient Panhormos, whose name shows it to have been a large inn. Defensive strength would be of some importance here among the mountains, and a guardhouse and harbour of refuge, Panhormos, was established on the summit, which was often deeply covered with snow in winter.

The Seljuk khans bear witness to the high development of art, but to a very unsound condition of society and government, in the Seljuk State. Such great, fortress-like buildings were not needed on the Roman roads and therefore were not built then. In the Seljuk time they were necessary, because the caravans, by which alone trade and communication were kept up between the cities, required shelter at night and protection from the nomads. The cities were islets in the ocean of nomadism; and the khans were harbours of refuge at short intervals in the dangerous voyage from city

---

[1] *Pauline and other Studies*, p. 385.

to city. Peace began to reign on the roads only when communication ceased, when there were no travellers to rob and no trade to plunder.

As for the model on which the khans of the Seljuks were built, I should, like Dr. Sarré, find it in an old Anatolian style of building; but not in hotels of the Roman or Byzantine time. The model was the old class of buildings called Tetrapyrgia, whose very name reveals their form. They were farmsteadings of quadrilateral shape, having at the four corners, towers, which were connected by walls and inner chambers, enclosing an open quadrangle. They were so strong that regular military operations were needed to reduce them;[1] and, given the shape just described, this implies a construction like the Seljuk khans, with strong outer walls and a single defensible gateway. The view of Zazadin Khan[2] near Iconium, given in Plate XV., may serve as a fair specimen of these buildings.

In those big fortified homesteads lived the large patriarchal households of the landholders, representatives of the conquering caste in a subjugated land, a class which is just beginning in recent investigation to appear before the view of history. From those landed families came some of the leading figures in early Church history, such as Basil of Cæsareia and Gregory of Nyssa. Their history may yet be traced more completely.

The cities of Turkey, isolated from one another and thus compelled to be each sufficient for itself, dwindled away. The old manufactures died, some sooner, some as late as the middle of the nineteenth century. It was my good fortune

---

[1] As Eumenes had to do (Plutarch, *Eum.* 8: *Studies in the History of the Eastern Provinces*, p. 373).

[2] See below, Article XII., No. 17.

that we began, my wife and I, to travel just at the end of the period of decay. We saw the end of the old and the beginning of the new. I remember riding into Konia, once the greatest and most splendid city of Turkey—of which the Turkish proverb said, "See all the world, but see Konia"; it was as if one were riding through a city of the dead, street after street seemed empty and solitary, like the enchanted city in the story of the Arabian Nights. But now Konia is rising again to be an important, though far from a splendid city, as the terminus of the Anatolian Railway and beginning of the Bagdad Railway. Its claims to magnificence are gone; the old walls were all torn down about twenty to thirty years ago; of the palace only the shapeless core of a tower remains; some of the beautiful old mosques are ruinous, some are patched in the coarsest way, yet even thus many of them retain enough of the past to be charming. In April, 1904, we noticed unwonted patches of white colour along the road from the railway station to the Government house, and on inquiry learned that the German Ambassador had visited the city a week before, and the mud walls had all been whitewashed along the road by which he drove to call on the Pasha. That is the cheap magnificence of the twentieth century in Asia Minor. One week after the gorgeous pageant there were still a few traces left of it!

Not merely did trade and manufacture die out. The land passed out of cultivation, except in so far as was necessary to feed a dwindling population. Nomads do not cultivate the ground, but live on their flocks, and only the city population required to be supported from the tillage of the ground. Thus a land which had been absolutely the richest in the world became one of the poorest. I have seen, especially in Palestine, bare hillsides where could be traced the old terraces, showing that the hills had once been cultivated to the very summit; but the terraces were neglected and gradually broken down, the soil was washed off the hillside, and there remained either bare rock or a uniform slope too steep to cultivate, if any cultivator appeared. There are many stretches of land on the edge of the hills which are now almost covered with stones washed down from above; yet round the villages some scanty cultivation exists, and corn struggles up amid the stones from a soil which is hardly visible under them, but which is so fertile that even thus it can grow a wretched crop to make bread for the villagers. There are vast plains of splendid soil where you could hardly see a stone in an acre—pure, rich soil but absolutely sterile because the water supply has ceased. Where the land has become so bare and smooth, the rain runs off as soon as it has fallen, because there is nothing to detain it. The irrigation channels in that soft, deep soil efface themselves as soon as they are neglected. Yet there is abundance of water near at hand, it only needs to be distributed. Over parts of such plain we rode once, my wife and I, for more than an hour, through water over two feet deep: in other years I have ridden repeatedly over the same road, and found the country hard and dry as a bone that had lain for years in the sun.[1]

I have seen miles and miles—and know there are many hundreds of miles—along the coast-land covered with a growth of wild olive shrubs, where now not a single olive is produced. All that country was once a great olive garden, teeming with wealth and population, where now are only a few black goats'-hair tents in the winter, and hardly a living

[1] This refers to the road from Konia to Kara-Bunar and the East generally: the precise part was west of Ismil. The most direct path from Konia to Ismil is passable only in the driest season of the year: the ordinary path keeps well to the north to avoid the inundating waters.

soul in the heat of summer. The olive dies out where the population is Mohammedan. It is the tree of civilisation, which can flourish only where order and security of tenure exist. Even in a disorderly land one may sow cereals and vegetables, the fruit of which may with luck be gathered in a few months; but the young olive takes fifteen to eighteen years to bring in any return, and an outlook over that length of time is too great for any Mohammedan population. The reason lies, not in any inherent necessity of Mohammedanism, but in the fact that no Mohammedan Government, except, perhaps, that of the Moors in Spain, has ever been able to produce the assurance in the minds of its subjects that property will be secure for so long that it would be worth while to make an olive plantation.

One example may be given of the contrast between the wealth of the past and the poverty of recent time. In 1882 I found a column, eleven feet high, covered on one side with Greek writing, in an upland village near Antioch of Pisidia. It records a list of subscriptions for patriotic and religious purposes, made on some occasion about 250 A.D. by a society which was fighting against Christianity.[1] The subscriptions amount to several hundred thousand denarii. The denarius had considerably depreciated in value at that date since the time when it was worth a franc; and the exact point of depreciation which it had reached is uncertain, but it can hardly have been lower than a thousand to the pound sterling in amount of metal. The total sum subscribed was certainly considerable. Twenty years ago you could not find in the whole village change for a coin of the value of four shillings. That one example may be taken as a not unfair measure of the ratio which the wealth of the country in

---

[1] *Studies in the History of the Eastern Provinces*, pp. 321, 372.

Roman times bears to the wealth of the present day. The difference is that between a well-cultivated and an ill-cultivated country. Four thousand years ago the peasant cultivator made the one; during the last millennium the soldier and the fanatic have made the other. The peasant cultivator, with peace and security of tenure, must be called in once more to repair through 50 or 100 years of patient labour the damage wrought by war and misgovernment.

Let me once more guard against a possible misunderstanding of my words. There is a considerable amount of land in Asia Minor which has never passed out of cultivation, and where the agricultural tradition and experience have been kept alive. A population of a good many millions had to be fed out of the produce of the country; and, if the population is less now, there is more exported than formerly. The best and most favoured land has remained under cultivation, and especially near the centres of population. Irrigation has never ceased and is still practised in certain districts, so that the essential principles of water-engineering have never been wholly forgotten. The wheat of the Ushak region is of remarkably fine quality, and I have been told by several independent authorities that it is not inferior to the finest in the world. In 1906, for example, I travelled for an hour on the Anatolian Railway with a Belgian gentleman of long experience in the country, and he mentioned that the Ushak grain commanded a higher price for certain purposes than even the best Canadian wheat. The Ushak district may be taken as a fair specimen of the land of the upper plateau. The figs of the Mæander valley (commonly known as Smyrna figs, because Smyrna is the harbour of exportation) have always been prized in commerce. Many other examples might be quoted to prove what may be expected from the restoration of agriculture over the vast areas where it has almost entirely ceased.

But the revivification of this almost dead land has begun. The cities are becoming busier. Industries are reviving. The nomad, even, is being changed into the husbandman by a process that will be long and painful.

The reason for the revivification of the country is not the beginning of good government, for the government is as bad as ever it was; government always lags behind the people, and is forced onward or dragged onward by the growing education and insistent demands of the nation. The reason lies in one phrase—the coming of the railways. Communication is now becoming possible and fairly safe; the life-blood is beginning to flow in the new veins; the body that was dead has begun to live again. Roads are improved—though the traveller fresh from Europe would be puzzled to detect where the improvement lay—and these help to feed the railways and restore circulation. With communication comes trade and the revival of old industries or the introduction of new ones. There has been an immense increase in the production of Turkey carpets, as it has become possible to send them to the coast at remunerative rates. Towns where not a single carpet-loom existed fifteen years ago have now hundreds of people engaged in the manufacture. Less than twenty years ago a friend who was engaged in the carpet trade, going up the Ottoman Railway as soon as it was extended to the Lycus valley, was struck by the ornamental possibilities of large, cheap kerchiefs made at the small town of Bulladann. He sent home a few specimens; about three years later he sent home 70,000 in one year, and others were also sending them to London and New York. The gathering and export of liquorice root, begun about sixty years

PLATE XXIII.

Zazadin Khan near Konia. *See pp.* 185-7.

PLATE XXIV.

The Gate of the Virgin-Goddess: looking over the Limnai.
To face p. 192.

ago, rapidly became the largest trade in Turkey. For a long time it has been sent exclusively to America to sweeten tobacco; thus the Tobacco Trust became the sole purchaser; and it used its position to seize the entire trade a few years ago.

In the revivification of Asia Minor the land has to be brought back into a state fit for cultivation by clearance, by irrigation, by planting and growing of trees. That means an expenditure of uncounted millions and a long lapse of time before any return for that vast expenditure can begin. Commercially, it is an impossibility. No one would risk his money in schemes which can at the best only begin to pay his children or his grandchildren when population has multiplied and there is a home market for produce; and the cost would be so tremendous that the money could not be raised. This work cannot be done by money. It can only be done by the labour of generations of men working and improving their own land for the benefit of their own families.

Here again I must guard against misconstruction. I do not make so foolish a statement as that capital cannot be judiciously used to supplement, direct and facilitate the restoration of agriculture, or that capital cannot be used remuneratively in the districts most favoured by nature, where irrigation can be restored most easily. In 1891 I saw a great irrigation channel on the outer sides of Taurus not very far from Ibriz as the crow flies, but very far distant as water flows; and we crossed it on horseback, not without difficulty owing to its depth, at a point high on the hill underneath the "strong castle of Hirakla". This channel was constructed, as I believe, several thousand years ago; and it carried an immense supply of water many miles to be dissipated at last in uncultivated lands. In 1902 I saw the same channel utilised in the middle of its course, but farther away from its source than the point under Hirakla where we saw and crossed it in 1891, by the Circassian people of a new village. The villagers had simply broken down the channel and turned the whole of the water (far too great a supply) at random over the country, making it difficult for waggons to travel on the road at the point where the water crossed it. The waste of abundant water supply at some points and the dearth generally constitute the problem which has to be solved. But the elements of a solution are for the most part present: only one element is entirely wanting, and that is security of property. There is no guarantee that he who labours shall profit. Without palace influence and palace favour no one can gather the fruits of his toil.

It is known, for example, that a good deal is being done on the soil of Mesopotamia, which has in great part passed into the possession of the Sultan himself in quite recent times (as have enormous estates throughout the Turkish Empire). Here there is security of property. Here the rapacity of the tax-gatherer does not step in to seize the fruits of labour, for no taxes are paid on Imperial property: all the profit belongs to the private revenue of the Sultan, and the State grows poorer as estate after estate has been added to his vast possessions. But many exaggerated and inaccurate reports about the facts in Mesopotamia are current, and have sometimes found their way into high-class journals in Europe. The real facts can be learned only by patient travel in that country, which is unknown to me.

This process of peasant-cultivation has recently been carried out on a small scale in the neighbourhood of Smyrna, where European influence is strong, and where the enlightened administration of Kiamil Pasha has been effective. Plots of waste land on the hillsides have been given to peasants on condition that good cultivation is applied to them, and the result has been a great enlargement of the area of productive land. This improvement has taken place in spite of the notorious insecurity of the country, due to the increase of brigandage caused by the war in Arabia. The soldiers for that war are drawn mainly from Anatolia. Arabian service is regarded as equivalent to a sentence of death; the conscripts desert in numbers, and all deserters, as outlaws, take to the mountains, *i.e.*, become brigands. A brigand must go where there is the opportunity of earning a livelihood; therefore they abound near Smyrna, where there is industry and money, while the poverty-stricken inner country is fairly safe.

Among the creators of those vineyards on the hillsides near Smyrna there existed a knowledge of method and a tradition of viticulture. The skill gained through the experience of generations was put into the work of reclamation. The peasant cultivators in this case were merely the representatives for the moment of the eternal peasant, the embodiment of slowly acquired knowledge. The superhuman power, which is above and independent of the ephemeral mortal workman, must be brought to bear on the land. The old artist at Ibriz tells us so in his sculpture. The peasant-god, the divine nature, that is what reclaims the soil for the use of mankind. It is a work of the race, not of the individual.

To knowledge must be added labour, the toil of generations. Money is here of no avail. This work is antecedent to money: the foundations have to be made on which civilised life, with intercommunication, trade, and money as the common measure of value and the instrument of exchange, may be built up. In the savage state, or to the civilised man on a desert island, money is valueless, and much building is needed before it can acquire value.

That truth is sometimes not appreciated in discussions on this subject. Recently I chanced to read an article in a popular magazine[1] on the crofters in the Highlands of Scotland, in which the writer proved that the crofter system was more expensive than the landlord system. Draining the croft would cost £150, building a house £300. The crofter would have to pay the bank five per cent. for this money: the landlord could borrow it at four per cent. The increased annual burden was fatal to the crofter-system. The draining and irrigation of the land of Anatolia cost no money: it cost the work of generations: it was paid by the lives of men, and not by coin of the realm. The restoration of agriculture can be made and paid for only in the old way. Unless the crofter can make personal work serve instead of money, he and his system are certainly doomed. The peasant-god had no bank from which to borrow at five per cent.

Thus we have briefly described how the country of Asia Minor was made by long hard labour suitable for agriculture, and how the agriculture was destroyed and the land allowed in great part to relapse into its primitive state. The restoration of the Anatolian land to agriculture can take place only in the same way as the creation of agriculture was originally achieved, by slow patient labour directed by intelligence through a succession of generations. The process may be facilitated by utilising the other natural products of the country, especially the mineral wealth: an increasing population will need a larger supply of food. But to the writer

[1] *Blackwood's Magazine*, August, 1906.

the special interest of this investigation lies in the connection with religion. Religion led the way and fixed the rules for the creation of agriculture; and it has degenerated along with the agriculture and civilisation of the land. The connection is apt to escape notice among modern scholars, because in European countries a widening gulf separates religion from practical life, and there has thus been induced a habit of thinking that the history of religion proceeds apart from and unconnected with the development or deterioration of civilisation. But this is a grave error. The development of a nation's life is in the long run the history of its religion.

Note.—As bearing on the permanent sanctity attached to certain sites in Asia Minor through all mutations of the external form of religion, I use this opportunity of correcting my description of the sacred place on the Limnai (*Cities of St. Paul*, p. 293). This place, still regarded as holy and made the scene of an annual panegyris in September in honour of the Virgin Mother of God, was, beyond all question, once a sanctuary of the Virgin Artemis of the Limnai. There is at this spot both a small cave high up in the rock (which here drops steeply down to the lake), and near it on the shore a very curious great arch of rock, apparently natural, through which one looks out over the lake. At the panegyris mass is celebrated in the cave, which has a rude niche like a roughly hewn apse to the West, not East; this apse has been partly destroyed. But the natural phenomenon of the arch probably originated the sanctity of the spot.

I am indebted to Miss Gertrude Bell for the description and for the photograph of the archway, Plate XXIX.

The question arises, whether this natural doorway is the

Dipylon, which on one theory was the sacred place of Great Artemis, the goddess of the Limnai. In the Tekmoreian inscriptions the sacred ceremony, according to the restoration of an inscription printed in my paper on the subject,[1] took place in the Dipylon. Now Dipylon strictly implies two doors; but it might indicate a temple like that of Janus, a gateway with its two faces (as stated in *Studies in the History of the Eastern Provinces*, p. 349).

[1] *Studies in the History of the Eastern Provinces*, p. 319: ἐν τ]ῷ διπυ]λῳ. On p. 349, I mentioned another restoration τ]ῷ διπύ[ρῳ without ἐν (which occurred to me too late to be discussed on p. 319). This restoration is advocated by Mr. A. J. Reinach (who does not observe that I suggested it) with weighty but not quite convincing arguments. Perhaps the photograph here given may turn the scale in favour of the old reading: though after thinking of διπύρῳ I long preferred it.

VI.

THE RELIGION OF THE HITTITE SCULPTURES AT BOGHAZ-KEUI

VI.

THE RELIGION OF THE HITTITE SCULPTURES AT BOGHAZ-KEUI

[NOTE.—The following paper is left practically as it was written in the year 1881, with only some slight verbal changes. The writer had not the opportunity of correcting the proofs before the paper was published in the *Journal of the Royal Asiatic Society*, 1882. The view which is here taken of the religion of Asia Minor has not been universally accepted; and several scholars would reject the idea that so important a part in the cultus belonged to the feminine element. On the other hand, those who maintain this view have developed it in much greater detail than appears in this short paper. But it seems better to reproduce the original statement of the writer's views, partly because sentences and paragraphs from this inaccessible paper have been quoted in several works, partly because of a recent discovery in Ephesus. Mr. Cecil Smith, in publishing the remarkable ivory statuettes found by Mr. Hogarth in the foundations of the ancient temple of Ephesian Artemis, expresses the opinion [1] that one of them represents the Eunuch priest of the goddess; he compares it with the priest who so frequently appears in the rock-sculptures of Boghaz-Keui, and he supports by new arguments the interpretation of that figure which is stated in the present article. The support accorded by so judicious and so com-

[1] *Archaic Artemisia of Ephesus*, p. 173.

petent an authority is a sufficient justification for reprinting a paper written twenty-seven years ago.

This paper contains the germ of many of the writer's subsequent speculations about early Anatolian religion. It has been developed, improved, carried out in more detail in those later speculations; but it needs no change, for it simply expresses the facts as they forced themselves once and for ever on the writer's mind. I do not mean that I would now maintain in every detail the opinions here expressed; and I doubt if I should now have courage to state so positively the general theory which is here formulated. But at least nothing has been discovered to make me withdraw from the rather bold position which I then took up. The paper made no attempt to explain the sculptures as a whole. Probably, if it had done so, one would not have been able to reprint it. But, as that old article was written under the first inspiration of a visit to the site, and described what I thought I saw in certain parts of those wonderful sculptures, it may be worth while to place before the reader the record of the impression produced by them.

The range of illustration is small, because the writer at that time had seen hardly any of the Hittite sculptures, and had had very little practice in estimating the character of rock-sculpture. The visit to Boghaz-Keui and Euyuk occurred on the first journey which I made in the interior of the country, about thirteen months after first landing in Asia Minor. With twenty-eight years' experience I should now be much better able to profit by studying the rock-monuments than I was then. I may recall with deepest gratitude the debt which I owe to the late General Sir Charles Wilson for having invited me to accompany him on this journey. But his official duties did not permit him to remain at any place except modern centres of population and government, hence we had only a hurried view of the great city and the rock-sanctuary.]

M. Perrot has rightly argued that the wonderful rock-sculptures near Boghaz-Keui are a series of religious representations.[1] But, while his account is in general accurate and sympathetic, I believe that further progress in the interpretation of their meaning is hindered by one misconception on his part: many of the figures which he considers male seemed to me undoubtedly female. I came to Boghaz-Keui fresh from the perusal at Ancyra of the only copy of M. Perrot's *Voyage Archéologique* that exists in Asia Minor; but, after two hours' examination, Sir C. Wilson and I both came independently to the same conclusion, that the majority of the figures were female.[2] We were fortunately able to remain a second day, and I spent about five hours examining every figure in this regard. In many cases the sex is quite uncertain; but only a few are certainly male, and a large number are certainly female. On the whole, I came to the conclusion that the sculptures were the monument of a religion in which the female sex played a much more important part than the male, and that in various cases where the sex was doubtful, the probability lay on the female

[1] These notes are printed solely from the wish to call attention to a remarkable series of sculptures, which have as yet been almost completely neglected. In our hurried visit, 1881, there was no opportunity of examining them sufficiently. Now Herr Hermann has been charged with the duty of bringing casts to the Berlin Museum, and there is every reason to hope that the sculptures will soon be accessible to study. [This hope was only partly realised.]

[2] [I may add that the impression was produced on both of us, quite independently and unexpectedly, of something characteristically feminine in the face; this impression is not conveyed by the photographs, where shadows and angle of view exercise too strong influence: see also concluding note to this article.]

side. Bachofen (*das Mutterrecht*), amid many untenable opinions and crude hypotheses, has shown how great an influence belonged to the women in Asia Minor, and this influence is of course creative of or dependent on religious sanction: and Gelzer has proved that the Lydian religion attached special importance to the female (Rhein. Mus., xxxv., p. 516). The character of the sculptures at Pteria is therefore in accordance with the analogy of Asia Minor.

Two facts suggest a false idea as to the sex of the figures. In the first place, the great mass of the figures fall into two long lines directed towards a central point. The series of figures on the left is headed by three gods, that on the right by a goddess; almost all the figures on the right are clearly female, several of those on the left are equally clearly male. Hence the idea arose that the figures of the right are female, of the left male. But this idea cannot be carried out completely. The goddess who leads the procession on the right is followed immediately by a youthful god standing on a leopard; and in the series to the left there are several female figures.

In the second place, the wearing of the short tunic has been generally regarded as proving that more than half the figures are male. Closer examination makes this doubtful. Most of the figures are armed, and it is obvious that if women are going to fight they cannot wear long sweeping robes. Female warriors were one of the most distinctive characteristics of the religion of Asia Minor and particularly of Cappadocia; and I should not hesitate to consider the twelve armed figures [1] in the narrow passage opposite the most mysterious and perhaps the most sacred figures of the whole to be Amazons.

[1] Perrot, *Voyage Archéologique*, pl. 52.

All that occurs on earth must have its prototype and its origin in similar divine phenomena. Accordingly, the idea of women as fighting and as warlike, finds its religious justification in the warlike goddess who was one of the chief manifestations of divinity; and the masculine air, the short dress, the flatness of the bosom, are quite in the spirit of a religion, of which it is characteristic to raise itself above the distinction of sex. Its essence [1] lies in the adoration under various forms of the life of nature, that life subject apparently to death, yet never dying, but reproducing itself in new forms, different and yet the same. This perpetual self-identity under varying forms, this annihilation of death through the power of self-reproduction, was the object of the enthusiastic worship of Asia Minor with all its self-abandonment, its periods of complete immersion in the divine nature and of superiority to all moral distinctions and human ties, its mixture of obscene symbolism and the most sublime truths. The mystery of self-reproduction, of self-identity amid diversity, is the key to explain all the repulsive legends that cluster round that worship, and all the manifold representations or embodiments of the divine life that are carved on the rocks of Boghaz-Keui [and Frahtin, and the palace walls of Euyuk]. The parent is the child, the mother is the daughter, the father the son; they seem to men different; religion teaches that they are the same, that death and birth are only two aspects of one idea, and that the birth is only the completion of the incomplete apparent death.

[1] I must here assume unproved that theory of the character of Anatolian religion which seems required by the facts of its history. [It is stated more fully in the article of " The Religion of Greece and Asia Minor " in Hastings' *Dictionary of the Bible*, v., p. 110 ff.]

One of the central ideas in the religion is that the distinction of sex is not ultimate, but only an appearance, and not a real element of the divine life. In its essence that life is self-complete, self-sufficient, continually existent; the idea of death comes in with the idea of sex, of incompleteness, of diversity. The goddess is the earth, the Mother; the god is the Heaven, the Father; the ultimate divinity comprehends both heaven and earth, both god and goddess. Hence arises the widespread Anatolian idea of the androgynous god—an idea which appears in Greek art as the Hermaphrodite—merely a rude symbolical expression of the unreality of sexual distinction. Hence also arises the tendency to confuse or to obliterate the distinction of sex in the gods, to represent the goddess with the character of the man, the god as womanly and effeminate; while the priest of the religion must be neither male nor female.

The wearing of bracelets and earrings is of course not peculiar to women, but has been practised in many countries by men. In the rock-sculpture at Ibriz in southern Cappadocia[1] both the husbandman-god and the bearded king wear earrings; so also did Lydian men.[2] But in the sculptures of Boghaz-Keui and Euyuk I could not find them on any figure certainly male with one exception, and this exception furnishes a presumption that they were in northern Cappadocia a feminine ornament. This is a figure that occurs three times at Boghaz-Keui, and twice at Euyuk,[3] and M. Perrot rightly comes to the conclusion that it must represent the high priest; and we can easily recognise in it the

[1] See above, p. 174.
[2] Xenophon, *Anabasis*, iii., 1, 31.
[3] Perrot, pl. 42, 47, 50, 51, 56. Euyuk is five hours north of Pteria. Here, out of the side of one of the large artificial " mounds of Semiramis," appear the doorway and front, covered with sculptures, of some great palace or temple.

effeminate character, the soft outlines, the long sweeping dress, and the ornaments of the eunuch high priest, Archigallos, so well known in the cultus of Cybele.[1] This view to which M. Perrot inclines, is made quite certain by the subject of the following slab at Euyuk, which was not seen by him: Sir C. Wilson got the villagers to turn over a block, and disclosed one of the most interesting scenes of the whole series.

The accompanying plan of the entrance to the palace at Euyuk shows the position of this slab, which is lettered Z.

It is on the right hand as one enters the great doorway, guarded by the two Sphinxes, 9 and 10. The two sculptured blocks on the left side of the entrance, 7 and 8, are each 6 feet 6 inches long; so that the length of the entrance way is exactly 13 feet. Now Z is 7 feet 3 inches long, and the adjoining block, 11, is 5 feet 9 inches long, so that these two exactly fill up the right side of the entrance way. It is remarkable that there is no sculpture on the long side of block 11; while on its short end, which forms the first slab of the series on the right hand front wall, a seated deity (Perrot, pl. 66) is carved. Both the blocks 7 and 8 on the left side of the entrance way are adorned with reliefs; one of those on the right side is carved, and the other is left plain. I know no explanation of the apparent anomaly.

9	10
8 |	| Z
7 |	| 11

FIG. 1.

At the right hand of the scene on slab Z a deity sits with the feet resting on a footstool, one in front of the other; the figure is much worn, but in all that remains it is exactly the

---

[1] On the Archigallos in Phrygian religion see *Studies in the History and Art of the Eastern Roman Provinces*, pp. 246 f., 343.

VI. *The Religion of*

same as the seated goddess on pl. 66, and in the accompanying drawing it is restored accordingly. Towards this deity a procession of four figures advances, headed by the priest. His dress is the same as in all the scenes where Perrot has engraved him: in his right hand he, as usual, holds the long curved staff (*lituus*), while with the left he pours from an oinochoe a libation, which falls on the front foot of the seated deity. Behind him is the priestess, with her hands in the position that seems to be characteristic of women in the art of Cappadocia. The right hand holds out some round object in front of her face, the left hand carries some object

FIG. 2.

to her mouth. She is dressed in the same long sweeping dress which she wears in other scenes on these monuments, but it is now impossible to tell whether she wore earrings. Behind her come two other figures, which are much worn; they were dressed in short tunics and cloaks which hang so as to cover one leg and leave the advanced leg bare. The figures at the extremities of this slab have been injured by the small stones on which it has fallen; but fortunately the two in the middle have not suffered so much. From the position of these two figures it is not open to doubt that they are the chief priest and priestess of the cultus.

The same view is suggested by the scene on pl. 56 (Perrot), in which also the subject seems to be a procession approaching the divine presence. An altar of peculiar shape is placed in front of a small figure of a bull, evidently a religious symbol, standing on a high pedestal.[1] The same two priestly figures, wearing the same dress, approach the altar: the priest carries in his right hand the *lituus*, and the priestess wears earrings. [Three altars of this peculiar mushroom form have been discovered at Emir-Ghazi (seventy-five miles east of Iconium), which is probably the Kases or Kasis of Byzantine writers, the Khasbia of Ptolemy; but unfortunately two of them are much mutilated. An altar of similar form appears twice in the rock-sculptures at Frahtin; but here the circular basis is not plain (as at Euyuk), nor surrounded with zones of hieroglyphics (as at Emir-Ghazi), but ribbed obliquely, like the dress of the priestess from the waist downwards in the two annexed figures.]

At Boghaz-Keui the priest is seen three times (pls. 42, 47, 50, 51, Perrot).[2] In Fig. 3 he is represented walking beside a tall figure, whose arm is affectionately twined round his neck. Perrot would fain make this pair a man and woman, but is obliged to acknowledge that the little figure is clearly male; and he suggests that they represent the king and the priest grouped as a pair. To our eyes the tall figure is as clearly female as the small figure is male. It is in high relief, and the face stands out from the rock with an exquisitely delicate contour—bold, determined, and yet feminine. The figure is far the finest of all the series, and looks

---

[1] [Many bronzes representing a bull standing on a raised platform or altar have been found in other Hittite sites (Chantre, *Mission en Cappadoce*, and unpublished examples elsewhere). On Frahtin see the *Pre-Hellenic Monuments of Cappadocia* in Maspero's *Recueil de Travaux*, etc., vol. xiv.]

[2] Perrot, pls. 50, 51.

210   VI. *The Religion of*

almost like the creation of a different art. In the midst of rude work and inartistic symbolism, it recalled to me the

Fig. 3.

Amazons of the Maussolleum frieze.[1] It is evidently the Νικηφόρος θεά of an inscription of Comana (*Journ. Philol.*,

[1] One who looks at the plates in Perrot, 50 and 51, will at once say that I am wrong on this point, and that the figure is certainly male. But, before

1882, p. 147), the warlike goddess who was characteristic of the Asia Minor worship. Like the Lydian Omphale, she bears the weapons, and her male companion is the effeminate and unwarlike god, Heracles, sunk temporarily to be a woman.

This companion is Atys, at once her favourite and her priest, her son and her paramour. The god as the first priest was the type of all succeeding priests, who at Pessinus bore his name as an official title: each priest wore the insignia, and was said to imitate the self-mutilation of the god. That priests and priestesses should wear the dress, bear the name, and represent the personality, of the god deity whom they served, was common in Greek religion also. The priests of Bacchus were Bacchoi, the female celebrants Bacchai; the priests of Sabos or Sabazios were also called Saboi; and many other examples may be found.

The frequency with which the priest appears in these religious sculptures shows how great was his importance in the religion, and his influence among the people. He was the embodiment of the god living always among his people and explaining to them always through the oracle, which was a never-failing accompaniment of the Anatolian religion, the will of heaven. This is in complete agreement with all that we know of political organisation and government among the people of Asia Minor, before they were affected by Greek influence. Either the priesthood comprehended the kinghood in itself and exercised supreme power, or the priest was at least second to the king in dignity and rank

judging, one should bear in mind that the photograph on pl. 51 is useless, and that the drawing on pl. 50, being made by one who thought the figure male, loses all the feminine character.

and social powers.[1] The same thought is suggested by the scene on pl. 47 (Perrot). Here the priest is represented as of superhuman size, standing with his feet on two large objects, in shape like cones with rounded points; these are quite different in character and shape from the mountains on which the gods stand. The priest is evidently here portrayed as the apparent god, co-ordinated with the other manifestations of the divine nature on the rocks around, smaller in size than the greatest of these, but larger than many of them.

In all the three cases where this figure occurs at Boghaz-Keui, it is accompanied by a remarkable symbol: this symbol is not always the same, but the three are only slight modifications of one type. The variations are doubtless of great importance, and will in time perhaps throw much light on the scenes in which they occur. They are all composed of symbols, such as occur in the hieroglyphic inscriptions that are characteristic of the rock-sculptures of Asia Minor, so placed together as to form something like a *naiskos*, bounded on each side by two Ionic columns: the whole being crowned by the winged solar disk.

[Fig. 4 shows an ivory statuette found under the temple of Artemis at Ephesus, and beautifully reproduced, both plain and in colours, in *Excavations at Ephesus* (Hogarth and others, 1908), Plates XXI. 2 and XXIV. 7, 11. Mr. Cecil Smith, on p. 173 of that work, recognises in it the Megabyzos or Eunuch chief-priest of the goddess. He mentions that "Newton in his *Essays*, p. 230, has drawn attention to the quasi-regal supremacy of" this priest. Of the ten complete human figures in ivory found under the temple, "no less than nine are undoubtedly statuettes of

[1] Str., p. 557, 672 [where kinghood and priesthood were united, mutilation of the priest could only be a fiction; and there are some traces of such fictions, as when the Archigallos is distinct from the priest].

women ".[1] The tenth is this figure of the Megabyzos, which has some male characteristics, while "the sleek, rounded forms of the face, the arrangement of the hair, and the long-sleeved chiton, would naturally suggest a woman". I must add that, in spite of the sleek forms, the type of the face, with its thick features and "the broad fleshy nose," seems to me to mark the figure as male even more clearly than the delicate and spiritual type of the warrior figures at Boghaz-Keui stamp them as female. "The chain which hangs round his neck is probably his chain of office [2] . . . the curious fez-like cap, the broad decorated belt and the mode of dressing the hair, with a plait looped in front of each ear, may be regarded as part of the same ceremonial costume." The slight maeander ornament on the lower part of the dress may be compared and contrasted with the elaborate ornamentation on the priest's dress at Ibriz.]

It follows from the nature of this religion that on the rocks of Boghaz-Keui we must expect to find in the diversity of divine personages many various manifestations of the one divine

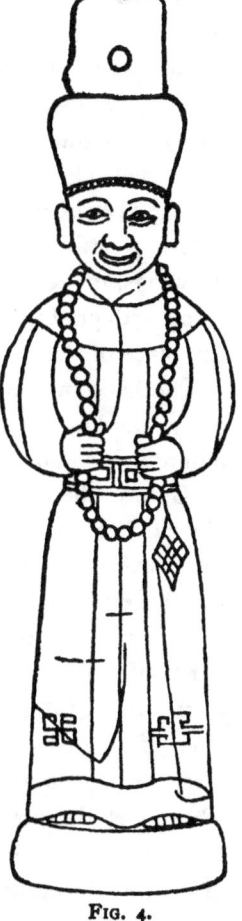

FIG. 4.

[1] [The preponderance of the female element in hieratic representations, alike at Ephesus and at Boghaz-Keui, is noteworthy.]

[2] [Mr. Smith compares the position of the hand grasping the chain with a statuette published by Chantre, *Mission en Cappadoce*, p. 151.]

life. The attempt to explain them must begin by studying the cases where the same figure is repeated with slight variations, and must have at its disposal either the original sculptures or satisfactory representations of them. The photographs published by M. Perrot, welcome as they are, cannot be made the basis of a satisfactory discussion. In every figure I could see numberless details which are quite invisible on the photographs: the light is very bad among the rocks, the apparatus often can not be put at the proper position, and nothing except either a series of careful drawings, made with the help of photographs and studied along with photographs, or a complete set of casts, can supply the place of the originals.

The head of the series of figures on the right is a female deity standing on a lion, which has its feet placed on four mountains. On her head is the turreted crown, which was in Greece the distinguishing mark of the Asian goddess Cybele, but which, from its frequent occurrence at Pteria, can hardly be more than the mark of womanhood, of the female sex in its properly female function and not as setting aside the distinction between male and female. She holds her hands in the attitude which is characteristic of women in the art of Cappadocia; the right hand raises a symbol in front of her, the left holds some object towards her mouth. She is followed by a youthful god standing on a leopard, whose feet also are planted on mountains. In this pair one must recognise the mother and son, Cybele and Atys in one of his manifestations, Demeter and Dionysos. The leopard on which the god stands is the favourite animal of the Greek Dionysos. A few other examples of the connection between the sculptures of Pteria and the religion of Phrygia and Lydia have been given in *Journ. Hell. Stud.*, 1882, pp. 40-46.

But few of the figures on these rocks have their character so plainly expressed as these examples; and without better material for study, the whole set must remain unexplained.

[*Note*.—I have in this reprint avoided using the name Pteria for the city at Boghaz-Keui, not because I think the identification (accepted in the article originally and in my *Historical Geography*, pp. 29, 31, etc.) wrong, but because the form of the name is uncertain. Herodotus uses the expressions τὴν Πτερίην, τὴν Ἐφεσίην, in adjectival form. Many others have suggested that Ptara, the Lycian city-name (Patara in Greek), is the noun; and this seems highly probable; but the further suggestion that Ptara means "city" seems not so acceptable. Perhaps Ptara, like Ptagia in Pisidia, is connected with the divine name Pta (in Greek Meter Ipta), which was used in Eastern Lydia: see *Studies in the History of the Eastern Provinces*, p. 369.

That Croesus, when he crossed the Halys, would march direct on the capital of his enemy, may be assumed as certain. Now Boghaz-Keui is marked by its size and remains as the capital of a great Anatolian Empire: see *Historical Geography*, p. 28, and the first part of the article here reprinted; also above, p. 127.]

Fig. 5.—The Apollo of Lystra: a third-century votive relief (see p. 167 f.).

VII.

THE MORNING STAR AND THE CHRONOLOGY OF THE LIFE OF CHRIST

VII.

THE MORNING STAR AND THE CHRONOLOGY OF THE LIFE OF CHRIST

THE connection between the two parts of the above title is not obvious at first sight. It is the merit of Colonel Mackinlay, in the book which we propose to review, on *The Magi: How they Recognised Christ's Star*,[1] to have shown that there is a very real connection. His title is, perhaps, not very well chosen, for it does not allude to any of the parts and topics which seem to me to be the most important and interesting in his work, while it emphasises what is most speculative and least convincing. Although the present writer has written a brief preface to the book, it seems not out of place for him to review it; indeed it appears justifiable, and almost obligatory, to state more fully than was possible in the few paragraphs of his preface the reasons which make him consider that the book deserves careful reading.

That men, when conversing familiarly with one another, usually draw any figures of speech or any symbolic expressions which they may chance to employ from the range of their own interests and knowledge, is a principle that cannot be denied, and will be freely admitted by every one. The lawyer uses legal metaphors, the stockbroker the slang of the exchange, in explaining his meaning. The contrast in this respect between St. Paul's language and that of most of the writers in the Bible is well known, and has often been

[1] Hodder & Stoughton, 1907.

pointed out. He rarely goes to nature, but uses the language of city life and of education, and, to some extent, of business and trade. On the contrary, the Bible generally contains a far larger proportion of metaphors and imagery drawn from the phenomena of nature, the wind, the rain, the storm, the heavens, sun and stars, the growing and dying or harvested vegetation of the earth, etc.; except Paul the writers whose works are contained in the Bible were men of the country, not men of the city.

In regard to the imagery of this latter class a second principle may be observed. Those who live and talk in the open air tend to draw their illustrations from what is present and visible to, or in the mind of, their hearers and themselves at the time. Probably every expositor and preacher has occasionally drawn his inspiration more or less unconsciously from this principle, and every careful reader has sometimes observed particular instances of its application. But the formal commentators do not make sufficient use of it. It is not obvious to the secluded scholar in his study amid the atmosphere of books. You feel it most strongly in the world of life. Sir Isaac Newton, however, though he was (so far as I know) unused to life in the open air as well as unfamiliar with the Mediterranean lands, perceived this principle, and stated it in a very interesting passage which is quoted by Colonel Mackinlay. It is not one of the least of the merits of his book that it gives prominence to this excellent observation of a great man; if I may suppose that the passage is as unfamiliar to the world of scholars as it was to me. "I observe that Christ and His forerunner John in their parabolic discourses were wont to allude to things present. The old prophets, when they would describe things emphatically, did not only draw parables from things which offered themselves, as from the rent of a garment (1 Sam. xv. 27, 28) . . . from the vessels of a potter (Jer. xviii. 3-6) . . . but also, when such fit objects were wanting, they supplied them by their own actions, as by rending a garment (1 Kings xi. 30, 31); by shooting (2 Kings xiii. 17-19), etc. By such types the prophets loved to speak. And Christ, being endued with a nobler prophet spirit than the rest, excelled also in this kind of speaking, yet so as not to speak by His own actions—that were less grave and decent—but to turn into parables such things as offered themselves. On occasion of the harvest approaching He admonishes His disciples once and again of the spiritual harvest (John iv. 35; Matt. ix. 37). Seeing the lilies of the field, He admonishes His disciples about gay clothing (Matt. vi. 28). In allusion to the present season of fruits, He admonishes His disciples about knowing men by their fruits. In the time of the Passover, when trees put forth their leaves, He bids His disciples 'learn a parable from the fig-tree; when his branch is yet tender and putteth forth leaves, ye know that the summer is nigh'." This admirable passage is quoted from Newton's *Commentary on Daniel*, a work which is proverbial in modern times for fanciful and strained interpretations, and which I confess that I have never even seen; but if there is much more in it like this paragraph, it must be better worth reading than some modern commentaries, for this is original and true.

The author mentions several other examples in corroboration of Newton's principle. One pair of examples is peculiarly interesting. In Matthew xx. 1-16 occurs the parable of the householder, who went out early in the morning to hire labourers into his vineyard. Every one who studies ancient literature or life knows the strong prejudice that was entertained against hired labourers alike in Palestine and in Italy in ancient times. The "hireling" was despised as untrustworthy and idle, an unwilling labourer who worked for money and not for love of the work or of the master whom he served. He was always looking for the reward and the pay for his labour, not aiming at doing it well for its own sake (Job vii. 2). John x. 12 f. contrasts the cowardly hireling with the true shepherd; the former neglects the sheep, and flees when the wolf approaches, but the true shepherd defends them to the death. So in Italy *mercennarii* or free hired labourers were always disliked, and contempt is often expressed for them. A man who wanted important or delicate work well done employed the members of his own family, especially his household slaves.[1] Every person who attempts to explain to pupils the spirit of ancient Roman life has constant occasion to insist on this; and it applies also to Greek life, though it is not there so strongly forced on one's attention.

Why is it that the Kingdom of Heaven, the prophets and the servants of God, are compared by Matthew in this passage to hirelings, who all receive the same pay at the end of the day, whether they have worked in the vineyard one hour or a whole day? In Matthew xxi. 28 it is the owner's son who works in the vineyard; in John xv. 2 the owner himself is the workman. What is the reason for this difference? In the first passage there is no stress laid on the trustworthiness or untrustworthiness of the hired labourers. The only point of comparison lies in the reward that is given to all alike: so much is true, but this does not

---

[1] That household slaves were a part of the family, and regarded as specially trustworthy servants, is a fact of immense importance in the study of ancient society.

quite satisfactorily and fully explain the choice of this parable.

The Author points out that the passage in Matthew xx. 1-16 relates a conversation held about midwinter or January, whereas Matthew xxi. 28 and John xv. 2 were spoken in the middle of March. Wherein, then, lies the difference? He very aptly quotes Mr. W. Carruthers, F.R.S., who writes, "For tilling the ground and keeping it free from weeds in winter, hired labour would be sufficient; but for cutting off the rapidly growing shoots in March or later, so as to prevent the energy of the plant from being directed to mere vegetative development, an intelligent workman would be needed". The delicate labour of pruning must be intrusted to one who has both skill and interest in the result; but unskilled labour was sufficient to turn over the soil and to destroy the weeds. Moreover, there is a great deal more of tedious labour involved in the latter; and it must often have been necessary to get in more hands to do the winter work in the vineyard.

In both cases the illustration was drawn from what was actually being done at the moment. Speaker and hearers saw the suggestion of the parable taking place before their eyes, as the words were spoken. Similarly I have elsewhere tried to point out[1] how inevitable it is that, when Christ said to Nicodemus "the wind bloweth where it listeth, and thou hearest the voice thereof, but knowest not whence it cometh and whither it goeth," the two were not in some cellar in Jerusalem, but out on the side of the Mount of Olives, with the wind of spring moving gently around them. The character which is impressed on speech and thought by life in the open air, is apt to escape the reader who is used to live

[1] *The Education of Christ*, p. 74.

and think and study and address audiences in a room; for he often assumes unconsciously that scenes must have occurred in closed spaces, though something of the vitality is lost on this assumption. Part of what is called the Oriental character of the Bible should more correctly be called the open-air character.

These cases may be generalised as a principle. Those who live in the open air and draw their imagery from the visible phenomena of nature must be to a large extent guided in their choice by the present circumstances. A man who converses while sitting or walking in the open air is not likely to talk about the beautiful bloom of the fruit-trees, if the trees in an orchard close by are bare in the winter season or loaded with fruit. If he talked of the beautiful flowers that clothe the trees, you know that the conversation occurred in the spring-time. The careful reader can tell in many cases the time of the year when such illustrations were spoken, and thus a system of annual chronology can be established. Every reader of literature can illustrate this from his own experience or study. There are few commentators on any ancient author who have not sometimes employed reasoning of this class. Colonel Mackinlay's merit lies in employing it more systematically and thoroughly, and with greater attention to the facts and habits of ancient Palestinian life and surroundings, than any other person (so far as the present reviewer's knowledge extends), and in establishing on this basis, which is theoretically a perfectly sound one, a complete chronology of the life of Christ. In doing so he rests his reasoning on many acute and subtle observations, which are well worth careful reading.

This method of reasoning has, of course, its dangers and its defects. It is almost inevitable that the reasoner should press some of his observations too far, and should be too subtle and too ready to take more from a passage than others (and especially the hasty reader) think it can stand. But there is always that danger in the cumulative method of reasoning: one brings in everything, large or small, that can add to the pile. I would illustrate this, and explain its limits, by quoting a parallel case.

Mr. Hobart has been blamed in the same way for bringing into his proof that the writer of the Acts and the Third Gospel was a physician many details which add little or nothing to the strength of his demonstration. This is quite true, and Mr. Hobart was as fully aware of it as any of his critics. But when his critics go on to maintain that this detracts from the strength of his reasoning, they are altogether mistaking the character of cumulative evidence. The valuelessness of one detail, the lightness of one stone, does not take away from the strength and the weight of the other details, though it may annoy and mislead the hasty reader, who judges by a sample and, by chance or design, takes the poorest. Moreover, the critic who is accustomed to the more fascinating and brilliant method of deductive reasoning (in which, however, the weakness of even one link in the chain is fatal to the strength of the whole) is apt to forget that cumulative reasoning is not of the same kind. Each has its distinct character, its own peculiar merits and defects.

Accordingly, Colonel Mackinlay may lose in the reader's estimate several of his props, and yet retain enough to support an edifice which continues to stand and to be habitable. The chronology of the life of Christ is difficult and obscure; and every attempt to reason out a new line of proof ought to be heartily welcomed. The reasoning in this case proceeds from a mind which assumes at starting the complete trustworthiness and perfect accuracy of the Gospels. This will at once discredit the book with many of the prejudiced and arbitrary class of scholars, whose mind is already completely made up and closed to any new evidence; and it may be granted that the prejudice in the Author's mind does in some cases produce what I must call a certain weakness in the argument, where he abandons the cumulative method of observing details and facts, and proceeds to reason from general principles, as for example about the character and conduct and past life of the Magi in his Chapter VII., in which he no longer stands on what can be considered firm or safe ground.

While the present reviewer is personally most interested in the thorough-going chronology of the life of Christ month by month, or at least season by season and feast by feast, which the Author works out, it is certain that many, probably most, readers will follow with more lively interest his observations on the meaning of particular sayings and their relation to the surroundings of time, season, atmospheric phenomena and the position of the familiar stars. Although in regard to the phenomena of the heavens almost all interest in and knowledge of even the more striking stars has been lost in Western society, yet the true scholar must try to place himself in the mental atmosphere of ancient Palestinian life, when a certain familiarity with some of the stars was possessed by all and was made an essential part of their thought and expression and used as a guide in their ways and times of life. One or two examples may therefore be given of the class of observations on which the Author's system is founded.

When Christ saw Nathanael under the fig-tree, this may

be regarded as an indication of summer or autumn. In Matthew xxiv. 32, when the branch of the fig-tree "is now become tender and putteth forth its leaves, ye know that the summer is nigh". The fading of the leaf of the fig-tree is alluded to by Isaiah xxxiv. 4. Between those limits lay the scene when Nathanael retired under the fig-tree. He was astonished that any one could see him, and therefore he must have been hid from view by the thick foliage. Moreover, the Author points out that he had evidently gone there to pray in quiet and secrecy, as "an Israelite without guile". This was about the beginning of the Ministry of Christ; the Baptism and the Temptation had already occurred; but there seems to have been no great interval between them. The Temptation apparently followed the Baptism immediately, and lasted forty days. The Author places these events in August and September.

Some time previously occurred the first appearance of John the Baptist as a teacher. The Author points out that three expressions in his early teaching refer to the season: (1) "The axe is laid to the root of the tree": the decision to cut down a useless tree would be taken later than the pruning season in March, when it had become evident that the tree was no longer productive. (2) "Every tree that bringeth not forth good fruit is cut down." This emphasises the same allusion. Both point to April. (3) "Whose fan is in His hand and He will thoroughly cleanse His threshing-floor; and He will gather His wheat into the garner." The season is harvest and the locality was the deep hot valley of the Jordan, where harvest was very early. The preaching of John, therefore, began to arrest the attention of the Jews in April and the time immediately following. The imagery quoted from him belongs to the months April-

June. After a certain interval, a few weeks or months probably, Jesus came to be baptised. As John passed like a meteor across the sky of Palestine, or rather like the Morning Star heralding the light of day, there is no reason to place the Baptism in a later year than the first appearance of John. On this point there is a practically universal agreement of opinion. All these events belong to the spring and summer and early autumn of the same year. Since the Baptist is so consistently spoken of as the Morning Star, it must have been shining at his appearance and gladdening the eyes of the crowd of his followers every morning. The custom of so designating him arose among those who saw the Star[1] marking him out as the Herald. The cycle of appearances of Venus as the Morning Star prove that this year was A.D. 25.

To take another example of the influence which the seasons and the state of agriculture exerted on the customs of the people among whom Christ lived and taught, we take one from the sphere of action and no longer from that of mere language. The Author points out on p. 120 that at the feeding of the five thousand Jesus "commanded the multitude to sit down on the grass" (Matt. xiv. 19). To us who live in the moist northern islands this conveys no intimation of the time of year, but in the dry soil and under the hot sun of the Levant lands, it means that the season was spring. Only in spring is there grass, which withers early along with the flowers under the summer sun. This fact plays an important part in the economy of farm life; and the traveller is often reminded of it, when he seeks to hire horses at that season: they are all out at grass. A free life on the grass for the short time during which this food can be got is regarded

---

[1] This is emphasised below, p. 231.

as necessary to their health and vigour. Their keep costs nothing during that time, but they cannot do hard work on grass. Hence the traveller, if he insists on getting horses in that season, must tempt the owners by a higher price. Such are the facts in Asia Minor, and I have no doubt that they are similar in Palestine.

The brief phrase which Matthew uses may seem to some —especially to those who have not had the opportunity of familiarising themselves with the kind of thought and expression which arises from the rarity and value of grass in such countries—to be an insufficient basis to support the Author's inference as to the season. But, as he points out, Mark vi. 39 speaks of "the green grass," and John vi. 10 says, "there was much grass in the place". Moreover John vi. 4 mentions that the time of the year was just before Passover.[1] The inference from the scanty phrase of Matthew is perfectly confirmed.

The Author points out well that this is the season of the year when bread is scarce and dear for people who live on the fruits of their own soil and are not affected by imported grain. The produce of the last harvest is coming near an end, and is often exhausted or almost exhausted by this season, while the new harvest is ripening, but not ready to eat. People have often to go hungry, and prices rise high. In this time of dearth the relief which Christ gave was really needed, for the villages (none of which were even near) would be also on the verge of scarcity.

[1] The inference from Mark and John is, of course, familiar and common, and has been used as an argument against Hort's unfortunate suggestion that τὸ Πάσχα in John vi. 4 is an interpolation. But my object is to demonstrate that the brief word of Matthew would alone be sufficient evidence, though I suppose that some European scholars would have scouted such an assertion, if it were not supported by the clearer testimony of John and Mark.

While in this case the individual character of the scene and the suitability of the surrounding conditions are extremely well marked, one must observe that the details which give life to the incident are lacking in the story of the feeding of four thousand (Matt. xv. 32 ff.; Mark viii. 1 ff.), except that there the people sit down on the ground: there was no longer grass to sit on at this season. But that is the general state of the soil: the other scene gathers individuality and life from the unusual character of the circumstances.

When the Author attempts to find an allusion to the varying seasons in Luke x. 3, "Lambs in the midst of wolves" (dated February or beginning of March), as compared with Matthew x. 16, "sheep in the midst of wolves" (in harvest-time, about May, "the young sheep by this time would no longer be considered lambs"), I do not think his reasoning can be accepted. In my experience the term "lamb" is used in Asiatic Turkey for a young sheep at any season of the year, and any flesh of sheep that is sold as fit to eat is "lamb". The flesh of a sheep in its second year is already coarse, and not considered eatable except by poor and hardy peasants.[1] Moreover, the Author himself dates the words of John the Baptist, "Behold the Lamb of God," in the autumn, whereas his principle would require a date about February to April. No safe inference, therefore, can be drawn from the use of the terms "lamb" and "sheep".

The main feature of Colonel Mackinlay's book is its insistence on the importance of the Morning Star in the symbolism of the Gospels. Some of the references to this Star in the Gospels are so emphatic and distinct that they cannot be misunderstood. This species of symbolism was employed freely, as every reader knows, in the Gospels. The Author,

[1] This is mentioned and illustrated in my *Impressions of Turkey*, p. 17.

however, shows that it was carried very much farther than has been hitherto observed; and some of the passages in which he detects the use of this symbolism gain much effect from his interpretation. John the Baptist was the Forerunner, the Morning Star. Christ was the Sun, the Light of the World. On p. 16 the Author protests against the mistaken idea in Holman Hunt's picture, "The Light of the World," where Christ is represented as illuminating the world with a lantern. It was as the Sun that He illumined the world; and He used the words about Himself at the end of the Feast of Tabernacles, which "reminded the Jews of their deliverance from Egypt and of the Divine leading by the pillar of fire in the wilderness (Neh. ix. 1, 9, 12, 19)". At this Feast large lamps were "lighted in the Temple court, which were reminders of the ancient guiding pillar of fire in the wilderness; He said in effect, I am like the sun which gives light to all in the world,—a greater blessing than the Hebrews had of old, when they followed the pillar of fire".

Similarly in John ix. 5, where "the Light of the World" is Christ, the allusion must be to the sun, for there is in the context a contrast between day and night. The Author also compares xi. 9; xii. 35 f., 46; i. 9; 1 John ii. 8; Luke i. 78; ii. 32; Acts xiii. 47, in all of which Christ is the Sun. The usage persisted as it had been originated; just as John the Baptist was always the Morning Star and Forerunner of the Sun.

In the first chapter the Author is careful to show how much larger a part the Morning Star plays in the life and language of the peoples in the Levant lands than it does among the late-rising nations of the dark North. The Morning Star begins the day for the nomads and the agriculturists of those southern regions, and even in the cities people work at a very early hour; in southern countries generally people rise very much earlier than they do in the cold northern lands; and, where artificial light is scanty and bad, few sit up long after dark, and there is less disposition to lie late in the morning. Moreover, where sunlight is abundant, one seems to feel much less need for long sleep than in dark countries. The Author touches on the question whether the ancients knew that Venus, the Morning Star, assumes at times a crescent form (which they probably did), and how they acquired this knowledge. He is disposed to think that they sometimes employed artificial aids to vision, as a lens was found by Layard at Nemrud; and that the naked eye could not discover the crescent form though people who know what to expect can see it or think they see it. But one of my friends, a distinguished Professor of Mathematics, tells me that the crescent form could be detected by a careful watcher of the skies, if he saw the planet against the edge of a sharp upright cliff. At any rate it is certain that the ancients "observed the planet with the utmost attention" and gave it a prominent place in their religion under the names Istar and Ashtaroth and Venus and so on.

Now, just as John the Baptist about May-June A.D. 25 drew his illustrations from the harvest and the threshing-floors, which were busy at that season, and just as about December A.D. 27 the sowing which was busily going on all around suggested the parables in Matthew xiii. 3-32; Mark iv. 26-29, so the Author maintains that, when John preached "He that cometh after me is mightier than I," drawing his idea from the Morning Star, herald of the Sun, that Star must have been in its morning phase at the time, guiding the conduct and plain to the eyes and touching the minds of all his audience every day before dawn, when they rose at its summons. So with several other expressions, as, "he was the lamp that burneth and shineth" (John v. 35), "behold I send My messenger before thy face" (quoted in Matt. xi. 10, as people applied to him the prophecy of Malachi iii. 1).

Incidentally we must notice that such accounts as those mentioned in the beginning of the preceding paragraph are not to be understood as reports of what John and Jesus said in one single speech. They should rather be taken as expressing the gist and marrow of the teaching at a certain period, as the general purport crystallised in the memory of certain auditors.

In the Apocalypse xxii. 16 Christ is called the Morning Star, but in the Gospels He is the Sun, while the Baptist is His Herald, an image taken from Malachi iii. 1 ; iv. 2, as seen in Luke i. 76, 78 ; Mark i. 2 ; Luke i. 17 ; John iii. 28 ; Matthew xi. 10 ; Luke vii. 27 ; Paul in Acts xiii. 24 ; John i. 7, 8, etc. The comparison in the Apocalypse belongs to a different period and another circle of thought. Its meaning may be illustrated by the expression in the letter to the Church at Thyatira, "he that overcometh . . . I will give him the Morning Star" (Rev. ii. 28). In this phrase there lies probably more than is allowed for in the *Letters to the Seven Churches of Asia*, p. 334. We must understand that the Star is the dawn of a brighter day and a new career. To the victor there shall be given the brightness and splendour and power that outshine the great Empire, and the promise of and entrance upon a higher life. It is the same thought as afterwards suggested the term *dies natalis* for the day on which a martyr died: this day was his birthday, on which he entered into a nobler life. After the same fashion

VII. *The Morning Star*

Christ calls Himself in Revelation xxii. 16 the Morning Star, as the herald and introducer of a new era. In the Gospels the point of view is so different as to show that they belong to an earlier age and another style of thought, not contradictory, but the result of different surroundings and conditions.

In Chapter VI. the Author discusses the length of Christ's Ministry, and concludes that it was three and a half years. It has long seemed to me that this was the true length; and the shorter periods assigned by many scholars appeared to be based on misconceptions. The estimate of one year (or, more strictly, one year and some months) is due to misinterpretation of Luke iv. 19, where "the acceptable year of the Lord" is taken as the period of Christ's Ministry. This is an almost inexcusable error, for it supposes that the period of one year and several months could be called one year by the ancients. This period would have been called two years, according to the universal rule.[1] Some of the early Fathers, who were uninterested in and careless of chronological exactness, are responsible for this misinterpretation,[2] which ought not to survive when it is recognised that the Ministry must have lasted over at least two Passovers, together with some months before the first.

The Author passes over this estimate as requiring no notice, and inquires only into the possibility of the middle estimate that the Ministry lasted two years and a half. Besides the much debated question of the number of Passovers that occurred during the Ministry, he also discusses the number of Feasts of Tabernacles. In regard to the

---

[1] See the article on "Days, Months, Hours" in Hastings' *Dictionary of the Bible*, vol. v.

[2] Clement of Alexandria and Origen both said so.

former question there is, of course, nothing new to be said. The arguments have all been already drawn out to endless length; and the Author passes over them in a brief paragraph of seven lines. The latter question opens up a topic of considerable extent, on which the Author has much that is quite novel to say, and which he insists upon a great deal in other chapters also. He points out that the reading of Isaiah lxi. by Jesus in the synagogue at Nazareth must have taken place at the beginning of a year, at the beginning of a Sabbatic year, and at the Feast of Tabernacles. His reasoning on this subject is extremely ingenious and interesting, and merits the most serious consideration. Chronologically, this would settle the question, if it should finally stand scrutiny. My own impression is that it will establish itself; but I may be prejudiced, as it confirms my own chronological views in all except one point, which is of merely speculative interest, *viz.*, the year of Christ's birth. The length of Christ's Ministry and the year of His death are matters of the utmost importance for the right understanding and for the historical value of the Gospels; but it makes little difference in those respects whether He was born in any year between B.C. 8 and 5. Colonel Mackinlay has maintained that the Birth was in B.C. 8 at the Feast of Tabernacles; and he has advanced distinctly stronger arguments for this view than can be brought forward in favour of any other year. A year later than 5 or earlier than 8 would be fatal to the historicity of Matthew and Luke;[1] beyond that the date is a matter only of chronological importance. Incidentally we must here observe, as a consequence of the very early date, that the residence of the

---

[1] A date later than B.C. 5 would place the Birth after Herod's death; a date earlier than B.C. 8 would put the Ministry too early.

Holy Family in Egypt would have to be longer than is usually supposed; but there is absolutely no ground in the words of Matthew to support an argument that the residence in Egypt could not have lasted so long as five years and a third, which is the period assigned by the Author.

The Sabbatical year necessarily began in the autumn. If it had commenced in spring, the beginning would have occurred after corn had been sowed, and the land could not have lain fallow for the year. It was inevitably implied in the idea of a Sabbatical year that it should begin at the end of the annual cycle of agriculture and before the next annual cycle opened; *i.e.*, it must begin near the autumn equinox at the Feast of Tabernacles. This was fixed by the Law of Moses, whereas the ordinary arrangement of the Calendar in the South-Syrian lands made the year begin in spring.

The Author maintains that the Sabbatical year began at the Feast of Tabernacles in the autumn of A.D. 26.[1] This then was the time when the scene in the Synagogue at Nazareth occurred; and Christ had been speaking in public previously for some time. The conclusion which I have reached as to the beginning of the Ministry (*Christ Born at Bethlehem*, p. 201) is that "in the later months of that year A.D. 25, John appeared announcing the coming of Christ, and very shortly thereafter Jesus came and was baptised by John in the river Jordan. Some months[2] thereafter occurred the Passover on 21st March, A.D. 26." Colonel Mackinlay would place these events earlier by a few months. He leaves a longer interval between the appearance of John and of

---

[1] There is some controversy as to the incidence of Sabbatical years; but the view which Colonel Mackinlay takes seems to be the right one.

[2] In the original text I printed "one or two months thereafter," but this was too precise, and I would substitute the vaguer expression.

Jesus, *viz.*, about four to five months; and places the Baptism about forty-five days before the Feast of Tabernacles A.D. 25. The preaching of Jesus would then begin about that Feast. I see no objection to this, though the evidence is too slender to demonstrate it. Thus he finds the first two occurrences of this Feast within the Ministry A.D. 25 and 26.

The third Feast he places at the time of Matthew xii. 18-21; the Sabbatic year was now ended, and the period "of special invitation to the Jewish nation" was past. Now begins a new period; and in the words quoted from Isaiah in this passage of Matthew Christ is twice described as the Saviour of the Gentiles.

The fourth Feast of Tabernacles, in the Author's scheme, synchronised with the Transfiguration, which suggested to Peter's mind the idea of making the three tabernacles. The ordinary view seems to be that which is stated by Dr. Plummer in his Commentary on Luke ix., "if they were to remain there they must have shelter". Why superhuman personages like Moses and Elias should need the shelter of booths in order to remain on a mountain does not appear very clear. But, if the Jews were everywhere making booths at that very moment in order to spend in them the sacred week, it seems a not unnatural suggestion of Peter's to construct three booths for the three superhuman personages to keep the Jewish feast: "one for Thee, and one for Moses and one for Elias".

The Author's suggestion agrees with the very slight indications that can be gathered from the context.

The Transfiguration (Matt. xvii. 1 ff.; Mark ix. 2 ff.; Luke ix. 28 ff.) occurred later than the Passover of A.D. 28 (about which time, as we have just seen,[1] must have occurred

---
[1] See above, p. 228.

the incident mentioned by Matthew xiv. 14 ff., and John vi. 4 ff.); but the visit to the borders of Judæa beyond Jordan (Matt. xix. 1; John x. 40), the opening of the final period of the Saviour's life, about the end of 28 and the beginning of 29, had not yet occurred. This approximate date for the Transfiguration is, of course, evident and universally accepted; but its connection with the Feast of Tabernacles is not a matter of general agreement.

Now, Jesus spent part of this Feast at Jerusalem (John vii. 14); but it is mentioned that He would not go up at the beginning of the Feast, but remained some days in Galilee, and appeared in Jerusalem, "when it was now the middle of the Feast," the third to the fifth day. On the Author's theory we have thus a quite remarkable chronological agreement between John and the Synoptics; and the agreement is so striking that it could hardly be purely accidental. On that theory the Transfiguration occurred at the time when the Tabernacles were being constructed, *i.e.*, either on the day at whose sunset the Feast began or on the first day of the Feast. In that event Jesus was manifested as the Son of God, not publicly, but to three spectators, on a solitary mountain-top; and the three were ordered to keep the event secret until after the Resurrection (as Mark and Matthew mention, though Luke deliberately omits [1] this sequel to the event). John vii. 4 mentions that when this "Feast of Tabernacles was at hand," the brothers of Jesus urged Him to go up to Jerusalem, to abandon His privacy and secrecy, and "manifest Thyself to the world". Jesus refused to go up at present, on the ground that "My time is not yet come".

[1] This remarkable omission of part of his chief authority must make the scholar chary of allowing any weight to the argument that Luke knew nothing about any event or speech, because he does not record it.

When the rest went up to Jerusalem to the Feast, " He abode still in Galilee ". But afterwards He went up, "not publicly, but as it were in secret"; and suddenly, "in the midst of the Feast," He appeared in the Temple. There He preached the remarkable discourse, beginning, " I am the light of the world ".

All that John mentions in this passage fits in so perfectly in tone and in chronology with the Synoptic record as to make it evident to any one possessed of the literary and the historic sense that the two narratives, which complete one another so remarkably, although neither of them mentions any detail or any saying that occurs in the other, must be founded on personal knowledge or first-hand evidence about actual facts. The only other theory that would account for such a singular coincidence amid difference is that there has been deliberate and wonderfully skilful invention of a series of incidents, and partition of them between two separate narratives dovetailing perfectly into one another. Such a theory, whether in the form that the two narratives were concocted by agreement at the same time, or that one was invented subsequently to suit the other which was already in existence, is not likely to be advanced at the present day by any scholar, for there are too many obvious difficulties (which it is needless to state here). This agreement of the two authorities[1] is so important a point as to deserve fuller notice.

Take, first of all, the sequence of events.

1. Jesus went forth into the villages of Cæsarea Philippi. He asked His disciples, "Who do men say that I am?" They answered that He was taken by some for John the Baptist, by others for Elias or one of the prophets. He then

[1] Mark is the authority on whom Luke and Matthew both rely.

asked, "Who say ye that I am?" Peter answered, "Thou art the Christ". Thereupon He bade them tell no man of Him (Mark viii. 27-30).

2. Jesus now began to tell them of His approaching sufferings and death and resurrection. This He stated openly. Peter rebuked Him for speaking thus, and was sharply reprimanded (Mark viii. 31-ix. 1).

3. Now the Feast of Tabernacles was at hand. His brothers advised Him to go to celebrate it in Jerusalem, and reveal Himself publicly to the Jewish world for what He claimed to be; but He refused, because His time was not yet fulfilled; and He abode in Galilee (John vii. 1-9). John's narrative here presumes as well known the statements made by the Synoptics about the claims now being advanced both openly and in private to His disciples (headings 1 and 2).

4. Six days later He took Peter and James and John into a high mountain apart. Here occurred the Transfiguration; and the thought of the Feast suggested to Peter that the three heavenly ones should celebrate the Feast of Tabernacles, and the three earthly ones should enjoy the spectacle. Afterwards, as they descended from the mountain, Jesus again charged them to tell no man until the Son of Man be risen from the dead. They questioned one another what was the meaning of this rising from the dead. And Jesus explained (Mark ix. 2-13).

5. Jesus then went up secretly to Jerusalem and appeared in the Temple on the third or fourth day of the Feast, and taught, so that the people wondered. He asked why they sought to kill Him. He explained that He would be with them only a short time, and would then go "unto Him that sent Me". He publicly offered instruction to all, drink to any that thirsted. And some said that this was the prophet,

others the Christ. But the conclusion was that, since He was of Galilee, He therefore could not be the Christ ; [1] and no man laid hands on Him. He declared Himself in the Temple to be the light of the world, to be not of this world, but sent by His Father. And He went out of the Temple (John vii. 10-viii. 59). Presumably, John at least accompanied Him to Jerusalem (probably all the three disciples), and thus knew what happened there; but no other person was informed, and the visit was little talked about in Galilee.

6. They rejoined the disciples,[2] and He travelled in Galilee, keeping Himself secret; and He taught the disciples about the resurrection; but they understood not the saying and were afraid to ask Him (Mark ix. 14-32).

Secondly, it is plain that the two accounts are agreed about the importance of this moment in autumn A.D. 28. Jesus was now beginning to make His fate known; in Galilee He spoke only to His disciples[3] about the coming events; but though He told them repeatedly, they failed to understand the drift of His words. John alone adds that He made a secret journey to Jerusalem and gave similar teaching in a guarded symbolic fashion to the Jews in the Temple. Both accounts agree that His death was now often mentioned by Him, but that no one realised what He meant.

How is this remarkable agreement as to time and subject to be explained? I cannot see any opening for doubt (1) that it arises from the personal knowledge and memory of

---

[1] The irony of this conclusion escapes many scholars. Their reasoning was sound; and their conclusion was inevitable, if the starting-point was correct. They thought it was correct; but they were in error. Hence their reasoning was really a witness to the truth: Christ must be born in Bethlehem, and Jesus (unknown to them) was born there. Such is the meaning of the Fourth Gospel.

[2] Luke alone says "on the next day" after the Transfiguration.

[3] Except once the expression "openly": see above, heading 2.

John; and (2) that John knew the Synoptic narrative (not necessarily all three accounts, of course). It is impossible that John should so exactly fill up what is omitted by the Synoptists, without repeating anything that they tell, unless he was deliberately completing, with full knowledge of the facts, a narrative which he regarded as incomplete, though true. The irony of John (which is conspicuous in the touch regarding the supposed birth of Jesus in Galilee) is seen to be much more thoroughgoing when his report of the words in the Temple is taken as a veiled and symbolic statement to the multitude of the teaching which was given in Galilee to the disciples alone before and after the Transfiguration, and which was as little understood by them as it was by the multitude in the Temple. There is irony in this, but how much greater is the pathos than the irony! This is what the disciples afterwards discussed among themselves and mourned and marvelled over, in the days that followed the Resurrection.[1]

An agreement of this kind between two documents, lying so much beneath the surface, yet so complete, would in the criticism of non-Christian works be regarded as a weighty proof of trustworthiness and authenticity, unless the supposition of elaborately concocted fraud was established; but frauds so elaborate and skilful are unknown in ancient literature.

In favour of this dating Colonel Mackinlay's arguments, together with the reasons now advanced, seem to be conclusive. From it follow several interesting results, which he has not neglected to observe, and probably many more which fall outside the scope of his book. One topographical inference would be that the Mount of the Transfiguration could not

[1] See above, p. 89 f.

be Mount Hermon (which always seemed to me very improbable and incongruous with ancient habits and ideas), but some mountain farther south and nearer Jerusalem. It would be impossible without extraordinary exertion (possible for a trained athlete, but not for ordinary human beings) to be on the top of Mount Hermon at the beginning of the Feast and in Jerusalem on the fourth day of the Feast. If Tabor or some other peak of Galilee were the scene, the circumstances are quite in accordance with ordinary life.

The Nativity also is placed by the Author at the Feast of Tabernacles. This seems highly probable, and may even, I think, be regarded as approximating to certainty. It has been pointed out frequently that the circumstances of the Birth are inconsistent with a winter date, for the sheep are folded at night in winter, whereas they were feeding out on the upland plains near Bethlehem on the night when Christ was born: that is the custom only during the hot season of the year. Considerable part of the summer is required for the operations of harvest and thrashing in various parts of Palestine, which take place earlier or later according to the elevation above the sea; and it would have been impossible to order any movement of the people until those operations were fully completed. Accordingly the conclusion has been drawn, "we may say with considerable confidence that August to October is the period within which the numbering would be fixed" (*Christ Born at Bethlehem*, p. 193). Now, at the Feast of Tabernacles there was always a considerable movement of the Jews from the northern parts towards Jerusalem; and it was natural that the king should avoid the disturbance caused by two movements near the same time, and should make the numbering coincide with the Feast, only requiring that all should go up on this occasion to the town of Judæa, which was their original home. I have pointed out how necessary it was that the prejudices and customs of the Jews should not be interfered with; an Oriental despot may be extremely cruel without offending public feeling, and indeed may be all the more successful by virtue of his cruelty; but he must not run counter to the national genius and habits, and this Herod seems to have carefully refrained from doing. The journey to Jerusalem which many were undertaking at the autumn Feast could be combined with the enforced repairing of each to his own city, for it must be remembered that these northern Jews at this period were of the two tribes, not of the ten.

An interesting discovery has been made in Egypt bearing on this point: an order dated A.D. 104 that every Egyptian must repair to his own home in preparation for the numbering of the households. Mr. Kenyon and Mr. Bell append the following note to this document: "It is a rescript from the Prefect requiring all persons who were residing out of their own homes to return to their homes in view of the approaching census. The analogy between this order and Luke ii. 1-3 is obvious." [1]

This may be taken as a parallel to the similar order at the first numbering in Palestine; and it tends to show that when Herod issued his command, he was acting under Roman orders, and had no choice but to obey. It was not a device which he had chosen himself with his skill in kingcraft;

---

[1] *British Museum Papyri*, iii., p. 124. I am indebted to Professor J. H. Moulton for directing my attention to this important document. Previously I had been inclined to think that the method of carrying out the enumeration on the principle that each man should be counted in his own city might have originated from Herod. This possibility is now definitely eliminated. The method was Roman, and the origin may therefore be assigned with perfect confidence, as Luke assigns it, to the Emperor. See Moulton in the *Expository Times*, 1907, p. 41 (October).

it was one that was forced on him, and which he had to carry into effect.

It is an unfortunate circumstance for the convincingness of the Author's argument that he states "harmonies" as if they were arguments. They are in his estimation and from his point of view arguments; but in the modern view they have no value as proof. It would have been a wiser plan to separate the "harmonies" from the evidence. The harmonies are in some cases interesting, but, in view of the feeling in the Bible, what value could it have (even if proved) that Christ was baptised at a Full Moon? Such "harmonies" are valueless coincidences.

The very idea of "harmonies," as Colonel Mackinlay works them out, will be found repellent by many minds. But his system of chronology rests, as I am strongly inclined to think, on a thoroughly sound basis of reasoning. One cannot yet say that the basis is certain. The subject is still too obscure and the evidence too scanty. But, in the words of Professor J. H. Moulton (in the passage just quoted), "We are getting on. One of the census papers of the Nativity year will turn up next." When the chronology is settled, the "harmonies" come in as very noteworthy coincidences, in which there may be more than can as yet be comprehended: the whole structure may be compared to that of the great Pyramid, in the construction of which astronomical facts certainly played a part, though it is not easy to determine where design ends and coincidence begins.

It becomes only more clear to the reader of this book that the Gospels are a remarkable structure, resting on fact and observation, and full of the sort of detail which can originate only in the actual life of a real personage.

Note.—I may add that my object in the book, *Was Christ Born at Bethlehem?* was to demonstrate the historical possibility of Luke's narrative. I did not try to prove that Christ was born in B.C. 6; but showed that this date offered a perfectly reasonable and credible historical sequence of events in perfect harmony with all other evidence, except the testimony of Tertullian, who gave the date B.C. 8. The proper year for the Enrolment was the one mentioned by Tertullian; but I showed that a delay of two years was not inconceivable, and in a subsequent article in the *Expositor*, November, 1901, p. 321 ff., quoted a parallel case of long delay. But the testimony of Tertullian is now confirmed by Colonel Mackinlay's argument that the Enrolment took place in the proper year B.C. 8; and this date may now be accepted provisionally as the only one which has all the evidence in its favour.

VIII.
A CRITICISM OF RECENT RESEARCH

VIII.

A CRITICISM OF RECENT RESEARCH

A GOOD many years ago I expressed (I think in the *Expositor*) the opinion, forced on one who lived far from Oxford, that Dr. Sanday was to some degree giving up to a single University what was meant for mankind. This reproach—if that can be called reproach which was merely the recognition of a zealous and strict devotion to the immediate duty—can no longer be uttered in view of the books with which the Lady Margaret Professor of Divinity has enriched us in recent years. One perceives that these are the result of the long period of probation and preparation to which Dr. Sanday's work has been submitted. The marked characteristic of his writing is its maturity and fulness of thought rather than its ingenuity. His books derive their value, not from bold and brilliant views, which seem to carry both the writer and the reader away with them and almost to overmaster the judgment, but from the impression they convey of a reserve of power that lies still unused behind the written word, of a methodical toning down of expression to the standard that is inevitable and convincing. He never strikes one as speaking too strongly, but always as having pondered over the expression of each opinion till it is the last and completest word that has to be said from that point of view. There is no modern writer who more strongly impresses me with the sense of the moral element which is a necessary part of high intellectual power. It is a truth which one has often to impress on students at college, that mere cleverness is a poor and even a dangerous part of a scholar's equipment, adequate by itself only for the winning of entrance scholarships and class prizes, but having no staying power in the race of life. One feels in Dr. Sanday's work that it is founded and built up on the intense desire to reach the truth, and that this intense desire has directed the method, and concentrated the faculties in the path of knowledge.

The book is made up of a series of lectures and reviews which have no connection with one another except in two very important respects, they all belong to one stage and one period in the evolution of the Author's views, and they to a large extent spring from a single purpose, *viz.*, to sum up and estimate some leading tendencies and results in the present stage of scholarship. That the various surveys which are taken of separate parts of the whole field were worked up to suit different occasions gives an appearance of disjointedness; but the appearance is really only superficial, and might by slight changes have been in great measure eliminated, if there were anything to gain by eliminating it.

The opening chapter on the Symbolism of the Bible is a very simple expression of much careful thought: many problems have been pondered over for a long time before it was written, yet they hardly appear above the calm surface. On p. 14, as we see gladly, Dr. Sanday recognises that "from the very first sacrifice was expressive of ideas". The use of the plural shows that he would not admit the explanation of the origin of the rite of sacrifice from a single idea, as some scholars would maintain. Sacrifice is the expression of the human mind in its relation to God, and is as various as the human mind. The thought of primitive man was simple, but it can never be reduced to one idea alone. The man who can explain the origin of sacrifice from one idea is perilously near the discovery of the key to all mythology, and he who has found that key is hopelessly lost. You can with sufficient ingenuity always explain—verbally—anything out of anything; and thus you can draw out—on paper—a process of development whereby all mythology and all sacrifice evolve themselves from a single origin; but this process has nothing firmer to rest upon than the paper on which it is written. Dr. Sanday's words might easily be taken as indicating the view that there are only two really primitive ideas in sacrifice, the gift and the sacrificial communion; but I think that this would be a misconception, and that, when he speaks of "two ideas that we can trace farthest," he does not intend to restrict the number to two, but merely expresses his conviction as to the reality and certainty of at least these two.

On the other hand, I confess that I cannot entirely sympathise with the point of view expressed in the paragraph at the foot of p. 9: "We are not surprised to find that in the early books of the Bible, where dealings take place between God and man, the Godhead is represented under human form. Man was himself the noblest being with which he was acquainted; and therefore, in conceiving of a being still nobler, he necessarily started from his own self-consciousness; he began by magnifying his own qualities, and only by degrees did he learn, not only to magnify, but to discriminate between them."

This is, in a way, perfectly proper and sensible. It is what every one says—perhaps what every one must say—and yet I do not feel that it is vital or illuminative: it seems to leave out the true principle. I should not venture to attempt to define the true principle: the task is above my power. But I cannot recognise it in this statement, which is apt to suggest that the conceptions of the Divine nature current among the Hebrews began by being anthropomorphic. This does not convince me. I should rather approach the problem from the point of view that the early Hebrew conceptions were undeveloped, vague, and capable of future growth in more than one direction. They might have degenerated into anthropomorphism, as the Greek conception did. They were equally capable of development in another direction; and they did in fact, under the impulse of a succession of prophets and thinkers, develop in a nobler and truer way. But how to describe the unformed germ of early Hebrew thought I know not.

Difficulties of various kinds impede the attempt to express oneself clearly on this subject. You cannot speak precisely about what is essentially vague. It is difficult to project oneself into the mind of primitive man, or to picture to oneself what was in his mind. It is also hard for us, who are accustomed to aim at clearness and precision and definite outlines, to sympathise with or understand the Oriental expression which rather shrinks from these qualities and prefers the vague, the allusive and the indirect. The difference between the European and the Asiatic mind is, to a large degree, a mere matter of education lasting through generations and centuries, but perhaps it is to a certain extent due to difference of nature and sympathy and endowment. Most of what Dr. Sanday says on this hard subject seems to me excellent, illuminative and suggestive; but not all.

I much prefer his other term "indirect description" to

the word "symbolism" by which he more frequently designates the Hebrew and Oriental style of expression.

The term "symbolism" which Dr. Sanday prefers, not as perfect but as the least objectionable, is open to the objection that the person who speaks symbolically is conscious of the difference between the symbol and the real thing, and consciously employs the one to stand in place of the other. That is the case with the symbolic actions of the prophets, described in the first section of this opening chapter of the book which we are reviewing, as when Agabus took Paul's girdle and bound himself with it in token that Paul would be bound if he went to Jerusalem: the symbolism here was conscious and intended, and Agabus explained its meaning.

But, as the Author himself says on p. 11, the earlier Hebrews often did not regard the "symbol" as different from the thing symbolised: the "symbol" was the thing symbolised. How are we to understand or to describe a stage of thought when ideas are so vague and so unformed that they thus pass into one another without any consciousness of the transition? Take the genealogical fiction, which plays so important a part in the early history of many peoples, not merely of the Jews. It was not a fiction in primitive thought: it expressed a truth in the simplest and most direct manner in which the natural mind could express it, though to us the manner seems indirect. The Rev. Dr. White of Marsovan gives an admirable example that came within his own experience, where a wandering dervish used this mode of expression: "He told me that he was a Shukhbazari; and then, to enlighten my ignorance, explained that Arabs, Circassians and Shukhbazaris are own brothers, children of one father and one mother. He used a Scripture form of expression to make me understand that the three peoples possessed the same traits of character." The dervish was merely eager to emphasise the close resemblance in character between the three peoples. He could think and speak only in concrete terms: he could not generalise or deal in abstractions. Yet out of his language, in the process and hardening of thought, there might rise naturally and easily a genealogical fiction: the common father and mother acquire names, and the three peoples become three sons.

Nor is it merely real similarity of character that may give origin to this genealogical expression of history. Geographical contiguity may cause it, or the speaker may express by it little more than a common diversity from himself. He looks out over the world, and distinguishes from himself several peoples of the north-west as being children of one father different from his father. So in Genesis x. 4 we have "the sons of Javan: Elishah, and Tarshish, Kittim, and Dodanim".

The "genealogical fiction" then, has to be understood correctly, and it becomes valuable history. Only the unsympathetic and unintelligent historical criticism of forty or fifty years ago, the period of Grote and Cornwall Lewis and the *Tübinger*, would be content to regard it simply as legend, and leave it out of the sphere of history. But, in order to understand aright any genealogical myth, we must put ourselves at the point of view of the person or people who originated that particular expression. It tells us something about the peoples whom it correlates to one another: it tells us more about the person or people who originated it: it tells us most of all about the standard and range of knowledge, the limits of geographical outlook, and so on, in the period when it took the form in which we have it.

Again, what was the conception in the mind of the ancient

Hebrew, when he spoke of the messenger (or angel) of the Lord who conveyed certain knowledge to the mind of a human being? Who shall define this conception, or express exactly the distinction between it and the thought in the mind of another Hebrew, who used the expression that the word of the Lord came to a man? These two phrases belong to two different stages in the thought of men, who had a simpler and less clearly defined way of conceiving and expressing their relation to the unseen Divine power which surrounds and is always pressing upon man. It is not mine to define these Hebrew ideas. I do not understand them. But I do at least feel that they are radically different from the anthropomorphic conception of the Hellenes. And I feel in a vague way that Luke the Hellene has unconsciously and unintentionally transfused a Hebrew view into a Greek view, when he described the angel of the Annunciation. He seems to have thought of such an appearance as Iris makes in the *Iliad*; but I doubt if that was the idea in the Hebrew mind of her from whom the story came. It is not to be supposed that Luke added or invented any detail. The name Gabriel beyond all question comes from the Hebrew authority and belongs to the obscure later Hebrew development of the angelic idea, when the power of God, conceived as acting in different directions, was endowed with various names; and in this stage there was certainly a certain approach to anthropomorphism, as Hebrew thought was being misdeveloped and clothed with defined but false form. Luke, however, was simply translating into Greek a Hebrew narrative, rethinking it and then expressing it, but in rethinking it he unavoidably gave it a more Hellenic form.

But here lies the problem that is proposed to the modern

student of ancient history. He must entirely dissociate himself from the accepted method of investigating the ancient documents—what is called the "critical" method. He must forget the modern dichotomy of the world into the "educated" and the "savage" races. He must separate the primitive man alike from the "educated" and the "savages" of modern time; for men in the early stage were neither one nor the other, but contained the possibility of both.

In the second half of this most interesting chapter, Dr. Sanday proceeds to apply to the Gospels the inferences which he has drawn from the use of "symbolism" in the Old Testament. The discussion of the Temptation of Jesus occupies the largest space in this part, and is of peculiar interest to the present reviewer. The Temptation is in Dr. Sanday's view entirely a parable (if I am not wholly misunderstanding him). His idea of the Temptation is expressed in the picture by W. Dyce—"a monotonous landscape and a Figure seated upon a stone, with the hands clasped, and an expression of intense thought on the beautiful but by no means effeminate features". Not that he regards this as the only correct representation of the Temptation. As he says, "it would be a mistake if we were to insist too much upon this contrast [*i.e.*, the contrast between the subjective modern view, and that of Tissot with a conventional fiend, or of mediæval painters with every detail sharp and definite], as though the modern presentation were right and true, and the ancient or mediæval wrong and untrue. Each is really right in its place: they mean fundamentally the same thing, and it is only the symbolical expression that is different."

With Dr. Sanday's view I find myself on the whole in

thorough sympathy. That the story of the Temptation is largely of the nature of parable seems established by the Gospels themselves. I venture, as being the briefest way in which I can express my criticism of the present study, to quote part, and to abbreviate part, of what I once wrote on the subject (*The Education of Christ*, p. 31 f.): "The authority obviously is the account given by Himself to His disciples; and we are told that 'without a parable spake He not to them'. How far the details partake of the nature of parable, intended to make transcendental truth intelligible to the simple fishermen, we cannot precisely tell, and no man ought to dogmatise. But no one can doubt as to the essential truth that lies under the narrative." Jesus counted the cost before He began His career: He thought of other possibilities, brilliant and tempting; and He rejected them as temptations. It is involved in the Temptation, when He described it to His disciples, that He was already conscious of the superhuman powers and opportunities that were His, if He chose to use them for personal ends. If you regard the story as anything beyond pure fiction, you must accept the superhuman consciousness of Him who was tempted by means such as are here brought to bear on Jesus. As a whole the temptations are meaningless and absurd, if applied to an ordinary man. It is mere trifling or sarcasm to say to a man who is hungry, "command that these stones become loaves".

If Jesus could think and speak of this as a temptation, He must have been conscious of His own superhuman power; and at the time when He related the incident to His disciples, He must have been already regarded by them as possessed of such power. Even the idea that the Temptation was either partly parable, or entirely and purely a symbolic way of explaining a thought too high for the capacity of simple uneducated fishermen and rustics to comprehend, implies in the person who related this story about Himself the consciousness of powers and opportunities beyond the range of mere humanity and the knowledge that His hearers had some vague sympathetic conception of this nature. Accordingly, those who hold and carry out logically the theory that Jesus was a mere human being and that He was during His lifetime regarded only as a human being by His associates, must necessarily dismiss the story of the Temptation as pure legend, the invention of a later age, and must deny to it the character of a parable spoken by Jesus.

If I understand Dr. Sanday rightly, there is nothing in this statement that would disagree with his views. The only word of question that I would make with regard to his expression of them, is whether in the desire to give clearness to his lecture (such was the original form of the first chapter) he has not made it in some parts too clear and sharp and definite in outline, too strongly modern in tone: though the quotation which I have extracted from his book attests his recognition of the fact that every age must and may look at the Temptation with different eyes, and all perhaps equally rightly.

Some may probably be afraid that Dr. Sanday's use of symbolism may, from his premises, be quite logically carried very far, much farther than he carries it or they would like. But in an admirable concluding page he sums up the true attitude of mind and the right temper in which historical study ought to be carried on. With certain obvious modifications, what he says here is applicable to every department of ancient history. A certain sympathy for peoples and times and ideas remote from our own, an intense desire to comprehend them, a determined effort to throw off the fetters of nineteenth century views and to rise to a freer outlook, a contempt for narrow reasoning and hard logicality (which in these historical problems is often thoroughly illogical in the higher sense of the term logic), all these are needed in the reconstruction of ancient history and the interpretation of ancient literature. But hear how delicately and finely Dr. Sanday describes this attitude of mind: it "consists mainly in three things :—

" 1. In a spirit of *reverence* for old ideas, which may perhaps be transcended, but which discharged a very important function in their day;

" 2. In a spirit of *patience* which, because those ideas may be transcended, does not at once discard and renounce them, but seeks to extract their full significance ;

" 3. In an *open mind* for the real extent of this significance.[1] We have our treasure, perhaps, in earthen vessels, but the vessels are themselves very deserving of study. I would say rather that, for the purpose before us, we should not think of them exactly as earthen, but as made of some finer and more transparent material which permits us to see through to the light within."

A survey of recent research would be an impertinent and valueless production if it were simply a cataloguing of faults and a statement of dissent. One is familiar with the criticism written by the able young graduate, fresh from the schools, whose condescending recognition of merit is as rare as a grain of wheat in a bushel of chaff, whose principal aim seems to be to show how much better he could have done the work,

---

[1] The mind open to hear evidence is what we all desire, but none of us fully possesses. We are all to some extent prejudiced by training, predilection, etc. The truest scholar has the most open mind. See above, p. 34 f.

if he had cared to undertake it, than the author, and who has evidently never made any serious attempt to understand the book which he criticises, but merely touched it on the outside and gone off at a tangent. Criticism of this kind is *unerquicklich wie der Nebelwind*.

Totally different is the character of Dr. Sanday's work. He appreciates thoroughly the high principle that it is the function of true criticism to find excellences, not defects. He tells us what he finds that is good in each of the authors whom he criticises; he expresses his dissent only where necessary to bring out the state of modern opinion; and he expresses it in very gentle and gracious terms. The sharpest statement of disapproval which I observe is that on p. 171; and yet how much it is qualified by preceding sentences of genuine hearty praise. I quote the whole passage: "I have a sincere respect, and even admiration, for perhaps five-sixths of his work, including particularly—I should like to say in passing—his reviews of the literature of Patristics, in which he has been at once just and generous to some of my friends here in Oxford. I repeat that the pamphlet from which I started is not only good but in many ways very good. One may go on for wide stretches in his books and find only occasion to admire. And yet every now and then one is pulled up sharp by passages like those of which I have been speaking, which, I confess, move me to indignation, so narrow are they, and so hard, so deficient in sympathy and in intelligence for the difference between one age and another."

A quality in Dr. Sanday which strikes me as peculiarly admirable — perhaps because I lack it too much — is his power of learning from writers who are so antipathetic to him. If a commentator is devoid of sympathy for the ancient author about whom he is writing, or lacks insight into the more delicate and subtle aspects of the text which he is discussing, I can hardly force myself to read him; he has nothing for me; and I neither learn from him (except that he sometimes makes me understand through antagonism passages which I might otherwise have failed to comprehend) nor criticise him. But we have just seen how Dr. Sanday can respect and admire five-sixths of an author whose remaining sixth part moves him to indignation.

Now let us see how he expresses himself about another writer, who "has directness and ability, and never minces matters; as I have said, he belongs to no school, and repeats the formulæ of no school. But he writes in the style of a Prussian official. He has all the arrogance of a certain kind of common sense. His mind is mathematical, with something of the stiffness of mathematics—a mind of the type which is supposed to ask of everything, What does it prove? It is a mind that applies the standards to which it is accustomed with very little play of historical imagination. If it cannot at once see the connection of cause and effect, it assumes that there is no connection. It makes no allowance for deficiencies of knowledge, for scantiness of sources and scantiness of detail contained in the sources, for the very imperfect reconstruction of the background that alone is possible to us. If there is upon the surface some appearance of incoherence or inconsequence, it is at once inferred that there is real incoherence and inconsequence. And the narrative is straightway rejected as history; though a little reflection would show that life is full of these seeming inconsistencies, and would be fuller still if our knowledge of the events going on around us did not supply us with the links of connection which make them intelligible. He argues as though we could exhaust the motives of the actors in events that happened nearly nineteen hundred years ago, whereas nothing is more certain than that we cannot in the least come near exhausting them."

On one somewhat important matter I find myself, to my great regret, distinctly in opposition to my friend the Author (to whose counsel and help and never-failing encouragement I owe so much). He seems to me to estimate too highly the possibilities of discovery which purely literary criticism offers: while I seem to him to undervalue them. This is a question that requires more space than can here be given to it; but my impression is that the great and epoch-making steps in advance come from non-literary, external, objective discovery, and that the literary critics adopt these with admirable and praiseworthy facility as soon as the facts are established, and quickly forget that they themselves (or their predecessors) used to think otherwise, and would still be thinking otherwise, if new facts had not been supplied to them. Nothing gives me such interest, and so illustrates human nature, as to observe how principles of literary criticism of the Old Testament, which were accepted as self-evident when I was studying the subject under Robertson Smith's guidance about 1878, are now scorned and set aside as quite absurd and outworn by the modern literary critics. But it was not literary criticism that made the advance: it was hard external facts that turned the literary critics from their old path, and they have utterly forgotten how the change came about.

Moreover, it sometimes seems to my humble judgment that Dr. Sanday is unconsciously guided by the prepossession that there must be a certain residuum of truth in some clever treatise which he has been reading; and he finds this residuum by dividing the writer's total estimated result by 10 or by 100.

He finds the English scholars on the whole to be nearer the truth, the Germans to be more educative and suggestive. I agree with him to a certain extent. I owe to the Germans almost all the stimulus of my early years, and I owe to several of them also almost all the encouragement which I received at the beginning when I needed it most, and for which I can never be sufficiently grateful to them. But now I find the English most useful, because they often give me facts without views, while the majority of the German writers start from a definite and fixed theory, which one may almost call a prejudice. They assume—many of them—the whole in the opening paragraph of the book; and often it seems as if one could draw out the whole reasoning of a treatise in inexorable logic after reading the opening assumptions.

I must find room for another saying, which seems profoundly true and far too generally neglected: "The fact is that the Judaism of the time of Christ had a wider and more open horizon than that of a hundred years later. The result of the terrific and almost superhuman efforts that the Jews made to throw off the Roman yoke was a long reaction that has lasted almost to our own time. When the great effort failed, Judaism withdrew into its shell: it contracted its outlook and turned in upon itself. It gave up the hope of Divine intervention that had at one time seemed so near, and was content to brood upon its past." Several times, in a quite different line of thought, I have had to protest against the prejudice that the later Jewish customs and thought can be regarded as the norm according to which we must judge about Jewish practice and views in the first century before and after Christ. Dr. Sanday here states the true historical principle in a direct and uncompromising fashion; and the passage from which I have quoted a few words is as well worth study as anything in the whole space of these carefully thought-out lectures.

In the style one is often also struck by an apparently unconscious tendency on Dr. Sanday's part to use military metaphors, to think like a soldier, and to count and marshal his thoughts as methodically as a general estimates and orders his force, not after the bold and creative fashion of a Cæsar, who discomfits his opponent by sheer audacity and almost superhuman rapidity, and who imbues his army with something of his own genius and resourcefulness, but after the fashion of a capable leader, trained to make the best use of the forces that are placed at his disposal. So, for example, "exactly five-sixths of Jülicher's work is good and even admirable"; and "the histories of Elijah and Elisha are much nearer—indeed quite near—to the events".

Other examples of similar character are:—

"Weinel's book is up to a good average, and Steinmann's perhaps somewhat above it" (p. 44).

"I welcome much of his criticism both on the right hand and on the left" (p. 44).

"With us dashing and desultory raids are apt to take the place of what is in Germany the steady disciplined advance of a regularly mobilised army" (p. 42).

"Whatever advance is made is made all along the line" (p. 41).

Taken in conjunction with what is said in the opening paragraph of the present article, these extracts seem to be indicative of the methodical character of the Author's mind and the orderly progress of his studies. The development of a scholar is always an interesting study, certainly to other scholars, and probably also to the world at large; and this quality seems to lie at the basis of the Author's intellectual power. In this connection I need make no apology for another observation, even though it may perhaps seem to some people to savour of a too personal scrutiny.

In this book which now lies before us I am struck with one difference, and, as I venture to think, improvement in the style from his earlier writings—I am not referring to English composition but to scientific exposition of opinion. Dr. Sanday uses the simple first person singular more frequently than he did in an earlier period of his work. This usage is not necessarily egotistic; in scientific work it is rarely egotistic; it is the briefest and most direct way of calling attention to the subjectivity, and therefore necessarily the uncertainty, of a statement : it is a danger flag, not a claim of personal ownership. When a view seems to be proved and trustworthy, one states it in the impersonal language of science; when it is advisable to call attention to the subjective element in a view, and to warn the reader that it is as yet only opinion (as one believes, true opinion), but not thoroughly reasoned and assured knowledge,[1] one uses the personal form.

[1] In Platonic language, it is ἀληθὴς δόξα, but not ἐπιστήμη.

IX.

HISTORICAL GEOGRAPHY OF THE HOLY LAND

IX.

HISTORICAL GEOGRAPHY OF THE HOLY LAND

In venturing to write a review of Professor G. A. Smith's *Historical Geography of the Holy Land*, I feel somewhat like "the man in the street" attempting to criticise a work of fine scholarship. But the wish that I should do so has been expressed by those whom I am unwilling to disobey; and perhaps the impression made by the book on a bystander, who is interested in the game of Old Testament study, though not himself able to play, may possess some slight interest, and warrant the following paragraphs in appearing before the public. Besides having myself studied with some minuteness the *Historical Geography* of another part of Western Asia, I have had the advantage of frequently talking about the early history of the Hebrew people with my friend Professor Robertson Smith, and of reading under his guidance in 1878 everything that he thought most valuable on the criticism and interpretation of the Mosaic books and the historical books of the Old Testament—a long piece of work which afterwards proved a most valuable education for the problems that face the historical investigator in Asia Minor. Naturally, after such a course as was marked out by Robertson Smith, one retains a permanent interest in the subject; and this interest has made me welcome most heartily a book which attacks that fascinating problem in a new way, bringing new methods of analysis to the investigation, and applying them with a union of boldness and caution and free, wide view that is most refreshing after the niggling way in which many of the recent investigations about Asia Minor (over which I have had to spend too much time) are composed. Here we have an investigator who sets himself to master the problem as a whole, who tries to conceive clearly the general disposition and character of the land about which he is to treat, to view it always in association with man and with history, and to understand the interrelation of its parts, and then proceeds to take his readers along the same path that he has trod. He has seen the places with the reconstructive eye and the warm, creative imagination of the historian; he has inhaled the atmosphere with the love and enthusiasm that breathe through his pages, and make the reader fancy that he can catch the same breath.

A writer on Historical Geography could get nowhere else so favourable a field as Professor G. A. Smith has found. Not only does an eternal interest cling to it; it is also a land of singularly well-marked features, easy to understand and easy to bring home to the reader's understanding; and further, it is a small land, which can be pictured with that breadth and fulness of treatment that are necessary to make the scenes and facts live before the reader—and yet within reasonable compass. And, having a good subject, the author uses his advantage to the full, giving us a book which is of the first importance as opening up a fresh path of study. It applies the modern methods of united historical and geographical investigation to the department where prepossessions and inherited prejudices were strongest, and where methods too purely literary absorbed the energy of the more free and unprejudiced scholars. It applies them, too, with a spirit of free, lofty and generous enthusiasm, that makes it fascinating from the first to the last page. It is, of course, far from completing its task; it is really only the first opening up of what will hereafter prove a fruitful field of study. No one appreciates that fact better than Professor Smith himself; and when the critic tries to estimate the future that is opened up before us by this book—in other words, the problems that it leaves unattempted or unsolved,—he feels that the author himself would be best able to look out over the vista in front.

There remain many sites which have to be localised much more precisely before the full bearing of the incidents connected with them becomes plain. This important part of the subject Professor Smith has avoided—wisely and rightly for his immediate purpose—but it must be faced hereafter either by him or by others. See, for example, pages 221, 222, where Professor Smith brings out very clearly both the local character and vividness of the tale of Samson, and also the obscurity in which it must remain involved until the localities are more fully identified.

Book II., Western Palestine, nearly 400 pages in length, is the main part of the volume, and shows Professor Smith at his best. He is most familiar with this part of the country, and he has put forth all his strength on the elucidation of the many incidents which he has to introduce. Every page, almost, seems more interesting than the preceding; one must go through it steadily with the map and the authorities by one's side in order to appreciate the character of the book. The only criticism which one can make on it in reasonable compass is—read it.

Book III., on Eastern Palestine, seemed to me less satisfactory than any other part of the book. The questions which have to be treated here are not so purely Hebrew, but take us into a wider range of history. Perhaps it is due to the necessity of bringing the book, already a long one, to an end; perhaps it arises from the fact that much of the history of the East country appeals to a different class of readers; but the treatment as a whole is thinner in this part; the subject has not naturally the same interest as that of Book II., and is, I think, not handled with so sure a touch as the main part of the work. To take one example: there are on page 635 several statements from which I must express dissent. Professor Smith is here giving examples of the difference of tone between Christian and pagan epitaphs in the Hauran; and contrasts the hopelessness of the latter with the "quiet confidence" of the former. Such a contrast is often obvious in literature; but I doubt whether it can fairly be traced in the epitaphs of either the Hauran or of Asia Minor.

He says "καὶ σύ, Even thou, is a common *memento mori*". I have always thought that this is the supposed reply of the deceased to the greeting presumed to be uttered by the passer-by; it occurs sometimes in the fully expressed form, χαῖρε· χαῖρε καὶ σύ, *i.e.*, "Farewell," "Fare-thou-well also". Again we read that "'thou hast finished' is a common epitaph". But the verb τελευτάω had come to be used regularly in the sense of "to *die*" from the fifth century B.C. downwards; and no such connotation as Professor Smith supposes could, I think, have been present to the epitaph-writers of the Hauran. Hence the epitaph which he next quotes must be translated, "Titus, Malchus' son, farewell! Thou hast died ere thy prime (at the age) of twelve years—Farewell." The last word is the reply of Titus to the greeting, and the epitaph is far from favouring the contrast which Professor Smith draws. Still less do his next examples support his case: "the dead are told that theirs is the inevitable fate, no one is immortal". But the formula on which he relies, οὐδεὶς ἀθάνατος, is very often Christian, and not, as Professor Smith argues, pagan. Once or twice it occurs in doubtful cases, but Waddington 2032, 2050, and Ewing 163,[1] are epitaphs containing the common and typical Christian formula, ἐνθάδε κεῖται, Here lies——; while Waddington 2459 is, as the editor remarks, clearly Christian (being one of the most interesting Christian epitaphs of Eastern Palestine, belonging probably to the third century, and being engraved while Christian formulae were still fluid, and had not yet become fixed and stereotyped). Waddington 1897 is also almost certainly Christian; the name Domitilla is one of the most interesting of early Christian names. The formula θάρσει, Be of good cheer, which often precedes οὐδεὶς ἀθάνατος, would alone be almost sufficient to mark the whole as Christian, and to show that the hopelessness which Professor Smith finds in the phrase is not really there: the precise sense in which the words should be taken is "no one is free from death," rather than, as he maintains, "no one is immortal".[2] It is quite probable that the phrase was adopted from pagan epitaphs[3] by the Christians, as many

---

[1] Mr. Ewing's inscriptions will be published in the ensuing *Quarterly Statement* of the Palestine Exploration Fund by Mr. A. A. G. Wright and Mr. A. Souter, two of my recent pupils in Aberdeen.

[2] In n. 4 he quotes Wadd. 1986 as pagan, but Waddington considers it as Christian (in my opinion rightly). In n. 5 "Wadd. 2429" seems to be a wrong reference.

[3] [Examples probably pagan occur in *Bulletin de Corr. Hell.*, 1902, pp. 175, 186; but it is elsewhere usually Christian (see *Studies in the Eastern Roman Provinces*, 1906, p. 129). Fourteen years' further experience has shown how frequently the exclamations, which are treated in the text, occur in Christian inscriptions.]

other forms were, but most of the cases in which it occurs are clearly Christian, and the contrast which Professor Smith founds on it cannot be maintained.

In another interesting little inscription, mentioned on the same page, Professor Smith restores μετὰ πάντα τά(φος), After all things a tomb; but on the analogy of common formulæ, such as ὁ βίος ταῦτα, Life is—this, I should prefer μετὰ πάντα τα(ῦτα), After all—this.[1]

I have dwelt on this page at some length, because the line of demarcation between Christian and non-Christian epitaphs is a very delicate one, and there is no point in antiquity on which more mistakes are made, while it is of peculiar interest and even of importance to notice the gradual steps by which the Christians separated themselves from the customs and ways of ordinary society around them, and created a code of manners and forms distinctive of themselves.[2]

Perhaps some readers may find the discussion of general principles contained in Book I., The Land as a Whole, the least interesting part of this fascinating volume; but for my own part, it appeals to me with almost greater interest than Books II. or III. The descriptive part of Book I. is luminous and most successful, but I confess to being rather dis-

---

[1] An excellent parallel in thought and in expression occurs in an inscription of the Phrygian Hierapolis, which seems to Waddington No. 1687 (as well as to myself) to be Christian, εἰδὼς ὅτι τὸ τέλος ὑμῶν τοῦ βίου ταῦτα. It is given more accurately in many points as No. 28 in my forthcoming *Cities and Bishoprics of Phrygia*. In *Bulletin de Corr. Hell.*, iii., p. 144, a long metrical epitaph and curse ends with ταῦτα in a line by itself: "So much".

[2] I notice also that on p. 544 Professor Smith remarks that Tacitus (whom I had quoted on my side in a discussion of the name Ituræi) is against me: he must have made some mistake, for the MSS. and all good editions are with me. Some school editions and English translations use the term Ituraea as a noun, which is unknown (as I have proved) to the ancients.

appointed with the general reflections on the bearing which Historical Geography has on the criticism of the Hebrew authorities. These are rather vaguely and slightly indicated; they seem to express the general ideas with which one might approach the subject for the first time rather than the cream of the results which one gathers from the doing of the work; and I should imagine that chapter v., in which they are contained, was written before Book II., and did not spring from a mind filled with the facts and the method applied in that part.

The first four chapters of Book I. deal with "the place of Syria in the world's history," and with the form, climate and scenery of the land; and, finally, chapter vi. places the reader at two points of view from which to acquire a general idea of the effect produced by the characteristics described in the preceding chapters, *viz.*, on the deck of a steamer[1] and on the top of Mount Ebal beside Shechem. The relation of Arabia to Syria (including Palestine) and of Syria to the outer world are set before us very suggestively in chapter i. The Arabian tribes, always in process of growing too numerous for their bare and barren land, are ever also in process of forcing themselves into the surrounding countries, sometimes in peaceful emigration, generally in the guise of marauders or conquerors; but of the four paths open to them, the path of Syria is the easiest, and the one most trodden by them throughout history. The frontier tribes of the Arabian wilderness have been constantly pressing in on the fertile lands of Syria. So long as Syria has been held by strong, energetic rulers the nomads are kept back, or are

---

[1] On p. 119 there is a harshness of expression. The steamer is sailing *north* from Jaffa, but the places seen are enumerated as going south. Yet we cannot read *south* for *north*.

allowed to enter only as peaceful emigrants or as useful mercenaries in the service of the Syrian Government; for, while their warlike and restless character makes them a terror to the settled Syrian peoples, who become steadily less fit for war by continuance of peace, it also makes them excellent soldiers to recruit the Syrian armies. Thus it is impossible for any Arabian tribe to continue very long a frontier-tribe; an unvarying law pushes on each in succession towards and over the frontier; and this constant immigration tends to invigorate the Syrian population and keep it from stagnating in Oriental peasant life. So the Hebrews forced their way into Canaan. So also the Ituræans, whom we first hear about in the late period when Chronicles was composed[1] as warring on the eastern frontier against Reuben, Gad and Manasseh, gradually forced their way on towards Anti-Lebanon (in the position where they are represented in the maps attached to Professor Smith's work) and even penetrated in part across Anti-Lebanon into the fertile valley of "Hollow Syria," taking advantage of the disorganisation caused by the decay of the Seleucid Empire after B.C. 190. Had not the Seleucid power been soon replaced by the strong hand of Rome, in all probability the Ituræi would have overrun Syria entirely, in pursuance of that eternal law of succession by which the effete dynasties and peoples of the East are swept away by fresh vigorous conquerors, a process which the support of Europe, propping up the worn-out stock of Turkish or Hindu or other dynasties, has sometimes stopped, always to the great detriment of their subjects.

There seems to be a curious and deep-seated variation

[1] While these wars are projected into a remoter period by the writer, it is probable that he took the name of this nomad tribe from the facts of his own time. The Septuagint reads 'Ιτουραῖοι in 1 *Chron.* v. 19.

between two different points of view as regards the religion and development of Israel. We read, *e.g.*, "Monotheism was born, not, as M. Renan says, in Arabia, but in Syria" (p. 113); and Professor Smith goes on to argue that, as the character of Syria and its peoples is so opposed to monotheism, we are driven to "the belief that the monotheism which appeared upon it was ultimately due to direct superhuman revelation". So also on page 90, "those spiritual forces which, in spite of the opposition of nature, did create upon Syria the monotheistic creed of Israel".

Such passages as these are quite in accordance with that view of Hebrew history which sees in it a gradual rise towards a loftier and purer conception of God and of the Divine nature, as the people under the guidance of its prophets disengaged itself step by step from the grosser religion which was once shared by the Hebrews with the other Semitic races. On that theory it would be quite natural to assert positively that the Hebrew monotheism arose in Syria, not in Arabia. But alongside of this view, sometimes even in the same paragraph with it, we find another, which seems—so far as I can venture to judge—to be inconsistent with it, and to involve an opposite view of the character of Hebrew history, *viz.*, the traditional view that the lofty character of Hebrew religion was impressed on it, once for all, in Arabia, not in Syria, that constant lapses from the purity of this religion occurred amid the seductions and temptations of Syrian surroundings, that the prophets resisted these lapses and recalled the people to the original purity of their faith, expounding and unfolding in detail the character of that faith, and applying it to each new political and social situation that arose, but not making it loftier or purer, for it was absolutely lofty and pure from the first. Take, for example, the words on page 89: "the conception of Israel's early history which prevails in Deuteronomy, *viz.*, that the nation suffered a declension from a pure and simple estate of life and religion to one which was gross and sensuous, from the worship of their own deity to the worship of many local gods, is justified in the main—I do not say in details, but in the main—by the geographical data, and by what we know to have been the influence of these at all periods in history".

But, in truth, what are called the moderate critics seem all—in the rough judgment of ignorant outsiders, such as the present writer—to be involved in the same double point of view, and to be attempting to combine two different (and I would add irreconcilable) theories in their attitude towards the history of Israel. I am, of course, not speaking about the recognition of the composite nature of the law-books and the older class of historical records: those who do not recognise that fact occupy a position so diametrically opposite to mine that we can see nothing alike, and there can be no profitable discussion between us. But to those who recognise that fact there remains a further, and, I think, far more important question, *viz.*, as to the relation between the various component parts of these books—one might say between the different *strata*, were it not that the very word *strata* implies and presupposes a settled opinion in regard to the question which is put before us for settlement. That question has been answered by almost all critics in one way, *viz.*, the relation between the components is one of time, and the differences between them are due to gradual development of religious feeling and organisation in the nation. Those critics who carry out that principle logically and consistently form the extreme critical school; those who accept it, but shrink with wise caution from the full consequences of their own position, are the moderate critics. Professor Driver puts the point in his usual clear, well-defined and unmistakable way, in his *Introduction*, page 80: "Can any one read the injunctions respecting sacrifices and feasts in *Exodus* xxiii. 14-19 beside those in P (*Lev.* i.-vii., *Num.* xxviii.-xxix., for instance), and not feel that some centuries must have intervened between the simplicity which marks the one and the minute specialisation which is the mark of the other?" Any one who feels compelled to give to that question the answer that Dr. Driver desires is making the assumption that the principle of the extreme critical school is right, though his natural practical sense makes him shrink from carrying it out with ruthless logic. Neither the wise statesman nor the wise scholar can permit himself to be thoroughly consistent in carrying into practice the one-sided and incomplete principles which occasionally he does not shrink from enunciating in theory. It is a fair answer to Dr. Driver's question to say that other reasons besides lapse of time have been found sufficient to cause differences of this class,[1] and that no sufficient reasons have yet been brought forward to prove that no other cause except progressive development can account for the great difference which all

[1] For example, if in A.D. 1860 two able American statesmen, deep in practical politics, but of opposite parties, had been set separately to the task of formulating the principles of the American constitution, they would have produced very different books, at variance on many most fundamental points. Of course the many centuries of organised civilisation that lay behind them would have forced on them a great amount of similarity in other points; whereas no causes existed to produce such similarity in the case of the Hebrew tribes, who brought with them into Palestine, as we assume, a lofty religion and moral law, which none of them had fully comprehended and worked into their nature, much less developed into a practical working system of ritual and life.

of us wish to understand. I entertain no opinion on the point: I am merely seeking for information; and I do not find any one who faces fairly the question as a whole. All seem to me to start with their faces set determinedly towards one side of it alone.

When I say "no sufficient reasons" for the answer expected have been given as yet, it is necessary to except the thorough and "advanced" critics, whose position is quite logical and complete. They carry out thoroughly their view that a gradual, progressive and perfectly natural development took place on the soil of Syria, and infer that those parts of the Hebrew documents which imply a declension from a primitive revelation spring from a late misrepresentation of early history, in which the steps of ascent were described as successive recoveries from lapses and errors. Professor Smith seems in some places to use this principle, and yet on the whole to declare that geographical study is opposed to it. But it would lead us too far to exemplify and make clear the results which, if I may venture to criticise his method, seem to me to spring from this unconscious inconsistency in principle.[1] I may however say that, if a fuller discussion of the subject were possible, I should take exception to Professor Smith's fundamental con-

[1] A few slips of expression may be noticed here, which it would be well to correct in a later edition: p. 25, l. 5, Africa was not made a Roman province till B.C. 146; pp. 22-23, *note*, read Kronos for Chronos, and βαίτυλοι for βετυλαι (a form which is not given in the *Thesaurus* of Stephanus) twice; p. 17, *note*, it is too vague to quote "Porphyry in the *Acta Sanctorum*," for there are over sixty folio volumes of that work; p. 35, l. 13, the number fifteen is too small (I notice often a tendency to state numbers rather low), Nazareth is decidedly more than that from Cæsarea, and is not within fifteen miles of any point on the coast, if the maps are right. The accentuation of Greek words is often incorrect or wholly wanting (see, *e.g.*, pp. 4, 22, 23, 356, 406, 415, 442, 455, 483).

trast between most of the Semitic religions on the one hand as being purely polytheistic, and, on the other hand, the three [1] monotheistic religions, which arose among the Semites. I cannot agree with the view that the character of the other Semitic religions is adequately expressed by calling them "polytheistic": the term "multiplicity-in-unity" seems to express their nature better.[2]

[1] "Three" on p. 28, "two" on p. 29, by a natural variation in the thought.

[2] See above, pp. 12 f. and 200. The present article (published in 1894) is reprinted mainly in order to illustrate the difficulty that we of the West experience in attempting to understand the Semitic and Oriental ideas of religion; and to show how they have been turned over in the writer's mind year after year with a growing appreciation of the difficulty. Much that we call "Oriental" in religion is really only early and undeveloped, and our difficulty is to project ourselves into a primitive period and to sympathise with inchoate thought.

X.

ST. PAUL'S USE OF METAPHORS FROM GREEK AND ROMAN LIFE

X.

ST. PAUL'S USE OF METAPHORS FROM GREEK AND ROMAN LIFE

THE late Dean Howson, in an interesting little book on the *Metaphors of St. Paul*, well described the difference between the Old and the New Testaments in regard to the range and character of figurative language. In the New Testament "we find ourselves in contact with circumstances far more nearly resembling those which surround us in modern life; we are on the borders or in the heart of Greek civilisation and we are always in the midst of the Roman Empire". Especially is this the case with St. Paul. He was a master of all the education and the opportunities of his time. He turned to his profit and to the advancement of his great purpose all the resources of civilisation. He draws his illustrations from a certain range of thought and knowledge, and this reveals the scope of his education and his interests.

Dean Howson points out that "his metaphors are usually drawn, not from the operations and phenomena of the natural world, but from the activities and the outward manifestations of human life," and that in this respect he stands in marked contrast with most of the writers in the Bible. "The vapour, the wind, the fountain, beasts and birds and serpents, the flower of the grass, the waves of the sea, the early and latter rain, the sun risen with a burning heat—these are like the figures of the ancient prophets, and there is more imagery of this kind in the one short Epistle of St. James than in all the speeches and letters of St. Paul put together."[1]

Paul's favourite figures are taken from the midst of the busiest human society and city life, *e.g.*, from the market—"Owe no man anything but to love one another" (Rom. xiii. 8), "I am debtor both to Greeks and to Barbarians" (Rom. i. 14), "Make your market to the full of the opportunity"[2] (which the world offers, Eph. v. 16; Col. iv. 5), "wages" (Rom. vi. 23)—and the word "riches" is a specially characteristic mark of his style. Another metaphor of this class is "I count," λογίζομαι; but this word, though strictly it was a figure taken from the keeping of accounts, was in such familiar and habitual use that Paul may often have employed it without any clear consciousness of the metaphor, simply adopting it from ordinary semi-philosophic language. The Romans were particularly methodical accountants, and it is noteworthy that Paul uses this and other terms of the same kind[3] more frequently in writing to the Romans than anywhere else, as if unconsciously his mind was thinking in a more Roman fashion. But the idea is Greek, although such metaphors were less frequently used by the Greeks than by the pragmatic and methodical Romans; and Paul of course had no need to go to Roman life in search of it. Still the fact remains that the Romans make much more frequent use of the metaphor, "enter in the account-book," than the Greeks. In Cicero's letters this metaphor is extremely frequent.

The Romans also carefully distinguish between entering on the credit and on the debit side of the account-book (*ferre expensum* and *acceptum referre*), whereas λογίζομαι is

[1] Howson, p. 131.   [2] *St. Paul the Traveller*, p. 149.
[3] ὀφειλέτης, ὀφείλημα, four times in Romans, once in Gal., not elsewhere.

used for both. In Rom. ii. 26, iv. 3, 4, 5, 6, 9, 11, 22, 24, ix. 8; 2 Cor. v. 19, xii. 6; 2 Tim. iv. 16, λογίζομαι means "reckon to the credit of". It means "reckon to the debit" (πάλιν, *per contra*, on the opposite page) in 2 Cor. x. 7. It means simply "enter in your accounts" in Phil. iv. 8, iii. 13; Rom. viii. 18, iii. 28, vi. 11; Hebr. xi. 19.[1]

Paul is rarely interested in the phenomena of nature or the scenery of country life. Where he draws his illustrations from the country and from agriculture, he chiefly "deals with human labour and its useful results". There are, of course, some isolated exceptions, as when he spoke to the uneducated rustic mob of Lystra, a small town dependent on agriculture and pasturage, not on commerce and exchange, about the "rain from heaven and fruitful seasons".

Yet the idea of fruit which occurs in this Lystran address is peculiarly characteristic of Paul. The idea of development, of growth culminating in fruit, a process leading to an end in riches and usefulness—this always appeals strongly to him. It occurs, *e.g.*, in Philippians i. 11, 22, iv. 17; Galatians v. 19-23; Colossians i. 6, 10; Ephesians v. 8, 9, 11; Romans i. 13, vi. 21-23, vii. 4, 5, xv. 28; 2 Corinthians ix. 10; Titus iii. 14, etc. His philosophy rests mainly on this idea of growth and development. He looks on the world as the development of a purpose; the world is to him always fluid and changing, never stationary; but the change is the purpose of God, working itself out amid the errors and the wickedness, the deliberate sin, of men.[2]

He is specially fond of expressing this idea of the Divine power making and moulding the mind of man through a

---

[1] See Rev. Griffith Thomas in *Expository Times*, 1906, p. 211; Sanday and Headlam on Romans iv. 3.
[2] See *Cities of St. Paul*, Pt. I., § II., where this idea was worked out subsequently in a fuller way.

metaphor taken from the stadium. The person in whom the purpose of God works, redeeming him from his sin and setting him in the Divine path, fulfils the course marked out for him and runs the proper race. He uses this figure very often—about the word of the Lord (2 Thess. iii. 1; compare Heb. xii. 1); about John the Baptist (Acts xiii. 25); about himself (Acts xx. 24, 2 Tim. iv. 7, Phil. ii. 16, Gal. ii. 2); and in a general way, Romans ix. 16; 2 Corinthians ix. 24, 26; Galatians v. 7, etc. This figure of the runner in the foot-race is peculiar in the New Testament to him and the writer of the Epistle to the Hebrews (who was certainly a Hellenistic Jew). A strait and narrow Hebrew, hating all things Greek and Western, could never have compared the Divine life to the course in the stadium: still less could he have done this so persistently as to show that the thought lay in the very fabric of his mind (see Note, p. 298).

Again, the general terms connected with the athletic ground are frequent in Paul, and in him alone in the New Testament. These terms (derived from ἀγών and ἀθλέω) might refer to any common athletic sport, but are probably to be generally understood of the race-course:[1] sometimes the context makes this certain.

In 2 Timothy iv. 7-8, "I have fought the good fight" is not a military, but an athletic metaphor: "I have played a good game" is the correspondent in modern slang. The whole sentence is literally, "I have competed in the honourable contest, I have run the race to the finish,[2] I have observed (the rules of) the faith". Similarly in 1 Timothy vi. 12, there is no reference to fighting (as the Authorised and

---

[1] There is one exception: see following page.

[2] τὸν καλὸν ἀγῶνα ἠγώνισμαι · τὸν δρόμον τετέλεκα · τὴν πίστιν τετήρηκα, where the last three words mean, "I have observed the rules which are laid down for this race-course of faith." (See p. 290.)

Revised Versions have it); but the instructions to Timothy are, "Compete in the honourable contest of faith,"[1] a more compressed expression of the same comparison as in 2 Timothy iv. 7.

The race in this honourable contest is described most fully in Philippians iii. 12-14, " It is not as if I had already got the prize or finished the race, but I am rushing on hard, to see if I may seize that for which I was actually seized by Christ; brethren, I do not count myself yet to have seized (the prize); but this one thing only, forgetting everything that lies behind, and straining forward to what is in front, I rush on with the goal in my view so as to reach the prize"; and the prize is defined by the following words, " of the summons on high of God in Christ Jesus". The metaphor is concealed in several other cases in the English Version under the term "contention" (1 Thess. ii. 2) or "striving" (Col. iv. 12).

In this respect we must class with him the other great Hellenist of the New Testament, the writer of the Epistle to the Hebrews, who uses the word ἄθλησις (see p. 291). Some of the latter's metaphors seem almost to depend for intelligibility on the familiarity of the readers with Paul's metaphors from athletics. As this writer was addressing Jews,[2] he cannot have depended on his readers' familiarity with games. He used the metaphors because they rose naturally to his mind.

It was chiefly the race-course that furnished St. Paul with these metaphors; but the boxing contest also suggested itself to his mind in one case at least. " I so box as one that does not beat the air" (with his fists: 1 Cor. ix. 26): my effort is really effective.

[1] ἀγωνίζου τὸν καλὸν ἀγῶνα τῆς πίστεως.
[2] I assume here the point touched on in the following paper.

The prize in the foot-race and other athletic contests was the crown; and the person who thinks of the Divine life as a race towards a goal must think of the culmination of the Divine life as the gaining of the victor's garland. But there are two important differences: (1) in the games only one can obtain the prize, whereas every runner in the Divine race of life may gain it; (2) the crown in the one case is an evanescent garland, which soon withers, whereas in the other it is permanent and unfading (1 Cor. ix. 24-27).

The analogy which Paul has in his thought is not confined to the eagerness of spirit and concentration of purpose and to the prize which is aimed at. The athletic competitor must live a life of training and strict discipline before the actual competition begins. So for the Divine race, " I keep my body under and bring it into subjection," to avoid the danger of being led away and shipwrecked by passion and self-indulgence. This training was guided by certain rules and instructions.

The athlete must "strive lawfully" and observe all the rules laid down by the trainers and the guardians of the course, not merely for conduct in the course, but also during the preparation for it (2 Tim. ii. 5); and similarly in the Christian life it is Faith, like the arbiter, who lays down the laws of the competition (2 Tim. iv. 8: p. 288, note 2).

The metaphors of this class are confined almost exclusively to St. Paul in the whole range of the Bible, and with him they are extremely frequent. The Paulinistic author of the letter to the Hebrews is almost the only other writer who uses such figures, and with him they are only few. The author of Revelation ii. 10 is hardly an exception: "The crown of life," which in that passage is the reward of the victor, is in a sense the garland of victory; but the crown was suggested to the writer's mind rather by "the crown of Smyrna" than by the garland of the games;[1] and the idea of victory which so often occurs in the Seven Letters seems hardly to be consciously connected in the writer's thought with the games, but rather with war. The crown was not peculiar to the Greeks nor was it restricted among them to athletic contests; and, before assuming the connection, in any case, it is necessary to prove that the idea of athletics lies in the passage as a whole. That is not the case in any of the non-Pauline passages where the crown is mentioned, except in Hebrews.

St. Paul stands alone in this respect; and his language came to him because of his early training. It is quite impossible to suppose that a method of illustration which is so frequent and characteristic was deliberately chosen, contrary to the Apostle's nature and convictions, in order to suit his readers in Gentile Churches. The Hellenist who wrote to the Hebrews used metaphors of this class once or twice in spite of the prejudice of his readers against those pagan habits. See final note, p. 298.

St. Paul was free from the prejudice; he found that the keenness and enthusiastic, passionate attention, which were lavished on athletic contests in the world where he had been brought up, furnished the best illustration for the spirit in which the Divine life must be lived. He could not have appreciated this fact unless he had been brought up amid those surroundings and had experienced the strength of those feelings. If he had been educated in the same way as the narrow strait-laced Jews, to whom such things were an abomination, it is impossible to suppose that he could have used these comparisons.

[1] *Letters to the Seven Churches*, p. 275.

The frequency of these gymnastic metaphors, with the depth of feeling shown in them, is a striking fact. They show real understanding of the intensity of feeling that the competition rouses in the athlete. It is only in youth, and especially in boyhood, that this can be learned. A Jew brought up in Palestine to abhor such sports, which were conducted by Gentiles in the Greek fashion of nudity, could never come to understand this intense feeling, if he merely saw the games in later life while living as a preacher in Greek cities. Paul had been educated in a Hellenic city where he had seen for himself that athletic sports are not wrong or abominable;[1] he had understood sympathetically the feeling of the competitors; he knew that this feeling contained an element of nobleness and self-sacrifice, and he utilised it to express the intensity of the religious life. There certainly was no idea in his mind that such comparisons degraded religion. The narrow Jew could not free himself from that idea; but it evidently had no place in Paul's mind, which had been formed in other surroundings than those of Palestine. He sympathised with the Gentile; he had learned from the Gentile; he was a debtor to the Gentile.[2]

We must infer that this department of Paul's vocabulary and thought originated in his early experiences as a child, brought up amid the surroundings of a Hellenistic city and familiarised with the conduct of the race-course. The spirit

[1] The Jews of Jerusalem had begun to learn this fact early in the second century B.C.; and the building of a gymnasium (to which the priests hastened after service in the Temple), with the spread of Greek fashions and increase of heathenish manners in Jerusalem (especially the wearing of hats by the young men)—which were not forced on the people by the tyrant Antiochus (as modern writers often assume), but suggested to him by the "progressive" party among the Jews themselves—are mentioned as having provoked the Maccabæan rebellion (2 Macc. iv. 12-14).

[2] Compare Rom. i. 14.

of the competitors in the course was, on the whole, one of the best and healthiest facts of Greek city life. Paul had learned this from participating in the life of a Hellenic city as a boy; there is no other way in which the lesson can be learned so thoroughly as to sink into the man's nature and guide his thought and language as this topic guides Paul's.

When Ignatius compares the Christian life to a religious procession, with a long train of rejoicing devotees clad in the appropriate garments, bearing their religious symbols and holy things through the public streets, we see that he was at times ruled insensibly by old ideas and scenes familiar to him in earlier life. As a general rule, he regarded his old pagan life with shame as a cause of humiliation; yet thoughts and associations connected with it directed his mind and his expression. No Jew brought up from the beginning to regard pagan ceremonial as simply hateful could have used the comparison.

Just as the experience of Ignatius in the Pagan Mysteries, and his understanding of the intense religious feeling which they roused in their votaries, coloured and formed his language in describing the deepest and most mystic elements in the Christian faith,[1] so Paul's language was coloured and formed by his experience in Tarsus. A man whose mind was thus moulded could not long have remained in sympathy with the Jews of Jerusalem. A common hatred for Him whom they thought an impostor united them all for a time to resist the religion of Christ. But his nature had been formed in a freer fashion than the Palestinian, and he soon burst their narrow bonds. His nature drove and goaded him on into a wider field, and he found it hard to "kick against the goads".

[1] *Letters to the Seven Churches*, ch. xiii.

It would be useful to compare the Pauline metaphors with the language of Philo, who was born and brought up in the Hellenic city of Alexandria. In him also illustrations taken from the stadium and the palaestra are very frequent, though they are (I think) more common in the form of similes than of metaphors, and are therefore not so wrought into the fabric of the thought as is the case with Paul's metaphorical language.

But it is easy to carry this method to an extreme which lands it in absurdity. Dean Howson, in his *Metaphors of St. Paul*, the last chapter of which we praised and freely used in the preceding pages, devotes two chapters to the military metaphors and the architectural metaphors in the Apostle's letters. If his estimate of these is as reasonable as we consider his account of the athletic metaphors to be, then, by the same train of argument, Paul must have been as familiar with and interested in Roman military methods and Greek architectural details as with the spirit and eagerness of the victorious athlete ; which is absurd.

But, when you look at the military and architectural metaphors, there is hardly one which is not of a quite vague and general kind. Wherever Dean Howson finds the word "fight" or "build," he detects an allusion to a Roman army or a Greek temple. But there were soldiers before Rome was heard of, and houses were built before the form of the Greek temple had been evolved. The most pacific and unmilitary of mortals will often use the word "fight". Persons absolutely ignorant of the shape of a Greek temple may habitually use the word "build". Even Hellenes were not always thinking of a temple when they employed that metaphor.

These and many similar words have passed into the universal language of mankind, and are constantly used without any distinct thought of the original department of life from which they are adopted. They are not peculiar to St. Paul in the New Testament. The verb "to build" occurs there thirty-one times outside of his writings and ten times in them: the word "builder" once outside, while he never uses it.[1] The noun "building" is not so unfavourable to the Dean's view: it is found four times outside the Pauline letters, and fifteen times in them; moreover Paul shows a marked tendency to employ the word in the moral sphere to describe the building up of character and holiness. But this peculiarity is not favourable to the supposition of architectural experience and training, for in comparison with other writers in the New Testament he displays less familiarity with the original process, and inclines to use the word only in the transferred sense, which implies that he was not consciously thinking of the metaphor, nor making the metaphor for the first time, but was adopting a previously existing mode of expressing the moral fact—a mode which had been long familiar to him.

It is different in the case of the athletic metaphors. In many of them it is quite clear from the passage that Paul was consciously and deliberately using the metaphor as such; and it is highly probable that he was the first to strike out this Christian use of the words. The Greek language of Christian theology was created by him, and never wholly lost the character he had impressed on it: so Tertullian was mainly influential in devising a Latin expression for the Greek Christian theology.

The whole of Dean Howson's discussion of architectural

---

[1] The statistics refer to the Greek words οἰκοδόμος and οἰκοδομέω. He uses once the word ἀρχιτέκτων, which is rendered "builder" (1 Cor. iii. 10).

Pauline metaphors comes to practically nothing, so far as concerns his thesis that the Apostle was thinking in them of the classical Greek temple. In so far as Paul was conscious of his architectural metaphors—and in some places he was clearly conscious—he was generally thinking rather of the house than of the temple. It is a necessary rule in estimating the nature of metaphor that it must be presumed (apart from any special reason) to be drawn from the realm that is most familiar to the writer. Now Paul was certainly quite familiar with the process of building a house; but he may never actually have seen a Greek temple in building. Yet Dean Howson is convinced that it was the classical temple, resting on columns and splendidly decorated, that floated always before Paul's mind and determined his expression.

The degree to which the Dean presses his statistics is shown by the following: on page 47 he says that the verb "edify" and its substantive "edification" occur about twenty times in the New Testament, and are with one exception used by St. Paul alone, and the one exception is in Acts, a book "written almost certainly under his superintendence". The passage of Acts is ix. 31, and it is straining facts to rely on this as an example of Pauline influence. Moreover, the very words "being edified and walking in the fear of the Lord," prove that the writer had no sense of the original realm from which the metaphor was derived, but was using a word which had passed into the language of Christian moral philosophy (quite possibly and even probably through the influence of Paul, who in his turn used it rather philosophically than with conscious metaphor). Such statistics from the English Version are misleading. We have stated the facts regarding the Greek words for building, and they are not favourable to the Dean's view.

Throughout the military metaphors, some of which are clearly conscious and intended, there are none which even in the slightest degree suggest any real interest in or familiarity with military matters; they are all quite popular; and there are only two which are certainly Roman in character. All the rest are simply military in general; they are not Roman any more than they are Greek: they relate to the popular conception of the soldier *in genere*. Even the allusion in 2 Tim. ii. 3, 4, which probably implies a professional soldier, who "does not entangle himself with the common affairs of life," would be quite well satisfied by the mercenaries who were a common feature of the later Greek or Graeco-Asiatic kingdoms and armies.

The two indubitably Roman military metaphors are the two striking allusions to the triumph, which are resonant of the dignity and majesty of Rome.

The first is in Colossians ii. 15 (14): "the bond (consisting in ordinances) which was opposed to us he hath taken out of the way, nailing it to the cross: (15) having stripped off from himself the principalities and the powers, he made a show of them openly, celebrating a triumph over them in his crucifixion".

The other passage is a more detailed picture of the long train of the Roman triumph, with incense and spices perfuming the streets, when the chiefs of the defeated people were taken into the Mamertine prison on the side of the Capitol and there strangled, as the procession was ascending the slope of the Capitoline hill. "Thanks be to God, who always leads us (His soldiers) in the train of His triumph,[1]

---

[1] Lightfoot on Col. ii. 14 seems to take this in the sense "celebrates his triumph over us as his conquered foes". I think the meaning taken above is better: "we were the soldiers who march behind him in his triumph," as the soldiers of the victorious army always did.

and makes manifest through us the fragrance of His knowledge in every place: for we are a fragrance of Christ unto God, in them that are being saved and in them that are perishing."

In these passages speaks the Roman; and they are the only two passages in all the letters of Paul in which I fancy that one can catch the tone of the Roman citizen. Nothing is sufficient to express the completeness and absoluteness of the Divine victory except a Roman triumph. How different is this from the way in which the writer of the Apocalypse strives to find expression for the same idea.

There is in these two Pauline passages a striking analogy to the passage just cited from Ignatius, who found nothing so suited to describe the Christian life as a religious procession through the streets of a city. As in the one passage you recognise the pagan and probably the priest, so in the other you recognise the Roman citizen. It would be a perfectly legitimate inference to deduce from these passages that Paul was a Roman; but, had he himself not mentioned his standing in the Empire, the inference would have been derided by the critics as fanciful and incredible.

NOTE to p. 288, l. 15.—Now the full force of this observation is apparent only when we take into account that this question had been raised for a long time back in Jewish circles, and that opinion on the subject differed sharply. It was almost a mark of the broader Jewish thought to regard athletics without reprobation. It was a characteristic of the narrower Jewish patriotic party, which abhorred foreign ways, to abominate and reprobate the sports of the palaestra or the stadium: see p. 292, note 1.

XI.

THE DATE AND AUTHORSHIP OF THE EPISTLE TO THE HEBREWS

XI.

THE DATE AND AUTHORSHIP OF THE EPISTLE TO THE HEBREWS

THE problem treated in the present paper is not soluble in the sense of demonstrating absolutely that one view is true and all other views are false. There is too little available evidence, internal or external.

But there is a strong probability—almost amounting to certainty—that the true view will be found to be widely illuminative, will make clear much that is obscure, and will show the Epistle not merely as a marvellous picture of " the spiritual character of the readers," [1] but also as an important passage in the history of the first century.

Tried by this test, all the common theories of date and manner of origin fail. The Barnabas theory, the Apollos theory, throw light on nothing, not even on the Epistle itself. A date under Domitian, a date about A.D. 64-66,[2] make the document more enigmatical and isolated than it is when one has no theory on the subject.

It is not a matter of mere idle curiosity to reason as to the time and place at which the Epistle was written. It is true that the work is independent of those external circumstances, and can be understood and valued as a great book without

---

[1] Westcott on *Hebrews*, p. xli.
[2] The latter view formerly commended itself to me (*Church in Rom. Emp.*, p. 307). Longer study shows it to be untenable.

a thought about them. But the history of the Apostolic Age is a subject of serious importance; and while that great blank remains in it, while the doubt continues as to whether the work belongs to Domitian's or Nero's time, whether it was addressed to a Jewish or Gentile Church, there must be a doubt as to the security of the foundations upon which the history rests. So closely related to one another are all the other phenomena of early Christianity, that, while this wonderful book stands apart in such isolation, we cannot (or ought not to) feel the same confidence in our conception of the rest of the history.

The historical questions relating to the date and circumstances of the composition of the Epistle to the Hebrews have been brought nearer to an answer in a series of noteworthy papers by the Rev. W. M. Lewis. While in some respects the view stated in the following remarks differs from that advocated by Mr. Lewis, it agrees with his theory as regards all the main circumstances of the time and place and (to a considerable extent) the manner of composition of the Epistle; and it would certainly not have been attained so soon, possibly not at all, had I not been guided and stimulated by his earlier series of papers.[1] While writing the present article, I have also had before me his more recent articles,[2] which only confirm my general agreement with, and my occasional dissent from, his opinion.

It will also be clear to any reader how much the writer has been indebted to Westcott's great edition of the Epistle. Very often the turn of a sentence or the expression of an opinion is borrowed from him, with only the slight modification that a great man's words always require when they are

[1] In the *Thinker*, Oct. and Nov., 1893.
[2] In the *Biblical World*, Aug., 1898, April, 1899.

seized and thought anew by even a humble disciple. I have also made frequent use of the Rev. G. Milligan's judicious and scholarly book;[1] but he is farther removed than the Bishop of Durham from the opinion which I hold. Their arguments are tested against those of Professor McGiffert, as the best representative of the opposed point of view.

Deliberately and intentionally, here and elsewhere, I use the words of others as much as possible, and preferably of those who do not hold the opinion which I advocate. This procedure is the best preventive against overstatement of the reasons on which my opinion is founded.

The theory advanced by Mr. Lewis is that the Epistle to the Hebrews was written from Cæsarea during Paul's imprisonment in the palace of Herod (Acts xxiii. 35).[2] He considers that Luke, in a series of interviews (Acts xxiv. 23), was instructed as to Paul's views, and directed to embody these in the form of a letter. The part of the theory which takes Luke for the author of the Epistle can hardly be accepted. But as regards the important matters of the place and time and situation in which the letter originated, this theory seems to be remarkably illuminative, and therefore probably true.

The intention of the following remarks is not to recapitulate Mr. Lewis's arguments, which ought to be studied in his own statement; but to state my own reasons for thinking that he has come near the truth.

Stated briefly and dogmatically, the view to which this paper leads up is—

[1] *Theology of the Epistle to the Hebrews*, 1899.
[2] Mr. Lewis usually states the date in this wide way. In one passage, however, he places the Epistle at the end of the imprisonment, after Festus had succeeded Felix. That seems to me a little too late, and inconsistent with xiii. 23, as will be shown in the sequel.

that the Epistle to the Hebrews was finished in the month of April or May, A.D. 59,[1] towards the end of the government of Felix;

that it treats certain topics which had been frequently discussed between Paul and the leading men of the Church at Cæsarea during his imprisonment, and embodies the general impression and outcome of those discussions;

that it purported to be, in a sense, the Epistle of the Church in Cæsarea to the Jewish party of the Church in Jerusalem; this implies that the writer, practically speaking, was Philip the Deacon (Acts xxi. 8); he generally speaks as representing the Cæsarean Church, using the first person plural, but occasionally he employs the author's first person singular, "I may almost say" (ix. 22 plural in the Greek), "what shall I more say?" (xi. 32);

that the plan of composing such a letter had been discussed beforehand with Paul, and the letter, when written, was submitted to him, and the last few verses were actually appended by him;

that its intention was to place the Jewish readers on a new plane of thought, on which they might better comprehend Paul's views and work, and to reconcile the dispute between the extreme Judaic party and the Pauline party in the Church, not by arguing for or explaining Paul's views, but by leading the Judaists into a different line of thought which would conduct them to a higher point of view;

---

[1] The chronology advocated in *St. Paul the Traveller* is assumed throughout; those who follow another system can readily modify the dates to suit.

and finally, that the letter, as being a joint production, which was addressed to a mere section of a congregation, was not prefaced by the usual introductory clause of all ordinary letters, "So-and-so to So-and-so": presumably the bearer of the letter would explain the circumstances.

That there is at this period an opening for a letter in which Paul was interested will at once be conceded. That is proved by the fact that many excellent scholars have placed, and some still place, during the Cæsarean captivity three letters which Lightfoot, supported by the almost universal opinion of British scholars, places in the Roman captivity.[1]

No progress is possible until a definite and unhesitating opinion is formed whether the ancient title "Epistle to the Hebrews" is approximately correct or wholly erroneous, *i.e.*, whether the letter was written to Jews or to Gentiles. Some recent scholars have argued that the letter was written "to a Church or group of Churches whose membership was largely Gentile, where the Jews, as far as there were any, had become amalgamated with their Gentile brethren so that all race distinctions were lost sight of".[2] With all due respect to the distinguished scholars who have argued in favour of that view, I must express what I think—that it would be difficult to find an opinion so paradoxical, so obviously opposed to the whole weight of evidence, so entirely founded on strained misinterpretation of a few passages and on the ignoring of the general

---

[1] Harnack, in the table appended to his *Chronologie der altchr. Literatur*, p. 717, gives both possibilities, but leans to the Roman date.

[2] McGiffert, *Apostolic Age*, p. 468, who gives a clear résumé of the arguments of Pfleiderer, Van Soden, etc., on this side.

character of the document. "The argument ... cannot be treated as more than an ingenious paradox by any one who regards the general teaching of the Epistle in connection with the forms of thought in the Apostolic Age."[1]

For example, it is argued that Hebrews ix. 14—" How much more shall the blood of Christ cleanse your conscience from dead works to serve the living God?"—could not be addressed to Jewish disciples, but only to persons who had been heathen. One would have thought that "dead works" was precisely what the Jew as Jew trusted to for salvation, and that Hebrews vi. 1, 2—" repentance from dead works, and faith toward God, the teaching of baptism, and the laying on of hands, and of resurrection of the dead and of eternal judgment "—is clearly a summary of the first steps[2] made by the Jew towards Christianity, and a most improbable and uncharacteristic way of describing the first steps of a pagan towards the truth. Obviously there is an irreconcilable difference in the fundamental ideas about history and early Christianity, when two sets of scholars can look at words like these and pronounce such diametrically opposite opinions on them.

Contrast with one another such judgments as the following:—

| There is no trace of any admixture of heathen converts; nor does the letter touch on any of the topics of heathen controversy (note xiii. 9) (Westcott, p. xxxvi.). | Not simply is there no sign that the author was addressing Jewish Christians ... there are some passages which make it evident that he was addressing Gentiles (McGiffert, p. 467). |

[1] Westcott, p. xxxv.

[2] What the writer calls "the foundation": he exhorts his readers not to confine their attention to this, but to proceed onwards to the more complete knowledge of what Christianity is.

The widening breach between the Church and the Synagogue rendered it necessary at last to make choice between them, and "the Hebrews" were in danger of apostasy: ii. 1, 3; iii. 6, 12 ff.; iv. 1, 3, 11; vi. 6; x. 25, 29, 39 (Westcott, *loc. cit.*).	Nothing whatever is said about apostasy to Judaism. . . . There is no sign that the author thinks of such apostasy as due to the influence of Judaism, or as connected with it in any way (McGiffert, p. 466 f.).

To put the matter in brief, Pfleiderer and his supporters neglect the obvious fact that the Epistle is addressed to persons who believed in the Jewish Scriptures, and were half-hearted in proceeding therefrom to Christianity; whereas Gentile Christians were persons who accepted the authority of the Old Testament Scriptures because they first had become Christians. "The Old Testament belonged to the Gentile as truly as to the Jewish wing of the Church, and an argument drawn from it had just as much weight with the former as with the latter."[1] That is perfectly true; but how different is the spirit in which the Old Testament is appealed to in the two cases. In addressing a Jew the preacher began his first approach by showing that the Old Testament pointed him forward to Christ. In addressing a pagan audience the preacher would complete the last steps in his approach by appealing to that prophetic preparation for Christ. Dr. McGiffert compares Hebrews with Clement, and finds that the latter "makes even larger use of" the Old Testament than the former. But how different is the manner! We also rest our case on the same comparison.

But it is not the intention of this paper to argue that point. Those who agree with Pfleiderer will not care to read any further, as we look from incompatible points of historical view. They may be referred to the arguments of Westcott and Milligan; and if they do not listen to those scholars, they would not listen to me.

[1] McGiffert, p. 46 f.

But one more specimen of the arguments that are used to prove that the Epistle could not have been addressed to the Jews of Palestine, and specially of Jerusalem, must be given, because important inferences depend on it: "The reference to the great generosity of those addressed, and to their continued ministrations to the necessities of the saints, does not accord with what we know of the long-continued poverty of the Church of Jerusalem".[1] When reduced to a syllogism, this argument may be thus stated:—

No poor man can be generous.
The members of the Church at Jerusalem were poor.
They therefore were not generous.

If the major premise is correct, the syllogism is perfect. But who will accept the major premise, when it is put plainly before him?

The argument is a glaring fallacy, and a libel on human nature.

Moreover, the Greek word which is rendered "generosity" is $\dot{a}\gamma\acute{a}\pi\eta$. Surely the writers who employ that argument were writing, not with the eye on the Greek text, but with a modern commentator before them. Surely, not even Pfleiderer himself, who of all moderns is the least trammelled by the actual facts of nature and of history, would knowingly and intentionally assert that a poor Church cannot show love ($\dot{a}\gamma\acute{a}\pi\eta$).

Let any one who is interested in probing the matter travel in the East for some months or years, and travel not as a Cook's tourist, with tents, and beds, and cooks, and stores of food, and " a' the comforts o' the Sautmarket" (which Baillie Nicol Jarvie could not take with him into the Highlands), but live in dependence on the inhabitants, and come into

---
[1] McGiffert, p. 464. Heb. vi. 10.

actual relations with them. He will learn how true it is that generosity and hospitality may be practised by very poor people even towards travellers with plenty of money, and may be lacking in the rich.

Or, if he cannot travel in the East, he may learn at home, provided that he does not keep himself shut up in his study, but comes close to real life, to appreciate Matthew Arnold's sonnet about the tramp who begged only from labouring men, because

> She will not ask of aliens, but of friends,
> Of sharers in a common human fate.
> She turns from that cold succour, which attends
> The unknown little from the unknowing great.

The truth is that Jerusalem was pre-eminently the city in which there was most opportunity for even the poorest Christians to show the virtues of generosity and hospitality, because it was crowded at frequent and regular intervals with strangers, many of them poor. Corinth and similar "wayside" stations on the great through route of traffic had many similar opportunities;[1] but even Corinth in that respect could not be compared to Jerusalem. These opportunities afforded admirable opening for the Christians to come into friendly relations with the Jews of distant lands; and there cannot reasonably be any doubt that they used these opportunities. It was certainly in this way, through the frequent journeys of Jews to and from Jerusalem, that the Gospel spread so early to Rome and Italy; and it is the reason for the friendly relations that evidently existed between the Roman Jews and the Christians, as we shall see in the following pages.

It may be regarded as incontrovertible that the Epistle

---

[1] *Church in Rom. Empire*, pp. 10, 318 f.

was not written by Paul. Origen's opinion, "every one competent to judge of language must admit that the style is not that of St. Paul,"[1] will not be seriously disputed, and is echoed almost unanimously by modern scholars. The few exceptions in modern times, such as Wordsworth and Lewin, may be taken as examples of the remarkable truth that there is no view about the books of the Bible so paradoxical as not to find some good scholar for its champion.

But are we therefore to disconnect it absolutely from the Apostle Paul?

If that were so, it is difficult to see how such a strong body of early opinion should have regarded it as originating indirectly from Paul, and as conveying his views about a great crisis in the development of the Church. Clement of Alexandria and Origen, while both recognising that the language is not that of Paul, suggest different theories to account for what they recognise as assured fact—that the views and plans are those of Paul.

Now how did Clement and Origen come to consider the connection of Paul with the Epistle as an assured fact? It was not because the views and ideas are those which Paul elsewhere expresses, for, on the contrary, the Epistle presents a different aspect of the subject from the ideas expressed in Paul's Epistles. It obviously was because an old tradition asserted the connection.

Further, this belief and tradition is most unlikely to have arisen without some real ground. Mere desire to secure canonical authority for this Epistle is not sufficient reason, for the Epistle differs so much from Paul's writings that general opinion, in seeking for an apostolic author, would have been more likely to hit upon one of the Apostles, separ-

[1] Westcott, p. lxv.

ated for a time from the community addressed, and hoping soon to revisit it (xiii. 19). " The true position of the Epistle . . . is that of a final development of the teaching of 'the three,' and not of a special application of the teaching of St. Paul. It is, so to speak, most truly intelligible as the last voice of the Apostles of the Circumcision, and not as a peculiar utterance of the Apostle of the Gentiles" (Westcott, p. 41).

This tradition of a Pauline connection was so strong as to persist even though there was prevalent already in the second century a clear perception that the style was not that of Paul.[1] It was common in early manuscripts to place Hebrews in the midst of Paul's Epistles, even between Galatians and Ephesians (as was the case in an authority on which our greatest manuscript, B, was dependent). Origen mentions that "the primitive writers" were positive as to the connection of Paul with the Epistle.[2]

A very ancient tradition, therefore, of the strongest character guaranteed that Paul stood in some relation to the Epistle. While it evidently did not assert that Paul was the author in the same sense as of Romans or Corinthians, it did assert that the thoughts in the Epistle either emanated from him, or were approved by him when written,

[1] Origen mentions theories already current in his time that Clement of Rome or Luke had written the thoughts of Paul in their own words. Clement of Alexandria thought that Paul had written in Hebrew, and Luke translated. These prove that speculation was already active when they wrote.

[2] Οἱ ἀρχαῖοι ἄνδρες: compare Wordsworth, p. 356, on the meaning of this phrase. How Dr. McGiffert can say, "the idea that Hebrews was Paul's work appears first in Alexandria in the latter part of the second century, and seems to have no tradition back of it" (p. 480 note), is to me unintelligible: and equally so his words, "the only really ancient tradition that we have links the Epistle with the name of Barnabas (Tertullian, *de Pud.* 20)". That is a third century statement, and Dr. McGiffert himself concedes that the Pauline connection has second century authority.

or in some way were stamped with his authority, and that the Epistle must be treated as standing in the closest relation to the work of the Apostle.

The persons addressed had been Christians for a considerable time, "when by reason of the time—because they had been Christians so long—they ought to have been teachers, they were themselves in need of elementary teaching": such is the implication of v. 12.[1]

They had not heard the Gospel from Jesus Himself, but only from those who had listened to Jesus. "(Salvation), which, having at the first been spoken through the Lord, was confirmed unto us by them that heard" (ii. 3). It is, however, a mistake to infer from this that the writer and the readers were Christians "of the second generation," and therefore the Epistle must be as late as Domitian. All the 3,000 who were converted on the fiftieth day after the Crucifixion might be addressed in the words used in ii. 3.

But, indubitably, the writer and the readers were all alike persons that had not hearkened to the preaching of Jesus, but had only heard the Gospel at second hand from men who knew the Lord.[2] This indication of their position must be combined with another.

"They were addressed separately from their leaders."[3] This remarkable fact has not as a rule been sufficiently studied, though almost every commentator from the earliest times notes it. The words—"salute all them that have the rule over you"—in xiii. 24, imply "that the letter was not addressed officially to the Church, but to some section of

---

[1] Westcott, p. 132.

[2] It is evident that Paul would never have classed himself in the category so described, ii. 3.

[3] Westcott, p. xxxvi.

it".[1] The inference is correctly drawn by Theodoret: "they that had the rule did not stand in need of such teaching" as it is the object of the Epistle to convey.

There is implied in these words (1) a marking off and separating of a body holding rule in the community (of which those addressed formed part): there was a distinct class of persons recognised generally as "the leaders"; (2) a certain distinction between the views entertained by the leaders and the views entertained by the persons addressed.

In what relation does this peculiar and remarkable fact stand to the history of the period, so far as we know it?

There was one community in which the leaders were a distinct and well-marked body. At Jerusalem James and the Twelve were a clearly defined body with a peculiar standing and authority. That is implied throughout the narrative, and is formally and explicitly recognised in various passages in Acts and in the Epistles. But along with them must be classed the original disciples that had listened to the words of Jesus. Wherever they were, clearly those who had followed the Lord Himself were recognised as possessing dignity and character which none converted by men ever attained. In Jerusalem this class must have constituted a certain considerable body even as late as A.D. 59. In no other Church is there likely to have been more than a very few, if any, resident and settled members of this class.

The writer, himself a convert at second hand, does not presume to address his "word of exhortation" to any one who had followed Jesus personally.

Further, these leaders are conceived both by Paul and by the author of Acts as differing in opinion from at least a

[1] Westcott, p. 451, quoting Theodoret.

certain considerable section of the Christian community in Jerusalem. It is beyond doubt that Paul claimed (and Luke confirmed the claim) to be in essential agreement with the leading Apostles. It is an equally indisputable fact that Paul was at variance with a large section of the Jewish Christians in Jerusalem, who regarded him as an enemy of Jewish feeling and as bent on destroying Jewish ritual.

There was no other community in which such marked divergence of view between the leaders and the congregation existed, so far as our records show. There was no other community in which it is at all probable that such a division existed. We learn of divisions and differences of opinion existing in several other congregations; but there is not the slightest appearance or probability that in any of them a body of leaders took one side and the congregation as a mass took the other side, while in some cases it is clear that the lines of division were quite different in character. In fact, there is no allusion to anything like a body possessing higher position in any congregation except that of Antioch (Acts xiii. 1); and that isolated case hardly seems to be one that would justify us in speaking of a class of ἡγούμενοι.

Further, the subject on which the Epistle dilates is the subject on which divergence existed between the leaders and the general body of the congregation in Jerusalem— *viz.*, the relation of Judaism and the Law to Christianity and Faith. It is precisely on that subject that it would be least easy to address the leaders and the mass at Jerusalem in the same terms.

Moreover, in Acts xxi. 20-24, James, speaking evidently on behalf of the leaders, recognises that many myriads of the Christian Jews held very different views from what he himself entertained about Paul's views on the Jewish ritual.

They thought Paul was an enemy bent on destroying that ritual: James and the leaders knew that Paul practised that ritual personally, and James urged Paul to show publicly his adhesion to and belief in the value of the ritual.[1] The writer of the Epistle, similarly, is bent on bringing out the true character and value of the Jewish ritual, on proving that Christianity does not destroy that ritual but perfects it, and on showing that the Christian principle of Faith was already a powerful factor in the life of the ancient Jews.

It is therefore certain that the situation implied in the Epistle existed in Palestine during Paul's last stay in the country; and there is no evidence that it existed anywhere else.

This argument is based on the supposition that the narrative in Acts is authoritative, that the picture which it gives of the harmony between Paul and the leading Apostles is trustworthy, and that Paul was justified in claiming Peter and James and John as friends and sympathizers. Against this view the almost unanimous consensus of modern scholars is that the anticipations which Paul entertained about the right development of the Church were out of harmony—some say to a less, some to a greater degree, while some assert that they were utterly discordant—with the views of the older Apostles. This modern opinion seems to me erroneous, not merely to a certain degree, but wholly and absolutely. It is the main source of difficulty in first century Christian history (along with the topographical error about Galatia which is closely linked to it). Here it is the greatest cause of the

[1] It must, of course, be assumed that Paul regarded the ritual as having a distinct value for Jewish Christians. He continued through life the attention to Jewish ritual in which he had been trained. Accordingly some modern scholars regard the story of James's advice given to Paul as invented and unhistorical.

difficulties which the Epistle to the Hebrews offers to the historical student. If you accept Luke's presentation of the Apostolic history, there is no difficulty, and everything becomes simple.

In xv. 24 the writer conveys to the readers the salutation of "those from Italy". It is grammatically quite possible to understand this Greek phrase as meaning simply "those who belong to Italy"; and this might imply that the writer conveys from some place in Italy, where he composes the letter, "the salutations of the Italian congregations generally" to his readers. But, as the Bishop of Durham (from whom I quote) goes on to say, "it is difficult to understand how any one could give the salutations of the Italian Christians generally"; the writer would more naturally give the greeting of the Church of the city in which he was writing (οἱ ἀπὸ ʹΡώμης or the like);[1] hence "it appears more natural . . . to suppose that the writer is speaking of a small group of friends from Italy who were with him at the time".

The conclusion which the Bishop considers more natural is, of course, imperative on our theory of Cæsarean origin. There must have existed near the writer, and in communication with him, a company of persons belonging to various towns of Italy.

Now, are there any circumstances in which a company of persons from Italy are likely to have been at Cæsarea?

---

[1] Westcott, p. xliv. It is not inconceivable either that the writer was on a circular mission to the Italian Churches, or that he wrote from a city, Rome or Puteoli, where representatives of several Italian cities had met. Both suppositions, however, are improbable, and difficult to harmonise either with the Epistle or with what we know about the history of the time. A circular mission through Italy was not the experience which would naturally suggest a letter of this kind; and a meeting of representatives is also unlikely in itself, and would probably be explained by the writer, so that the readers might understand who were the persons that saluted them.

Obviously this was quite a natural thing. A company of Jews on pilgrimage would be pretty certain to use a ship from Puteoli to Syria (joining it either at Puteoli or at some of the harbours in Southern Italy, as it coasted along). There were undoubtedly such pilgrim ships sailing every spring. It was on board a ship of that kind that Paul dreaded a conspiracy against his life (Acts xx. 2, 3).[1] The Roman Government had often guaranteed the right of safe passage of Jewish pilgrims to Jerusalem. In B.C. 49 Fannius, the Governor of Asia, wrote to the Coan magistrates on the subject: the pilgrim ships naturally passed by Cos, which had been a great Jewish centre of trade and banking as early as B.C. 138 (1 Macc. xv. 23). Compare the letter of Augustus quoted by Josephus, *Ant. Jud.*, xvi., 6, 2.

Every spring, then, a company of Italian Jews passed twice through Cæsarea on their way to and from Jerusalem. Now it is obvious that such a company is most unlikely to have consisted wholly of Christian Jews: it may be regarded as certain that there would be a majority of non-Christian Jews, but also it is probable that both Christian and non-Christian Jews would travel in one company in the same ship. Except Paul the Christian Jews had not yet come to be regarded as foes by the Jews outside of Palestine.

But is it not unlikely that such a company of Jews would come into social and religious intercourse with Paul and Paul's friends, considering the relations in which Paul stood to the Jewish authorities of Jerusalem? Surely not at the period in which our theory places the letter. A body of Italian Jewish pilgrims would be received hospitably by Cæsarean Jews, and it is in the last degree improbable that the Christian Jews of Cæsarea would fall short of their non-

---

[1] *St. Paul the Traveller*, p. 287, compare p. 264.

Christian brethren. Certainly, so far as Paul had any influence with the Cæsarean Church, the Italian Jews would be welcomed and generously entertained.

But we are assuming there must have been some Christians among the company of the Italian pilgrims. The question may be raised whether this is not improbable?

Certainly not! If Paul went on pilgrimage, why not the Italian Jewish Christians of Italy, who were still on far more friendly terms with the Jews than he was?

Further, the friendly spirit which we suppose to have existed between the Italian pilgrims and the Cæsarean Christians harmonises excellently with the facts recorded in Acts xxviii. 17 ff. The friendly tone of the Roman Jewish leaders towards Paul, their ignorance (or rather diplomatic ignoring)[1] of any hostility between him and the Jews, their perfect readiness to hear what he has to say, is precisely the tone which we suppose in Cæsarea. The one incident throws light on the other. The narrative in Acts xxviii. 17-28 has always been regarded as a serious difficulty: it is mentioned by Dr. Sanday[2] as one of the four striking "real difficulties" of the book. It has been counted a difficulty, because it was thought inconsistent with the presumption from other recorded facts. It ceases to be a difficulty when we find it in perfect harmony with the situation revealed in this Epistle. Moreover, as Dr. Sanday proceeds: "the indications which we get in Romans xvi. as to the way in which Christianity first established itself in Rome would be consistent with a

---

[1] It is noteworthy that they do not deny having heard of the proceedings against Paul. They have no official report by letter, and no one has reported to them any actual crime of which he had been guilty. They expressly say that they are aware of the general bad feeling which existed against Paul among Jews.

[2] *Bampton Lectures*, 1893, p. 329, note.

considerable degree of ignorance on the part of official Judaism ". The "difficulty" solves itself when the evidence is fairly looked at as a whole.

It is clear that, if we are correct in this, a common interpretation of Suetonius, *Claud.* 25, must be abandoned. The Latin historian's words, *Judæos impulsore Chresto assidue tumultuantes*, cannot be taken as an allusion made through Roman ignorance to quarrels which occurred between Christian and non-Christian Jews; such quarrels seem to belong in Rome only to a later period than the time of Claudius (A.D. 41-54).

The salutation of the Italians would of course be sent to Jerusalem on their homeward journey, not on the way up to the Holy City, when they would carry their salutations in person. On the return journey they would naturally send greetings to their late hosts and the whole community from which they had just parted, if they happened to be passing through Cæsarea at the time when a public letter was about to be sent to Jerusalem.

This seems to be self-evident to any one who understands the circumstances and accompaniments of ancient travel; but it may be better to discuss the situation more fully, inasmuch as there is a widespread idea that in that period people generally, and early Christians especially, were governed in practical life by totally different conditions from ordinary human beings; and commentators or critics, who write in the study and know or care little about the practical facts of ancient travel, sometimes fail to see what must inevitably have happened. Moreover, a consideration of this case throws light both on the situation in which the Epistle to the Hebrews was written and on the relations in which Paul and his companions stood to Cæsarea and its congregation when they arrived in A.D. 57 from the Aegean lands (Acts xxi.).

In the first place, it may be assumed that the Italian pilgrims when they landed in the harbour of Cæsarea on their way up to Jerusalem in A.D. 59,[1] would rest there some days before they began the land journey of about sixty miles to Jerusalem (just as Paul and his company had done two years previously). After a long voyage in an ancient ship with its cramped space and uncomfortable circumstances, such opportunity of refreshment was urgently needed. Tacitus mentions that troops, which had been sent out to the East by Nero in A.D. 68, and brought back again forthwith to Italy, were incapacitated by the voyage and its discomforts for military service in the war of A.D. 69.[2]

During these days of rest the pilgrims would be in friendly intercourse with the Jews and Jewish Christians at Cæsarea. Hospitality to pilgrims and travellers was a duty, incumbent on Jews and Christians alike, and this duty was especially insisted on by the early Church.[3] But there would be no motive for the Cæsarean Church to send to Jerusalem the salutations of pilgrims who were themselves going up to Jerusalem and would arrive there almost or quite as soon as the letter. When the pilgrims were hiring horses and making their preparations for the land journey,[4] the Jewish Christians were quite as likely to help them as the old Jews. Strangers in an eastern town are always exposed to many troubles and many attempts at overcharge and cheating; and residents who were willing had abundant opportunity of doing much service at small cost to the pilgrims. In this way, both by hospitality in their houses and by kindness

[1] On the year, see below.
[3] See p. 309.
[2] Tacitus, *Hist.*, i. 31.
[4] *Pauline and other Studies*, p. 266 ff.

and help in other ways, friendly relations were established between the pilgrims and the Cæsarean Church before the former went up to Jerusalem.

Secondly, in Jerusalem there was abundant opportunity of a similar kind for establishing friendly relations between the pilgrims and the Church of the Holy City; and, as we have seen above, it must be regarded as certain that the opportunity was systematically used by the wise policy of the Christian leaders.

When the pilgrims returned, probably after several weeks, to the port of Cæsarea, their former relations with the local church were, of course, resumed. Again an interval of at least a day or two would almost invariably occur before a suitable ship was found sailing to Puteoli and preparations for the long voyage completed.[1] In this interval the Italian pilgrims, οἱ ἀπὸ 'Ιταλίας, were again in intercourse with the Cæsarean Church, and sent a message of greeting in the letter which that church was composing and sending to Jerusalem. Very probably Paul himself was interested in the pilgrims and in their message.

The message in itself contributes to the effect which the Epistle aims at. The writer, while explaining and placing on a well-reasoned basis the true relation between Judaism and Christianity as the less and more perfect stages of one faith, desired to facilitate and preserve harmony between the

---

[1] Although ships, indubitably, were on the outlook for the pilgrim trade, and there were thus ships carrying large parties of pilgrims, it cannot be supposed that the same ship in which pilgrims had come to Cæsarea always lay in the harbour waiting till they returned. In many cases it would find another cargo too soon, and would sail as soon as it was loaded. Even if in some cases the ship waited for the pilgrims, it had also to load; and arrangements could not be so exactly made that the ship would sail a few hours after the party arrived. Things move more slowly in the East.

Jews and the Jewish Christians; and the salutation exemplifies and confirms the harmony.

Incidentally the passage shows the exact date when the Epistle was composed. The final words were written shortly after the Passover ended; about April-May, either A.D. 58 or 59. The latter year is preferable, as the analogies of Hebrews are to Paul's last defence before Agrippa and Festus (Acts xxvi.), not to his earlier speeches in Jerusalem and Rome. Moreover the Epistle represents the outcome of a long period of thought and quiet discussion, after the stormy period at the beginning of the Cæsarean captivity was ended.

The relation of the writer to the persons addressed is shown most clearly in the conclusion. He was in some way prevented at the moment from being with them (xiii. 19); he does not state what cause is detaining him against his will. Yet immediately afterwards he says confidently that he expects to see them shortly. He therefore regards it as practically fixed that he is shortly to be in the place where the persons addressed are. Accepting Delitzsch's view[1] that the last few verses were appended by Paul himself, we make the following inferences.

When Paul was at Cæsarea, it is clear from xxv. 9 and from the general circumstances of the case, that if the formal trial of the prisoner occurred, it was almost certain to be held at Jerusalem, where the evidence was most readily accessible, and where the Jews wished it to be held. Every historical student knows how much influence the general wish of the provincials exercised on every Roman

---

[1] The change of author was marked, not merely by change of handwriting, but probably also by a break, or some other device, which was lost in the later manuscripts.

governor. It is therefore natural and probable that at some time during his long imprisonment Paul expected that the trial would not be longer delayed, and that he would shortly be in Jerusalem. This was, of course, written before the plot to assassinate Paul on the way up to be tried had been discovered (when, in despair of a fair trial in Palestine, he was driven to appeal to the Emperor), in the summer of A.D. 59.

The reference to Timothy in xiii. 23 is obscure on every theory. It touches facts of which we are wholly ignorant. But the intention is clear that, if Timothy be not detained too long by possible hindrances, he will accompany the writer to the city where the persons addressed live. Timothy, moreover, is an intimate and dear friend of the writer, who therefore expects this dear friend to accompany him. Timothy at the moment is away at a distance, and there maybe impediments to his speedy arrival; but, if he comes in time, it is a matter of course that he will accompany the writer.

Timothy, it is certain, accompanied Paul to Jerusalem in A.D. 57 (Acts xx. 4). We need not doubt that he and the other delegates soon followed Paul to Cæsarea. It is, however, in the last degree improbable that the delegates all remained in Cæsarea throughout the two years' imprisonment. It may be taken as certain that Paul carried out his usual policy of sending his coadjutors on missions both to his churches and to new cities, and that mission work went on actively during that period. Paul then says: "Know that Timothy has been sent away on a mission,[1] with whom, if he returns quickly, I will see you".

In the Epistle "we" generally denotes the body of Chris-

[1] This interpretation, advocated by Lewis, seems more probable than "set free from prison": cp. Acts xiii. 3, and *St. Paul the Traveller*, p. 67 f. But it seems self-contradictory to suppose that his mission was to carry the letter to Jerusalem, as has been suggested.

tians not immediate hearers of the Lord, in particular the writers in Cæsarea and the readers in Jerusalem (though, of course, in several places what is said would apply to all Christians). Sometimes, however, "we" and "you" are distinguished and pointedly contrasted as the writers and the readers, as in v. 11, vi. 9, 11. Moreover, "we" sometimes (as ii. 5), and "you" often, denote the single body of writers or of readers respectively. The writers express themselves always as a group, for the first person singular in xi. 32[1] is an instance of literary and impersonal usage, not an indication of personality; and the last few verses we with Delitzsch take as added by Paul with his own hand.

The personality of the writer and his relation to Paul are the points in which Mr. Lewis's theory seems to require serious modification.

(1) The Jewish nationality of the writer seems as certain as that of the readers: Mr. Milligan, on p. 36 of the work quoted above, says, "The writer, who was clearly himself a Jew". Probably this will be disputed by no one, and least of all by Mr. Lewis himself. He, as we may gather, would explain that, when Luke (whom he considers to be the writer of the Epistle) writes as a Jew, he does so because he is expressing the thoughts of Paul. This brings us to the second point.

(2) Mr. Lewis seems to attribute too little independent action to the writer. He hears only Paul speaking through the words of Luke. He holds that Luke was, if not the amanuensis, yet the mere redactor of Paul's thoughts. That appears a somewhat anomalous and improbable position. One can understand that Luke might act as secretary, and

---

[1] The first person singular is used in the English translation in ix. 22, but not in the Greek text: here also it is a mere literary form.

reproduce as faithfully as he could the words and thoughts of Paul; but one sees no reason why Paul should instruct Luke as to his ideas in a series of short interviews,[1] and leave him to express them in his (Luke's) own words and style, without making sure that he succeeded in expressing them correctly. If the writer was striving simply to express Paul's thoughts and ideas, he was not successful. The opinion of scholars is practically unanimous, that the letter is not Paul's because the ideas expressed in it are not Paul's, though related to them. The truth is that the Epistle is clearly not an attempt by another to express Paul's ideas, but an independent thinking out of the same topics that Paul was meditating on and conversing about at Cæsarea. The person who wrote the Epistle was not trying unsuccessfully to express Paul's ideas as to "Faith" and "the Law," for example: his own individuality and character are expressed in the use which he makes of those terms—not contradictory, but complementary to, and yet absolutely different in nature from, Paul's ideas.

It has just been said that Paul was thinking at Cæsarea about the same topics that the Epistle discusses. Mr. Lewis has treated this subject excellently, and it should be studied in his own words. I give only a few examples.

In the first place, he quotes from the address to Agrippa and Festus expressions which show that Paul had recently been dwelling on the topics of the Epistle. The idea— "The hope of the promise made of God to the fathers, unto which promise our twelve tribes, instantly serving God night and day, hope to come" (Acts xxvi. 6, 7)—moves in the same sphere as Hebrews. The insistence upon the cease-

---

[1] One can hardly accept Mr. Lewis's interpretation of διὰ βραχέων (Heb. xiii.) as "in snatches" during brief interviews.

lessness of the ritual, the conception that the Law may be regarded as a system of ritual, and " a scheme of typical provisions for atonement,"[1] are noteworthy in Paul's words, and are characteristic of the Epistle. Again, "the sufferings of Christ, as distinguished from his death," are a characteristic feature of Hebrews, but not of any of Paul's Epistles. In Acts xxvi. 22 f., " I continue unto this day witnessing to both small and great,[2] . . . that Christ should suffer ".

These are quoted as examples of Mr. Lewis's striking demonstration of the parallelism between Paul's defence before Agrippa and the Epistle, especially in respect of points which are not characteristic of Paul's Epistles.

Secondly, Mr. Lewis gives some important arguments to show that topics and ideas and expressions used in Hebrews must have been in Paul's mind at that period, in order to effect the transition from his earlier to his later Epistles. These topics lead on from Corinthians and Romans, and are presupposed in Ephesians, Philippians, Colossians.

An interesting little point of expression lies in Paul's use of the Song of Moses, Deuteronomy xxxii. 1-43: he makes the following quotations or references to it:—

Deut. xxxii. 4 in 1 Cor. x. 4;
„   „   17 „ 1 Cor. x. 20;
„   „   25 „ 2 Cor. vii. 5 ;
„   „   35 „ Rom. xii. 19 and Heb. x. 30;[3]
„   „   36 „ Heb. x. 30;
„   „   43 „ Rom. xv. 10 ;
„   „   43 „ Heb. i. 6.

---

[1] Westcott, p. lii.

[2] Hebrews viii. 11, "from the least to the greatest ". Mr. Lewis says that no similar expression occurs in the Epistles of Paul.

[3] The two quotations are in identical words, yet differing both from the Septuagint and the Hebrew text.

On the other hand, among ideas which are characteristic of the later Epistles, but not of the earlier, Mr. Lewis quotes the headship of Christ over the Church, the use of ἄφεσις, "forgiveness of sins," in Hebrews ix. 22, x. 18; Ephesians i. 7; Colossians i. 14, and in the defence, Acts xxvi. 18, etc.;[1] also Lightfoot's note on the analogy between the context of Colossians i. 12 and Acts xxvi. 18, "where all the ideas and most of the expressions occur," points us to the fact that both "are echoes of an argument entered into at length previously in Hebrews".

These brief notes are not intended as an adequate treatment of the subject. That would require a detailed examination of many passages in the Cæsarean light, and a discussion of several well-known arguments. In fact, the present article is simply a justification of, and a preface to, a historical commentary on the letter.

In conclusion, it may be added that probably the most important result of the Cæsarean view is the light it sheds on the relation of the Cæsarean Church to Paul on the one hand and to the Jewish-Christian party on the other. The reconciliation between the two parties in the Church was making good progress. It is an argument of my chapters on Christian Antiquities in *Cities and Bishoprics of Phrygia* that the reconciliation was nearly complete in Asia Minor. Moreover, as has been shown, it justifies in a remarkable way the historical accuracy of the book of the Acts. You have only to take the right point of view, and always you find Luke a safe guide.

NOTE.—Dr. Harnack in a paper which attracted much notice has attributed the Epistle to Priscilla. In his argu-

---

[1] It must, however, be noticed that the word is used by Paul also in Acts xiii. 38 (thrice by Peter, Acts ii. 38, v. 31, x. 43).

328   XI. *The Epistle to the Hebrews*

ment he does not quote from the Epistle itself any words or thoughts characteristic of a woman. It seems to be an indispensable part of such a theory that some proof of womanly character should be shown in the letter. The allusions to milk, and to folding up as a garment, cannot be considered to indicate authorship of a woman, for they are customary; and Dr. Harnack himself evidently thinks so, for he does not allude to them as furnishing any support to his theory. If one could find the slightest indication of a woman's feeling in the letter, one might think of Philip's four daughters, prophetesses; but, as it is, there seems to be absolutely nothing on that side to lay hold of.

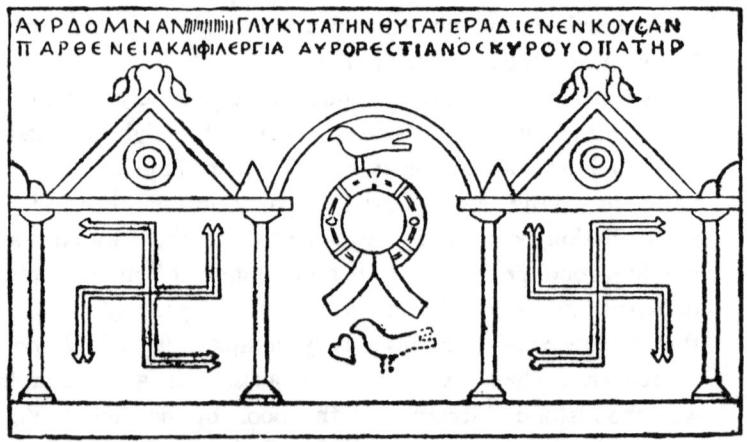

FIG. 6.—The Dove in the Art of Isaura (see p. 385).

XII.
THE CHURCH OF LYCAONIA IN THE FOURTH CENTURY

FIG. 7.—The Cross in Lycaonian Ornamental Style (see p. 406).

FIG. 8.—The Fish in the Art of Isaura (see p. 403).

XII.

THE CHURCH OF LYCAONIA IN THE FOURTH CENTURY

THE country of Lycaonia has furnished the largest body of early Christian inscriptions, with the exception of the Catacombs in Rome. At some time it is proposed to publish the whole collection, amounting to many hundreds, mostly unpublished; but the number known increases so much every year that it is premature to attempt to do so at present. It is, however, a useful task to select a certain number of the most typical texts, to exhibit their value as evidence for the development of Christianity in its earliest Anatolian seat, to describe the problems which they raise, and to suggest a partial solution of some of these problems.

They form a group around Iconium as centre, and they therefore represent one of the earliest and strongest bodies of Christian opinion, whose origin goes back to St. Paul's first missionary journey in Asia Minor, and whose ecclesiastical organisation was practically completed in its permanent and final form at an earlier period probably than the Church of any other Roman province. The bishops of every city of Lycaonia and of all the region in immediate connection with Iconium were present at one or other of the two great Councils of the fourth century, in A.D. 325 and 381;[1]

[1] Psibela was not represented; but I believe that it was then subject to Laodiceia and became a city and a bishopric only at the end of the fifth century under the name Verinopolis. Also Sinethandos became a bishopric only in the eighth century.

and this could hardly be the case unless the ecclesiastical organisation was practically complete in the third century. It was a long journey from Lycaonia to Nicæa or to Constantinople, where those Councils were held; yet the Lycaonian bishops were far more completely represented than those of provinces which lay within easier reach of the Councils. Taking this in conjunction with the fact that one of the earliest Councils was held at Iconium in A.D. 236, we must regard Lycaonia as having been very important in Christian history during the third century.

It would, therefore, be useful to study the Church organisation, the priests and other ecclesiastical officials, and the relation in which they stood to the ordinary population in this old Christian land during the fourth century. The method must start from the inscriptions and compare them with contemporary literature. A few initial steps are made in this paper, which may facilitate the way for deeper study, and show what value and interest belong to the work.

The following table gives a list of the bishoprics from which are drawn the documents which are here described. As the political organisation varied greatly in the Roman period, I give a statement of the Provincial system at different epochs. The original Province of Galatia included almost the whole of these bishoprics, until a few of them were detached at the formation of the triple Province Cilicia-Lycaonia-Isauria, probably about 135 A.D. After South Galatia was made into a separate Province called Pisidia about 295, the majority of them were finally detached from Galatia. In 372 a new Province Lycaonia was formed out of parts of Pisidia and Isauria.

in the Fourth Century

	BISHOPS A.D. 325.	BISHOPS A.D. 381.	PROVINCE IN ST. PAUL'S TIME.	PROVINCE IN THE THIRD CENTURY.	PROVINCE A.D. 295-372.	PROVINCE AFTER A.D. 372.
Iconium	Eulalius	Amphilochius	Galatia	Galatia	Pisidia	Lycaonia
Lystra	—	Paulus	,,	,,	,,	,,
Misthia	Patricius	Darius	,,	,,	,,	,,
Amblada	Theodorus	—	,,	,,	Isauria	,,
Vasada	Cyrillus	Cyrillus	,,	,,	,,	,,
Homonades	Tiberius	—	,,	,,	,,	,,
Ilistra	Paulus	—	Kingdom of Antiochus	Lycaonia	,,	,,
Laranda	—	—	,,	,,	,,	,,
Derbe and Possala	Stephanus	Daphnus	Galatia	,,	,,	,,
Barata	Theodorus [1]	—	Kingdom of Antiochus	,,	,,	,,
Hyde	—	Theodosius	,,	,,	Pisidia (?)	,,
Isaura Nova	—	Hilarius	Galatia	Galatia (?)	,,	,,
Corua	—	Inzos (Inzas [?])	,,	,,	,,	,,
Savatra	—	Aristophanes	,,	Lycaonia	Galatia (?)	,,
Perta	—	Leontius	,,	Galatia	,,	,,
Canna	—	Eustathius	,,	Lycaonia (?)	,,	,,
Egdaumava and Drya	Erechtius	—	,,	Galatia	,,	,,
Laodiceia	Julius Eugenius [2]	—	,,	,,	Pisidia	Pisidia
Pappa	Academius	Eugenius	,,	,,	,,	,,
Sinethandos	—	—	,,	,,	,,	,,
Isaura Palaia	—	Severus in 372	,,	Isauria	Isauria	Isauria

[1] This is a very doubtful attribution; Theodorus Usensis seems the best form, but this bishop, last in Pisidia, is omitted in many MSS. In *Histor. Geogr.*, p. 393, I attributed him to Zorzila Pisidiæ. Gelzer takes him as of Vasada, and regards Theodorus of Vasada in Isauria as a blunder; but Vasada was certainly in Isauria at this time,
[2] Not present at the Council of Nicaea: see No. 1,

XII. The Church of Lycaonia

I. The basis of all historical study must be the chronological arrangement of the documents; but as we approach the Christian inscriptions of Lycaonia, we encounter the initial difficulty of specifying the period to which they belong. Whereas the Phrygian Christian inscriptions are frequently dated exactly by year, month and day, and the dated texts form a fixed and certain series alongside of which the undated can be arranged with an approximation to certainty, not a single Lycaonian inscription has been found dated according to an era, such as was used in Phrygia; the custom of dating by an era was rarely, or not at all, practised in Lycaonia. Except where an Emperor or other known person is mentioned, no Lycaonian inscription can be fixed by external and indubitable evidence; and among the Christian inscriptions that means of determining the period is, of course, rarely available. The only useful method is to arrange them in classes, according to the formulæ used, then to place these, as far as possible, in chronological succession, and finally to try to determine approximately the period when the earliest class began and when the others were in use.

A first question that arises in this connection is whether there is any reason to expect that in Lycaonia Christian inscriptions should begin later than in Phrygia. So far as regards the time when the new religion became so general in the country that a large number of Christian epitaphs could be openly set up, there is no reason to think that Asian Phrygia was more quickly Christianised than the country about Iconium and Pisidian Antioch, *i.e.*, the Southern Galatia of St. Paul's time. On the contrary, Christianity seems, so far as the indications afford ground for judgment, to have penetrated farther to the North, and therefore presumably more rapidly, from Iconium than from the first centre in Asian Phrygia (*viz.*, the Lycus valley, where Colossæ, Laodiceia and Hierapolis were situated). So far as this consideration goes, we should expect Christian inscriptions to be numerous in Lycaonia at an earlier time than in Phrygia.

But, on the other hand, ordinary Pagan epigraphy seems to have spread from the West eastwards, and to have been generally practised in Phrygia earlier than in Lycaonia or Galatia or Cappadocia. Epigraphy spread along with the Greek language and education. From this point of view Christian epigraphy was probably affected by the general principle, and should be dated later in Lycaonia than in Asian Phrygia. But the difference in time cannot have been very great, especially as it seems clear that Christianity was an effective agent in spreading the knowledge of Greek and killing the native languages in Anatolia.[1] It seems safe to suppose that Christian epigraphy was not more than fifty years later in Lycaonia than in Asian Phrygia. Now the earliest Christian epitaphs known in Phrygia are fixed about A.D. 192 and about 224, while about 250 the dated inscriptions become numerous.[2]

On this line of argument we should have to look for the earliest Christian epitaphs in Lycaonia about A.D. 240, and expect that about 300 they should be common; but as 300 lies within the time of the severest persecution, we should rather regard 310-400 as the time when they were frequent. A.D. 250-360 is the period when the rich Christian epigraphy of Nova Isaura (between Lystra and Derbe) has been placed

[1] See *Zeitschrift f. vgl. Sprachforschung*, N.F. viii., p. 382 f., and *Oesterr. Jahreshefte*, 1905, *Beiblatt*, introd. to art. on " Later Phrygian Inscriptions "; also above, p. 146.
[2] *Cities and Bish. of Phr.*, ii., pp. 526, 713.

according to a careful examination and argument;[1] but it is mostly of an earlier type than Lycaonian epitaphs in general.

As a general rule it is certain that formulæ which approximate in form to, or are identical with, Pagan formulæ were earlier in origin than those which are overtly Christian in character. As has been frequently pointed out, Christian society and social customs were only slowly differentiated from the common everyday society and customs of the time. This then must be taken as a principle to start from, that epitaphs expressed according to a form ordinarily used by the Pagans are to be arranged earlier in chronological order than those which are purely Christian in character. This principle will, at once, simplify our task greatly. The following criteria of date may be enumerated.

It will, I think, be found that several formulæ, which probably most scholars were formerly disposed to consider as quite late and purely Byzantine in period—as was formerly the present writer's view—had come into use in Lycaonia at least as early as the fourth century; and there is some probability that part of the earliest Christian symbolism in art originated or at least was very early adopted in common use in that country.

(1) The overwhelming majority of Pagan epitaphs in the central regions of Asia Minor under the Roman Empire follow the form that such and such a person constructed the tomb for himself, or for some other person or persons, or for both himself and others. The construction of the tomb was a religious duty; and the document began by mentioning the performance of this duty. The Christian epitaphs, which are expressed in this form, may be placed

---

[1] See Miss Ramsay's paper in *Studies in the Art and History of the Eastern Roman Provinces*, 1906, p. 1 ff.

in the earliest period. Certain individual epitaphs of this class present various other features, which point to an early date, and thus confirm the general principle. The names and the lettering are, as a whole, of an early type; neither of these criteria are sufficiently definite to date, or even fix the order of, the inscriptions, but occasionally they furnish in isolated cases strong and even complete evidence. The presumption is that epitaphs with this formula are not later than the fourth century; and the change to a new form probably began soon after 350.

In some cases the name of the person buried is placed first (accusative) and the maker of the tomb is mentioned at the end (nominative). One might at first be disposed to regard these as indicating a transition to the second class of epitaphs, and to place them later than the straightforward formula; but the examples that occur do not suggest a late date.

(2) The formula, "here lies so-and-so,"[1] is of a later period. It was imitated from the Latin *hic jacet*, and is more characteristic of the cosmopolitan religion Christianity than of the more localised paganism; but it is not confined to the former. It is a sign probably rather of the fourth century or later, than the third. The employment of this formula, with the preceding one introduced in a supplementary way at the conclusion of the epitaph, characterises a series of grave-stones which probably belong to the period A.D. 340-380: they are chiefly metrical epitaphs. A more overtly Christian form, "here has been laid to rest,"[2] may be regarded as a later development, and assigned to the end of the fourth century and later. These classes of formula

---

[1] ἔνθα or ἐνθάδε κεῖται or κατάκειται.
[2] ἐνθάδε κεκοίμηται, κεκήδευται, ἐκοιμήθη: the last is probably latest.

lasted very long through Byzantine time. The periods specified here represent merely the probable beginning.

(3) The name Aurelius (usually Aur.), employed in Greek incorrect fashion as a prænomen, indicates the period A.D. 220-330 (see commentary on No. 15).

(4) The name Flavius (usually Fl. or sometimes Fla., *i.e.*, Phl. or Phla.), employed in the same fashion, marks the influence of the Constantinian dynasty; and belongs to the period A.D. 330-400 or later. Such cases are much less numerous than the use of Aur., as the Latin style of using two and three names passed into desuetude, and the Greek fashion of the single name became predominant. Moreover inscriptions became rarer after A.D. 400.

(5) The *nomen* Julius is, on the whole, remarkably common in these epitaphs. It occurs too early to have been suggested by the occurrence of the name in the later Constantinian family. Nor is it likely to have originated from a short-lived Emperor like Philip. More probably it belongs to older usage, which persisted through the centuries. Especially among the Jews Julius Cæsar and the early Empire roused strong partisanship; and the name Julius is likely to have been much used among them. They were strong in the chief Lycaonian cities.

(6) The name Valerius belonged to the dynasty of Diocletian, and was not likely to be favoured by Christians except through its connotation (as connected with *valere*, to be strong).

(7) The use of the Roman triple name is an indication of early date. In rural Lycaonia it seems to have ceased before A.D. 400.

(8) The formula " Here lies the slave of God " (ὁ δοῦλος τοῦ Θεοῦ), followed by the name of the deceased, belongs to a

much more developed stage of Christian expression. It cannot safely be dated before the fifth century, and it lasted long.

II. The only Christian inscription of Lycaonia that can be dated with exactness is the following, about A.D. 338-340. It confirms the conjectural dating of these inscriptions, adopted from the general criteria above stated, and published in the *Expositor*, 1905-6.

1. Laodicea Katakekaumene on a sarcophagus.

Marcus Julius Eu[gen]ius, son of Cyrillus Celer of (the village) Kouessos and senator (of Laodicea), after having been a soldier in the Governor's maniple in Pisidia, and having married Gaia Julia Flaviana, daughter of Gaius Nestorianus, a man of (Roman) senatorial rank; and having gained military honours; and after the command had meanwhile gone forth in the time of Maximin that the Christians should sacrifice and should not retire from military service; and after having endured very many tortures under Diogenes, Governor (of Pisidia); and after having succeeded in retiring from military service, guarding the faith of the Christians; and after having spent a short time in the city of the Laodiceans; and after having been constituted bishop through the will of the Almighty God; and after having administered the episcopate during 25 full years with much distinction; and after having rebuilt from the foundations the entire church and all the adornment around it—*i.e.* (consisting) of stoai and tetrastoa and paintings and screens and water-tank and entrance gateway along with all the constructions in masonry—and having, in a word, set everything in order; and

XII. The Church of Lycaonia

Μ. Ἰού[λ.] Εὐ[γέ]νιος Κυρίλλου Κέλερος Κουησσέως βουλ|(ευτοῦ),
στ[ρ]ατευσά[μ]ενος ἐν τῇ κατὰ Πισιδίαν ἡγεμονικῇ τάξι,
καὶ γήμα[ς θ]υ[γ]ατέρα Γαίου Νεστοριανοῦ συνκλητικοῦ
Γ]α. Ἰουλ. Φ[λα]ουιανήν, καὶ μετ' ἐπιτευ[μ]ίας στρατευσάμε |νον,
5 ἐν δὲ τῷ μεταξὺ χρόνῳ κελεύσεως φ[ο]ιτησάσης ἐπὶ | [Μ]αξιμίνου
τοὺς Χρ[ε]ιστιανοὺς θύειν καὶ μὴ ἀπα[λ]λάσσεσθαι τῇ | ς
στρατεί[α]ς, πλείστας δὲ ὅσας βασάνου[ς] ὑπομείνα |ς
ἐπὶ Διογένους ἡγεμόνος, σπουδάσας δὲ ἀπαλλα | γῆναι
τῆς στρατείας τὴν τῶν Χρειστιανῶν πίστιν φυλάσσω | ν,
10 χρόνον τ[ε] βραχὺν διατρείψας ἐν τῇ Λαοδικέων πό | λι
καὶ βουλήσει τοῦ παντοκράτορος θεοῦ ἐπίσκοπο | ς
κατασταθείς, καὶ εἴκοσι πέντε ὅλοις ἔτεσιν τὴν ἐπισκ | οπὴν
μετὰ πολλῆς ἐπιτευμίας διοικήσας, καὶ πᾶσαν τὴν ἐκ | λησίαν
ἀνοικοδομήσας ἀπὸ θεμελίων καὶ σύνπαντα τὸν | περὶ αὐτὴν
15 κόσμον—[τ]ουτέστιν [σ]τοῶν τε καὶ τετραστόων καὶ
ζωγραφιῶ[ν] καὶ κεντησέων κὲ ὑδρείου καὶ προπύλου (σὺν) καὶ πᾶσι τοῖς
λιθοξοικοῖς ἔργοις—καὶ π[άντ]α⟨ς⟩ ἁπλῶ(ς) κατασκευάσ[ας, ἀρνούμ]ενος τε τὸν τῶν ἀνθρώπων
βίον ἐποίησα ἐμαυτῷ πε[λτα] καὶ σορὸν ἐν ᾗ τὰ [π]ρ[ογεγραμμένα] ταῦτα ἐποίησα ἐπυγρ(ά)φιν ε-
(ἰς τύμβον ἐ)μὸν τῆς τε ἐκ[δοχῆς] τοῦ γένους μου.

Faults in the text: (4) στρατευσάμενον, accus. for gen. ; (16) καί for σὺν καί ; (17) πάντας ἀπλῶ for πάντα ἀπλῶς ; (18) at the end made the engraver's eye pass on to the ἐ of ἐμόν, and he omitted several words. He omitted α in ἐπυγρφιν.
In 17 τελούμενος, ἀπαλλαξόμενος, λεψόμενος, all are unsatisfactory: but the meaning is clear. On the use of middle for active in Phrygian Greek, see my note in *Philologus*, 1888, p. 754 f.

renouncing the life of men (for a hermit's), I made for myself sepulchral buildings (*pelta*) and a sarcophagus, on which[1] I caused to be engraved all these afore-mentioned words, to be my tomb and that of the succession of my race.

This inscription, which was found by Mr. W. M. Calder of Christ Church, Oxford, in July, 1908, and published by him in the *Expositor*, November, 1908, is one of the most remarkable documents of the kind that has ever been found, and a historical authority of the first importance. It ranks next in interest to the epitaph of Avircius Marcellus in the list of Christian inscriptions; and is so full of historical suggestiveness, that one finds it hard to restrict the commentary on it within moderate limits.

Marcus Julius Eugenius was, like so many of the leading men in the early Christian history of Anatolia, born of one of the wealthy families,[2] which could afford to give the higher education to their scions. In accordance with his birth from a leading provincial family, he entered the Imperial service, the door of which was through a military career. He was enrolled in the body of troops attached to the immediate service of the Governor of the Province Pisidia. He must therefore have been stationed at Pisidian Antioch. There he married Gaia Julia Flaviana, daughter of Gaius (Julius) Nestorianus, who was a member of the Roman Senate, and therefore belonged to the aristocracy of the Empire. It is not open to doubt that Julius Eugenius was an officer, but he intentionally refrains from stating his rank, whether because he thought that this was of too purely mundane interest, or because an officer was obliged, not

---

[1] The inscription is said to be on the sarcophagus, not on the *pelta*.
[2] On the importance of this fact, see *Pauline and other Studies*, p. 376.

merely to acquiesce tacitly in pagan ceremonial (as the private soldiers were), but to take an active part in the religious ritual of the regiment; and he was unwilling to lay stress on this aspect of his career. He mentions, however, that he served with distinction, which may be taken to mean that he gained decorations and medals.[1]

Meantime there went forth an Imperial decree in the time of Maximin that the Christians should offer sacrifice (in the State religion) and should not retire from military service. This is a novel and striking record, which throws unexpected light on the character of the persecution ordered by Maximin. Here is absolutely contemporary evidence, and the circumstances in which it was written down place it beyond all suspicion of being intended for temporary effect or suggested by controversy.

During the persecution of Diocletian, A.D. 303, the intention was at first to clear the army of Christians, and Christian soldiers were in the opening stage of the persecution given the choice between dismissal from the honour of service and compliance with the Imperial decrees enforcing sacrifice.[2] A large number of soldiers, preferring their religion, forthwith abandoned their career. Thereafter persecution, which had not originally been contemplated, was begun; and soldiers were executed on their confession. And again at a later time, when Licinius was preparing for the final struggle against Constantine in A.D. 315 and 323, he tried to purge his army of Christians.

In contrast with this policy it appears that in the time of Maximin, A.D. 307-313, an Imperial decree forbade Chris-

[1] *Donatus donis militaribus.*
[2] Eusebius, *Hist. Eccles.*, p. viii. i., Lactantius, *de Mort. Persec.*, x., quoted by Harnack, *Verbreitung* (ed. 2), ii., p. 46 f., and *Expansion of Christianity*, ii., p. 211 f.

tians to give up military service (doubtless attempting to coerce them into compliance with the State ritual). Beyond question, the reason must have been that the enforced retirement of so many Christian soldiers was weakening the army too much. It is certain that the armies of the Eastern Empire were largely composed of Christians, and Maximin found that the earlier policy was dangerous. If Licinius recurred to the older policy, the reason was easy to see. His enemy, Constantine, was recognised as the champion of the Christians; and Licinius was afraid to trust Christians to fight against him. This war was fought by Licinius as the champion of paganism.

Already, in the time of Diocletian, it is apparent from the Acta of St. Maximilian that Christians were being compelled to enlist: Maximilian, in spite of his protests that he was a Christian and could not be a soldier, was measured and put through the first stages of enforced conscription.[1] Apparently, it was hoped that he would submit and accept the position when he found there was no escape; and probably the suspicion was entertained that he was merely shirking service under the plea of religion. When he persevered he was executed.

The Imperial and ecclesiastical orders regarding military service form a remarkable series which throw light on one another and on the relation of the Church to the State.

(1) Diocletian and Maximian in A.D. 303 ordered Christians to leave the service. They must have relied on the men's loyalty or the attractions of the army to make Christians abandon their faith; and, evidently, these proved strong influences.

(2) Maximin forbade Christians to leave the service, when

[1] Harnack, *Verbreitung*, p. 48 (ed. 2); *Expansion of Christianity*, ii., p. 214; Ruinart, *Acta Sincera Mart.*, p. 341 (Ratisbon, 1859).

the Eastern army was being dangerously weakened by the loss of the Christian soldiers, who abandoned the service rather than their religion.

(3) The Council of Arles forbade soldiers to lay down arms in time of peace. This implies that the Church now took the side of the Christianised Empire of the West and ordered Christians to remain in the army and not to abandon the service on grounds of conscience.

(4) Licinius in his war against Constantine, 315 and 323, ordered Christians to leave the army of the East. He could not trust them to fight for him against Constantine.

(5) The Nicene Council in 325 decreed very severe penalties against those who, after having left the army, had resumed service. This cannot be taken as referring to ancient events in the persecution of Diocletian or of Maximin. It applies to those who had returned to the army in 323 and fought against Constantine. Licinius evidently tried to attract the Christians back to the ranks and succeeded: some were even eager to return. Here again we find the Church officially siding with the Christian Emperor, and using ecclesiastical penalties to enforce loyalty. The Church at Nicæa definitely takes one side in a political question, and begins the close alliance with the Imperial Government, on which see Article IV. in this volume.

The edict under Maximin must have been issued shortly after his accession to the Imperial dignity in A.D. 307. It was followed by the arrest and torture of the young officer in Pisidia by order of the governor Diogenes. The official in question, Valerius Diogenes, is known from other documents[1] to have governed Pisidia about this time. His date is fixed by the fact that at Apameia he erected a monument

[1] *C.I.L.*, iii., 6807, 13661.

in honour of the Empress Valeria, who fell into unmerited disgrace and had to flee from court in A.D. 311. Diogenes, therefore, was governor before that year; and, as there is no reason to think that duration of office was longer at this time than previously, it is probable that Julius Eugenius suffered shortly before the persecution was stopped by edict of Galerius in A.D. 311. The edict of Maximin, in that case, would be a supplementary decree issued during the long persecution 303-311, and not mentioned by Eusebius in his History.

But the possibility must be considered that Diogenes may have governed Pisidia for a longer period, and that the time when Eugenius suffered was during the recrudescence of persecution in the East under Maximin in A.D. 312 and 313. In that case, however, it is difficult to reconcile this edict of Maximin with the description of his conduct as given by Eusebius: he did not issue any formal edict annulling Galerius's act of toleration, but contented himself with sending letters and practically setting aside the edict of grace, until at last just before his death he issued a new edict of toleration. All reasons, therefore, point to the earlier date.

We conclude, then, that Eugenius suffered about A.D. 310, and that his escape from death (which is contrary to the other evidence about the character of the great persecution) may have been due either to the fact that towards the end feeling was changing and punishments were not always carried so far, or to the mildness of persecution in Pisidia (see No. 28).

Julius Eugenius obtained permission to retire from military service, and settled in Laodicea, where he was soon made bishop, about A.D. 314-316 (see p. 351). He devoted himself to the restoration of the church, which had evidently been destroyed in the great persecution and had to be rebuilt from the foundations. This is in striking agreement with the History of Eusebius, who, immediately after the final edict and the death of Maximin, proceeds to describe the restoration of the churches. The new churches were far more splendid than those which had been destroyed. Christianity was now dominant and prosperous; money flowed in; and the Imperial bounty contributed to the rebuilding.[1] The emperors had always made a practice of contributing liberally to works of public utility; and churches were now regarded as a necessary part of municipal equipment. As here the Laodicean church was restored, ἐκ θεμελίων, so Eusebius tells that they were rebuilt ἐκ βάθρων. As Eugenius mentions the "adornment" or "equipment" (κόσμος) of his church, so Eusebius, x., 4, in the panegyric which he addressed to Paulinus, bishop of Tyre, on the dedication of his new-built church, speaks of "the splendid ornaments of this temple" (τὰ τοῦδε τοῦ νεὼ περικαλλῆ κοσμήματά).

We may fairly take the rest of Eusebius's very full description as of the church at Tyre as an illustration of what Eugenius did. Paulinus used the old site, which had been purposely polluted with all kinds of impurities, so that the cleansing of it was a troublesome work. In the old establishment, the outer gates (πύλαι) had been cut down with axes, the holy books had been destroyed and the church had been burned;[2] but Paulinus built a new, much larger and more magnificent church and series of constructions, surrounded by a wider enclosing wall (περίβολος). On the east side he built a large and lofty entrance (πρόπυλον), calculated to attract the attention even of strangers and enemies, to

[1] Eusebius, *Hist. Eccles.*, x., 2, and the African donations, x., 6 (Calder).
[2] ἐνεπύρισαν ἐν πυρὶ τὸ ἁγιαστήριον τοῦ Θεοῦ.

astound them by the contrast of the present splendour and the former desolation, to afford them, as they stood far outside, a good view of all that was inside, and entice them to enter. Passing through the outer gateway or Propylon, the visitor or the devotee came next into a wide square space, open to the heavens, surrounded by four covered porticoes supported on columns. From column to column stretched screens of wooden lattice-work.[1] This atrium is what Eugenius calls a tetrastoon. In the open space of the atrium there were fountains of flowing water, so that all visitors might enter the holier buildings purified and not with unwashed feet. Opposite the outer entrance he made another gateway (πρόπυλον) with three gates, the largest and loftiest in the middle. These caught the rays of the rising sun, like the outer gateway. The church itself (ναός, βασίλειος οἶκος, ὡς ἂν βασιλίς) was surrounded with porticoes (στοαί) on both sides. In the church the holy place (θυσιαστήριον) was partitioned off by beautifully wrought wooden screens of lattice-work,[2] to the admiration of spectators. He made the pavement of marble, and on each side he constructed chambers and exedrai for various hieratic purposes of purification, baptism, etc.

The analogy of this contemporary church at Tyre not merely shows what was the arrangement and appearance of the Laodicean buildings, but also proves that the same type was widely accepted in the Christian world of the fourth century. Another example has recently been uncovered in the excavations conducted by Dr. Wiegand at Miletus.[3]

[1] στοαῖς κίοσιν πανταχόθεν ἐπαιρομέναις· ὧν τὰ μέσα διαφράγμασι τοῖς ἀπὸ ξύλου δικτυωτοῖς ἐς τὸ σύμμετρον ἥκουσι μήκους περικλείσας.

[2] τοῖς ἀπὸ ξύλου περιέφραττε δικτύοις, εἰς ἄκρον ἐντέχνου λειτουργίας ἐξησκημένοις, ὡς θαυμάσιον τοῖς ὁρῶσι παρέχειν τὴν θέαν.

[3] Sechster vorläufige Bericht, p. 28 ff. (Berlin, 1908; Anhang zu den Abhandl. d. Akad.).

Here also the Propylon leads to an atrium of the usual form; and through the atrium one enters the church (which has the form of a basilica). A variety of other buildings are grouped closely around, forming one single complex structure. The entrance is from the west, not from the east, as at Tyre.

There is, therefore, no doubt as to the character of Eugenius's constructions. The whole was surrounded by an enclosing wall or peribolos. This wall is implied by the entrance gateway ($\pi\rho\delta\pi\nu\lambda\text{o}\nu$), and is summed up among the works of masonry, which are comprehensively mentioned at the end of the list. The enclosure was entered by a gateway, which admitted to an open space in which there were at least two atriums or square spaces open to the sky and surrounded by porticoes. The church also was bordered by porticoes. There was a water-tank instead of the fountains of the Tyrian church. The church and perhaps the atria were decorated with paintings. There remain the $\kappa\epsilon\nu\tau\eta\sigma\epsilon\iota\varsigma$, a word not elsewhere quoted in the technical sense here employed. There can, however, be no doubt that Mr. Calder is right in taking the word to denote carved work, made by piercing holes in wood. I should unhesitatingly identify them with the lattice-work screens, which were used at Tyre both in the church and in the atrium: see also No. 11.

Eusebius in his panegyric makes no reference to the municipal side of this great work. He regards it as intended for the faithful alone, and speaks only of its ecclesiastical purpose. The pagan strangers look from outside, and the hope is entertained that the interior splendour may allure them to qualify for entrance. But it is clear that these great structures were intended to be a centre of social life for the faithful; and, as the cities became entirely Christianised, the church buildings formed the centre of city life generally.[1]

This architectural enterprise must have absorbed all the energy of Bishop Eugenius for the twenty-five years of his episcopate, and was perhaps the reason why he did not attend the Council of Nicæa in A.D. 325 (though the situation of Laodicea on the great road made it easier for him to attend than it was for such distant bishops as those of Barata, Isaura, Vasada, and others in Pisidia and Lycaonia). It was necessary for him to find the workmen and the money, as well as to exercise constant supervision over the work. The well-known letter of Gregory to Amphilochius about the much smaller building which he intended to erect at Nyssa [2] shows how much depended on the bishop in such a case.

In later life Julius Eugenius, according to the old Phrygian custom, proceeded to prepare his own grave and sepulchral monument. It consisted of *pelta* and a sarcophagus. The curious term *pelta* is frequently used in Lycaonian, Pisidian and Phrygian epitaphs. It is probably a native word (used as a neuter, πέλτον, in Greek); and is explained with high probability by Keil in *Hermes*, 1908, p. 551, as denoting a palisade or partition surrounding the plot of ground on which the sarcophagus was placed, and which was the property of the maker of the tomb. The palisade was, according to Keil, composed of staves—(δόρατα); and we are reminded of the screens in churches of that period, on which see especially No. 11. Such *pelta*, originally wooden, were likely to be made also of stone, and to retain the old name.

---

[1] See above, p. 153 ff.

[2] It is translated and commented on by Bruno Keil in Strzygowski's *Kleinasien ein Neuland der Kunstgeschichte*, p. 77 f. This church was only a martyrion or memorial of a martyr; and was a single small church of the usual memorion type.

Within the palisade there was probably a large basis or sub-structure on which the sarcophagus was placed: the substructure is called in West-Phrygian epitaphs by various names indicating the whole or parts.[1]

Following the example of St. Avircius Marcellus, a century and a half earlier, Eugenius caused to be engraved on his sarcophagus a record of his life, and this record has been revealed by Mr. Calder's important discovery. Contrary to the usual custom, the bishop makes no mention of his immediate family except in the vague general phrase of the conclusion (which shows that he had children). He mentions his wife at the beginning in such a way as to suggest that her noble birth was a cause of pride to him; but he does not say that she was to be buried in the same grave. Possibly, she was already dead and buried at Pisidian Antioch, the city to which her family probably belonged. The bishop's attention, however, was fully occupied in the task of compressing into the brief limits of an epitaph the account of his own career; and we must be grateful to him for bequeathing so noteworthy a record of this critical period, which furnishes striking confirmation of Eusebius's historical sense in selecting for record the typical facts and processes of the time.

It is clear that Eugenius was a bishop of the fully developed monarchical type, head of the Laodicean Church, controller of its finance, director of its work, speaking in its name. He rebuilt the old Church, as he says; but there can be no doubt that he employed all the resources of the local Church, as well as his own, for this end. The organisation of each city-Church in Lycaonia must therefore be understood as completed on the same type at this time. Yet he

---

[1] βαθρικόν, σύγκρουστον, γράδοι, etc. (*Cities and Bishoprics of Phrygia*, ii., p. 367).

uses the old native formula of epitaph, not a new Christian style. As he made a point of retiring (σπουδάσας ἀπαλλαγῆναι) from service as soon as the law was relaxed in 313 by the last edict of Maximian, and as he resided only a short time in Laodicea before he was made bishop, his elevation is not likely to have been later than 316. Apparently, his sufferings and his rank caused him to be selected without passing through the lower orders. His twenty-fifth year of office, then, was A.D. 340 or earlier.

III. While it is impossible here to enter on the vexed question of the relation between bishops and presbyters—nor is the writer qualified to do so—it is equally impossible to ignore the fact that these inscriptions throw some light on the character of the presbyterate in the fourth century, and that the information serves to complete in some ways the accepted views. I may take Dr. Hatch's article, "Priest," in the *Dictionary of Christian Antiquities*, ii., 1700 ff., as a fair specimen of those views: to the effect that where the bishop existed he was from the first the manager of the Church finance and custodian of the Church funds, and that through this and other functions he gradually became, first of all, president of the whole body of Church officials, as *primus inter pares* of the *presbyteroi*; and thereafter ruling and monarchical bishop; that "by the beginning of the third century the organisation of almost all Churches had begun to conform to a single type, bishop, presbyters and deacons," though "in some places the older organisation lingered on" through the third century; and that "the functions of the presbyterate in this fully organised and generally accepted type may be mainly grouped according as they relate (1) to discipline, (2) to the sacraments, (3) to teaching, (4) to benediction".

The most important of the inscriptions relating to the duties of the presbyter in Lycaonia is

2. Alkaran, near Nova Isaura (R. in *Journal of Hellenic Studies*, 1902, p. 167) :—

Helper of widows, of orphans, of strangers, of the poor, [Nestor? son of Nestor?], presbyter of the sacred expenditure : i(n) (remembrance).[1]

This epitaph may be assigned with much confidence to the latter part of the fourth century, but the earlier part of the fifth is possible. The disuse of the older form of epitaph prohibits an earlier date. The individual characterisation and full description of the deceased is unfavourable to a later date. There is nothing of a stereotyped and formulated character. It reads like the free expression of an individual mind, and formulæ were likely to grow out of this expression in subsequent time.

The preceding sentence was printed in the *Expositor*, December, 1905, p. 445. In 1908 I observed a remarkable confirmation of it in the opening of the *Acta Sanctorum Anthousae Athanasii*, etc.,[2] where the description here given of the presbyter is caught up and applied to Athanasius, Bishop of Tarsus, who is called "the protector of orphans, the champion of widows, the help of the oppressed, and the harbour of the storm-tossed ".[3]

The words of the *Acta* are only a turgid variation of the terms used in the epitaph : the four classes of persons aided

---

[1] χηρῶν ὀρφανῶν [ξένων ταλαι]πώρων ἀρωγὸς [Νέστωρ ? δίς ?], πρεσβύτε[ρ]ος τῶν ἱ[ερῶν ἀναλω]μάτων μ.χ. The name of the deceased is supplied conjecturally, to show the construction.

[2] *Analecta Bolland.*, xii., 10 ff. (ed. Usener), a longer and earlier form ; *Acta Sanct.*, August, iv., 499 f., a shorter but later form of the *Acta*.

[3] ὀρφανῶν ἀντιλήπτωρ, χηρῶν ὑπερασπιστής, καταπονουμένων βοηθός, καὶ χειμαζομένων λιμήν.

by the church officer remain, orphans, widows, strangers and wretched; but in respect of each class a special epithet is applied to the official, and "strangers" are fantastically called "storm-tossed," the "wretched" are styled "the oppressed". It is possible that the words of the epitaph are taken from some religious work of the fourth century; and that the expression became customary in the south-eastern part of Anatolia,[1] and thus came to be known both to the composer of this epitaph and to the author of the *Acta*.[2] But at least it is evident that the epitaph gives the simple and early form, while the expression used in the *Acta* is later in date and pedantic in phraseology.

In this inscription the Presbyter is described as dispenser of charity and hospitality, which implies control of the funds for those purposes. If the restoration of the conclusion be accepted, he was in control of the entire finance of the Church. Yet this duty is supposed to have been the most characteristic and determining function of the bishop's office.

The only other restoration that seems possible at the end is that which Professor Cumont suggested at the time when

[1] The verb connected with ἀντιλήπτωρ was used in this region: see No. 43.
[2] The scene of the *Acta* lies in this Province. The time is given as the reign of Valerian, when Cilicia, Isauria and Lycaonia formed the Province called the "Three Eparchiæ" (p. 332): Anthousa belonged to Seleucia of Isauria, yet her two Christian slaves were tried and suffered at Tarsus of Cilicia, metropolis of the whole Province. This seems so strange to the author of the earlier *Acta*, that he omitted the specification of Anthousa's city (which, however, is retained in the later *Acta* and in the Menologia, and even in § 4 of the earlier *Acta*). This author wrote much later than A.D. 295, when Cilicia was disjoined by Diocletian from Isauria. Usener, ignoring the provincial facts, maintains in his edition that Anthousa belonged to Tarsus; his sole reason is that she saw Athanasius, Bishop of Tarsus; but a journey was needed before they met. He rightly observed that the longer *Acta*, which he published, are older than the shorter *Acta*.

I found the inscription, τῶν ἱ[ερῶν πραγ]μάτων; he compared the words applied in *Apostol. Const.*, ii., 35, to the priest, διοικητὴς τῶν ἐκκλησιαστικῶν πραγμάτων. But this seems to require in the inscription the use of a preposition ἐπί, and the longer word suits the large gap better. Moreover, the reading "expenditure" is, perhaps, demanded by the circumstances here: the last words furnish the explanation for the opening words. The deceased presbyter was the helper of widows, etc., because he was in charge of the expenditure of the Church. It is therefore clear that the word ἱερῶν in the one case is practically equivalent to ἐκκλησιαστικῶν in the other: "the expenses of the Ekklesia" are "the sacred expenses".

The word "strangers" is a pure restoration; but some word is required by the context, and this word almost imposes itself as necessary. The duty of hospitality was strenuously insisted on in the early Church from the very beginning.[1] Charity and hospitality formed a most important part of the ecclesiastical establishment.

The restoration "strangers" is further confirmed by inscription No. 3. Moreover, we remember the great foundation built by Basil near Cæsarea,[2] including almshouse, hospital and place of entertainment for strangers.

In the village church where this presbyter officiated, we find ourselves in the same surroundings as those which Basil had in his mind. The Church is the centre of practical work in social organisation, charity and hospitality, the Church of the people.

In early documents the duty of presbyters to take care of widows is strongly emphasised: Dr. Hatch quotes Polycarp,

---

[1] *Pauline and other Studies*, pp. 118, 385.
[2] See above, p. 154.

ad Phil., 4; *Epist. Clement. ad Jacob.*, 8; *Apost. Const.*, iv., 2.[1] Hermas rather associates this duty with bishops, and so does Ignatius, *ad Polyc.*, 4.

The question arises whether this epitaph can be supposed to describe one of a body of presbyters, on the theory that the various ecclesiastical duties were apportioned among them.[2] This view seems to be impossible, as there is no reason to think that the various functions of the presbyterate were ever divided in this strict businesslike way among the members of the body, or that one presbyter superintended finance, charity and hospitality, another taught, a third dispensed the sacraments, and so on. Division of duties *inter pares* was voluntary, not permanent and official.

It is preferable to suppose that the deceased is described as having discharged certain of the duties of his office with special zeal and success, without implying that he did not also discharge all the other functions of the presbyterate. We must remember that in the many village churches there was no bishop, but only a presbyter in charge; and this presbyter necessarily exercised all the powers which in a great city church were exercised by a bishop and presbyters. In that view the village presbyter was simply the village priest; and, as we shall find in other epitaphs, he was often called *hiereus*. Lycaonia was covered with innumerable villages, and the remains show that in each village there must have been at least one church, which needed its priest. In a small city like Barata there were quite thirty churches. But in the entire Province of Lycaonia there were only eighteen bishops. The presbyter or *hiereus* of

---

[1] The second and third authorities may be called early from our point of view in the present article.

[2] Formerly I inclined to this view, *Expositor*, Dec., 1905, p. 447 ff.

the village church had, therefore, to discharge all the various duties which the Orthodox Church regarded as its sphere of work: he managed finance, charity, hospitality, as well as the strictly ecclesiastical and hieratic functions; and in his epitaph it is those social duties that are emphasised. They were what endeared the presbyter to his people and made him live in their memory. The Orthodox and Imperial Church was still the Church of the people.[1]

That a presbyter administered a village church in this way in the fourth century is proved by a reference in Basil's letter 188, 10, a difficult passage which is discussed at length in my paper on Pisidia in *Annual of the British School of Athens*, 1902, p. 266 f. It seems in this passage to be presupposed that in the unnamed village under discussion there was only one presbyter, Longinus. When the district was in A.D. 371 transferred and placed under Iconium, Amphilochius the metropolitan of Iconium found that Longinus (who had been favoured by the metropolitan of Isaura, his former head) was unworthy; and ordered another presbyter, Cyriacus of the village Mindana, to perform his duties.[2]

Again in letter 54 Basil, addressing his Chorepiscopi (village-bishops or country bishops) reprimands them for admitting, without proper examination and without reference to himself, numbers of persons into the lower order of the ministry. This practice they had carried so far that in every village there were many ministers,[3] but often not one

---

[1] See above, p. 152.

[2] Professor Holl, *Amphilochius*, p. 20 (Berlin, 1906), comes to different conclusions. He quotes only my *Historical Geography*, not my later article, on the topography; and topography is the key to the whole incident.

[3] These ministers are defined as subdeacons in the Benedictine annotation. The priestly order (ἱερατεῖον, τάγμα τῶν ἱερατικῶν) is usually extended by

single person worthy to perform the service of the altars. He requires that a strict investigation be made as to the ordination and the personal character of the ministers in every village, and the unworthy relegated among the laity.

It seems therefore that in this region of Asia Minor a village church usually had a presbyter with deacons and subdeacons. The presbyter evidently must have stood in the same relation to these subordinate clergy, as the bishop did to his presbyters and deacons in the church of a city; and similar functions in regard to finance fell to the lot of the bishop in a city and the presbyter in a village.

The relation of the presbyter in a village to a village-bishop or country-bishop (χωρεπίσκοπος) remains uncertain, as the exact position of the latter is not strictly defined. There was not a country-bishop in every village. Basil had fifty country-bishops under him; but in the vast disocese of Cæsarea there must have been hundreds of villages. It seems from his letter 104 that a village-bishop had to look after more villages than one.

The ill-defined relations between the country-bishops and the other clergy, superior and inferior (as attested by Basil, *Ep*. 104), were probably the cause of their suppression. Basil mentions, *Ep*. 190, that there was a tendency to do away with them [1] already in his time.

Now the question arises whether there was not some special term to denote a church which was administered by

---

Basil to include these lower orders, though the synod of Laodicea distinguished them (according to the Benedictine note), and though Basil himself defines τοὺς ἱερωμένους as presbyters and deacons (excluding subdeacons) in his letter 104. He mentions in letter 54 that fear of the conscription was driving many persons into the ministry.

[1] The bishops of small cities or large villages, whose suppression he there speaks of, are probably χωρεπίσκοποι.

a presbyter, as distinguished from a church which was administered by a bishop and a board of presbyters. On a later inscription I shall advance reasons for thinking that such a church was sometimes called a *presbyterion*.

This epitaph and No. 4 seem to have arisen in the same surroundings of thought and custom in which chapter 35 of the *Apostolic Constitutions,* ii., grew up; but the latter is expressed in more formed and almost stereotyped phraseology. "Thus will your righteousness surpass [that of the scribes and Pharisees], if you take greater forethought than they for the priests and the orphans and the widows: as it is written, He hath scattered abroad: He hath given to the poor.[1] . . . For thy duty is to give, and the priest's duty to manage, as manager and administrator of the ecclesiastical things."

The term "ecclesiastical" seems to indicate a more advanced state of organisation than the word "sacred," which is used in the corresponding part of the epitaph. Moreover the manager (οἰκονόμος) is in the next sentence of the *Constitutions* said to be the bishop, while in the epitaph the presbyter is the administrator. The title manager (οἰκονόμος) is used several times in the Lycaonian inscriptions to indicate apparently a presbyter, not a bishop—one who was charged specially with the duty of managing the money of the church devoted to charitable purposes. Thus it seems to be implied that in each Lycaonian church there was a certain fund, contributed by the congregation, as the *Constitutions* state, and distributed to widows, orphans and poor (perhaps also to strangers in the form of entertainment) by the bishop or presbyter, who was entitled Oikonomos in performance of this duty. When the Lycaonian inscriptions speak of the

[1] τοῖς πένησιν: in the prose epitaph ταλαιπώρων is the word.

presbyter in relations in which the *Apostolic Constitutions* would probably mention a bishop, we must understand that the idea in the minds of every one is "priest": bishop and presbyter alike are priests. In the *Constitutions*, ii., 30, is given an elaborate statement of the relation of the deacon to the bishop; exactly the same might be said about the relation between the deacon and the presbyter: "Let the Bishop be honoured by you in the place of God, and the Deacon as his prophet, for as Christ without the Father does nothing, so neither does the Deacon without the Bishop; and as Son is not without Father, so neither is Deacon without the Bishop; and as Son is subordinate[1] to Father, so also every Deacon to the Bishop; and as the Son is messenger and prophet of the Father, so also the Deacon is messenger and prophet of the Bishop". Moreover, in the *Constitutions*, ii., 19, the name bishop is roughly used in a still wider generic fashion, to include the entire clergy as distinguished from the laity: "Listen, ye bishops; and listen, ye laymen". In this and in the following chapter 20, it is clear that the generic distinction between guide and guided, shepherd and sheep, is in the writer's mind, and that the clergy, higher or lower, are the shepherd, but only the head and representative of the clergy is named on behalf of the whole order. Where the bishop is, the rest of the clergy does not act except as ministers of his will and policy; but, as doing so, they share in his honourable position and dignity; and where he is not, the next in order acts for him, and is the father and shepherd of the people.

"Let the laymen honour the shepherd, who is good, love him, fear him as father, as lord, as high priest of God, as

---

[1] ὑπόχρεος; in No. 4, line 6, the presbyter is ὑπουργό[s] to the bishop (unless the deacon is really meant: see commentary).

teacher of piety. . . . In like manner let the bishop love the laity as his children." One feels that the Lycaonian epitaphs might use the same words about the presbyter.

Here it seems probable that in the *Constitutions* the relation of deacon and bishop is generically the relation of deacon to the higher order of the ministry, and practically includes the relation of deacon to presbyter. I do not mean that bishop and presbyter were the same thing; but that the term bishop could still be used, and was sometimes used, as a generic term to include presbyters and bishops.

3. Alkaran near Nova Isaura.

Koulas to Solon, a stranger, i(n) r(emembrance).

This is a practical example of the last duty of hospitality in ancient usage. The stranger received the honour of a tomb from his host. There is no proof that the inscription is Christian or ecclesiastical; but in the late period and in the circumstances of that period, both are probably true.

4. Dinek near Nova Isaura.[1]

σήματι τῷδ'] ἐνέπω παριόντι φ[. . .]οε χαίρειν   1
χ]ρόνοις [π]α[λα]ιο[ι]s ἱερε[νεν] ἀρο[ύρ]ης   4
πᾶσι παρερχομ]ένοις · σύ δέ μοι χαρίσαιο προσελθών,   2
καὶ τερφ]θεὶς [ἐπ]έεσσι, μαθὼν δὲ σαφῶς ὅτι Νέστωρ   3
5 σεμνὸς πρεσβύ]τερος, μετρίων χηρῶν ἐπαρωγός ·   5
αὐ]ταρ [ὅδε ἐν]κρατιης ὁ διάκονος ἐσθλὸς ὑπουργός
ἡμετέρ]ης θησαυρὸς ἐπαρχίης ἐπίλεκτος
δό[γματος οὐ]ρανίου ὁ διδάσκαλος ἠιθέοισιν.
καὶ σοφὸς [ἐν μερόπ]εσσι δικάσπολος ἔπλετο πιστός
10 ἡγεμόσιν ξ[υνέδρευε τ' · ἴ]σασι δὲ μυρία φῦλα.
καὶ μνησθεὶς φιλότητος ἐμ[ῆς κεδν]ῆς σοφίης τε
σπε[ύ]σεν ἐμοὶ στενάχων ἀπὸ σω[ματος, ἐμ]πάλι χαίρων
ἡμετέρης φιλίης μεμνημεν[ος ἥματ]α ⟨πα⟩πάντα
τὴν σεμνὴν φιλαδελφὸν C . . . ο π[αρακοιτ]ιν ἀρίστην

[1] I have received much help from Mr. J. G. C. Anderson, Professor Sanday, and Professor T. Callander; and to them the best restorations are due. Line 1 is most uncertain. Perhaps restore only ταῦτα at the beginning, and five syllables after χαίρειν.

15 Τηλεφίδην Μαμμεῖν [ἡ σεμνοτάτ]η ἱε[ρ]ε[ι]ῶν
   πιστὴν ἐνκρατίης οἰκονόμον, ἔ[κ τε προν]οίας
   μνημ[οσύν]ης μ[νή]μης [τ]ε χάριν [θ]εράπενά[τε Χριστοῦ
                                     ὅχ' ἄριστος ἐν ὕμνοις
   τεῖσεν ἀπὸ σφετ[ερ
20 ἄ]σματα [κ]αλὰ [φρ]άσουσι καὶ ἐσσομένοισ[ι πυθέσθαι

I described in the *Journal of Hellenic Studies*, 1905, p. 349, the circumstances which made my copy in 1901 defective and unsatisfactory. In 1905 I saw the inscription again, but it had suffered much in the interval. My eyes are not sensitive to very delicate effects, and I should be accompanied on another visit by some persons with sharper eyes for faint lines. This stone also lies far away from the pressing needs of exploration, and would require two long days of travelling and one day of work to copy it properly. Such conditions add immensely to the cost of a single inscription, but this one would reward the expense. The stone is broken down the middle, and on the right and left sides, but complete at top and bottom. The two halves lie separate, and one is in a very awkward position so that the copier can hardly see it except upside down. Only a facsimile would be sufficient to give a fair idea of the state of the text, as the surface is often broken in parts.

I have never known an inscription in which so many letters are preserved, yet so much of the meaning remains entirely obscure, and restoration is so difficult. There seems to be no proper connection between the parts, and thus the restorer has no foundation to work on. Accordingly I have been forced at last to the hypothesis—almost the last refuge of despair—that the second line is misplaced. The first line is engraved on the square capital of the stone (which is shaped like an ornate altar). Then I conjecture that the following second and third hexameters were engraved on the shaft of the stone, and that the stone-cutter accidentally omitted the fourth hexameter. Finding his error too late, he engraved the omitted words on the retreating face between the first line and the second. It is not a rare thing to find words thus omitted in an inscription and added at the side or the end. Where the inscription is complete, the correct order can easily be detected (though some strange errors have been made in publishing inscriptions that contain such misplaced letters or words, because the editor failed to notice the misplacement). Here, where the inscription is incomplete, and where there are lacunae both at beginning and end of every line, and sometimes also in the middle of the lines, the difficulty is almost insuperable, especially as the hexameters do not correspond to the lines of the engraved text. Elsewhere I have pointed out more than once that the engraver of such epitaphs generally had a written copy to work from. Thus it comes about that the misplaced words here are not exactly a hexameter. There is generally a little more than a hexameter in each line of the text.

If we try to correct the misplacement, the meaning of the opening lines would be :—

By this sign (or stone) I bid the passer hail, and all who go by; but do thou show me favour, approaching, and taking pleasure in my words and learning clearly that Nestor in old times was priest in these lands [a revered presby]ter, the help of virtuous widows.

A salutation to the passers-by is a common feature in ancient epitaphs: it was sometimes placed at the end, sometimes at the beginning. Such salutations were taken over from pagan custom into early Christian epitaphs. In the present case the use of the salutation must be regarded as a sign of comparatively early date. The salutation was evidently closely connected in construction with the following line (line 3 on the stone).

The description of the duties and position of Nestor as presbyter, and several other points of interest in the sequel, make this epitaph an important document, and it is unfortunate that a good deal of the interpretation has to rest on conjectural restoration :—

> that Nestor in ancient times was priest in these cultivated lands, a revered presbyter, helper of virtuous widows; moreover, he (was) the minister of continence, excellent subordinate worker, chosen treasure of our Province, the teacher of the heavenly decree to young men ; and he was a trustworthy judge among men, and he sat among the governors, and a thousand nations know this.

Here, as in the previous inscription, the stress is laid strongly on the presbyter's work as a dispenser of charity. The practical side of the Church's work is dominant in the popular estimation. The judicial or disciplinary side of his work, and the teaching side, are also strongly emphasised in lines 9, 8 and 6. The other two more ritualistic or hieratic sides of the presbyter's work (as enumerated by Dr. Hatch in the passage quoted above), relating to the sacraments and to benediction, seem to have been much less regarded in the Lycaonian world ; they may be supposed to be summed up in the verb ἱέρευεν. As to the general description "select treasure," that vague expression refers rather to his popularity in the Province: Nestor, like Timothy, was well spoken of and well esteemed in Iconium and the whole country. The word "deacon" in line 6 would naturally be taken, at first sight, as a parenthetic reference to a deacon who was subordinate minister to Nestor; but I have been unable to work this into a satisfactory interpretation of the document. I take the two expressions ὁ διάκονος in 6 and ὁ διδάσκαλος in 8 as both parts of the description of the presbyter's work, understanding that the former is not used in its official sense but as defining one side of Nestor's duties: he was the minister of self-restraint, and the teacher of the divine ordinance.

We notice here the same thought that appears in the opening words of the preceding inscription. The priest was the helper of virtuous widows, and dispenser of charity. It is important to find that he is described as both presbyter and *hiereus*[1]: the two terms are therefore synonymous. The bishop was archiereus (No. 37), and it is probably to the bishop of Nova Isaura that Nestor was a good subordinate worker. As the deacon was a helper and subordinate to the presbyter, so the presbyter was an assistant to the bishop.

The strong expression in line 10 seems to imply that Nestor acted as assessor or associate to the civil officials of the Province in the administration of justice and discipline; and suggests that very grave powers were entrusted to the presbyters. Everywhere we are struck with the strength of the influence which the Church exercised over society.

In lines 11-13 we pass to Nestor's domestic relations. It is clear that his wife made the tomb. The exact restoration is doubtful and difficult; but the meaning seems to be that Nestor, as he thought of his wife's love and prudence, departed sorrowing, and then again rejoicing when he remembered her continuous affection.

Lines 14-16 describe at length the character of the

---

[1] The term ἱερεύς is involved in the verb ἱέρευεν, a restoration not certain (letters here very faint), and in the fem. ἱερε(ι)ᾶν.

wife, Mammeis, daughter of Telephus. The expressions are all in the accusative, except that [σεμνοτάτ]η ιερειῶν is nominative, which I have tried to explain by using the relative and understanding the verb ἦν. In this description she appears as a "trusty dispenser of continence," as Nestor was a minister of continence. Extremely important is the rather bold restoration which makes her " most holy of priestesses ". The reading ἰε[ρ]έων seems certain, and, on account of the feminine termination preceding, this can only be taken as a slip of the engraver for ἱερειῶν.[1] In that case we should have a clear example of the use of *hiereia* in the sense of " wife of a *hiereus*". It is certain that in Latin documents of the sixth century and later *presbytera* and *presbyterissa* were used in the sense of "wife of a presbyter," but no similar example has been found as yet in Lycaonia, except that in No. 21 *hierissa* perhaps means the wife of a Christian *hiereus*.

A restoration like "handmaid of Christ"[2] seems to be required: similar expressions are often found in Lycaonian epitaphs (see No. 44 f.). The meaning of the last lines seems to be that Mammeis, handmaid of Christ, in remembrance, made the tomb and honoured the dead; and that certain persons will sing beautiful hymns, for posterity also to learn. The last line perhaps refers to some sort of service for the dead, or ritual celebrated at the grave: in a Phrygian metrical epitaph a relative of the deceased " sends up holy hymns ".[3]

In lines 16, 17, is a clear proof of the carelessness of the engraver. The text . . . οἴας μνήμης μνήμης τε χάριν is

[1] " Descendant of priests " is not impossible; but the other is much more satisfactory, as it preserves the metre.

[2] The nominative, as restored, seems to point to a verb following: θεράπενα[ν Ἰησοῦ] also suggests itself.

[3] See *Studies in the History of the Eastern Prov.*, p. 226 (Anderson).

unmistakably a poetical working up of the formulæ εὐνοίας χάριν and μνήμης χάριν¹; and the repetition of μνήμης twice must not be charged against the composer, but undoubtedly against the engraver. I have supposed that he by a slip omitted four letters in the first μνημης, which in the copy supplied to him was μνημοσύνης. This restores the metre.

5. On a stone high up in the front wall of an early Turkish khan, on the left hand as one enters the gateway in the important village of Suwerek, the ancient Psebila² or Pegella. The khan is a very fine specimen of Seljuk work, and part of it seemed to be a Byzantine church, on one of whose capitals was the dedication in letters not of a very early period: "The vow of John [and of] his [household]".³ The building is well worth an architect's careful study.

> Nestorios, Presbyter, lies here, who shone a star among the Churches of God⁴ [one hexameter and a half lost: D]iomedes lies here.⁵

We notice here, first of all, the reminiscence of Homer, "shone like a star,"⁶ showing that the composer of the epitaph was a person of some education. But far more important is the unmistakable reference to the Stars of the Apocalypse. The Stars were held in the hand of Him who walked in the midst of the Churches, symbolised by the

---

¹ Epitaphs often show double, sometimes (as here), triple cumulation.

² See above, p. 138.

³ Other restorations of the missing letters after Ἰωάνου are possible; but the above is the most probable.

⁴ Νεστόριος πρεσβύτερος ἐνθάδε κῖτε
   ἀστὴρ ὃς ἐνέλαμπεν ἐν ἐκλησίεσιν θεοῖο.

The ν before θεοῖο makes the metre needlessly bad. It was impossible to get close to the stone, which also is upside down. The letters are too faint to permit an impression. Hence Professor T. Callander and I both failed to read the middle part.

⁵ The gap ought to be re-examined: the stone is upside down.

⁶ ἀστὴρ ὃς ἀπέλαμπεν, *Iliad*, xix., 381, and elsewhere.

golden lampstands. The Stars were the Angels of the Churches. Nestorios, then, was the angel who shone among the Churches of God.

The verb used by Homer, ἀπολάμπειν (to shine forth), is varied in this epitaph to ἐνλάμπειν (to shine in), for the evident purpose of making it suit better the scene alluded to in the Apocalypse.

It seems also highly probable that the six-rayed rosette, which is so common an ornament on Christian gravestones in Lycaonia, may have been understood as the Star of the Church. The position so often assigned to the rosette on those stones, balanced symmetrically against a more or less elaborately ornate cross, seems to prove that it had a meaning in the symbolic ornamentation of Christian stones.[1] This is not at all inconsistent with the suggestion, No. 10, that it was a developed form of the monogram of I and X, implying that Jesus Christ was the Star of the Church. Rather it seems to be implied that the presbyter (bishop) stands to the Church in the same relation as God does, a very similar stage of thought to that which appears in the *Apostolic Constitutions*, ii., 30: see the quotations given above on No. 2, *e.g.*, "let the Bishop be honoured by you in the place of God".

This seems to corroborate strongly the view which we have already stated as to the picture of the office of presbyter given in the Lycaonian inscriptions, and perhaps justifies us in speaking even more positively and emphatically. The term presbyter in those inscriptions is used in very much the same sense as hiereus and episkopos. The presbyter was

---

[1] It was, of course, used also as an ornament on pagan stones; practically every Christian symbol was previously employed by pagans, as the cross, the vine-branch, etc.; but the Christian symbolism turned those pagan ornaments to its own purposes.

not simply one of a board of elders in the congregation; he was the head and priest and leader of the local Church. The presbyter administered the revenues of the Church, cared for the poor, the stranger, the widow and the orphan, and was assisted in these duties by the deacon his subordinate.

This description applies to the country churches. A city church had a bishop at its head, and there was doubtless a board of presbyters under his presidency. What relation there was between these presbyters and the board surrounding the bishop, cannot be determined from the inscriptions. But probably the presbyters of the country churches came into the city to sit at councils where the bishop presided. In each congregation there were deacons and deaconesses, and subdeacons, also perhaps readers, evangelists, confessors, etc. (the last very rarely mentioned in the inscriptions).

Fig. 9.

6. Nevinne, in the hills above Laodicea (T. Callander).

I, Aur. Eugenius, son of Maximus, raised to my sweetest brother Palladius and to my sweetest children Basilis and Eugenia in my lifetime in remembrance.

IV. The above, an early inscription, is specially remarkable on account of the ornamentation. There is here the most patent and indubitable intention to employ the monogram of X and P (indicating the name of Christ) for a decorative purpose, symmetrically on each side of a circle over the inscription. This monogram was of later origin than that of I and X (on which see No. 10). From the latter, as I believe, arose the Christian use of the six-rayed star or rosette; and it is sometimes placed on one side of an epitaph to correspond to a cross on the opposite side. The cross with bent arms, swastika, was another decorative variety: see No. 11.

The monogram of I and X seems probably to belong to the third century, of X and P to begin about 300 A.D., while the upright monogrammatic cross[1] is not earlier than 350 A.D. in common use (see *Cities and Bish. of Phr.*, ii., p. 739; De Rossi, *Inscr. Crist.*, No. 127; Le Blant, *Inscr. Chrét. Gaule*, No. 369, and *Manuel*, p. 29).

V. Nova Isaura (*Journal of Hellenic Studies*, 1905, p. 172).

7. Claudia adorned Aur. Thal[]ais[2] her husband honourable oikonomos in remembrance.

Though there is no proof that Claudia's deceased husband was an ecclesiastic, yet it is highly probable that the honourable oikonomos here should be understood in a similar sense to the oikonomos of No. 4. One aspect of the bishop's or presbyter's duty, which was specially appreciated by the congregation, is emphasised and consecrated to memory (as has been mentioned on No. 2).

The date is early, as appears from the name Claudia, from the pseudo-praenomen Aur., from the use of the simpler term honourable (ἔντειμον) instead of the superlative τιμιώτατον (which occurs in No. 12, and was stereotyped before the time of Basil), and from the absence of all overtly ecclesiastical character. The epitaph is to be ranked along with that of Septimia Domna (see No. 16), and, like it, probably belongs to the third century. The oikonomissa in No. 22 is not earlier than the late fourth century.

---

[1] An example at Syracuse dated A.D. 416, *Röm. Quartalschr.*, 1896, p. 48.
[2] There are probably one or two letters lost in this name.

8. An unnoticed example of Oikonomos used simply as a title, implying probably presbyter or bishop as administrator of a village church, occurs in the district of Drya, the extreme northern bishopric of Lycaonia (united with Gdamava).

Gallikos the oikonomos of the people Plommeis.[1]

It would be quite contrary to analogy, and perhaps to the allowable possibilities of usage,[2] to take Gallicus here as a slave of the emperor stationed in this village (after a fashion illustrated for Laodicea and Zizima in *Classical Review*, Oct., 1905, p. 369).

The presbyters mentioned are very numerous. With regard to them we note that in many cases they were married. The number of cases where marriage is proved by mention of wife or children or both is so large, that this was evidently the ordinary custom in the Lycaonian congregations, and the unmarried presbyters were exceptional. Some of the inscriptions in which they are mentioned may perhaps be as early as the end of the third century : *e.g.*—

9. I Aur. Nestor erected this titlos to my sweetest father Callimachus, a Presbyter, in remembrance.

This is marked as early (1) by the formula ; (2) by the use of Aurelius as a *prænomen;* (3) by the term "titlos," which is frequent in inscriptions of the earlier type, and disappears from later epitaphs.

VI. The earliest known Christian inscription of Lycaonia is probably the following from Isaura Nova, published in *Studies in the Art and History of the Eastern Roman Pro-*

[1] Anderson, in *Journ. of Hell. Studies*, 1899, p. 124, No. 136. The symbols, basket on table and cooking-pot on a portable charcoal fireplace, which are shown under the inscription, are common on tombstones of the district, pagan and Christian alike. I have copied many examples. They point to a time not later than the fourth century.

[2] *Exactor reipublicæ Nacolensium*, C.I.L., iii., 349, is hardly a sufficient defence.

vinces, p. 22 ff., by Miss Ramsay, most of whose commentary is adopted here. This is one of the most interesting Christian

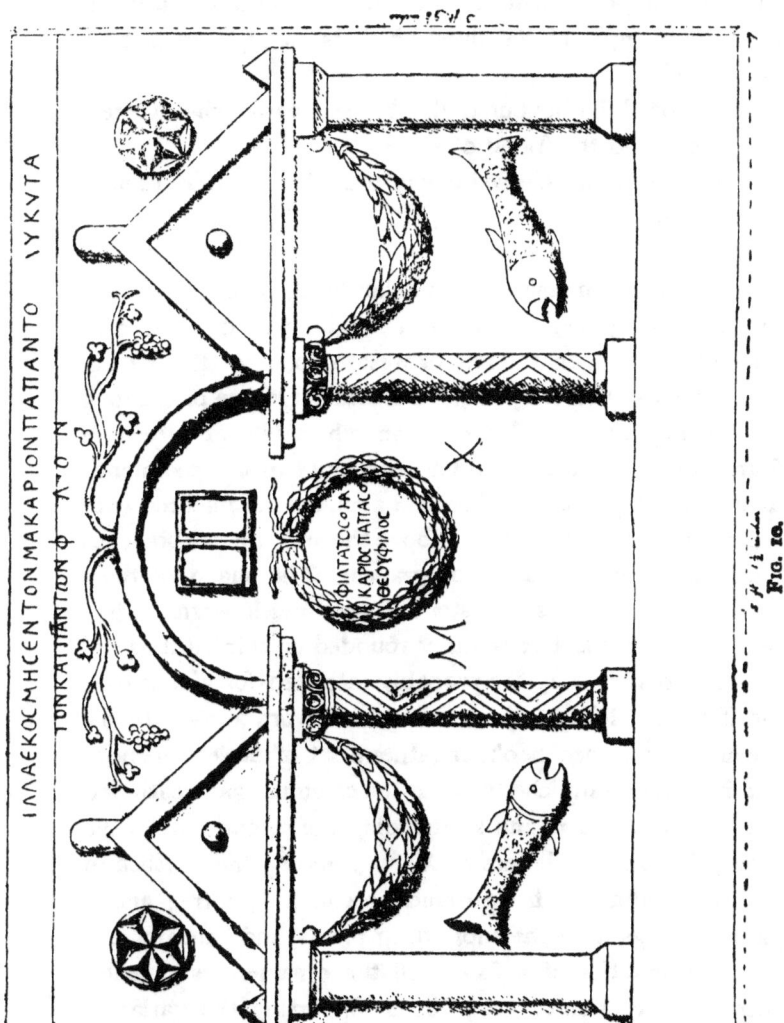

Fig. 10.

inscriptions that have as yet been discovered, coming after, though at a long interval, the recently discovered No. 1, and the epitaph of Avircius Marcellus. The ornamentation is the best example of the class, which is exemplified also by Nos. 11 ff.

10. [Non ?] illa honoured the blessed papas, the sweetest one and the friend of all.

Very dear is the blessed papas, the friend of God (Theophilus).

In remembrance.

The stone, a massive rectangular block 5 feet 1½ inches in length by 3 feet 9¼ inches in height, was discovered in 1901 on the hill on the left or western bank of the stream that flows through the village of Dorla. On one of the long sides is an architectural decoration, which takes the form of four columns supporting a round arch and two side pediments. The pillars supporting the central arch are ornamented with a pattern in incised lines, and above the arch are two branches with leaves and bunches of grapes. The shape of these leaves is doubtful, as the stone is very much worn. They seem to be trefoils, but whether rounded or pointed it is impossible to say: they are probably intended for vine-leaves, but if so, the delicate points have been worn away. Below the arch is an open book, or rather a set of tablets opened; and in the central niche between the columns is a wreath tied above with a ribbon, and surrounding the second part of the inscription, and the letters M X, for μνήμης χάριν. Each of the side pediments has a round boss in the centre; and a garland hangs from the supporting pillars, and beneath it is the representation of a fish. All the ornament is in relief, with the exception of the ribbons supporting the garlands, and the fins of the fish, which are merely incised. The larger part of the epitaph is inscribed above the ornament, close to the upper edge of the stone.

The tomb is evidently that of a bishop. In the expression the blessed papas (ὁ μακάριος πάπας), papas must be either the name or the title of the person buried there, probably the latter. Judging from the general character of Anatolian inscriptions, I came to the conclusion, in view of the stone in 1901, that it was not later than the second half of the third century, and that papas was the title. But this epitaph shows the remarkable peculiarity that the title supplants the actual name, in imitation of the pagan custom according to which a priest who became "hieronymos" (like the principal priests at Eleusis and in various of the great Anatolian cities) dropped his own name and was known simply by his title. This peculiarity is suggestive of a very early date; and that the stone is an early one, prior to the time of Constantine, is shown also by the lettering and by the general character of the epitaph and the ornament.

The title πάπας employed in this inscription is extremely interesting. It proves what was before probable, that this title was at first employed much more widely and was gradually restricted in use. The use of Papa to indicate the bishop in Roman inscriptions begins about A.D. 300, and from the sixth century it is confined to the Pope.[1] Dr. Harnack in *Berl. Sitzungsber.*, 1900, p. 990, points out that in the West Papa was, in early times, used only in Rome, but was there employed as the ordinary term for bishop, either of Rome, or of any other place. Tertullian uses it sarcastically of the

---

[1] Heraeus, *Archiv. für latein. Lexicogr.*, xiii., 157; De Rossi, *Inscr. Chr. Urb. Rom.*, i., p. cxv.; *Anth. Lat. Epigr.*, 656, 2; Cæsar, *de aet. tit. Christ.*, p. 65.

Roman bishop Callistus. In the East Harnack thinks it was used only in Egypt, and only of the Bishop of Alexandria, so that ὁ μακάριος πάπας was the recognised title of that bishop alone, while other Egyptian bishops were styled πατὴρ ἡμῶν. In the pre-Nicene period, as he says, the title πάπας is not known to have been used of any other Eastern bishop: but it was customary for the Alexandrian bishops from at least as early as 250. Only in the letter of Pseudo-Justin to Zenas and Serenus the title ὁ πάπας occurs. The phrase ὁ μακάριος πάπας is found several times during the third century in Egypt, and was a recognised title of the Bishop of Alexandria. This Isauran inscription shows that it was used also in Asia Minor during the same period. Dr. Sanday also quotes Gregory Thaumaturgus,[1] which implies that it was used in the province of Pontus about 250.

The name πάπας, applied to the priest of Malos Galatiae in Acta S. Theodoti, is quoted by a writer in *Anal. Boll.*, xxii., p. 327, as a proof that the document was not written by a contemporary, but belongs to a later age. In view of our inscription this argument falls to the ground, and the use of the term πάπας in that document is rather favourable to the view (advocated by the writer many years ago, and recently by Prof. Harnack and others) that the Acta S. Theodoti is a good document of early date.

The natural human feeling shown in the wording of the epitaph, "the sweetest one and friend of all" (τὸν γλυκύτατον καὶ πάντων φίλον), points to an early Christian period; the epithets applied to such persons as bishops afterwards became much more religious and stereotyped in character.

---

[1] *Ep.*, Canon i., οὐ τὰ βρώματα ἡμᾶς βαρεῖ, ἱερὲ (*v.l.* ἱερώτατε) πάπα (Routh, *Rell. Sacr.*, iii., 256).

Compare the tender expression, "dearer than light and life" (γλυκύτερον φωτὸς καὶ ζόης), applied by Aur. Xanthias to his son who died at the age of seven, in a Christian inscription of Rome, dated by the consuls of A.D. 238. The phrase πάντων φίλος is here used in an inscription which is undoubtedly Christian, and such moral sentiments are found on many Christian tombstones, but they cannot alone be taken as a proof of Christian origin.[1] In some cases similar sentiments were inscribed on non-Christian tombs as a counterblast to Christianity; these clearly belong to the pagan philosophical reaction.[2] It seems most probable that they were ordinarily Christian, and their occurrence on pagan stones is a proof of the strong influence which the new religion exerted even on its opponents. Another example is found in *Cities and Bishoprics of Phrygia*, ii., p. 386 f., No. 232. The expression πάντων φίλος occurs in an inscription of Tarsus, which may perhaps be restored [ἡ ψυχὴ ἐν] τῷ αἰῶνι ζῇ. Φωσφόρος ὁ πάντων φίλος κ.τ.λ.; the inscription continues in the ordinary style of epitaphs, though with some unusual features (published with some difference by Messrs. Heberdey and Wilhelm in *Wiener Akad. Denkschriften*, 1896, p. 5): it is evidently either Christian or of the reaction, when the aim was to show that paganism was superior to Christianity on its own lines. At Salonika τῷ πάντων φίλῳ Μυλάγῳ is probably pagan (*Mitth. Inst. Athen.*, 1896, p. 98).

Θεοῦ φίλος is probably a play on Theophilus, and thus reveals the real name of the bishop.

The fish, the common symbol of the Christians in the

---

[1] *Cities and Bishoprics of Phrygia*, ii., p. 495.
[2] Compare *Cities and Bishoprics of Phrygia*, ii., p. 506 f., and *Pauline and other Studies*, pp. 103-122.

early centuries, passed out of use at a comparatively early date, and the same is true of the open tablets which appear on this stone. This symbol occurs also on several North-Phrygian tombs, which were published in the *Expositor* in 1888 and 1905.

The character of the ornament on this stone also points to an early date, probably the third century A.D. It seems at first sight to be an earlier stage of the elaborate decoration common on Byzantine and Roman sarcophagi of the fourth century, a row of figures standing in niches, with highly intricate and elaborate tracery and architectural ornament. Here we have the semi-architectural schema, without the human figures. But, as one stone after another is discovered, we see that the schema is a traditional type in Nova Isaura, characteristic of the place, which is likely to have lasted for centuries, varied, but never essentially changed. The fact that it is a simpler stage of the fourth century sarcophagus style would not, taken alone, prove anything about date. But this monument is very much larger than the other Dorla monuments, and represents an attempt to improve upon and elaborate the native type. New elements are introduced on this tomb which are unknown on any of the other stones in Dorla; and yet it is indubitably among the very earliest of all the examples found in the village. This more ambitious style is a proof that more money, care, and work were spent on this stone. It was the tomb of an exceptional person (either through his wealth or through his rank), and it represented the highest stage of which local art was capable, elaborating the native schema by imported additions, especially the fish, that widespread symbol, which was certainly not invented in Nova Isaura, but introduced there from outside. Now, had this large and ambitious monument been built in the fourth century, it would probably have shown some of the Græco-Roman forms most characteristic of that time; taking into consideration the entire absence of those characteristic fourth century forms, and the fact that in the Dorla series this has all the appearance of being among the earliest, we must infer that it belongs to the third century. See on No. 11.

The ornament scattered liberally over the surface of the stone contains various elements; but none of these are necessarily borrowed from a formed Græco-Roman art. The fish was taken as a symbol, not as an artistic element, and is placed on the tomb to be significant, and not merely to be ornamental.

Other elements in the ornamentation, besides the fish, are almost certainly symbolical. The vine branch above the central pediment indicates that the bishop was a branch of the true vine, and the garland symbolises the crown of life. The open tablets, as has been pointed out in the *Expositor*, April, 1905, p. 296 f., are to be taken as representing the record of the covenant between God and man. It is there shown that the idea of the tablets is derived from Rev. v. 1 ff., and that "the book," which is mentioned in that passage, is really a set of double or triple tablets, with a document or covenant written in duplicate, one inside closed up, witnessed and sealed by seven witnesses, the other on the outside open and public (according to the usual Roman custom in regard to important business documents or wills). The book should be compared with the mosaic inscription of Naro in Africa (Hammam-Lif), *instrumenta servi tui*, on an open diploma: this inscription was in mosaic in a room beside the church, in which were kept the sacred books, etc. (*Rev. Arch.*, 1904, p. 368).

As is shown in this article, the Revelation is the one book of the New Testament which is often referred to in the Lycaonian inscriptions; and John is, next to Paul and Mirus (Wonderful), the commonest male name in those inscriptions during the fourth century.

It is probable that the six-leaved rosettes are also symbolical. The frequency of this rosette on Lycaonian Christian monuments, and the way in which it is sometimes employed, suggest that it is a modification of the early Christian monogram ✲, originally representing 'I ($\eta\sigma o \hat{v}s$) X ($\rho \iota \sigma \tau \acute{o} s$). See Nos. 5, 6.

Though a bishop is mentioned in this epitaph, the name Isaura never occurs in the Byzantine lists of bishoprics. It has been shown in an article on Lycaonia, published in the Austrian *Jahreshefte*, 1904, Part ii., that the two neighbouring towns, Isaura Nova and Korna, were bishoprics in early time, but were merged in the great autokephalos bishopric of Isaura Palaea, called Leontopolis, some time after 381, and probably at the same time that the name Leontopolis was given to Isaura, namely about 474. Basil himself, *Ep.* 190, dreaded this loss of independence "for the small states or villages which possess an Episcopal seat from ancient times," and in order to prevent it when the bishopric of Isaura Palaea was vacant about 374, he wrote to Amphilochius of Iconium and recommended the nomination of officials called προϊστάμενοι for the smaller towns or cities before a new bishop was appointed for Isaura. The grave of one of these officials at Alkaran, between Korna and Nova Isaura, is published in *Eastern Studies*, p. 29.

11. Nova Isaura (Miss Ramsay in *Eastern Studies*,[1] p. 35).

---

[1] This abbreviation is used here and below for the book quoted with fuller title in Nos. 10, 15.

Macer and Oa[s] and Anolis(?)[1] their sister adorned the bishop Mammas, friend to all men.

The ornamentation is similar in subject and arrangement to the preceding, but more conventional and therefore probably later. The object like a net between the columns on the right apparently represents one of the screens which are

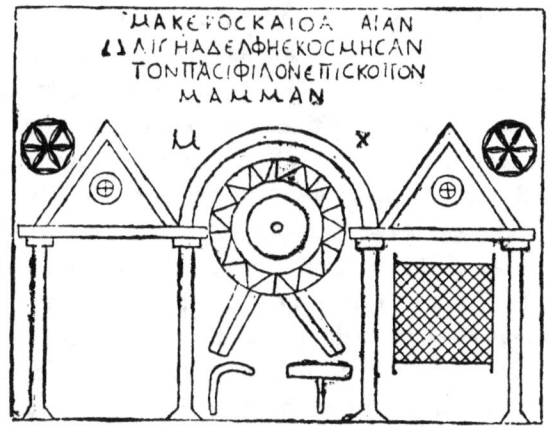

FIG. 11.

mentioned in the preceding commentary (No. 1): the screens at Tyre are described by Eusebius as being "made in net-fashion".[2] It might be possible to take the object here portrayed as a net, and to understand that the bishop is indicated symbolically as a fisher of men; but the architectural character of the ornamentation on the gravestones at Nova Isaura, and the skill of Isaurian masons,[3] make

[1] The names are all faint and uncertain.
[2] δικτυωτός.
[3] Their skill is described and proved by Professor Holl in *Hermes*, 1908, p. 242.

it practically certain that one of the wooden latticed screens used in the churches is here intended.

The origin of this symbol from the arrangement of the Christian church building, taken in connection with the architectural character of the Isauran scheme of decoration, makes it highly probable that this scheme has the same origin. We regard it as probable, therefore, that the typical Isauran decorative scheme on tombstones was suggested by some typical form of the Lycaonian Church, either the rounded arch of the apse between the two aisles, or the triple doorway at the west end with a round arch flanked by two pointed pediments.[1] The latter is perhaps the more probable. Some of the Isauran monuments show a pointed middle pediment between two round arches; and this might be explained as due to similar variety in the west doorways of churches. The weak point of the theory is that I cannot point to any example in the triple church doorways that remain; but these are all of much later date. The alternation of round and pointed occurs in a Roman building at Basilika Therma in Cappadocia, and also in theatres of the Roman period in Asia Minor (as Professor Strzygowski pointed out to me); and it may be quite plausibly supposed to have characterised the triple doors of early churches.[2]

The habitual use of wooden screens in the churches of central Asia Minor is, therefore, proved with certainty for the early fourth century and with probability for the third. These screens were made by piercing the wood with a sharp instrument called a *kenteterion*. The example shown on this

[1] Compare the Tyrian church door, p. 347, l. 13, and *Eastern Studies*, pp. 19-54. The pagan tomb was a temple, the Christian grave a church.

[2] Those who explain the scheme as originated by the interior view of the church with apse between aisles, will hold that the scheme with pointed middle is due to unintelligent variation of a form whose origin had been forgotten.

monument at Nova Isaura is very simple in kind, and might be made out of straight wooden staves; but the *kenteseis* of No. 1 probably imply a more elaborate kind of work. The importance of this fact about the use of woodwork in early churches appears, when one remembers the influence exerted on the development of art in later Roman times by oriental woodwork, as shown by Strzygowski (see especially his *Rom oder Orient*, a highly suggestive and truly *bahnbrechend* work, though with the faults that inevitably belong to a book of the pioneer type). In later churches we have found in several cases stone screens instead of wooden. Wood was scanty and expensive on the open plateau generally; but both Laodicea and Nova Isaura were close under hills where trees grew and wood was cheaper.

There was also an ornament between the left-hand pair of columns, but it has been carefully obliterated in modern times. The crosses placed so inconspicuously in the two pointed pediments might pass for mere ornament among pagans, while they would be significant to the initiated. Such was the character of early Christian epitaphs.[1] On the later gravestones the symbolism is more patent and unconcealed.

The use of the screen as a symbol might at first sight suggest a date about 330-350, when screens are mentioned in the churches at Laodicea (close at hand) and Tyre. But in all probability the use of screens in churches was of older origin, and characterised the pre-Diocletian Church as much as the post-Diocletian. The epithet of the bishop is not of the style which was usual in the fourth-century writers, but of an earlier kind. The concealed crosses strongly suggest the third century; and this date agrees well with the nomen-

---

[1] *Cities and Bishoprics of Phrygia*, ii., p. 502.

clature. The rustic symbols, mattock and sickle, are also of an early character. On the other hand the ornamentation is so exactly similar to that of No. 12 (an epitaph which distinctly belongs to about A.D. 350), that the two cannot be far removed from one another in date. We incline therefore to assign to the period A.D. 310-330 this monument.

The crown or garland in the central pediment was doubtless also symbolical.

The descriptive epithet "friend to all" ("friend of all" in No. 10), while it is in a sense a summary of a chapter in the *Apostolic Constitutions*, ii., 20, on the duties of the bishop, belongs to an earlier time than the stereotyped formulæ of honour assigned to ecclesiastical officials in the writings of the fourth century authors and in the epitaphs of that period. It was used in the pagan reaction A.D. 303-313,[1] and was therefore in older Christian use. Accordingly, we cannot assume that this epitaph is older than A.D. 303; but we can confidently believe that it is not very much later.

12. Nova Isaura (Miss Ramsay in *Eastern Studies*, p. 37).

> The most honourable deacon Tabeis, Nanna his mother and Valgius and Lucius his brothers, adorned (him) i(n) r(emembrance).

There is evidently no long interval between this monument and No. 10. Both were probably made in the same workshop. The screen (represented here in slightly different fashion) and the bent cross, are both Christian symbols. The latter is frequent on Isaurian Christian tombstones (p. 385). The formula of styling the deacon τειμώτατος is quite in the developed fashion, which was usual in fourth-century writers such as Basil.

13. Somewhat later than No 11, but probably earlier than

---

[1] See above, p. 375.

No. 12, and therefore of the period 290-320, is the following:—

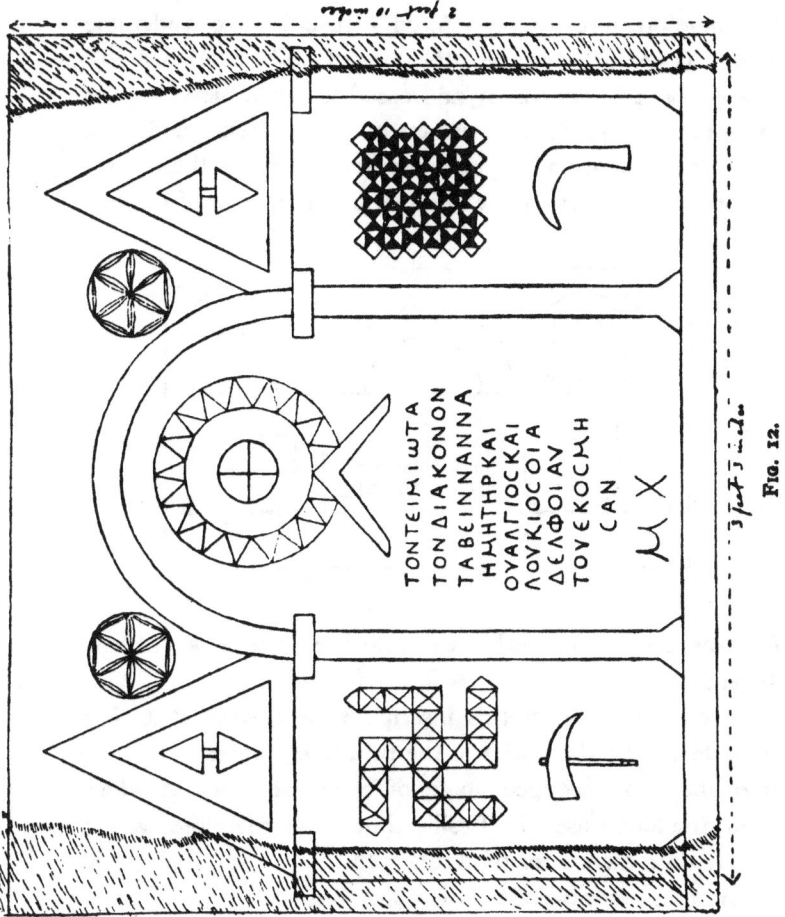

Fig. 12.

Nova Isaura (Miss Ramsay in *Eastern Studies*, p. 30). The very pure and sweet-voiced and with-all-virtue-adorned Sisamoas, bishop.

The epithets here differ from, yet have a distinct analogy to, those used of the bishop by Basil of Cæsarea about 370: the epithets are there quite conventional and stereotyped, and had therefore already been fixed in use for a considerable time. Take for example "the most God-beloved Bishop," ὁ θεοφιλέστατος ἐπίσκοπος, addressed as "your piety," "your perfection," "your God-fearing-ness," "your divine and most perfect consideration," "your comprehension":[1] these have all come to be used as polite designations and forms of address.

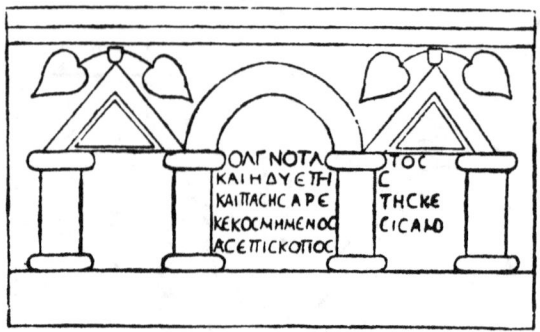

FIG. 13.

Contrast these forms with the simple direct expression of Nos. 10 and 11.

By comparison with this inscription we observe that Nos. 2, 4, describing the duties of the presbyter, present to us the free and unstereotyped stage of expression, out of which grew the forms used in Basil's time; and therefore we can hardly date them later than A.D. 350.

Another example of an early bishop is—

[1] Basil, *Ep.* 181 (dated A.D. 374), ἡ εὐλάβεια σου (frequent), ἡ σὴ τελειότης (172), ἡ θεοσέβεια σου (167), ἡ ἔνθεος καὶ τελειοτάτη φρόνησίς σου (141), ἡ σύνεσις σου (165). A presbyter, on the other hand, is simply "your perfect consideration," ἡ τελεία φρόνησίς σου, or "honoured head," τιμία κεφαλή (156).

14. Yuruk-Keui, near the base of the Kara Dagh.

Apas son of Kouanzaphees erected to his brother Indakos, bishop, just, beloved, in his own life-time and for himself, in remembrance.[1]

(Symbol.) (Leaf.) (Garland.) (Leaf.) (Symbol.)[2]

This unpublished inscription, found in 1905 between Nova Isaura, Derbe and Barata, is of the early class. The bishop who is here mentioned was indubitably a mere village-bishop (probably under Barata) or χωρεπίσκοπος of the fourth or even the third century.

15 and 16. Alkaran near Nova Isaura (Miss Ramsay in *Studies in the History of the Eastern Provinces*, p. 33).

Aur(elia) Domna sweetest daughter, who persevered in virginity and industry: her father, Aur(elius) Orestianus, son of Cyrus (honoured her with the sepulchral monument). *See Figure on* p. 328.

The scheme of ornament is the architectural type common in this Isauran region (see No. 10). The two doves, one holding a leaf in its mouth (Genesis viii. 11), are undoubtedly symbolical, and would alone be enough to prove the religion, which is also clearly indicated in the words of the epitaph. The doves are incised, and were added later (doubtless after purchase of the stone from the artist): the rest of the ornament is in relief. The bent cross, or swastika, occurs very frequently on Isaurian Christian gravestones.[3] On the dove, compare No. 19.

Beside the tombstone of Aurelia Domna was found the

---

[1] Ἀπᾶς Κουανζαφέους ἀνέστησεν ἀδελφῷ αὐτοῦ Ἰνδάκῳ ἐπισκόπῳ δικέῳ ἀγαφητῷ ζῶν κὲ ἑαυτοῦ μ.χ. The misspelling of ἀγαπητός is usual.

[2] The " symbols " in this line were defaced: they were enclosed within circles, and were probably either crosses or six-leaved rosettes.

[3] Sterrett, *Wolfe Expedition*, Nos. 56, 93, 220; and scores of other examples, then unknown to him, have been discovered since.

epitaph of "[L?] Septimia Domna, the sweetest and holiest wife" of [Aurelius?] Orestes, son of Cyrus. The two stones belonged to a family cemetery; and evidently were not very far removed in date from one another. L? Septimia Domna was almost certainly born about A.D. 200. The use of Aurelius as a sort of prænomen [1] began about A.D. 212, when the provincials were elevated to Roman citizenship by the Emperor Aurelius Caracalla. It lasted about a century. Hence Aurelia Domna may have died about the end of the third or the beginning of the fourth century. Her gravestone may be dated between No. 10 and No. 12. It is not so stereotyped as the latter, but it wants the freedom of No. 10.

The name Orestianos perhaps indicates a generation later than Orestes. Septimia, the wife of Orestes, might be by marriage the aunt of Orestianos, the father of Aurelia Domna. It is, however, not impossible that Cyrus had two sons, Orestes and Orestianos,[2] and that Septimia was the aunt of Aurelia Domna. Either supposition would suit the date suggested by the art, though the latter would tend to make No. 15 a little earlier than the former. There is nothing indicative of religion on the tombstone of Septimia Domna;[3] but the family was probably Christian. It was characteristic of the earlier period that the religion should not be obtrusively mentioned.

It cannot be inferred from the remarkable language of this epitaph that Aurelia Domna was officially a virgin ($\pi\alpha\rho\theta\acute{\epsilon}\nu o\varsigma$) in the church. But the Christian character is unmistakable in the phrase "persevering in virginity". See No. 29 ff.

[1] *Studies in the History of the Eastern Provinces*, p. 355. The custom is a Greek fashion, not true to Roman usage. The use of Aurelius as a *nomen* was, of course, older, and is found in the whole period 160-300 A.D.

[2] In that case Cyrus would be son of an older Orestes.

[3] The ornamentation is two rosettes and three leaves.

The "industry" which is also attributed to her was undoubtedly in the feminine arts of spinning and household work, which are often indicated on gravestones by the proper implements, distaff and spindle, pots and pans, tripod for supporting them, etc. In one inscription these are called the "works of Athena" (*Studies in the Eastern Prov.*, p. 70).

VII. The distinction between clergy and laity as separate orders is clearly marked in the Lycaonian inscriptions, hardly indeed in the earliest class, but certainly in those which may on our view be placed soon after the middle of the fourth century. The popular use of the term *hiereus* to designate a bishop or presbyter probably marks the full and general recognition of this distinction between the clergy and the ordinary congregation; and the correlative term *laos*, to indicate the laity, must have come into use at the same time.[1] It is true that the words were in Christian use from the beginning; but not hardened in the technical sense of contrasted orders of society. The distinction, however, is older than Basil.

The Anatolian inscriptions in which either term occurs seem generally to be as late as the fifth century; though some may perhaps be as early as the second half of the fourth. The fact that the term *hiereus* is much rarer in these inscriptions than *presbyteros* affords an argument that we have been right in placing a large number of the epitaphs before A.D. 350.

Further, any inscription which plainly neglects or is ignorant of the distinction between priest and laity is to be dated earlier than A.D. 350; and inscriptions or documents in which the occupation of the presbyter is mentioned are likely also to be earlier than that time.

[1] See an inscription of Northern Phrygia, given in the *Expositor*, Oct., 1888, p. 261.

17 and 18. Zazadin Khan (Cronin in *Journal of Hellenic Studies*, 1902, p. 361).

Two epitaphs from an ancient village beside the very interesting early Turkish building, Zazadin Khan, twelve miles north-east of Iconium, show the same metrical form applied to two *hiereis* or priests of the village. The lines were therefore a standing formula for epitaphs of priests.

> Here lies a man, priest of great God, who on account of gentleness gained heavenly glory, snatched hastily from Church and congregation, having the name Apollinarius [in the other case, Gregory], great glory of the congregation.

The formula, "here lies," is of later type than the epitaphs in which the maker of the tomb is mentioned; it is a mere translation of the Latin *hic jacet*, and marks the spread of Roman custom in the Greek-speaking districts of the East. Probably no example of it in Christian Anatolian use can be safely dated earlier than the fourth century.

One of the two epitaphs, that of Gregory, has two additional lines, worse in syntax and expression than the four stereotyped verses, and hardly intelligible: perhaps

> "A man who was a care to God through joyousness; E[lpidio?]s erected the stele and thus inscribed on the tomb."[1]

Here the older form of epitaph, mentioning the maker of the tomb, makes itself felt at the end, implying that that class was not yet forgotten or wholly out of date. In accordance with the principles on which we are working, it

---

[1] Rev. H. S. Cronin in *Journal of Hellenic Studies*, 1902, p. 362, No. 126; but I should prefer now to restore a proper name at the beginning of the fifth hexameter, E[. . .]s. The formula, so-and-so ἀνέστησεν the deceased, is common in Lycaonia.

would be impossible to place this inscription later than about 400 A.D. Now the formula of the first four lines was not composed for Gregory, but taken from an already stereotyped epitaph suitable for any priest; and when the composer of Gregory's epitaph tried to add something distinctive in the last two lines he sank to a much lower level and became almost unintelligible. The metrical formula, therefore, was a rather early composition, perhaps not later than 350, like several others in the same region.[1] No. 4, a metrical epitaph, probably contains the verb ἱέρευεν in l. 2, which would presuppose the use of the noun *hiereus*. Thus we can push back the popular use of the term *hiereus* in Lycaonia as far at least as about 350 A.D.

There is, of course, no difficulty in supposing that the distinction between priest and laity (ἱερεύς and λαός) was even older than this: the words are taken from the language of the Septuagint. Already in A.D. 218 an expression (quoted by Eusebius, *Hist. Eccles.*, vi., 19, 18) is found where the congregation (λαός) is set over against the bishop: the distinction is here latent though not explicit. At the same time it is certain that priests even late in the fourth century ordinarily lived by practising some trade, as Basil, *Ep.* 198, says, "the majority of them ply sedentary crafts, whereby they get their daily bread".

Another example of the relation of Hiereus and Presbyteros may be quoted—

19. Iconium (Cronin in *Journal of Hellenic Studies*, 1902, p. 124). Four rough hexameters.

Gourdos, good man, sleeps here like a dove. He was
    among men priest (*hiereus*) of the Most High God.

---

[1] For example, No. 25 of the New-Isauran inscriptions published by Miss Ramsay in *Eastern Studies*, p. 47.

To him Trokondas, his successor and comrade, made a stele in memory, doing him honour on his tomb.

(A Cross in relief on each side of the epitaph.)

Trokondas is called the comrade (ὁπάων) of the deceased; but the word, like the Latin *comes*, implies indubitably inferiority in position. Trokondas was probably a Deacon and Gourdos was his Bishop or Presbyter. The same Gourdos, perhaps, is mentioned in another inscription—

20. Aur. Gourdos, a Presbyter, erected (the tomb of) Tyrannos his adopted son (or foundling son) in remembrance (Sterrett, *Epigr. Journey*, No. 197).

The latter epitaph has all the marks of the earliest class of Lycaonian epitaphs; and it might very well be twenty or even forty years earlier than the former, which was engraved on the tomb of Gourdos. The omission of the praenomen Aur. in the former is no proof of diversity in the person: both because this praenomen is frequently found omitted and inserted in different references to the same person,[1] and because the epitaph of Gourdos is in hexameter verse, in which proper names were always treated more freely. The unusual name Gourdos (never elsewhere found) is not likely to have occurred twice in the case of a Presbyter and a Hiereus at Iconium during one century. The Presbyter and the Hiereus were assuredly the same person.

The epitaph of Gourdos is interesting in several respects. It unites the old formula with the new; "here sleeps" is a mere poetic variation of "here lies," while the concluding lines name the maker of the tomb. The occurrence of the old formula at the end in addition to the later formula at the beginning has been regarded above as belonging to the transition period, before the old formula had been forgotten;

---

[1] See *Studies in the History of the Eastern Provinces*, p. 355.

and most of the cases where the old and the new are united are in metrical epitaphs which seem to belong to the period A.D. 340-370.

The comparison to the dove is suggested by the type found (sometimes in relief, sometimes incised) on many tombstones of Lycaonia. One example from Isaura Nova is given as No. 15.

21. An inscription which must cause some hesitation is—
Papas and Gaius, sons of Titus Lorentius, to their father *hiereus* and Mania their mother *hierissa* in remembrance.[1]

I published this at first as an ordinary pagan inscription; but, since subsequently published epitaphs have shown that *hiereus* and *archiereus* came into ordinary use in Lycaonian epigraphy as technical Christian terms, it seems more probable that here we have a Christian epitaph involving the distinction between clergy and laity. The bare words *hiereus* and *hierissa* seem not to be in keeping with a pagan epitaph. In pagan usage a *hiereus* belonged to the worship of one deity, and as a rule either the name of the god to whom the *hiereus* belonged was expressed, or the context or situation left no doubt as to what deity and cult the *hiereus* was attached. At one of the great sanctuaries (*Hiera*) of Anatolia, where a single supreme priest stood at the head of the college of priests as representative of the god, it would be natural and was quite common to state a date "in the time when Noumenios was priest" without mentioning in any part of the document the deity or the cult; but the situation and facts in that case left no doubt, for dating was practised only according to the one supreme priest. Similarly, *archiereus* is often used absolutely, be-

---
[1] Laodicea, No. 7 (*Athen. Mittheil.*, 1888, p. 237).

cause it was a perfectly distinctive term, inasmuch as there was only one *archiereus* in the city or district. But the use of the bare terms *hiereus* and *hierissa* in an ordinary pagan epitaph in a city where there must have been many priests and *hierissai* seems so contrary to custom and difficult of understanding that it cannot be admitted with our present knowledge. Yet it is perhaps strange that T. Lorentius (popular pronunciation of Laurentius) and Mania were priest and priestess, perhaps a bishop and his wife, in Laodicea not later than about 360 A.D.

The explanation of these difficulties possibly is that this inscription belongs either to the pagan reaction A.D. 303-311, or to the time of Julian, A.D. 363-365, when something similar occurred. There was then a tendency to model pagan institutions, epitaphs, etc., on the established Christian usages; and we may suppose that the distinction of priest and laity was like many other Christian customs caught up by the pagan revivalists.[1]

It would certainly be impossible to take *hierissa* in this epitaph as indicating a special official position in the Church. If the inscription is Christian, *hierissa* can only mean "wife of a priest". This might, perhaps, be best explained as belonging to a quite early stage, when terminology was not properly settled and understood, and when the pagan custom, that man and wife should hold the offices of high-priest and high-priestess,[2] was still not forgotten. It seems, however, to have a parallel in No. 4, l. 15.

22. The interpretation might be defended by an inscription of Isaura Nova. (Miss Ramsay in *Journal of Hellenic Studies*, 1904, p. 283).

[1] On this most interesting phase of religion, which has never been properly studied, see a paper in *Pauline and other Studies*, p. 103 ff.
[2] See *Classical Review*, Nov., 1905, p. 417.

Doxa Oikonomeissa the revered (σεμνή).

In this case also it is improbable that oikonomissa indicated a special official position in the Church. It may perhaps be interpreted "wife of an oikonomos".[1] But perhaps the oikonomissa may have been an official in a nunnery. This epitaph is of the later type which probably began about A.D. 360; and there may have been a convent at Isaura Nova as early as A.D. 400.

Similarly, Presbyterissa would perhaps have to be taken as the wife of a Presbyter; but its occurrence is uncertain. The index of the *Corpus* of Greek inscriptions quotes it from No. 8624; but it depends there on a restoration, which is quite incorrect and unjustified by the copy. The Lexicon of Stephanus quotes it once, but the place does not bear on our purpose. If the inscriptions, which name many Presbyters and their wives, never use the term Presbyterissa, this would go far to show that a Presbyter's wife did not share his title in Lycaonia. See p. 365.

VIII. These cases suggest the question whether Diakonissa in the inscriptions of Lycaonia may mean simply the wife of a Diakonos, and not an official. In one case two sons raise the tomb to their mother Nonna, Diakonissa.[2] Another would probably be a test case, but the language is so ungrammatical as to be practically unintelligible. It is the epitaph of two persons, styled the excellent (and) blessed (dead), Flavius Alexander and Amia Diakonissa, belonging probably to the latter part of the fourth century, or the early fifth.[3] Here Alexander and Amia are certainly hus-

---

[1] Oikonomos is used as feminine (like Diakonos for Diakonissa) in the long metrical epitaph of Nestor the Presbyter and Oikonomos, No. 4. The wife of Nestor is there styled Oikonomos, like her husband.

[2] Anderson in *Journal of Hellenic Studies*, 1899, p. 130, No. 155.

[3] Anderson, *ibid.*, 1898, p. 126, No. 89.

band and wife. Alexander has no official title; but the doubt remains whether the omission is due merely to helplessness and inadvertence, the uneducated composer having a vague idea that the title Diakonissa might imply also that the husband had corresponding rank. If that could be assumed, the case would be conclusive that the official title of the husband was communicated to the wife. But it is more probable that Alexander held no office, and Amia was deaconess in her own right.

Less uncertainty attaches to another case.

23. Zazadin Khan (Cronin in *Journal of Hellenic Studies*, 1902, p. 359).

> Quintus, son of Heraklios, headman of the village, with his wife Matrona and his children Anicetus and Catillus, all four lie here in the tomb; and the wife of Anicetus, Basilissa, a diakonos, constructed the pleasing [1] tomb along with her only son Nemetorius, still an infant.[2]

Here the husband Anicetus has no title, and we cannot suppose that the title of Basilissa implied his official position. We must assume that she was deaconess during the life of her husband, who held no official rank. The tomb was evidently erected immediately after his death. Considering that marriages were ordinarily entered on at an early age, we must regard it as probable that Basilissa was still young when she made the grave.

24. In confirmation of the previous epitaphs showing that a deaconess was sometimes wife of a person who held no office in the Church, we may quote Laodicea, No. 65 :—

---

[1] ἀρεστός, not ἄριστος.

[2] Basilissa is called διάκονος, not διακόνισσα, perhaps for euphony; but the form diakonos often occurs where no such reason is possible.

Here lies Appas, the Reader (the younger tall son of Faustinus), to whom his mother Aurelia Faustina the Deaconess erected this heroön [1] in remembrance.

From these examples we must generalise the principle that in Lycaonia diakonissa (or diakonos in feminine) always denoted an official in the Church; and from the number of cases that occur, we must conclude that there were deaconesses as a rule in every congregation.

IX. An interesting little epitaph is the following from Tyriaion:—

25. Here lies (*sic!*) Heraklius and Patricius and Polykarpus Presbyters: in remembrance.

It is remarkable to find three presbyters in a common grave. The reason may probably be that they perished together in a persecution (like the five Phrygian "children, who at one occasion gained the lot of life": *Cities and Bish. of Phr.*, ii., p. 730); if so, their death might perhaps be placed during the last persecution, somewhere near A.D. 300; but, as that would carry the initial formula back further than we have hitherto put it, we must regard the point as uncertain. There is, of course, no reason why the Latin formula should not have been imitated in Lycaonia as early as A.D. 300.

X. The criterion by which in Phrygia many early Christian inscriptions reveal their religion—the concluding curse against the violator of the tomb in some such form as "he shall have to reckon with God" [2]—is almost entirely wanting in Lycaonia, where such imprecations are rarely appended to epitaphs. One example is published by Mr.

---

[1] *Athen. Mittheil.*, xiii., p. 254. Read ἀνήγιρε[ν] for ἀνηγιρ[θ]η: the two letters ЄH are better read thus: the formula is thus more typical.

[2] ἔσται αὐτῷ πρὸς τὸν θεόν.

Cronin from the copy of a Greek physician, Mr. Savas Diamantides, ending with the words, "Whosoever shall force an entrance, shall give account to God ".[1] The exact provenance of this epitaph is uncertain; but other examples occur in northern Lycaonia; and there can therefore be no doubt that in the region which was most immediately under the influence of Iconian Christianity, several varieties of this kind of Christianised imprecation were at one time in use. The reason why it was far commoner in Phrygia than in Lycaonia must be that it was an early formula, which passed into disuse in the fourth century. The Lycaonian inscriptions, therefore, which belong as a rule to the fourth century, rarely use it; some of the Lycaonian epitaphs in which it occurs belong beyond all doubt to that century, proving that it lingered on in a sporadic way.

26. Another example of the curse against violators of the tomb is the following from Laodicea, No. 45[2]:—

> The priest (hiereus) of the Trinity, Hesychius, wise, true, faithful worker . . . and if any one shall lay another in the tomb, he shall render judicial account to the living Judge.

The opening formula is of the later class, the allusion to a priest of the Trinity is of the developed ecclesiastical type, and the simple cross at the beginning is not early; and yet the concluding expression cannot be placed with any probability later than about A.D. 400, as this originally pagan, and in the strict sense non-Christian, habit of curse seems to be inconsistent with developed Christian custom, which

---

[1] δώσει θεῷ λόγον, *Journ. Hell. Stud.*, 1902, p. 354.

[2] *Athen. Mittheil.*, xiii., p. 249, ὁ τῆς Τριάδος ἱερὺς (!) Ἡσύχιος σοφὸς ἀληθὴς πιστὸς ἐργάτης . π . . ω, Μ[η]νόφιλος [τε . . . . . .]. ἤ τις δ' ἕτερον ἐπενβάλῃ τῷ τάφῳ κριτῇ τῷ ζῶντι λόγον ἔνδικον πο[ι]ή[σει. Iambics are rare in epitaphs: the last word is doubtful.

no longer set such value on the inviolability of the grave.

27. Another example, probably of the same period, occurs at Laodicea (No. 18) :—

——, son of Valerianus, quaestor, erected the inscription, while still living, to my sweetest wife Flavia Sosanna and my foster-child Sophronia in remembrance: if any one shall put another in (the tomb), he shall give account to God.

28. Here may be given in the way of contrast a developed Christian form of curse, from a rock in Phrygia near the site of Leontos Kephalai (see p. 140). It was copied by Professor Garstang of Liverpool. It belongs to a later time and style than the Lycaonian epitaphs. There is a large cross at the beginning.[1]

May he [who disturbs the tomb], and the accomplice privy to the act, and . . . have the curse of the three hundred and eighteen fathers.

The 318 fathers were the bishops present at the first Council of Nice, A.D. 325; but the use of the curse is distinctly later than the holding of the Council. It is remarkable that in Phrygia the Christian inscriptions are for the most part either very early or quite late. There is a marked absence of fourth century epitaphs; and the reason for this is found in the virulence with which Diocletian's persecution was carried out in Phrygia (*Cities and Bish.*, ii., p. 505). In Lycaonia, for some reason or other, probably the difference of character in the governor of the Province Pisidia, the persecution was apparently much less severe (see p. 345).

XI. A small series of inscriptions relates to that interesting

---

[1] νὰ ἔχῃ τὸν [τρ]ηακοσήον κὲ ὀκτὸ κὲ δέκα [π]ατ[έρο]ν τὸ ἀνάθεμαν ὁ . . . κ(ὲ) ἐπηαστήμονος κὲ. . . . The Greek is bad and late.

but enigmatical institution in the early Church, the Parthenoi or Virgins. One of these was found at Drya.[1]

29. Aur. Matrona (daughter) of Strabo, to her own daughter, a Virgin, Douda, erected in remembrance.

The name Matrona occurs not infrequently in Christian Lycaonian inscriptions. It is not in keeping with ancient custom that the epithet Parthenos should be added in a pagan inscription in prose simply to show that Douda died unmarried; I know nothing to justify such an opinion. The word must be taken in the ecclesiastical sense.

30. The following inscription of Laodicea (found at Serai-Inn in 1904) is probably of the late fourth century:—

Here has been laid to rest she who was kind to mortals and beauteous in form, by name Zoe, whom all held in great honour; and to her a tomb was built by her husband and also by her sister, Varelianos with Theosebia, very pious Virgin, a memory of the generation of men, for that is the privilege of the dead.[2]

The abbreviation of an already stereotyped epithet, εὐλαβ(εῖ) or εὐλαβ(εστάτῃ), proves that "Virgin" must here be taken in its technical sense as an ecclesiastical term. The prose epithet, "friend of all," which is characteristic of Christian epitaphs,[3] is here transformed for

---

[1] The most northern town of Lycaonia. The epitaph is published in *Journ. of Hell. Studies*, 1899, p. 121 (Anderson).

[2] ἐνθάδε κεκήδευτε φιλόβροτος ἀγλαόμορφος
οὔνομα (δὲ) Ζόη τὴν περτίεσκον ἄπαντες
τῇ δ' ἄρα τύνβον ἔδιμαν ἐὸς πόσις ἠδ' ἅμ' ἀδελφή,
Οὐαρελιανὸς σὺν Θεοσεβίῃ εὐλαβ. παρθένῳ,
μνήμην ἀνδρῶν γενέης, τὸ γὰρ γέρας ἐστί θανόντων.
In l. 2 δέ was omitted by fault of composer or engraver; but the metre requires it. In l. 1 δ was inserted, but the metre rejects it.

[3] See above, p. 375.

metrical reasons into the much poorer term "kind to mortals".

The date of this inscription is proved, also, both by the late formula, and by the shape of the stone, which I have observed only in the later Christian tombs: it is not a simple stele of the earlier class with pointed or rounded or square top, but one with a rude resemblance to a Herm, with circular head springing from broad shoulders. On the headpiece is incised an ornament like a six-leaved rosette, which was probably understood by the Christians as an elaboration of the old monogrammatic symbol ✶, *i.e.* ’Ι(ησοῦς) Χ(ριστός); yet the occurrence of the older formula in l. 3 makes it unsafe to date the tomb later than 370 or 380, on the principles which we have been following. Although the technical term εὐλαβ. in abbreviation is a mark of lateness, yet it cannot be doubted that Basil would have written in that way; and we may safely admit that the usage may have been practised as early as A.D. 375, in epigraphy as well as in handwriting.

A third is one of a pair found at Laodicea:—

31, 32. Gaius Julius Patricius erected to my sweetest aunt Orestina, who lived in continence,[1] in remembrance.

Gaius Julius Patricius erected this inscription to my dearest brother Mnesitheos in remembrance.

This pair of inscriptions on one stone is certainly early. The letters are fine and good, the formula is of the earlier class, and the full Roman name seems to have disappeared from popular use in this region during the fourth century. The widening of the area of Roman citizenship by Caracalla about 212, by giving every free man a right to the Roman

[1] ἐνκρατευσαμένη (*Ath. Mittheil.*, 1888, p. 272). Compare No. 16 above.

citizenship and the full Roman name, destroyed its distinctiveness and honourable character.

XII. It would not be safe to regard the word ἐνκρατευσαμένη here as necessarily a proof that Orestina stood apart from the Orthodox and Catholic Church, or was connected with any definite Enkratite sect or system. The use of the word ἐνκράτεια twice in the long metrical epitaph of the Presbyter Nestor, quoted below, shows clearly that no extravagant asceticism is implied by these terms, for in one case the quality is ascribed to the Presbyter's wife. But the following hitherto unpublished epitaph found near Laodicea shows that there was in that city a congregation of sectarian character, probably with Enkratite tendencies, and it may well be that Orestina belonged to that congregation.

33. Doudousa, daughter of Menneas, son of Gaianos, who became He(gou)menos of the holy and pure Church of God, to Aur. Tata my much beloved daughter and only child erected this tombstone, and of myself in my lifetime in remembrance.[1]

Here beyond all question Doudousa is described (regardless of gender) as the Hegoumenos of the holy pure Church of God. She seems to have been one of those female leaders of unorthodox religious movements, so many of whom are known in Asia Minor, from the lady of Thyatira (Rev. ii. 20) downwards. It is hardly possible to regard a female leader as belonging to the Orthodox Church; and the epithet "pure" applied to the Church in which she was a leader

---

[1] Δούδουσα, θυγάτ[ηρ Μ]εννέου Γα[ιανοῦ ?, γειν]αμένη ἱ(γού)μενος τῆς ἀγείας [κὲ] καθαρᾶς τοῦ θ(εο)ῦ ἐκλησείας, Αὐρ. Τάτᾳ τῇ πολυποθεινοτάτῃ κὲ μονογενῇ μου θυγατρὶ ἀνέστησα τὴν ἰστήλην ταύτην κὲ ἑαυτῆς ζῶσα μνήμης χάριν. The title ἰμενος, though not marked as an abbreviation (whereas θῦ is), can hardly be for anything except ἡγούμενος: the masculine form is remarkable.

seems perhaps to lay more emphasis on the ascetic tendency than the orthodox opinion approved.

"The Holy Church of God" is an expression that shows the fully formed ecclesiastical expression, and can hardly be dated earlier than the latter part of the fourth century. Its first employment as a common phrase cannot be placed later than A.D. 400, and is probably earlier, for we find it in an inscription copied by Hamilton (*C.I.G.*, 9268).

> 34. Aurelia Domna erected to my sweetest husband Tinoutos, the very pious deacon of the Holy Church of God of the Novatians, in remembrance.

The formula is of the early type. The *prænomen* Aur. is used, and the name Novatians in open use implies a date at least earlier than A.D. 420, when the sect and the name were proscribed. I should confidently regard this inscription as older than A.D. 340.

35. In 324-5 Gregory, father of the more famous Gregory Nazianzus, was converted from the sect of the Hypsistarii to the Orthodox Church. The sect took its name from its worship of the Most High God alone ($\theta\epsilon\grave{o}\varsigma\ \H{v}\psi\iota\sigma\tau\varsigma$); it is said to have adored light and fire, but to have used neither sacrifice nor images of God, to have kept the Sabbath and certain rules of clean and unclean foods, but not to have practised circumcision. Gregory of Nyssa about 380 speaks of a sect Hypsistianoi, who adored the one God, styling him Hypsistos or Pantokrator, but not Father.[1] Neither sect (if they are two sects, and not one) can be traced in that precise form outside of Cappadocia. About them we have only the untrustworthy account contained in the brief allusions of two of their opponents, whose hatred for

---

[1] *Contra Eunom.*, ed. Migne, vol. ii., p. 482 ff. Pantokrator is used in No. 1.

the Hypsistianoi makes it difficult to regard what they say as a fair account.

It is possible that the inscriptions of Iconium may throw some light on this obscure sect. There is every probability that a Cappadocian sect should spread also into Lycaonia, for there is no natural line of demarcation in the dead level plain where the frontier of the two Provinces lay. The epitaph quoted on p. 389 may commemorate a priest or bishop of the sect. At any rate it probably originated in circumstances similar to those which produced the Cappadocian sect. Gourdos is in that epitaph called "priest of the most high God";[1] but the style and character of the document seems to permit no doubt that it is Christian and did not emanate from a half-pagan, half-Jewish eclectic sect, such as the two Gregories describe. It is probable that their denial of the Christian character of the sect was merely the result of prejudice and ill-feeling, and that the Iconian epitaph is a fairer and safer witness to the character of the Hypsistarii than the malignant account of ecclesiastical enemies. If our opinion be not correct, the only alternative probably is that the epitaph originated in ordinary Christian circles, where the Cappadocian sect was unknown and where the typical epithet (which in Cappadocia would have proved the sect) was used as a right and orthodox term, occurring often in the Bible. But see No. 36.

36. A second epitaph partakes of the same character—

> The God of the tribes of Israel. Here lie the bones of the prudent deacon Paul; and we adjure the Almighty God [to punish any violator of the tomb?].[2]

---

[1] ἱερεὺς θεοῦ ὑψίστου (where the metre would require ὑψίστοιο).

[2] *C.I.G.*, 9270. The copy of Lukas has Φωτων instead of Φυλῶν. The correction made in the *Corpus* is probably right. Compare Nos. 26-28.

The abbreviations ΘC and ΘN for God mark this as the product of a more developed thought than most of the epitaphs of Lycaonia. Here the other typical epithet Pantokrator is used. The occurrence in two Iconian epitaphs of the two epithets marking the Cappadocian sect favours the opinion that both inscriptions originate from a branch of the Hypsistarii in Iconium. It is however possible that this second epitaph originated in a Jewish circle, though the most probable view perhaps is that a branch of the Jewish Christians survived in Lycaonia, and were nicknamed Hypsistarii by the "orthodox" Christians of the fourth century from their fondness for that favourite Jewish phrase, "the most High": they had been so far influenced by surrounding opinion as to abandon circumcision.

XIII. Deve-yuklu (Sarre, *Reise in Kleinasien*, p. 174; *A. E. Mitth. Oest.*, xix., 31 ff.).

37. Here lies Palladius, p(resbyter?) and high-priest of God for us: readers, pray for me.[1]

If the initial letter is rightly completed as "presbyter" (and I see no other way), the title high-priest, which seems more suited to the bishop, is given to a presbyter. Perhaps we have here also a trace of some non-Orthodox sect. The concluding formula is of developed Christian style; and the epitaph is of the fifth century or later.

XIV. The following epitaph, engraved on the tomb of a physician at Alkaran, near Isaura Nova, probably belongs to the period A.D. 330-350. The first two lines are in rude metre: the last two are in prose:—

38. Here earth contains Aur. Priscus, who was an excellent physician during the sixty years of his age. And

---

[1] ἔντα κατάκιτε Παλάδις π(ρεσβύτερος?) κὲ ἀρχιερεύς τοῦ Θεοῦ ἡμῖν· ὁ ἀναγινώσκοντες εὔξαστε ὑπὲρ ἐμοῦ.

(his tomb) was erected by his son Timotheos and his own consort Alexandria, in honour (*Figure*, p. 330).[1] This inscription is engraved above an elaborate ornamentation, partly incised, partly in relief, varied from the usual Isauran architectural scheme. There are the usual four columns supporting three pediments or arches, which, in this case, are all rounded.[2] In each of the three spaces between the four columns is a fish. The central arch is filled with the common shell pattern; the other two contain a doubtful symbol, perhaps a large fir-cone.

The ornament is executed in rude village work, quite different from the fine lines of the Dorla (Isauran) work, and implying the existence of the latter as model. Epigraphical reasons point to the same conclusion. The formula "Here the earth contains" is a mere poetic variation of "Here lies," the later formula which took the place of the older formula stating that "so-and-so made the tomb," or "honoured" or "set up" the deceased. These circumstances point to a later date. On the other hand, the second part of the physician's epitaph follows the old formula: "his son and wife set up". The mixture of the old and new formulæ, and the *prænomen* Aur., give a date about A.D. 340.

The praise given in this epitaph to the physician at the end of his long career is quite in the style of Basil, who says, in writing to the physician Eustathius about A.D. 374: " Humanity is the regular business of all you who practise as physicians. And, in my opinion, to put your science at the head and front of life's pursuits is to decide reasonably and rightly. This, at all events, seems to be the case if man's

---

[1] TIMI at the end: perhaps the beginning of τιμῆς χάριν, but the available space is exhausted, and the rest of the stone is crowded with ornamentation, so that the concluding letters were never engraved.

[2] In the ordinary Isauran scheme, the two side pediments are pointed.

most precious possession, life, is painful and not worth living unless it be lived in health, and if for health we are dependent on your skill" (*Epist.* 189).[1]

We notice also the emphasis which the ornamentation on the tombstone of Priscus lays on his Christian character. The connection of the physician with religion and his interest in it are emphasised in Basil's two letters to Eustathius (151 and 189). He writes: "In your own case medicine is seen, as it were, with two right hands: you enlarge the accepted limits of philanthropy by not confining the application of your skill to men's bodies, but by attending also to the cure of the diseases of their souls" (*Epist.* 189).[2] The letter to the physician Pasinicus (324) also shows on what friendly terms Basil wrote to men of this profession, and how much he seems to have esteemed their educated view of life; while he corresponded with Eustathius as a valued and respected friend on whose sympathy he could rely.[3]

39. A metrical epitaph found beside Derbe may belong to the tomb erected by one of those Christian physicians:—

Thou hast caused sorrow to thy companions (*i.e.*, by thy death) and in exceeding degree to thy parents; and thy name is Herakleon, son of Hermeros, physician.[4]

40. The initial formula of No. 38 appears in a somewhat more elaborate form in another epitaph, found near Isaura Nova in a bridge at Dinek Serai (*Journ. of Hell. St.*, 1905, p. 176):—

---

[1] and [2] Translation of Mr. Blomfield Jackson. See Harnack in *Texte u. Untersuch.*, viii., and list in a review *Anal. Boll.*, xii., 297.

[3] While respecting educated physicians, Basil was not above the belief in cures by words and charms, provided they were Christian, as the present writer has pointed out in more detail in the *Quarterly Review*, vol. clxxxvi., p. 427 (*Pauline and other Studies*, p. 380).

[4] MM. Radet and Paris in *Bull. Corr. Hellen.*, 1886, p. 510; Sterrett, *Wolfe Expedition*, p. 28.

> Here the bounteous earth, taking him to her bosom, contains Papas, who lived a just one among men, and whom Vanalis, his daughter, honoured with monument and beauteous muse, longing for the dead one.

The imitation marks the two epitaphs as of the same period, which is proved also by the presence in both of the new formula followed by the old. As one epitaph is Christian, the other may confidently be set down as also Christian.

XV. Allusions to the words of the Bible are rare in the epitaphs. compare No. 5 and the following.

> 41. Dikaios, measurer of corn for distribution, raised the stele to his wife Mouna, after a wedded life of 23 years, [ ] months, 20 days, and made (the tomb) for himself in his life-time. And the sarcophagus belongs to Him who knocks where the door stands before Him.

The allusion to Revelation iii. 20, " Behold, I stand at the door and knock," seems indubitable; though the Greek shows rather less similarity than the English.[1] It is possible that on the broken ornament of the top a personal name was engraved, and then the first line should be translated "a just measurer of corn". But Dikaiosyne occurs as a woman's name in a neighbouring village, and Dikaios is sometimes found as a man's name and probably so used here.

42. An epitaph from Suwerek, if the restoration be on the right lines, is important; and I should be glad to elicit either criticism or corroboration. See Fig. 7, p. 330.

> Aurelius Alexander [son of Alexander?], hoping in the

---

[1] κρούω and ἕστηκα ἐπὶ in Rev. iii. 20, κόπτω and ἐπέστηκεν (sic) in the epitaph; but the latter is composed by an uneducated villager, who made κόπτωνος the gen. of κόπτων, and remembered badly the words of the New Testament: he spoke Phrygian, not Greek.

after-life and joy, while living and of sound mind, made for himself a resting-place in remembrance.¹

This is an epitaph of the earliest class, and may quite probably belong to the third century. The formula, apart from the Christian hope, is of the early style, and the use of Aurelius as *prænomen* was commoner in the third century than in the fourth. The ornamentation shows the symmetrical use of crosses: compare No. 6 and *Studies in the Eastern Provinces*, p. 90.

XVI. The phrase "slave of God," δοῦλος θεοῦ, is the commonest in Byzantine epitaphs. Examples occur from about A.D. 400 or earlier to the latest time. Expressions, similar in sense but different in word, should be dated in the third or fourth century, before the common form was established. The phrase "slave of Christ," is, evidently, later than "slave of God," as being more remote from pagan forms of expression. The latter might quite conceivably be used by a pagan, though I cannot quote any case in which it was so used. The only inscription known to me in which δοῦλος Χριστοῦ occurs, is marked beyond question by other characteristics as of the developed Byzantine period; the title "Comes" occurs, and the detestable spelling (occurring not in rude village work, but on the tomb of a high officer) shows that the epitaph is likely to be of the seventh century or even later.

43. At Laodicea, published in *Athen. Mittheil.*, 1885, p. 43.

Athenodorus, house-servant of God, and Aelia Eupatra his wife while in life (prepared the grave) for themselves.

---

¹ A better restoration is suggested by my friend Mr. W. R. Paton, differing very slightly from that in the illustration; cp. 1 Pet. i. 13; iii. 17; Tit. i. 2 :—
Αὐρ . Ἀλέξανδρ[ος δίς], ἐλπίσας ἐπὶ [τὴν τῆς ἔπει]τα ζωῆς χαρά[ν, ζῶν τε κ]αὶ φρονῶν κ[ατεσκεύασεν ἑ]αυτῶ κοιμητή[ριον ἐνθάδε] μνήμης χάρ[ιν.

The term "house-servant of God" (οἰκέτης Θεοῦ) in itself might quite fairly be taken as a mere refinement of the commoner "slave of God," and therefore later in origin; but such an opinion is refuted by the character of this inscription, which is expressed in the earlier class of formula, mentioning first the name of the maker of the tomb. The names, too, are of an early type, especially the name of the wife Aelia Eupatra; and we may feel confident that the inscription must be as early as the fourth, and more probably the third, century. Looking at the style of letters, and the general impression given by the inscription as a whole, I should be inclined to place it in the third century.

The strange phrase " house-servant of God " (οἰκέτης θεοῦ) might be interpreted by some as a variation of the technical "home-born slave of Caesar" (*verna Caesaris*). But the term *Divus*, θεός, was applied only to a deceased emperor; and it is contrary to an otherwise unbroken rule to speak of a slave of the deified deceased emperor. At the same time it must be noted that many slaves of the emperor occur in epitaphs of Laodicea and the neighbourhood: they resided there to manage the estates and valuable copper and quicksilver mines belonging to the emperors in the mountain country immediately south of the city.[1]

It is also possible that Athenodorus, to indicate his religion, purposely chose an expression which was susceptible of another meaning. I have elsewhere pointed out[2] that in the

---

[1] The name Burnt Laodicea evidently arose from the furnaces for smelting the copper. Mr. Edwin Whittall pointed out to me that the ancients did not refine the ore (cinnabar) to extract the pure quicksilver, but used it in its raw condition as a colour. It was the red earth of Cappadocia, called γῆ Σινωπική, because it was brought to Greece by way of Sinope before the land Trade-Route to Ephesus came into use.

[2] *Cities and Bishoprics of Phrygia*, ii., p. 502.

earliest Christian epitaphs language was often employed which could be taken in a pagan sense by the uninitiated. This custom originated in the time when it was dangerous to profess Christianity; and after the numbers and influence of the Christians increased in any district, profession was made in more public fashion. If my suspicion be correct, this would be the earliest Lycaonian Christian epitaph. From the names and style there is no reason why it should not belong to the second century. According to ordinary rule one would class it as probably of that date.

The forms, attendant, companion, servant or slave of Christ (θεράπων θεράπαινα vary between those meanings; also παῖς δοῦλος) are found sporadically: cp. No. 4.

44. An example, found in Isauria, is published by Professor Sterrett (*Wolfe Exped.*, p. 60).

[So-and-so], while still living, faithful slave-boy of [Jesus] Christ, inscribed the stele for himself.[1]

45. Copied by my friend, Professor T. Callander, at Savatra in Lycaonia :—

The attendant of Christ, Paulus, I lie in this tomb, and the gravestone was set up by my young sister Maria in solemn remembrance to me her only brother.[2]

46. From the same place and authority: it is a mere concluding fragment :—

the brothers, attendants of Christ, constructed.[3]

47. A quaint inscription found in 1908 at Obruk (perhaps the site of Congoustos), eight miles east of Perta, concludes our survey of the Lycaonian Church.

---

[1] [ἔγρα]ψεν ἑαυτῷ παῖ[s Ἰησοῦ Χριστοῦ πιστός.

[2] XY θεράπων Πα[ῦ]λος ἐν τῷδε τύμβῳ κατάκι[μ]ε σῆμα δέ μοι τεῦξεν ἠΐθεος κασιγνή[τη] Μαρία μνήμης εἵνεκα σεμνῆς οἴῳ κασιγνήτῳ. θεράπων, like ὀπάων in No. 19. is equivalent to *comes*, subordinate companion.

[3] κασίγνητοι Χριστοῦ θεράποντες ἔτευξαν.

† Holy Trinity, protect the order of the deacons. Amen.[1]

This text perhaps indicates some disagreement between the deacons and the higher clergy; but other explanations are possible, and I publish it in hope of instruction on the point. The tagma of the clergy is mentioned by Basil (quoted on p. 356 *note*).

[1] ἁγία Τριάς, ἀντηλαβοῦ τοῦ τάγματι τῶν διακόνω(ν) · ἀμήν. A cross is cut at the beginning and a large cross below the letters.

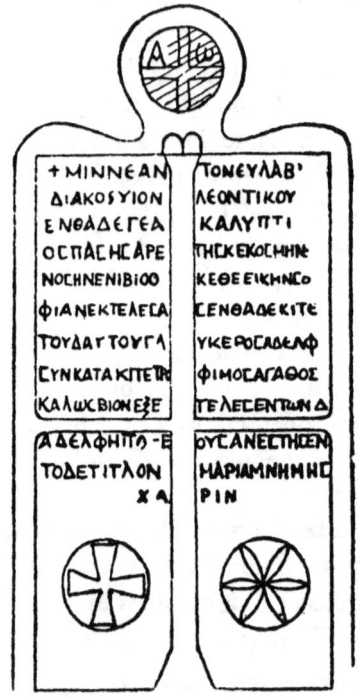

Fig. 14.—Anthropomorphic Lycaonian gravestone (see p. 399) with cross and rosette (monogram) as corresponding decorative elements. See pp. 330, 368 f., 406 f.

INDEX

Christian Inscriptions—
  Account to God, giving of, 396.
  Anthropomorphic gravestone, 399, 410.
  Aurelius as pseudo-prænomen, 338, 386, 390.
  Beginning of epigraphy in Central Anatolia, 335.
  Chronology of, 334 ff., 338, 369.
  Church of God, 401.
  Concealment of Christian character shows early period, 381, 408 f.
  Curse on violator of tomb, 395 ff.
  Fathers 318 of Nicæa, 397.
  "Friend of all," 375, 382.
  "Here lies," 337, 338, 388.
  Holy Church of God, 401.
  Reckoning with God, 396.
  Salutations on gravestones, 362.
  Slave of Christ, of God, 338, 365, 407 ff.
  Titles, growth of Byzantine Christian, 369, 384, 398.
  Trinity, 396, 410.
  Women's industry, 387.

Luke, 3-101, 220-46—
  Acts, conclusion of, 27.
  — chap. xv., 28, 60 f., 313 f.
  — credibility of, 58, 64, 87, 91, 315; see Luke *gen.*
  Annunciation, 255.
  Authorities, use of his, 58, 71, 80, 83.
  Birth narrative, 49 f., 219, 243-46, 255.
  Character, 31; see Hellenism of.
  Choice of details, 21.
  Connection with Antioch, 18, 35, 65-68.
  — — Ephesus, 21 ff., 35.

Luke, 3-101, 220-46 (*contd.*)—
  Connection with Corinth, 21, 35.
  — — Macedonia, 31, 34 ff., 48.
  Criticism of method in, 3, 8, 58, 60, 64, 72, 76, 87, 91, 315; see Luke *gen.*
  Hellenism of, 10 ff., 15, 255.
  House and roof, 46.
  Inexactnesses and inconsistencies in, alleged, 24 ff., 28 f.
  Jerusalem, 76.
  — and Hierosolyma, 51, 76.
  John, relation to, 29 f.
  Mark in Luke, 39 ff., 71.
  Marvellous in, 8-10, 65, 251-59.
  Method in criticism, see Criticism.
  — as a historian, 21, 34, 38.
  Omissions from his authorities, 238.
  Paulinism of, 12.
  Physician, 4, 6, 16, 27, 56 ff.
  Roof of house. 46.
  Ship, 36.
  Source, Lost Common Source of Matthew and, 71-101.
  Sources, 34, 38, 49, 55, 63, 73 f., 78 ff., 96 f.
  Speeches in, are they his composition? 22, 83.
  Style, 34. 44, 47 f., 50 f.
  Temptation in, 256 ff.
  Trustworthiness of, 4 f., 315 f., 327.
  Unity of authorship in his two books, 6 f.
  Use of his authorities, see Authorities
  Viper in Malta, 63 ff.
  We-passages in Acts, 15, 27, 33 ff., 37 f.
  Women in, 13, 30 f.

Miscellaneous—
  Agriculture, 179-98.
  — directed by religion, 197.
  Alphabet, see Greek.
  Anthropomorphism, 251.
  Arabs could not conquer Asia Minor, 114 f., 180 f.
  Asia and Europe, contact of, 105 ff., 143.
  Asia Minor, situation of, 105 f.
  — — roads of, 107 ff.
  — — dividing line in, 112 ff.
  — — contrast of coast and interior, 113.
  Aulokrene fountain, 108.
  Bull-god, 209.
  Clothes, philosophy of, 175.
  Coinage, origin of, 125.
  Commerce, methods in Asia, 125.
  Criticism, true, seeks excellences, not defects. 260.
  Crusades, influence on Europe, 125.
  Earrings worn by men, 206.
  Egoism not Egotism in literature, 265.
  First person singular, its use in exposition, 265.
  German Method, value of, 263.
  Germans do not read Hawkins and Hobart, 6.
  — Dr. Sanday on, 261 ff.
  Greek alphabet, entrance to Asia Minor, 123.
  Hieroglyphics, Hittite or Anatolian, 127 f., 159 f.
  Hired labour despised, 221 f.
  Huda-verdi, 132, 163 ff.
  Judaism, freer in first century than later, 263.
  Khans, 185 ff.
  Landscape of the plateau, 131.
  Legend, nature of, 100.
  Libation, 208.
  Lycaonia, organisation of, 332 f.
  Monotheism, origin of, 277.
  Morning star, crescent, 232.
  Nomadisation, 116, 181 ff., 275 f.
  Nomads. 180 f.; in Syria, 275.
  Old Testament criticism, 76 f., 262, 277 ff.
  Organisation of Lycaonia, 332 f.
  Pelta, 349.
  Semitic conception of God, 12 f., 250-55, 280 f.

Miscellaneous (continued)—
  Tekmoreioi, 197.
  Tetrapyrgia, 187.
  Turkish conquest of Asia Minor, 116, 181 ff.
  — art, 185 f.
  Water engineering, 129, 154, 164, 179, 188, 193, 348.
  Women warriors, 209 ff.

Paul, St.—
  Acts xv. and Gal. ii., 28, 60 f., 313.
  Architectural metaphors, 294 ff.
  Athletics, 288-94.
  Citizen rights, 25.
  Development and growth, idea of, 287 f.
  Ephesian Address, 22.
  Epistle to Hebrews, relation to, 304, 309 ff.
  — its relation to Paul's epistles, 326 ff.
  Galatians ii., 1-11, 28, 60 f., 313.
  — origin in teaching of Jesus, 96.
  Hellenism of, 15, 285-98.
  Language of, 219, 285 ff.
  Luke, his physician, 27.
  Metaphors, 285-98.
  Military metaphors, 294, 297.
  Name, 53 f., 76.
  Quotations from Deut. xxxii., 1, 326.
  Quoted in inscription? 407.
  Roman citizenship, 25.
  — metaphors, 297.
  Saul and Paul, 53 f., 76.
  Veiling of women, 175.
  Width of education, 285.

Religion, Christian—
  Acts, credibility of, 22, 28, 60 f., 87.
  Archiereus, 391, 403.
  Anatolian languages destroyed by, 146.
  Anthropomorphism in Bible, 251.
  Aristocratic birth of Church leaders, 187, 341.
  Asceticism, 400.
  Birth of Christ, date of, 235, 243, 246.
  Bishop of Laodiceia, Lycaonia, in fourth century, 153 f.
  Bishops, 350-60, 368, 385.

Index 413

Religion, Christian (*continued*)—
Book or tablets as symbol, 377.
Byzantine art, 145.
— Church, 143.
— — deterioration in, 161 f.
Chorepiscopus, 356 f.
Chronology of Gospels, 221-46.
Church architecture, 339, 346 ff., 366.
— as sepulchral monument, 156, 165.
— as a defensive power, 157.
— door on gravestones. See gravestone.
— Imperial contribution to expenses of, 346.
— the centre of social life, 153 ff., 348, 364.
Churches, thousand and one, at Barata, 155 ff.
Clergy and laity, 387 f.
Concealment of Christianity, 381, 408.
Continuity of pagan ideas, 133, 136, 138, 158 ff.
Deacons, 363, 410.
Diakonissa, 393 ff.
Diocletian, persecution of, 342 ff., 397.
Dove, symbol of, 385, 389.
Elohim, Jehovah, 76.
Epistle to Hebrews, 301-28.
— — — athletics in, 289, 291.
Epitaphs, 272 ff., 331-410.
Evangelists in church, 368.
Fig-tree, 227.
Freedom in the teaching of Jesus, 92 ff.
Genealogical expression in Bible, 253 f.
Gospels, 1-101, 219-46.
— later elements in? 14, 32.
— metaphors from life and nature, 219.
— trustworthiness of, 32, 87, 1-101, 219-65.
— sources not recoverable from internal evidence alone, 75.
Grass, sitting on the, 228 f.
Gravestone symbolises a church, and the tomb is a church, 380, also 328, 330, 371, 376, 379, 383.
Greek language spread by, 146.
Hegoumenoi. See Leaders.

Religion, Christian (*continued*)—
Herald, 233.
Heretics, 400 f.
Hiereus, 355, 365, 387 f.
Hierissa, 391 ff.
Hospitality, 154, 354.
Hypsistarii, Hypsistiani, 401 ff.
Industry of women mentioned on gravestones, 387.
Inscriptions of Lycaonia, 150 ff., 331-410.
Italian pilgrims, 316 f.
Jerusalem, Church of, division in, 313 ff.
Jews, relation to earliest Christians abroad, 317 ff.
John the Baptist, 227 ff., 232.
Kingdom of God, 85.
Latin and Greek Church, contrast of, 144 f.
Laity. See Clergy.
Leaders, separate class of, in one congregation, 313.
Legend, nature of, 100.
" Light of the World," 231.
Lycaonia, Christian in fourth century, 152.
Mark and the type of a Gospel, 82 ff.
Martyrs, 395.
Matthew, 4-101, 221-46.
— Logia of, 80.
Messenger of God, 13, 255.
Ministry of Christ, length of, 234.
Miraculous element in, 8 f., 65, 251-59.
Misunderstood at the time by disciples, 89 ff.
Morning star, 230-46.
Nineteenth and twentieth century view, contrast of, 9 f.
Official titles, growth of, 369, 384, 398.
Oikonomos, 358, 369 f., 393.
Oikonomissa, 393.
Open-air life, effect of, 223 ff.
Ornament, 367 f., 370 ff., 376 f., 378 f., 385, 399, 404, 410.
Orthodox Church, 143.
— — its alliance with the Empire, 147.
— — the Church of the people in fourth century, 152.
— — pagan survivals in, 159 f., 164, 174.

Religion, Christian (*continued*)—
   Pantokrator, 339 f., 401 f.
   Papas, 373 f.
   Permanence of religious feeling.
      See Pagan Religion.
   Physicians, 403 ff.
   Pilgrims to Jerusalem, 317 ff.
   Presbytera, presbyterissa, 365, 392 f.
   Presbyterion, 358.
   Presbyters, 351-65, 367, 370, 403.
   Q, 71-100.
   — source of knowledge of Christ's teaching, 85, 97 f.
   — date of, 81-89, 97 f.
   Reinvigorated the Roman Empire, 144.
   Revelation of John, 233, 378, 406 f.
   Sabbatical year, 236.
   Screens in churches, 347 f., 379 ff.
   Soldiers, 342 ff.
   Spread of Christianity, lines of, 134 f.
   Star, 230-46.
   Subdeacons, 356, 368.
   Symbolism in Bible, 250-59.
   — in art, 375 f.
   Tabernacles, feast of, 235-43.
   Teaching of Jesus misunderstood by His disciples in His life, 89 ff., 240 ff.
   Tekmoreioi, 197 f.
   Temptation, the, 256 ff.
   Transfiguration, 237-43.
   Trinity, 396, 410.
   Unified the Empire, 148.
   Virgins, 386, 398 f.
   Verbal criticism, 59 ff., 262.
   Water supply at churches, 348.
   Writing, early use of, 98 f.

Religion, Mohammedan—
   Accepted old religious sites, 132, 133, 138, 175.
   Art, 185 f.
   Bektash Dervishes, 155.
   Brotherhoods, an ancient institution, 155.
   Mosque built twice at Tyana, 114.

Religion, Pagan, 171-215—
   Amazons, 200 ff.
   Anatolian religion, 171-214.
   — — directed agriculture, 197.
   Asian influence on Greece, 128.
   Birth and death, 205.
   Bull god, 209.
   Confession, 178.
   Continuity of religious awe, see Permanence.
   Divine nature as feminine, 130 f.
   — — beneficence of, 132.
   — — on mountain peaks, 136.
   Domestication of animals through religion, 130.
   Ephesian priest, 212 f.
   Eunuch priest, 201-13.
   Feminine element in, see Mother-goddess.
   Grave as temple and church, 140, 165.
   — as a holy place, 173 f.
   High-places, 159 f.
   Huda-verdi, 132, 163 ff.
   Megabyzos, 213.
   Mother-goddess, 130 f., 203 ff.
   Permanence of religious awe, 133, 136, 138, 140, 159, 164 f., 174, 197, 336.
   Priest-king, 211.
   Religion the model and type of earthly life, 205.
   Sepulchral religion, 140.
   Virgin-Mother goddess, 134.

Roman Empire—
   Alliance with the Orthodox Church, 147.
   Emperor contributes to building of church, 346.
   Hellenism, its place in, 143.
   Lycaonia Province, 332.
   Mines, 408.
   Reinvigorated by Christianity, 144.
   Relation to Hellenism, 143.
   Slaves of the Emperor, 408.
   Three Eparchiæ, Province of, 332, 353.
   Unity of the Empire, religious, 148.

NAMES

I. Christian and Biblical—

Agabus, 25, 253.
Amphilochius, 151, 349, 356, 378.
Anthousa, 353 *note*.
Apollos, 301.
Athanasius, Bishop of Tarsus, 353 *note*.
Augustine, 12.
Avircius Marcellus, 341, 350, 372.
Barnabas, 20, 301.
Basil, 151 ff., 187, 354, 356, 378, 384, 387, 389, 404 f., 411.
Callistus, 374.
Clement (Alex.), 234 *note*.
— (Rome), 310.
Cornelius, 19.
Cyriacus, presbyter, 356.
Elias, 237.
Eusebius, 18, 65 f., 342 *note*, 345 ff., 379, 389.
Eutychus, 65.
Gabriel, 255.
Gregory, 401.
— of Nazianzus, 151, 401.
— of Nyssa, 151, 187, 401.
— Thaumaturgus, 374.
Hermas, 355.
Ignatius, 24, 293, 355.
Jairus, 58.
James, 240.
John, 24, 133, 220-241.
— Baptist, 227 f., 230 ff.
Longinus, presbyter, Lyc., 356.
Malachi, 233.
Mammas, Tribune, 156.
Maria, 409.
Mark, 4-101, 221-46.

I. Christian and Biblical (*cont.*)—

Mary, Virgin, 13, 63, 131, 133 f., 197.
Matthew, 4-101, 221-46.
Maximilian, St., 343.
Michael, 158.
Mnason, 19.
Naaman, 20.
Nathanael, 226 f.
Nicholas, Bishop of Myra, 123.
Nicodemus, 223.
Origen, 234, 310 f.
Papias, 80 f.
Paulinus, Bishop of Tyre, 346.
Peter, 55, 81 ff., 90, 237, 240, 407.
Phocas, St., 121, 123.
Polycarp, 354.
Pseudo-Justin, 374.
Publius, 16.
Stephen, 82 ff.
Tertullian, 373.
Theodoret, 313.
Theodotus, St., 374.
Theophilus, Bishop, 375.
Timothy, 288, 323, 363.
Titus, 17 f., 272, 287 f., 407.
Trophimus, 35.
Tychicus, 35.
Zacharias, 49 f.

II. Historical—

Aeschylus, 11.
Agamemnon, 124.
Agrippa, 322, 326.
Alexander the Great, 107, 126.
Al-Mamun, 114.
Anna Comnena, 180.
Aristides, 67.

II. Historical (*cont.*)—

Augustus, 317.
Barbarossa, Kaiser, 111, 166 f.
Bismarck, 9.
Caracalla, Aurelius, 386, 399.
Claudius, 319.
Constantine, 151.
Croesus, 110, 215.
Cyrus the Persian, 110.
Diocletian, 152 ff., 338, 342 f., 353 *note*, 397.
Diogenes, Governor of Pisidia, 344.
Dodanim, 254.
Domitilla, 273.
Domitian, 312.
Elishah, 254.
Eumenes, 187.
Galerius, 345.
Godfrey, 107.
Hadrian, Emperor, 133.
Harun-al-Rashid, 114.
Herod, 244.
Herodotus, 125, 215.
Homer, 367.
Ibrahim Pasha, 33 *note*.
Javan, sons of, 254.
Joannes Cinnamus, 180.
John Comnenus, 181 *note*.
Josephus, 67, 317.
Julian, 392.
Justinian, 133, 138.
Kiamil Pasha, 194.
Kittim, 254.
Licinius, 343 f.
Lucretius, 24.
Manlius Consul, 108.
Manuel, 110, 181 *note*.
Maximian, 351.
Maximin, 342 f., 345 f., 368.

II. Historical (cont.)—
Memluk Sultans, 117.
Nearchos, 66.
Nicetas of Khonai, 180.
Newton, Sir Isaac, 220 f.
Pindar, 11.
Philip, Emperor, 338.
Philo, 294.
Plutarch, 187.
Porphyry, 280 note.
Semiramis, Mounds of, 206 note.
Suetonius, 319.
Tacitus, 274 note.
Tarkuattes, Priest King, 160.
Tarshish, 254.
Valeria, Empress, 345.
Valerian, 353.
Valerius Diogenes, 344.
Verina, Empress, 138.
Xenophon, 119 f.

III. Modern Scholars—
Allen, 96 note.
Anderson, J. G. C., 360 note, 370 note, 393.
Arnold, Matthew, 309.
Bachofen, 204.
Bell, Miss Gertrude, 155, 159, 197.
Bell, Mr., 244.
Blass, Prof., 36, 47, 63.
Blomfield Jackson, Rev., 405 note.
Calder, W. M., 153 note, 341, 350.
Callander, Prof. T., 360, 366 note, 368, 409.
Carruthers, Mr. W., F.R.S., 223.
Chantre, 209 note.
Cronin, Rev. H. S., 388 f., 394, 396.
Cumont, Prof., 353.
Delitzsch, 322, 324.
De Rossi, 369, 373 note.
Diamantides, Savas, 396.
Dindorf, 67.
DoughtyWylie,Mrs.,174.
Driver, Dr., 279.
Foucart, 128.

III. Modern Scholars (cont.)—
Fränkel, 68.
Gardner, Prof. P., 125 note.
Garstang, Prof., 397.
Gelzer, 204.
Gibbon, 110 note, 181.
Grenfell, 67.
Hamilton, 401.
Harnack, Prof. A., 1-68, 305 note, 342 note, 373.
Hastings, Dr., 130 note, 177, 205 note.
Hatch, Dr., 351, 354, 363.
Hawkins, Sir J., 5 f.
Headlam, Principal, 287 note.
Heberdey, 375.
Heræus, 373 note, 374.
Hobart, 5 ff., 225.
Hogarth, 113 note, 201.
Holl, Prof., 146 note, 151 note, 356 note, 379 note.
Hook, Bryan, 64.
Howorth, Sir H., 181.
Howson, Dean, 285-89.
Humann, 203.
Hunt, 67.
Jülicher, 264.
Keil, 349.
Kenyon, 244.
Knowling, R. J., 17.
Körte, A., 124.
Layard, 232.
Le Blant, 369.
Lewis, W. M., 302 ff., 324 ff.
Lightfoot, 297, 305, 327.
McGiffert, Prof. A. C., 5, 26, 303 ff.
Mackinlay, Colonel, 219-46.
Maspero, 209 note.
Milligan, Dr. G., 303, 307, 324.
Mommsen, 144.
Moulton, Prof. J. H., 51, 60 note, 244 note, 245.
Newton, Sir C., 212.
Paton, W. R., 407 note.
Perrot, G., 203, 204 note, 206 ff., 212, 214.
Pfleiderer, 305 note.

III. Modern Scholars (cont.)—
Plummer, Dr., 237.
Radet, M., 125, 405 note.
Ramsay, Miss, 175, 336, 371, 378, 382, 392.
Reichel, Dr., 160.
Reinach, A. J., 198 note.
— Theodore, 118 note.
Renan, 277.
Sanday, Prof. W., 13, 98, 249-65, 318, 360, 374.
Sarré, 187, 403.
Sayce, 160.
Schürer, 9.
Sloman, A., 64 note.
Smith, Cecil, 201, 212.
— Prof. G. A., 269-81.
— Robertson, 77, 262, 269.
Souter, Prof. A., 18 note, 273.
Steinmann, 264.
Sterrett, Prof., 385 note, 390, 405 note, 409.
Strzygowski, Prof., 380.
Thomas, Rev. Griffith, 287.
Tissot, 256.
Trail, Prof. J. W. H., 64.
Usener, 353 note.
Van Soden, 305 note.
Waddington, 68, 273, 274 note.
Weinel, 264.
Weiss, Bernard, 55.
Wellhausen, 46.
Westcott, 301 note, 302, 306 note, 307, 310 note, 311 f., 313 note, 316 note.
White, Rev. Dr., of Marsovan, 253.
Whittall, Mr. Edwin, 408 note.
Wiegand, Dr., 347.
Wilhelm, 375.
Wilkinson, 72 note, 97 note.
Wilson, Sir Charles, 202, 203, 207.
Winckler, 127 note.
Wood (Ephesus), 133.
Wordsworth, Bishop, 311 note.
Wright, A. A. G., 273.

Index

IV. Pagan Gods—
Achilles Pontarches, 121 f.
Apollo, 108, 167, 216.
Archigallos, 207.
Artemis, 197 f., 201.
Ashtaroth, 232.
Athena, 108.
— works of, 387.
Atys, 211.
Bacchus, 211.
Cybele, 207.
Dipylon, 198.
Helena, 121.
Heracleids, 68.
Heracles, 179, 211.
Hermaphrodite, 206.
Hermes, 13.
Ida, Trojan, 119.
Ipta Meter, 215.
Iris, 13.
Istar, 232.
Janus, 198.
Kronos, 280.
Lityerses, 108.
Marsyas, 108.
Mother goddess, 206.
Omphale, 211.
Pta, 215.
Sabos, 211.
Tekmoreian, 198.
Venus, 232.
Zeus, 11, 168.

V. Places—
Achaia, 21 ff., 35.
Ak-Giol, White Lake, 172.
Akroenos, 137.
Alexandria, 122, 374.
Alkaran, 352, 360, 378, 403.
Amanus, 117 *note*.
Anava, the Salt Lake, 107.
Ancyra, 67.
Anthios, 140.
Antioch, Pisidian, 110, 134, 341; Plate XII.
Antioch, Syrian, 18 ff., 62, 66.
Anti-Taurus, 114.
Argos, 179.
Arles, Council of, 344.
Aurokra, 108 f.

V. Places (*cont.*)—
Bagdad Railway, 138, 188.
Barata, 150 *note*, 155 ff., 385; Plates XVI., XVII., XX.
Basilika Therma, 380.
Bin-Bir-Kilisse. See Barata.
Black Sea, 105.
Boghaz-Keui, 127, 201 ff., 212 f., 215.
Bulgurlar, 172 *note*.
Bulladann, 192.
Cæsarea of Cappadocia, 114, 154, 357.
Cæsarea Philippi, 239.
Cæsarea, Stratonis, 19, 320 ff.
Capernaum, 40.
Cappadocia, 153, 204, 401 f., 408 *note*.
Caspian, 105.
Caucasus, 105.
Celænæ, 107 f.
Cilician Gates, 109 *note*, 115, 139, 172 f., 186.
Comana, 210.
Congoustos, 410.
Constantinople, 116.
Corinth, 21 f., 309.
Crimea, 121.
Cyme, Æolic, 124.
Cyprus, 19, 122, 134.
Damascus, 20.
Deghile, 140; Plates XIII., XVIII., XIX.
Derbe, 335, 385, 405.
Deve-yuklu, 403.
Dindymos, 119.
Dinek, 360.
— Serai, 405.
Dorla. See Isaura.
Dorylaion, 107, 166.
Drya, 370.
Egypt, 231, 236, 374.
Eleusis, 373.
Emir-Ghazi, 209.
Ephesus, 21 ff., 119, 131 ff.
Eregli, 172.
Eski-Sheher, 107.
Euyuk, 205 ff.
Frahtin, 205.
Galatia, 23, 27.

V. Places (*cont.*)—
Galilee, 40, 42, 239, 241 ff.
Gennesaret, 44.
Halys, 215.
Hauran, 272.
Herakleia, 172.
Hermon, Mount, 243.
Hierapolis, 109.
Hierosolyma, 51, 53, 76, 335.
Hirakla, Castle of, 172, 193.
Holy Land, 269-81.
Huda-verdi, 132, 173 ff.
Ibriz, 171, 193, 206; Plate XXI.
Iconium, 151 f., 331 f., 356, 363, 402 f.
Isaura Nova or Dorla, 335, 352, 360, 370, 372, 376 f., 378 f., 385, 404 f.
Isaura Palaea, 378.
Jerusalem, 19, 25, 42, 51, 53, 76, 81, 223, 238 ff., 253, 320.
Jordan, 227, 236.
Judæa, 42, 244.
Kara-Bunar, 189 *note*.
Kara-Dagh, 163; Plates XIV., XV.
Kara-Hissar-Afion, 137, 140; Plate IV.
Kases, Kasis, 209.
Keramon Agora, 120.
Khadyn-Khan, 129.
Khasbia, 209.
Kizil Dagh, 160.
Korna, 378.
Kybistra, 172.
Laodicea, 153 f., 331 *note*, 335, 370, 381, 398, 407 f.
Laodicea, burnt, 408 *note*.
Leontopolis, 378.
Leontos Kephalai, 140, 397; Plate X.
Lerna, 179.
Limnai, 197.
Lycus, 107 ff.
Lystra, 65, 216, 335.
Macedonia, 23, 34 ff.
Maden-Sheher. See Barata.
Maeander, 107 ff., 119; Plate II.

Index

V. Places (*cont.*)—
Malta, 64.
Marsyas, 107.
Melitene, 114.
Mesopotamia, 110, 194.
Miletus, 347.
Mindana, 356.
Mount of Olives, 223.
Mycenæ, 139.
Myra, 122.
Naro in Africa, 377.
Nazareth, 40, 236.
Nemrud, 232.
Nevinne, 368.
Nice, Council of, 349, 397.
Nikopolis, 138.
Obrimas, 107.
Obruk, 409.
Oxyrynchos, 67.
Panhormos, 186.
Palestine, 44, 46, 188, 229, 243 f., 269-81, 292, 317.
Paphlagonia, 117.
Pegella, 138, 331 *note.*
Perga, 134.
Pergamos, 68.

V. Places (*cont.*)—
Pessinus, 211.
Philadelphia, 157.
Philippi, 27, 34, 46.
Phrygia, 395.
— Galatic, 48.
— Asian, 48, 335.
— Upper, 67 f.
Pisidia, 397.
Plommeis, 370.
Prymnessos, 67.
Pteria, 214.
Puteoli, 317.
Rome, 23.
Salonika, 375.
Sarus, 172.
Seleucia, 353 *note.*
Serai-Inn, 398.
Sinethandos, 331 *note.*
Sinope, 121, 408 *note.*
Sivri-Hissar, 138; Plate V.
Smyrna, 191, 195.
Stymphalos, 179.
Sultan Dagh, 140; Plate XII.
Suwerek, 366, 406.
Syracuse, 369 *note.*

V. Places (*cont.*)—
Syria, 107.
Tabor, 243.
Tarsus, 114, 120, 293, 375.
Taurus, 106, 112 ff., 115 ff., 137.
Temnos, 119.
Therma, 108. See Basilika.
Thessalonica, 35.
Thyatira, 233, 400.
Tomb of Midas, 139 f.; Plate VIII.
Trapesus, 120.
Troas, 27, 34 f., 48, 65.
Tyana, 172.
Tyre, 25, 346 ff., 379, 381
Tyriaion, 395.
Ushak, 191.
Verinopolis, 138, 331 *note.*
Yuruk-Keui, 385.
Zazadin Khan, 388, 394; Plate XXIII.
Zizima, 370.

www.ingramcontent.com/pod-product-compliance
Lightning Source LLC
Chambersburg PA
CBHW071137300426
44113CB00009B/998